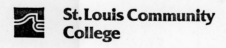

reluctant
REGULAT☐RS
THE FCC AND THE BROADCAST AUDIENCE

BARRY COLE
MAL OETTINGER

ADDISON-WESLEY PUBLISHING COMPANY
Reading, Massachusetts · Menlo Park, California
London · Amsterdam · Don Mills, Ontario · Sydney

Library of Congress Cataloging in Publication Data

Cole, Barry G
    Reluctant regulators.

    Includes index.
    1. Broadcasting policy--United States. 2. United
States. Federal Communications Commission.
I. Oettinger, Mal, 1932-   joint author. II. Title.
HE8689.8.C56   353.008'74'54   77-81629
ISBN 0-201-01039-9

ISBN 0-201-01039-9
ABCDEFGHIJ-MA-7987

To all the Coles
and all the Oettingers

Introduction

A now defunct television program used to tell us, "There are eight million stories in the Naked City." There are at least that many in the Federal Communications Commission.

Some of the more dramatic stories in this book involve confrontations between FCC regulators and groups and individuals who have no direct financial interest in broadcasting but who have learned, in Nicholas Johnson's phrase, "how to talk back to your television set." Only during the past decade have commissioners found themselves in a consumer's era, obliged to respond to the complaints and concerns of television viewers and radio listeners.

In the past, the FCC had been a tight little world in which commissioners enjoyed many personal contacts with the broadcasters they regulated (and their lawyers and lobbyists) and none at all with the amorphous public whose interest the agency supposedly protected. In recent years, community groups, media reformers, and representatives of minorities have burst into Commission hearing rooms, brandishing court decisions that spelled out their rights to participate. What these citizens were seeking, how commissioners reacted, and what the FCC did—or failed to do—to assure broadcasters' responsiveness to their audiences is a major focus of this book.

Representatives of the broadcast audience have made many demands and requests of the FCC. Some of these importunings are beyond the power of the commissioners to satisfy; others concern problems that commissioners have claimed to handle although they have in fact merely

postponed solutions. Over the years commissioners have developed policies and paid them lip service, then failed to adhere to them. Commissioners are fond of saying they have to walk a tightrope as regulators.
Often this is true. They deal with businessmen who have assumed
unusual public service obligations. They regulate journalists who are
protected by the First Amendment but who must present all sides of an
important controversial issue. They are forbidden to go into programming too deeply lest they be censors, yet they must determine that programs serve the needs and interests of a community. We have not chron-
icled the many times that seven commissioners have crossed the tightrope successfully; we tend to note the spills.

Commissioners must act under a number of constraints, and they
soon become aware of the limits on what they can do. Congress can
always reverse their policies—through legislation if necessary, though
a good public flogging at a congressional hearing will usually do the
trick. Commissioners need not be lawyers and, in recent years, a majority have not been lawyers. They often work out a solution to a knotty
problem with profound legal consequences through compromise, staff
advice, common sense and their own philosophical inclinations. Almost
every action they take is subject to review by a federal appeals court;
solutions to problems with which commissioners have grappled for
years may come unstitched when the court defines the legal ramifications.

Although we report on the actions and reactions of the individuals
who were commissioners and key staff members during the 1970s, we
are not singling them out for criticism. Earlier Commissions and staffs
faced some of the same problems and did little to resolve them. We
found also that political-party affiliations have little effect on what a
regulator will do in this area of broadcast policy.

The authors have observed the FCC over a number of years from
different vantage points. Barry Cole, a professor at Indiana University
who had lectured and written on broadcast regulation, came to Washington in the summer of 1970 to study and report on the FCC's licensing
process under a grant from the university. Cole was invited to discuss
some of his findings at a special Commission meeting on September 14,
1970, even though some members expressed apprehension about having
an outsider address a closed session.

Cole had been briefed that Dean Burch, the chairman, would be
willing to listen to him provided that his criticisms be specific and that
he have alternatives to offer, not simple carping. Cole spoke all morning
and presented recommendations for improving the renewal process. He
stressed that the responsibility for improvements lay with the commissioners, not the staff.

After the meeting, Chairman Burch met with Cole and offered him
a chance to be a consultant on license renewal for the FCC. "If you will
put off writing your book for a while," Burch said, "it may have a hap-
pier ending." Cole agreed, with the understanding that he retain his

commitment to write about the FCC's processes and that the materials to which he would be exposed might be part of that work. In fact, participants in Commission meetings would joke sometimes about how what they said would look in print some day.

As a consultant, Cole was given the same access to materials as a commissioner's legal assistant, was permitted to write agenda items and to speak at Commission meetings. Cole left the FCC in July 1975, after exposure to a number of aspects of broadcast regulation, in addition to licensing, his initial interest. As a consequence, this book has a broader perspective than it had as originally conceived.

Mal Oettinger has been following the vagaries of Commission policy since 1958, when he joined *Broadcasting* magazine and reported on the FCC for four years. From 1962 through 1966 he worked for the National Broadcasting Company in Washington, observing from a different viewpoint how the FCC regulates the stewards of the airwaves. As a freelancer from 1969 through 1974, Oettinger was the Washington editor of *Television/Radio Age* and reported regularly on the agency in a column called "Inside the FCC." He and Cole met during that period, and Oettinger became infected by Cole's enthusiasm for a book about the FCC.

The Commission is continuously modifying policies concerning broadcasters' responsibilities to the public and the court frequently orders new approaches. We recognize there may also be changes in the attitudes of the regulators toward public participation as citizen groups learn more about how to deal with the Commission. Even as we have been writing this book, events have moved inexorably to make some questions moot or to pose issues that had not arisen before. We are certain only that more changes can be expected in this volatile—and vital—area of broadcast regulation.

Explanatory Note: When we refer to the court or the court of appeals, we mean the United States Court of Appeals for the District of Columbia, unless otherwise specified.

We have cited the dates of publications containing articles that the reader might wish to explore further. When we omit dates, we believe we have quoted all the relevant passages. Readers are directed to the transcripts of Congressional hearings by subcommittee and date. Further information on FCC hearings, decisions and speeches may be found in the FCC Public Reference Room or through the Commission's Public Information Office.

Washington, D.C.   B.C.
July 1977   M.O.

Contents

THE PLAYERS

1
Watchdogs
of the Airwaves

The regulators, in significant part, have failed because their role calls for talents radically different from those possessed by the majority of men and women who have been appointed. The process by which the White House, under Presidents of both major parties, has selected the regulators tends to eliminate the person with talents for imaginative, aggressive regulation.

James M. Graham and Victor H. Kramer
Appointments to the Regulatory Agencies: The Federal Communications Commission and the Federal Trade Commission (1949–1974)

Old [FCC] Chairmen never die, they just fade away into the FCBA.

Richard E. Wiley, FCC chairman
Federal Communications Bar Association
luncheon, June 27, 1977

1 Many former commissioners of the FCC will tell you it's a thankless job—but there is never a dearth of applicants eager to take it. The pay is good ($50,000 a year), the tenure (seven years) is better than a senator's, the amount of work is generally up to the commissioner, and it's all indoors with no heavy lifting. Formal requirements for the job are vague although no more than four of the seven commissioners may be from the same political party.

The Commission came into being largely because of broadcasters who were distressed by the Babel-like situation of the 1920s. Everybody was talking on the air at once so that nobody could be understood. Herbert Hoover, then Secretary of Commerce and charged with overseeing the budding broadcasting business, said in 1922, "This is one of the few instances that I know of in this country where . . . all of the people interested are unanimously for an extension of regulatory powers on the part of the government." Ever an optimist, Hoover remarked in 1925, "We can surely agree that no one can raise a cry of deprivation of free speech if he is compelled to prove that there is something more than naked commercial selfishness in his purpose."

In 1927 Congress established a bipartisan Federal Radio Commission, with five members presidentially appointed from each of five geographical areas. The Secretary of Commerce still had some powers over radio broadcasting, and a staff of only 20 people was designated to aid the commissioners. The technical problems the FRC faced were staggering, but Congress was stingy with funds. The agency struggled along until 1934 when the Communications Act set up an independent regulatory agency of seven members (no more than four to be of the same political party) with jurisdiction over both wire and wireless communications, either interstate or foreign.

When the 1934 act was being written, the "communications" were just radio, telephone, and telegraph. Since then the technology of communications has galumphed along at a rate that makes the 1934 act simplistic, and yet the FCC must regulate complex modes of communications that were totally unforeseen in 1934.

In writing the acts, Congress adopted a phrase from the lexicon of public utility regulation: "public interest, convenience and necessity." This vague standard has been used ever since by FCC commissioners to justify whatever they have chosen to do. The phrase carries more weight than any five words should have to, and its meaning has been modified and refined by years of FCC decisions, judicial interpretations, and legislative actions.

On the face of it, a commissioner's job is overwhelming. He is called upon to decide questions involving radio and television programming and technical matters, telephone and telegraph rates, international communications by satellite and undersea cable, emission standards for microwave ovens and garage-door openers, citizens band radio, amateur radio, maritime communications, police and fire department communications, cable television, pay-television on air or by cable, data transmission services, educational broadcasting, antitrust considerations, and consumer electronics standards.

Considering the awesome responsibilities commissioners must bear, one would think that the President who appoints them and the senators who confirm them would take particular pains to ensure that each nominee is a legal-engineering-administrative paragon. Yet for many years, Presidents and members of Congress have been accused of using the FCC as a political dumping ground.

Is this accusation fair? In a remarkably readable, even gossipy, volume titled *Appointments to the Regulatory Agencies: The Federal Communications Commission and the Federal Trade Commission (1949–1974)*, prepared for the Senate Commerce Committee in 1976, lawyers James M. Graham and Victor H. Kramer conclude:

> Partisan political considerations dominate the selection of regulators to an alarming extent. Alarming, in that other factors—such as competence, experience, and even, on occasion, regulatory philosophy—are only secondary considerations. Most commission appointments are the result of well-stocked campaigns conducted at the right time with the right sponsors, and many selections can be explained in terms of powerful political connections and little else: Commission seats are . . . useful runner-up awards for persons who ricochet into the appointment as a result of a strong yet unsuccessful campaign for another position; appropriate resting berths for those who have labored long and hard in the party vineyards; and a convenient dumping ground for people who have performed unsatisfactorily in other, more important, Government posts.

A staff study by the House Subcommittee on Oversight and Investigations analyzed the prior employment of the 19 commissioners and the chairmen appointed and confirmed, from mid–1960 to mid–1976. Ten of the 19 had been employed in business or law practice that furthered industry interests. Only one of the 19 commissioners had demonstrated "consumer sensitivity" prior to Commission appointment, through full-time or part-time activity, in or out of government, promoting a consumer, environmental, or conservationist cause.

Graham and Kramer recommended that "a commissioner should have a demonstrated sensitivity to consumer and minority needs. In the past, a great deal of time has been spent on the question of whether a nominee is 'not insensitive' to those needs. What is required, however, is proof positive that the nominee begins with a clear understanding of the particular concerns of the so-called minorities within our society. The regulated industries have the resources at their command to insure that their viewpoints will be heard, argued and considered. This is not the case with other groups which have vital interests in an agency's performance."

Because most commissioners lack any demonstrated interest in the consumer, it is not surprising to learn that citizen groups have had little voice in selecting the commissioners. Speaking before a joint congressional committee in 1976, Victor Kramer emphasized that public interest and consumer groups are excluded from the process of identifying and selecting possible nominees:

> General public comment is confined to the time after the nomination is made, and consumer groups must necessarily center their efforts on the Senate and the confirmation hearing. To this day, selection of regulators is a closed process as far as consumer groups are concerned. Such is not the case with the regulated industries. With occasional exceptions, the White House allows and, at times, has actively solicited their reaction to a proposed commissioner in the critical period before a nomination is announced. Pre-nomination meetings and conferences between candidates and industry representatives are all too commonplace.

Commissioners traditionally have won appointment because they had friends in high office—or, more important, because they lacked powerful enemies. Regulated industries have been more successful in blocking appointments they feared than in promoting their own candidates. Citizen groups have testified in opposition to some FCC appointments and have campaigned with members of Congress to block appointments; usually the groups have been forced to settle for a statement from the nominee that he or she will deal evenhandedly with issues that concern the groups.

In one case, a citizen group scored a notable triumph. President Nixon in 1974 nominated Luther Holcomb to an FCC vacancy that under law had to be filled by a Democrat or an Independent. Holcomb, an ordained Baptist minister from Texas, had been appointed by Lyndon Johnson as vice chairman of the Equal Employment Opportunity Commission and reappointed by Nixon. For the FCC appointment, Holcomb had strong backing from the members of the Texas congressional delegation, both from Democrats and Republicans, and particularly from Nixon's former Treasury Secretary John Connally.

Holcomb's appointment was opposed by members of the Association of Spanish Surnamed Americans and by NOW (National Organization for Women), who felt he had been less than vigorous in carrying out EEOC responsibilities. But it was the Consumer Federation of America that sank the Holcomb nomination by revealing correspondence (on EEOC stationery) in which Holcomb told of his active campaigning for Nixon and other Republicans. At that point, Holcomb asked the President to withdraw his nomination.

During the years 1969–1972, the persistence of BEST (Black Efforts for Soul on Television) and its national coordinator, William Wright, helped persuade Sen. John Pastore (D.–R.I.), chairman of the Communications Subcommittee of the Senate Commerce Committee, to insist that the President nominate a black commissioner. In fact, Pastore ultimately refused to act upon other FCC appointments until a black was appointed; but BEST had little say in the eventual selection of the black commissioner. Judge Benjamin Hooks of Memphis was recommended by Sen. Howard Baker (R.–Tenn.), the ranking Republican on Pastore's committee.

A more representative example of citizen influence on the appointment process was the 1973–1974 attempt to block the confirmation of former Detroit broadcaster James Quello. The fact that Quello would be replacing Nicholas Johnson, the commissioner they held in highest regard, was especially upsetting to consumer advocates. Ralph Nader wrote Senator Pastore "on behalf of the millions of Americans who deserve at least one consumer spokesman on this important regulatory agency." Nader told Pastore that confirming Quello would be "bad government, an affront to the Senate and brazen disregard of the millions of viewers of the nation." A number of citizen groups wrote Pastore and other senators in protest; consumer and minority representatives, as well as Commissioner Johnson, appeared at the confirmation hearings to oppose Quello.

While this opposition made the hearings the longest ever conducted on an FCC nominee, only two of 16 Commerce Committee senators voted against Quello. By the time the nomination reached the Senate floor, the confirmation was affirmed by voice vote and, according to Associated Press, "without debate or dissent with just a couple of Senators on hand."

Political pressure hasn't deterred would-be commissioners. *Broadcasting*, an industry magazine, has noted that "White House talent scouts attest that FCC memberships are among the most sought-after appointive positions in government." Graham and Kramer emphasized that most commissioners "actively sought the job, wanted it desperately, and would have been crushed if they hadn't gotten it. The same is true in a reappointment situation." They also observed that prominent candidates for appointments who failed initially to get the nod often succeeded on their second or third attempts for the office.

Of the 52 commissioners who had served through the first half of 1977, about half were lawyers. Three of the 52 commissioners were women: Frieda Hennock (1948–1955); Charlotte Reid (1971–1976) and Margita White (1976–   ). Chairmen of the FCC, designated by the President, earn $2500 a year more than their six colleagues; the chairmen have a larger staff, considerably more public visibility, and the chance to steer the agency in the direction they want it to go. From 1934, when the FCC was established, until 1962, there was always an engineer, or a person skilled in the technical aspects of broadcasting, on the Commission. (Since then commissioners have relied for engineering expertise primarily on the Office of Chief Engineer or on engineering assistants on their personal staffs, though there has been a tendency in recent years for commissioners to hire an extra legal assistant or a generalist rather than an engineering aide.)

One reason people are so eager to win appointment to the FCC is the prospect of having a high market value in a regulated industry after their government service. Lawyers, particularly, have been known to forgo the higher salaries offered in private practice to put in an FCC tour and emerge as valuable legal commodities. Like other appointed government officials, many commissioners do not serve their full seven-year term before joining industry. The average chairman has served less than three years.

In *Economic Aspects of Television Regulation,* Roger Noll, Merton Peck, and John McGowan noted that of 33 commissioners between 1945 and 1970, 21 who left became affiliated with the communications industry, either as employees of companies regulated by the FCC or as lawyers and engineers practicing before the agency. Most of the other 12 commissioners retired after leaving the agency.

Between January 1970 and June 1977, nine commissioners left the FCC. Five of them became affiliated with the communications industry.

The Communications Act of 1934 prohibits commissioners who resign before their terms expire from practicing before the agency for one year. Some observers have suggested that this restriction isn't long enough to insulate commissioners from career considerations when they are setting policy and making judicial decisions.

President Carter announced early in 1977 that he would expect regulatory appointees to sign a pledge of their intention to complete the term to which they were about to be named. He later recommended that the time limit barring a previous appointee's participation in any matter before the agency be extended and that it apply to all commissioners, whether they complete their terms or not. Legislation was introduced "to close the revolving door" at all federal regulatory agencies.

With the prospect of future industry employment, commissioners naturally avoid fouling the nest to which they may fly. Nor are industry representatives reluctant to remind them.

One reminder was dropped in September 1976, when the Commission recommended to Congress that the Communications Act be amended to eliminate the provision that permits the filing of competing applications for a broadcasting facility that is up for license renewal. Under the current act, the Commission is obliged to hold a full-scale hearing to consider serious competing applications. After urging from Chairman Richard E. Wiley, the Commission recommended that competing applications be considered *only after* the incumbent licensee had been found disqualified to continue operation. Wiley told Barry Cole that communications lawyers had approached Wiley unsuccessfully with reminders that, "You're going to be out here practicing yourself before too long, Dick. You ought to keep it in mind that these hearings can be mighty lucrative, and they last for years."

Some commissioners and communications experts strongly oppose increasing the time during which a member is barred from practice after stepping down. When Sen. Lowell Weicker (R.–Conn.) proposed extending the waiting period in a 1976 regulatory reform bill, Commissioner Glen Robinson called the provision "quixotic and counterproductive." He said that an ex-commissioner's taking advantage of his or her former position and "inside information" to influence staff or former colleagues "is an imaginary problem." He maintained that existing law covers intentional abuses and cited such former commissioners as Fly, Porter, Minow, Loevinger, Cox, and Burch as examples of superior lawyers who might never have consented to serve if such a restriction had been in effect when they were appointed. In a later letter Wiley told the senators, "I agree with this assessment; it seems unreasonable to me to prohibit a person from practicing his profession in an area in which he has spent a great deal of his career and has expertise." Weicker's bill passed the Senate but died in the House after a jurisdictional dispute.

Cross-fertilization between the Commission and the private communications bar has led to legal challenges. Early in 1976 a challenger seeking the license of WNAC–TV, Boston, asked the FCC to disqualify the incumbent's law firm, Pierson, Ball & Dowd, because one of the firm's members was former FCC Chairman Dean Burch. The firm had represented the licensee for many years, and Burch was playing no part in the case; but the challenger claimed that Burch's presence in the firm was sufficient to affect the decision. The petition cited the United States code and American Bar Association rules to the effect that "the knowledge of one member of a law firm will be imputed by inference to all members of that firm." In May 1976 the FCC denied the petition, to the relief of the law firm and the licensee (which would have had to spend thousands of dollars bringing another firm up to date on the proceeding, which began in 1969).

Staff members who leave the agency can go into private practice immediately. Arguments similar to those advanced about commissioners have been marshalled favoring or opposing various restrictions on staff activities. In fact, in May 1935, the FCC passed a rule forbidding FCC attorneys from practice before the agency for two years after separation. The rule was rescinded after the commissioners heard complaints that the rule discouraged applications from talented lawyers.

Large staff turnover is a common phenomenon at all regulatory agencies. As Acting FTC Chairman Paul Rand Dixon told the House Appropriations Subcommittee in April 1976, his staff turnover was so rapid that "we've gotten to the point where we've got to think about contracting out some of our major cases." Rapid staff turnover certainly has prevailed at the FCC, especially in the broadcasting field where good outside opportunities are available.

During the first two and one-half years of Richard Shiben's tenure as chief of the renewal branch, for example, he says he went through "two and one-half staffs." Such rapid turnover increases the chances of what Ralph Nader calls "the deferred bribe," which is not money. Being cooperative is a way to keep career options open, to prove to prospective employers that one is knowledgeable, efficient—and agreeable.

One major reason that young lawyers left the Commission was (and presumably will continue to be) that they can get more money outside. A former high official in the Broadcast Bureau discussed the differences between working at the FCC and in private communications practice: "I worked 60 hours on a filing last week," he said, "and I got $4000. I worked 60 hours at the Commission during a week and got about $500." He volunteered that the work he'd done on the filing was far easier and wasn't subject to review by anyone but his client—who really didn't know much about the subject.

When important staff members leave the FCC, they are often Pied Pipers. In their wake come clients to their new law firms or consulting companies, often clients who have desperate problems with the FCC. Departing staff members may be able to lure subordinates to leave the FCC and move with them. If the staff member was sufficiently influential, he is like the advertising man who sets up his own shop with the personnel and clients from the advertising agency he just left. When established FCC staff members retire or leave the agency to start their own businesses, they have an additional advantage: those they placed in FCC positions over the years remain in those posts and provide important access to what the agency is up to. This phenomenon is governmentwide, of course, not restricted to the FCC.

Several Washington law firms include partners who were once FCC general counsels. For example, when John Pettit resigned that post in March 1974 to rejoin the law firm he had left two years earlier, two FCC attorneys, one of them Chairman Dean Burch's administrative assistant, soon joined him. AT&T, which had not previously done business with the firm, retained Pettit within months of his FCC departure; and the owner of two Arkansas TV stations, threatened with loss of license, also sought out the firm.

Not all senior staffers leave the Commission as the culmination of a carefully conceived program to increase their salaries and enhance their life-styles. Some turnover results from a basic change of policy and philosophy within the FCC.

Certain staff members with substantial responsibility are tenured under the Civil Service system and hold secure jobs, no matter who the commissioners are. When a tenured bureau chief or key staffer espouses policies at odds with those of the majority of the Commission, he may be made to feel unwelcome or harassed in a number of less than subtle ways until he volunteers to become a statistic in the agency's turnover.

Although most of the middle-level jobs are protected by Civil Service, the rate of departure for industry jobs is high among these employees, too. Frequently the motivation is opportunity for advancement, but sometimes it is disappointment in the standards of the agency.

Some lawyers leave the FCC because they are disillusioned with the nature of their jobs for reasons unconnected with the Commission's philosophy: they are disgusted with the boring and repetitive routines of their work; they feel they are filling out forms and going through motions that paralegal aides could handle; they feel cut off from the decision-making process. In short, they are not content to be cogs in the machine.

The longer Cole stayed at the Commission the more convinced he became, through observation and discussion, that staff members reach a point of no return. If individuals stay at the Commission beyond that point (often about five years), their entire careers, at least until they retire, will be as FCC employees; and they adjust their thinking accordingly. This phenomenon probably applies to most bureaucracies; certainly, the government's substantial retirement benefits are conducive to such patterns.

While not unique, the situation helps explain the weariness, cynicism, and indifference expressed by many staff members whenever a new commissioner was enthusiastic about a new idea. Many times the staffers had seen similar ideas circulate and then disappear. In coming to terms with their environment, the staffers had tempered their expectations.

After just a few years the feisty crusader who joined the Commission prepared to do battle with vested interests tends to abandon any quixotic posture and to be pleasant to those pleasant outsiders, generally representatives of regulated industries, who recognize his true worth. More significantly, the crusader learns to avoid the hassles that are the natural consequence of trying to fight the system. The atmosphere of the Commission is like that of a gentlemen's club. Troublemakers are politely ignored; their opinions are not sought. They are labeled by the collegiate members of the club as "radicals" or "obstructionists." Unless their presence is necessary to form a quorum or otherwise satisfy the club's ancient by-laws, they are generally excluded from the kaffee klatsches that constitute the club's primary business sessions. After many years the career employee has all too often established himself either as an eccentric, outside the mainstream of decision making, or as a functionary, dependable, but not very enthusiastic about anything.

On the other hand, staff members who are accomplished politicians and wily empire builders may find themselves with greater power than any single Commission member except, perhaps, the chairman. They will undoubtedly have greater expertise in their specialties than any commissioner has. Unless the chairman or a majority of commissioners has become distrustful of them, key staff members have the power to decide what information to bring to the Commission's attention and in what form. Sometimes staff members have chosen to delay certain matters or to keep them from commissioner scrutiny because they think the commissioners don't really want to deal with the situation. Or they may fear the Commission's decision and be holding the matter until a Commission more favorable to their point of view is installed.

When the courts or Congress—sometimes even citizen groups— castigate the FCC for its handling of some matter, the commissioners tend to blame the staff: "They never brought it to our attention in a form in which we could decide the issue." Conversely the staff laments, "The commissioners never told us what they wanted."

The vast majority of the FCC's decisions on routine matters are delegated to the staff. (An FCC organizational chart is in Appendix A.) And when the commissioners are to decide an issue that involves a close judgment on whether or not the agency should take action, the commissioners frequently have no idea of the debate raging below-stairs. A staff office or bureau presents to the commissioners a single recommendation on almost all matters, even though that recommendation may have been reached after a sharp split among staff members. Commissioner Johnson was continually urging that the staff offer alternatives. Cole thought this would be very desirable, too, when he first went to the FCC. Later, the process of rationalization, which becomes more highly developed the longer one stays at the Commission, made him sometimes agree with the staff that things were chaotic enough with just one recommendation. The commissioners seemed to have problems understanding the salient points of a single recommendation and reaching a decision. Alternatives might simply have bogged down the meetings even further; and major matters, which took years to resolve anyway, might have been delayed even longer.

Staff recommendations were often shockingly dependent on other data sources. For example, when two cable systems merged to form the nation's second largest cable system, the staff had to acknowledge its reliance on the trade publication *Television Digest* for information regarding the size and rank of the various systems, even though the FCC's Cable Bureau was supposedly gathering facts to determine whether the FCC should put limits on the size of any one cable operator's holdings. When the Broadcast Bureau, after years of delay, was pressed for information about whether FM stations should be permitted to duplicate programming of AM stations under the same ownership, the Bureau was forced to copy figures on FM growth from trade press reports.

The FCC's dependence on outside information sources stems from agency staffing weaknesses. There hasn't been a professional economist on the Commission in its history, and since 1970 only Commissioner Robinson consistently demonstrated an interest in economic fact-finding. Nor would the commissioners necessarily heed any economic data that might be presented, regardless of their source or persuasiveness. When the staff did bring information that contradicted data supplied by interested parties in a proceeding, a majority of the commissioners sometimes totally ignored the staff information in reaching a decision.

The staff seldom presented its own research findings or even findings from research done under contract. In July 1975, the Commission testified before the House Communications Subcommittee about its research efforts. Chairman Wiley was strongly criticized when he indicated that during the current fiscal year the Commission was going to spend only $750,000 for research, less than 1.5 percent of the Commission's total expenditures. The committee members would have been even more critical if they had realized that Wiley had inadvertently cited the $750,000 as one year's research budget when it actually represented a two-year total.

Most of the meager research funds are distributed through the Office of Plans and Policies, which was established in 1974. This office had a research budget of $400,000 for fiscal 1977. (The total FCC budget was about $57,000,000.) The Plans and Policies Office has helped somewhat to provide the Commission with independent data; but since it has only seven professionals, it contracts out much of its information gathering. One of the major duties of the office is to check each agenda item and determine whether its position agrees with the bureau's recommendation. During Wiley's tenure as chairman, the chief of this office normally reported his conclusions directly to Wiley, not to the full Commission.

Planning has never been one of the FCC's strong suits. The staff complains that it has no time for planning, that enormous effort is required just trying to reduce the backlog. The executive director's office has explored the use of computers and sophisticated management systems to try to improve the agency's efficiency. But old hands like Broadcast Bureau Chief Wallace Johnson have not been impressed; he said that the "thinkers" take up so much time asking questions that the "doers" can't get anything done.

Anyone who talks to a key FCC staff member (or attends a congressional hearing) will be told that the FCC is "overworked and understaffed." Is this true? Certainly a case can be made in such areas as citizens band radio where the glamour of the truckers' lore persuaded large numbers of people to buy CB radios and apply for licenses. The FCC was simply not flexible enough to get the staff to handle the inundation of applications.

Generally, however, the FCC proves the validity of Parkinson's rule that "the amount of work expands to fill the time available to do it." Many of the approximately 2150 employees at the FCC work long hours and accomplish a great deal; others sit around and do virtually nothing.

In a crisis the structure of the FCC is not flexible enough to permit the chairman or anyone else to move personnel freely and quickly to meet the needs of the moment, although chairmen are able to form special task forces for certain matters they feel deserve a high priority. Sometimes, if the most pressing problem is one that the commissioners do not want to handle, they will plead that they simply don't have the personnel to solve it—rather than undertaking a massive reallocation of the work force. For every complaint of FCC inefficiency in the broadcasting field, there are numerous complaints about how it mishandles cable, telephone systems, industrial radio, and other, less publicized responsibilities.

Nonetheless, most commissioners acknowledge freely that they specialize in problems concerning broadcasting. Some commissioners try assigning personal aides to other specialty fields, such as common carriers or special radio services. Once such assignments are made, commissioners tend to rely completely on the aide in the field. Other commissioners will specialize not only in broadcasting generally but also in specific areas of broadcasting. For example, Robert E. Lee has been a champion of UHF television (channels 14–83) development; Robert Bartley took a particular interest in cases involving concentration of control; Benjamin Hooks zeroed in on equal employment opportunity. From time to time commissioners have attempted to take an interest in every issue upon which they must vote—but they usually found themselves in the same position as the Cabinet officers who tried to follow President Carter's edict to read every regulation issued by their respective departments.

Cole asked almost all of the 14 commissioners who served during his five years at the Commission to estimate the proportion of their work time (including traveling and speech-giving) devoted to broadcasting. In most cases the estimate was at least two-thirds—and often even more.

The inordinate percentage of time commissioners spend on broadcasting stems partly from broadcasting's glamour and visibility and partly from the fact that broadcasting is something every commissioner knows something about and feels comfortable discussing. The disproportionate time could certainly not be justified in terms of new regulatory issues which needed attention. As Dean Burch once mentioned to Cole, there has been very little that's new in basic broadcast regulatory policy since the passage of the Radio Act of 1927. This lack of innovation is in sharp contrast to the new and complex issues arising in other areas of Commission regulatory activities, such as international (and satellite) communications and computer data-processing services provided by common carriers.

Nor can commissioners justify that large proportion of energy and time devoted to broadcasting on the grounds of the economic importance of most broadcasting decisions. Cole sometimes heard commissioners engage in lengthy debates over whether a radio station should be fined $500 or $1000—and then, before adjourning for lunch, take a fraction of that time to dispose quickly of a complex common carrier matter involving many millions of dollars.

The other FCC bureaus vie with the Broadcast Bureau for the commissioners' attention. Sometimes two bureaus lock horns over matters of mutual concern and overlapping jurisdiction. The battle for valuable spectrum space, for example, often pits the Broadcast Bureau against the Safety and Special Radio Services Bureau, which wants to allocate unused portions of the ultra-high frequency (UHF) television band to domestic land mobile users, such as police departments, and to transportation and commercial users, such as trucks and taxis, rather than to television broadcasting. The Common Carrier Bureau also has an interest in this battle because of its desire to expand frequencies for mobile radio users, including users of automobile telephones.

It is not surprising that the bureau chiefs and other key staffers tend to ally themselves with the industries that they regulate and whose representatives they see daily. A bureau chief becomes an advocate rather than a regulator. One senior official in the National Association of Broadcasters (NAB) told Cole he liked Broadcast Bureau Chief Wallace Johnson as a person, but found him "a poor advocate for the broadcast industry," and therefore wanted him replaced.

Bureau chiefs and key staffers tend also to ally themselves with the prevailing interests of the chairman or the majority of the commissioners. This alliance is particularly true of broadcasting, since the commissioners are especially interested in it and make their views known. Top officials of the FCC are selected by a vote of the commissioners; if the commissioners have a pro-industry philosophy, they are likely to select someone who agrees with them to head the day-to-day regulatory functions. The average commissioner may know no more about the candidate's other qualifications than about those of an FM station owner in Wichita. In practice, the chairman is given great leeway in personnel selection.

The power of the chairman varies considerably, depending on the energy, the skill, and the philosophy of the incumbent, and on the composition of the rest of the Commission. But the chairman's power is greater than that of any other commissioner. Besides being the President's main man, who serves as chairman at the President's pleasure, the chairman is also the agency's primary spokesman, and sets the Commission's agenda.

The real power of the chairman depends to a large extent on who his colleagues are and on how he relates to them. Richard Wiley may well have been the most powerful chairman in FCC history. Throughout his term, his six colleagues were appointed by a President of Wiley's party—either Nixon or Ford. Wiley was enormously hard-working, well informed, and well organized. He chose to involve himself deeply in certain matters, and his colleagues gave him a free rein because he was willing to compromise with them. Wiley worked hard to develop a consensus and was rewarded with near unanimity on most votes. He would try to ascertain the sentiments of the other commissioners before a meeting and would agree to language changes or to rule modifications to accommodate their strong feelings. According to *Access* magazine, during fiscal 1975 Wiley's vote was with the majority 98.9 percent of the time. Hooks, who had the most dissents, voted with the majority 96.3 percent of the time. As one of the other commissioners said of Wiley, "He's a good negotiator, a good bargainer."

Wiley once said, "I do try to get as many people under the umbrella as I can. A decision that's 7–0 is better than one that's 4–3; there's more confidence in it. You may have to change some language to do that, but I don't compromise on basic principles." His predecessor, Dean Burch, had a less tractable group of commissioners to deal with— and he was satisfied with a 4–3 vote if it went his way. He delegated far more authority to the staff than Wiley delegated, and Burch had no affinity for the close supervision at which Wiley excelled.

Wiley acknowledged he liked to "get out in front of issues" and use his power as chairman to shape the form of the final Commission action. Getting out in front has some disadvantages, however; criticism of the Commission is usually directed at the chairman. Because of Wiley's desire to decide things rather than sit on them and because of his tremendous capacity for work, the number of Commission decisions increased during his regime, and the number of opportunities for criticism (and court reversals) increased also.

Wiley met regularly with key staff members, told them what he wanted and expected, and set deadlines for execution. He explained that he wanted to hear any objections the staff had to his plans—if a compromise could not be worked out, the staff member was free to appeal to the full Commission—but he did not want to be surprised during Commission meetings by some argument he had not considered previously. Understandably, most staff members concentrated on pleasing Wiley. And there was no reason to believe he was not speaking for a clear majority of the Commission on almost all issues.

For readers who are never sure whether Laurel or Hardy was the fat one, here is a brief rundown of the commissioners who served on the FCC from the time Cole went to the agency in 1970 through the first half of 1977, and of how they got to be commissioners.

Robert T. Bartley, a Texas Democrat, is a nephew of the late House Speaker Sam Rayburn. In 1950 Rayburn wrote President Truman to seek an FCC appointment for Bartley, then Rayburn's administrative assistant: "I am more interested in this than any other recommendation I have ever made to you." Bartley got the first Democratic vacancy (in 1952) and won easy reappointment to two further terms, retiring in 1972 at the age of 63. His interest in the FCC began when he was director of the agency's Telegraph Division in 1934. After serving the SEC as a senior securities analyst from 1937–1939, he became an officer of the Yankee Network, a commercial radio system. He worked for the National Association of Broadcasters from 1943–1947 before joining Rayburn's staff.

Robert Emmett Lee, a Republican from Chicago, was first appointed to the FCC by President Eisenhower in 1953. Lee has served longer than any other federal regulator in history. Lee joined the FBI in 1938 as an accountant; J. Edgar Hoover appointed Lee chief clerk of the FBI in charge of all fiscal matters, and in 1946 recommended Lee to the House Appropriations Committee where he rose to director of investigations. In 1953 he aspired to become assistant comptroller general, but despite considerable congressional backing failed to win the post. An FCC commissionership offered Lee, then 41, was almost a consolation prize. Lee was proud of his friendship with the controversial Sen. Joseph R. McCarthy (R.–Wis.) and had worked in McCarthy's campaign to unseat Democratic Senator Millard Tydings in Maryland in 1950. This activity engendered opposition, and Lee was confirmed to the FCC by the unusually close vote of 58–25, giving the Republicans their first FCC majority. Lee's primary congressional sponsor, the powerful Republican Styles Bridges of New Hampshire, urged Eisenhower to reappoint Lee in 1960. The vote was 64–19 in the Senate, with the Democratic opposition citing agency scandals (which Lee hadn't been connected with). In 1967 Lyndon Johnson reappointed Lee even though his retention meant the Republicans would continue to hold a 4–3 FCC majority during a Democratic administration. Johnson's FCC chairman, Republican Rosel Hyde, wanted Lee reappointed; and Johnson, notoriously touchy about tampering with the FCC because of his broadcast interests, readily agreed. Senate confirmation was swift and unanimous this time. In 1974 Lee was appointed by President Nixon to an unprecedented fourth term.

Kenneth A. Cox, commissioner from 1963 to 1970, was a Washington state law professor who served as special counsel to the Senate Commerce Committee from 1956 to 1960. Committee Chairman Warren Magnuson (D.–Wash.) asked President Kennedy to appoint Cox FCC chairman in 1961; but Kennedy chose Newton N. Minow, a member of Adlai Stevenson's Chicago law firm and a friend of Robert Kennedy and Sargent Shriver. Magnuson's recommendation was sufficient to earn Cox appointment as chief of the FCC Broadcast Bureau in 1961, but not for a Democratic vacancy in 1962. The next year Kennedy did appoint Cox commissioner. When Cox's term ran out in 1970, President Nixon was eager to shift the 4–3 Democratic majority. Cox, 53, joined a Washington, D.C., law firm and became a vice president of MCI Communications, Inc., a specialized common carrier regulated by the FCC.

Nicholas A. Johnson was appointed commissioner in 1966 at the age of 31; for the previous two years he had been Maritime Administrator and had characterized shipping subsidies "a half-billion dollar a year theft from the American people." Shipbuilders, shipowners, and union representatives were eager to be rid of Johnson, and he himself wanted to try something new. Lyndon Johnson appointed him to the FCC. Nicholas Johnson was an Iowan and a member of the Texas bar who had clerked for Supreme Court Justice Hugo Black, taught law at the University of California, and worked for the prominent Washington law firm Covington & Burling. Johnson had known LBJ's press secretary Bill Moyers in Texas and one day went to see Moyers at the White House. While Moyers was busy, presidential aide Jack Valenti took Johnson on a tour, winding up in the Oval Office. LBJ, impressed by the bright young fellow with the appealing surname and Texas ties, offered him a spot in government. According to Johnson, the President withstood enormous lobbying pressures from maritime interests who wanted a new, less feisty administrator. McGeorge Bundy recommended Nicholas Johnson for the FCC post at a time Johnson said he was ready to leave government. Johnson clearly infuriated many broadcasters and members of other regulated industries and some politicians; but he served a full seven-year FCC term, leaving in 1973. After a narrow defeat in an Iowa Democratic congressional primary, Johnson became chairperson of the National Citizens Committee for Broadcasting.

H. Rex Lee, a Democrat, was appointed to the FCC in 1968 at the age of 58 after a long career of government service in various agencies and departments. President Johnson, then a lame duck, had been turned down by his first choice for commissioner, and was seeking someone who would be easily confirmed by the Senate. Lee accepted the appointment only after assurances from key senators that there would be no controversy. LBJ had visited American Samoa in 1966 during Rex Lee's term as governor and had been particularly impressed by the instructional television system Lee had established. In December 1973, ten days after Nicholas Johnson left the Commission, Lee resigned. For a while he was associated with the Public Service Satellite Consortium, a nonprofit corporation. In 1977 he went back to American Samoa to again serve as governor.

Dean Burch, former Republican National Committee chairman and manager of Sen. Barry Goldwater's presidential campaign, was appointed FCC chairman at 41 by President Nixon in 1969. White House memos revealed during the Watergate crisis indicated that some staff members expected Burch to apply political pressure to the media, but there is no indication that Burch responded. The Arizona lawyer left the FCC in 1974, after serving longer than any other chairman except James L. Fly (62 months), to become a special assistant to President

Nixon, who was under siege at the time. By year's end Burch left the White House although he remained an important political adviser to Gerald Ford. Burch joined the Washington communications law firm of Pierson, Ball & Dowd.

Robert Wells, a Kansas Republican and broadcast executive, was appointed in 1969 to fulfill President Nixon's 1968 campaign pledge—that he would name a broadcaster to the FCC. Wells had been campaign manager of Robert Dole's senatorial bid in 1968; Dole in turn campaigned for Wells's FCC nomination. A broadcaster since he was 17, Wells was general manager of a Great Bend, Kansas, radio station and of the Harris Radio Group when he joined the Commission at the age of 50. He left the FCC in 1971, ostensibly to seek the governorship of Kansas, but decided not to run for health reasons and returned to his broadcast interests. In 1976 Wells was reported to be a leading candidate to head the Office of Telecommunications Policy; but citizen groups and nonbroadcast communications interests opposed the choice, and Wells withdrew his name from consideration.

Thomas J. Houser was nominated to the FCC in December 1970 by President Nixon, whose first choice for the short-term vacancy that would provide a Republican majority was held up by an IRS audit. Houser, 41, was deputy director of the Peace Corps. He had been active in Illinois Republican politics and had managed the campaign of Sen. Charles Percy in 1966. Despite his political support, Houser was replaced after nine months on the FCC by Rep. Charlotte Reid (R.–Ill.), who had been promised appointment by Nixon. Houser returned to his Chicago law practice (including communications law) and helped organize the 1972 Illinois Republican campaign. In 1976 Houser was named to the Office of Telecommunications Policy post that Robert Wells had failed to get. The election of Jimmy Carter made this, too, a short-lived appointment; and in 1977, Houser opened a Washington law practice.

Charlotte T. Reid was named to the FCC in 1971, at the age of 58, after serving five terms in the House of Representatives. When President Nixon first discussed the appointment with her, she recalled, he said: "Have you ever considered the FCC? A woman with your congressional background and singing experience could make a fine contribution." From 1936 to 1939, under the professional name of Annette King, she was a featured vocalist on NBC radio and on Don McNeill's *Breakfast Club.* When her husband, Frank R. Reid, Jr., an Aurora, Illinois, attorney, died suddenly after winning the Republican nomination for a House seat in 1962, Mrs. Reid was selected to continue his campaign and won reelection four times. Her voting record was conservative; she never scored less than 96 percent in the Americans for

Constitutional Action ratings of voting records. Her district was to be reapportioned in 1972, and had she run she would have faced a primary against Leslie Arends, House Republican whip for almost 30 years. Mrs. Reid resigned from the FCC in 1976 and later became a consultant in Washington.

Richard E. Wiley was named to the Commission in 1972 after serving two years as general counsel—the first elevation of a staff member since Cox in 1963. Wiley, a Chicago lawyer, had worked for Bell & Howell and later became a partner in a law firm with no communications practice. He was active in the Nixon-Agnew campaign of 1968; and two years later a fellow campaign worker, then in the White House, arranged job interviews with FCC Chairman Burch and FTC Chairman Caspar Weinberger. Wiley was tapped for the FCC because Democrat Henry Geller was holding the important appointive position of general counsel. In 1974 when Burch went to the White House, Wiley was named chairman at the age of 39. President Carter permitted Wiley to remain FCC chairman after Wiley's term expired June 30, 1977.

Benjamin L. Hooks, the Commission's first black member, was a judge and an ordained Baptist minister. Besides serving as a pastor in Memphis and Detroit, he had been vice president of a Memphis bank. His appointment was the culmination of a long campaign by civil rights groups to have a black on the FCC. The groups had helped persuade Senate Communications Subcommittee Chairman John Pastore (D.–R.I.) and ranking Republican Howard Baker (R.–Tenn.) to insist that the White House appoint a black member. Hooks was Baker's choice although Hooks was a Democrat; and with Baker's aid, Hooks was chosen over other black candidates. He became a commissioner in 1972, at the age of 47; five years later he left the FCC to succeed Roy Wilkins as head of the NAACP.

James H. Quello was sworn in as a commissioner in 1974 at the age of 60 after what Graham and Kramer called "the most extensive inquiry ever conducted by the Senate into a regulatory nomination." During a 28-year career in broadcasting, Quello had risen from promotion manager of WJR Detroit to general manager and a vice president of Capital Cities Broadcasting Corporation. He retired in 1972 and early the next year issued a press release that he was seeking an FCC appointment. Over the years, he had made friends among the Michigan congressional delegation, and they supported his campaign. Minority Leader Gerald Ford apparently recommended Quello directly to Nixon; Senate Minority Whip Robert Griffin and Democratic Senator Philip Hart also backed Quello. Citizen groups opposed the nomination because of Quello's broadcast industry background. Quello saw no conflict of interest. He told *The Washington Star:* "I'm not using the appointment as a steppingstone to a high-paying job in the industry. I'm not a lawyer who's going to use it to obtain high-paying clients from industry." Despite a memo charging Quello with insensitivity to minority needs when he was a broadcaster, and the revelation that he, a Democrat, had contributed $1100 to Nixon's reelection campaign, the Senate finally confirmed Quello, 18 months after he had announced his availability for the job.

Glen O. Robinson won FCC appointment the third time he was considered; he was named to the unexpired portion of Burch's term, in 1974. Robinson was recommended to Alexander Haig, White House chief of staff, by Burch, then a White House assistant, and by OTP Director Clay Whitehead. Both were impressed by Robinson's law journal articles. Robinson was offered the position after Luther Holcomb withdrew his nomination. Robinson was 38, a law professor at the University of Minnesota. He had worked in communications law and antitrust at Covington & Burling. Robinson's term was less than two years. With his reappointment in doubt in 1976, an election year, Democrat Robinson announced he would join the law faculty of the University of Virginia. He is also associated with the Aspen Institute Program on Communications and Society.

Abbott M. Washburn was 59 when he was named in 1974 to fill the one-year unexpired portion of H. Rex Lee's term. Nixon was having trouble finding FCC candidates; the leading contender for the post was hastily dropped from consideration when he acknowledged he had written members of Congress urging Nixon's impeachment. As *Broadcasting* said, "Washburn had waged a long, quiet campaign for the nomination and had antagonized no one—an important qualification." In the 1940s he had reviewed radio scripts for sponsor General Mills. He was executive vice chairman of Crusade for Freedom (Radio Free Europe) in 1950, and he organized Citizens for Eisenhower clubs in 1952. For the next eight years, Washburn served as deputy director of the U.S. Information Agency. Washburn ran an international public relations firm until 1968 when he worked for Citizens for Nixon. From 1969 to 1971 Washburn was chairman of the United States delegation to INTELSAT and was an OTP consultant at the time of his appointment. In 1975 Washburn was named to a full seven-year FCC term by President Ford.

Joseph R. Fogarty was nominated to the FCC in July 1976 with the strong support of Sen. John Pastore, who was about to retire. Ten years before, Fogarty gave up his private law practice in Rhode Island to join the staff of the Senate Commerce Committee. Until 1975 Fogarty worked primarily on transportation legislation and East-West trade bills. He then joined Pastore's communications subcommittee as chief

2 Broadcasting was pioneered largely by businessmen willing to risk some money promoting their enterprises. Retailers and manufacturers of radios set up stations to broadcast programs in order to induce people to buy receivers. Newspapers aired tidbits of news in hopes of boosting their circulations. Department stores provided entertainment to promote radio sales and sometimes mentioned other merchandise they stocked. In the very beginning, no direct advertising was permitted, but some businessmen felt that identification with this new toy—this music and information service—would be good public relations. Religious groups and educators soon started stations to spread the word. Large businesses like AT&T, Westinghouse, and General Electric experimented with radio to determine whether it should have any place in their corporate plans. All of these pioneers were interested primarily in promoting their own products. Radio was strictly speculative in the early 1920s.

The initial development of television was delayed by World War II. Between the end of the war and September 20, 1948, the FCC authorized 123 TV stations (15 of them never got on the air) and had 303 applications pending. Eighty-two percent of the authorizations were issued to radio licensees, with most of the rest going to publishers, electronics manufacturers, and motion picture interests. These were companies with engineering savvy, advertising experience, and the money to invest at a time when television technical standards were uncertain and there was no prospect of immediate return on investment (because there weren't many receivers in homes). The 108 television pioneers were lucky in their timing as well as bold—the FCC hadn't anticipated the demand for TV channels and so granted the best channels in the top markets without a hearing. By September 1948, the FCC recognized that the existing allocation plan was technically deficient and declared a freeze on station authorization while the commissioners pondered how to allocate the remaining channels.

The Commission lifted the freeze in June 1952, when 716 applications for TV stations were pending. The Commission held numerous lengthy hearings to decide (on rather vague criteria) which of many competing applicants would best serve the public interest. But the person or company that *buys* a station and license today competes with no one—under the Communications Act the FCC is permitted to consider the qualifications of only that party to whom the incumbent licensee wishes to sell.

In the late 1970s broadcasting is a mature (not to say entrenched) industry. During three generations of development, many licenses have changed hands. At the 1977 NAB convention, a 33-year-old, self-proclaimed "second-generation broadcaster" commented to colleagues at a workshop: "We are businessmen and businesswomen first, and broadcasters second."

Most station owners operating these days bought their stations—instead of starting or inheriting them. *Broadcasting* reported that between 1954 and 1977, more than $4 billion changed hands in sales of 6618 radio stations (counting AM-FM stations sold together as one station), 623 television stations, and 239 radio/television combinations. Some stations were sold several times during the 23 years.

For comparison, here is the number of stations of various types on the air as of June 30, 1977, according to FCC records:

Commercial television—725 (including 514 VHF, channels 2 through 13)

Educational television—258 (including 101 VHF)

Commercial AM radio—4502

Commercial FM radio—2937

Educational FM radio—903

FCC requirements for becoming a broadcaster have always been minimal. A licensee must be an American citizen (or a corporation primarily owned and controlled by American citizens); must have enough money to run the station for a year, not counting any revenues it may produce; and must be of good character—the last qualification being open to generous interpretation. The licensee must also satisfy the FCC that there will be a staff engineer with sufficient knowledge to meet Commission technical standards, plus "adequate" studio and equipment plans "to effectuate to a reasonable degree" the programs to be broadcast.

STATION FINANCES

When one speaks of the broadcast industry, one envisions a powerful monolith, but actually about two-thirds of all radio stations have fewer than 10 full-time employees; roughly half of these have fewer than five full-time employees. Television stations range from a Mom-and-Pop station in Wyoming with two employees through major-market stations with hundreds of employees. The 15 television stations owned by the three networks have over 5000 employees.

Although broadcasting has a reputation for being a profitable business—and the major stations are indeed profitable (with 30 percent profit margins not unusual, especially in TV)—many radio stations and UHF (channels 14–83) television stations make small profits or report losses. For example, in 1976 the FCC reported that in the previous year, 2618 AM and combination AM-FM radio stations made profits (832 making less than $10,000) and 1677 reported losses. Among independent FM stations (those owned without an AM station in the same market), losers outnumbered gainers 373 to 278. In television for 1976 (as reported the next year), of 460 VHF stations, 10 made less than $25,000, and 42 lost money; of 178 UHF stations, 6 made less than

$25,000, and 59 reported losses. An NAB survey showed the typical UHF television station did not become profitable until 1972.

The profitability of a station is not necessarily dependent on the market it serves or on its number of employees. For example, a station that must compete for advertising revenues with a number of other stations may not be as profitable as, say, a station in a relatively small market that covers a wide territory without effective competition. A station in a large market with a large staff may be meeting such payroll expenses that its profit margin is not as impressive as that of a largely automated station with lower rates and fewer commercials.

The FCC garners its figures from its Form 324, the annual financial report required of broadcasters. The Commission has felt this form is inadequate to supply a clear picture of a station's fiscal operations and is currently investigating ways to revise the form, partly because accounting systems used by individual stations vary widely.

The Form 324 reports are kept confidential by the FCC. Citizen groups, believing that stations making profits ought to reinvest funds in local programming, have been eager to see station financial reports. The FCC has agreed with the broadcasters' vehement claim that revealing their profits and other financial data would leave them at a competitive disadvantage. In 1971 citizen groups filed a petition asking the FCC to make the reports public. The Commission, as of spring 1977, had gone to some pains to avoid voting on this petition. In 1975, for example, the staff had drafted an opinion turning down the request. Chairman Wiley said he didn't want the issue raised in a Commission meeting and would be happy "if I never see that item again." Had the Commission voted the petition down, the groups could appeal to the courts to order the FCC to make financial records public. As long as the petition was "under consideration," the FCC could turn down requests from citizen groups asking to see individual stations' Forms 324, on grounds that the agency was considering a broad rule and would not take the matter up case by case. The most recent FCC action on financial forms was to issue a public notice in December 1976 further restricting access to the forms to FCC employees with "an official need" to view them.

In December 1971, Commissioner Johnson revealed some financial information when he issued a dissent to staff renewals of California broadcast licenses. In his statement, he analyzed programming expenses and profits of 27 unidentified California TV stations. Johnson stated that "one of the most important aspects of the theory of Commission renewal that has not been fully developed is the need to link station resources with station performance." He found great variability in the ratio of what a station took in to what it spent on programs.

Johnson found that the proportion of total broadcast expenses devoted to program costs ranged from 0.4 percent to 62.4 percent. One station spent 0.3 percent of its revenues on programming; another station spent 86.5 percent. Johnson said this finding constituted a good reason to make the data available to community groups. "Doesn't such data contribute to a fair evaluation of a station's excuse that it can't do better in programming because it would cost too much? To me, it is hard to justify the failure to release such data when its use is almost essential if the renewal process is to be other than a charade."

In addition to programming expenditures, there are other gauges of a broadcaster's commitment to community service. About 470 commercial television stations and 2000 commercial radio stations subscribe to the NAB code, which sets advertising standards and program standards. Code members agree not to exceed certain commercial time limits during segments of the broadcast day; they agree also not to advertise certain products the code deems distasteful and to advertise others in only certain ways. For example, there is to be no advertising of liquor, and commercials involving beer and wine must avoid on-camera drinking. The code sets standards concerning children's programs, news and religious shows, and political broadcasts, too.

Some stations go beyond NAB code demands. Group W, the stations owned by Westinghouse, has refused to subscribe to the NAB code because, according to management claims, these stations have more stringent standards regarding commercial time than the code has.

Most stations that do not subscribe to the NAB code refuse to join because they believe the standards are too restrictive. Many stations choose simply to ignore the code. In the 1950s, 39 TV stations resigned because the code prohibited hemorrhoid remedy advertising; when the code ban was lifted, 30 stations rejoined.

THE NETWORKS

The biggest broadcasters of all—certainly biggest from the standpoint of audience—are the networks. The FCC does not license networks directly; in fact the word "network" does not even appear in the Communications Act. However, the FCC regulates network-owned radio and television stations. (Each of the three networks has its full quota of five VHF stations. The CBS owned-and-operated [O&O] stations, for example, in New York, Los Angeles, Chicago, Philadelphia, and St. Louis, cover roughly 25 percent of the nation's population.)

The three networks and their 15 O&O television stations accounted for more than 35 percent of the before-taxes income of the television industry for 1976. The 15 O&O stations alone showed combined pre-tax profits of $159 million on revenues of $487 million. This represented more than one-third of the three networks' total profits. For years ABC reported losses on its networking operations and claimed to be sustained by the profits of the stations it owned and operated. Similarly, radio networking operations are largely unprofitable, but O&O radio stations are profitable.

Attacking the various network problems from the agency's statutory regulatory power over stations, the FCC has passed rules regarding network affiliation agreements with stations and the amount of time network affiliates can accept from the networks during prime-time programming hours. About 85 percent of commercial TV stations and about one-third of commercial radio stations are affiliated with a network. The majority of the nonaffiliated TV stations are UHF stations with necessarily limited coverage areas and audiences; this limitation is the main reason efforts to launch a fourth network have been unavailing.

For many years members of Congress have introduced bills that would bring networks under direct FCC licensing, but these bills have died without a single formal hearing. Networks claim that the bills are unnecessary, that, through licensing network O&Os, the FCC has sufficient power to govern all it should.

Although Congress did not include networks in the Communications Act, in the course of hearings on the act, committees of Congress encouraged the FCC to regulate stations engaged in "chain broadcasting." In 1938 the FCC held its own hearings and passed chain broadcasting rules—dealing primarily with contractual arrangements between networks and affiliates.

As television became increasingly important between 1955 and 1957, the FCC held a thorough investigation of network practices and later formed an Office of Network Study within the agency. Few FCC rules regarding networks resulted from its investigation, but it heard charges that the networks dominated the television programming field through their ownership interest in programs they aired.

These allegations were revived by the Department of Justice in 1972 as the basis of an antitrust suit against the three networks. By the time the suit was brought, many of the circumstances outlined in the charges had changed. The networks claimed that the antitrust suit was politically inspired by the Nixon administration. The judge dismissed the case but gave Justice permission to pursue antitrust charges again if the department wished. NBC, in November 1976, signed a consent decree with Justice, conditioned on settlement with the other networks. A newly submitted case is pending.

In September 1976, Westinghouse (Group W), which owns five VHF television stations, two affiliated with CBS, two with NBC, and one with ABC, asked the FCC to institute a new network investigation. Group W charged that networks "are now exerting undue power and influence over affiliated local stations to the detriment of both the stations and the television viewing public." One major complaint of the group owner was that networks are supplying to stations programs with "excessive amounts of violence and adult material" without giving the individual licensees a chance to preview the material and decide if they want to air it. The FCC has always held the licensee, not the program supplier, responsible for whatever goes on the air. Group W asked the FCC to require networks to provide program previews for affiliates four weeks before air time.

Group W charged further that "the quasi-partnerships which once existed (between networks and affiliates) have now all but dissolved. Major decisions on expansion of network schedules, the content of programming, and compensation are now made unilaterally by the networks. Little incentive remains for serious consultation with or consideration of affiliates' views." A footnote adds, "Despite requests, one network even refused to discuss the matter of expanding the [network evening] news at its recent affiliates meeting." Group W continued, "The networks are trying to change local stations into mere extensions of the national network program pipeline. Each year local affiliated stations have less involvement in and responsibility for the totality of the programming carried over *their facilities* to the public in *their communities*. If this is allowed to continue, local affiliated stations will ultimately perform functions little different from cable TV outlets."

In January 1977, in response to the Group W petition, the FCC ordered an inquiry into the relationships between networks and affiliates and between networks and program sources. The Commission said, "What we contemplate at this time is solely a fact-gathering inquiry designed to provide the Commission with information necessary to a thorough understanding of television networking." This information, the FCC said, would be evaluated by a special staff of economists, lawyers, and other experts.

PUBLIC BROADCASTING

Compared with network broadcasting, public broadcasting attracted little FCC attention until recently. In 1976 the FCC proposed rules that would clarify the status of public broadcasting stations. The next year the FCC instituted an inquiry into fundraising practices and the underwriting of programs by corporations. On the whole, the previous attitude of commissioners toward public broadcasters was well expressed by Commissioner Robert E. Lee: "We pretty much left them alone."

The 258 public television stations are apportioned about equally among the following categories of licensee: universities, community foundations, and state or municipal school systems. Because most operate on UHF, only about two-thirds of the nation's population receives an acceptable signal. The 903 public radio stations are licensed to a wide variety of noncommercial operators; many of these stations operate on ten watts power on FM and their signals don't carry very far.

One of the seven commissioners is traditionally designated Education Commissioner; FCC actions regarding public broadcasting are supposed to originate in his or her office, and this commissioner serves as the agency's main liaison with public broadcasters. (The Education Commissioner is the one who will normally get the invitations to address their meetings and conventions.) Some commissioners have regarded this assignment more seriously than have others.

In addition, the FCC has had an educational branch within the Broadcast Bureau. For years this one- or two-person office has had little impact on FCC policy. The low priority of the educational branch was indicated when it was designated part of the Facilities Division during the Broadcast Bureau reorganization in 1976. The commissioners apparently did not consider establishing an Office of Education with advisory functions similar to those of the Office of Network Study; instead they placed the two-person "branch" in a division that handles applications for new or changed facilities.

The FCC's 1977 inquiry into fundraising methods and underwriting of public TV programs was instigated by commercial broadcasters' complaints of unfair, subsidized competition for advertising revenues. In 1972 the Corporation for Public Broadcasting asked the FCC to set more stringent engineering standards for noncommercial FM stations and to clarify the responsibilities of public radio stations to meet local needs. Four years later the FCC proposed rules that would clarify whether a station is obliged to offer educational programming and whether such programming must be instructional or "responsive to community needs of an educational, cultural and informational nature."

The Commission has devoted little regulatory effort to defining the service requirements of public stations. The FCC has avoided the question of what might be expected of public broadcasters because it believes that "the flexibility and freedom of the service is, in large part, fundamental to its existence."

COMMUNICATIONS LAWYERS

With rare exceptions, every broadcaster uses the services of a Washington lawyer specializing in communications to help him or her get a license or purchase a station. Some 760 lawyers, 80 percent of whom represent broadcasters, are members of the Federal Communications Bar Association (FCBA). Lawyers introduce the broadcaster to the mysteries of the FCC, and are usually successful in persuading the broadcaster to approach the Commission thereafter through a law firm.

Like dentists, the communications lawyers can tell their clients to come to them before they have trouble—or later when it will hurt worse. Lawyers point out that the FCC lacks clear guidelines on many important policies and procedures, that it sometimes enforces its rules in an arbitrary fashion, and that the FCC has traditionally preferred a "case-by-case" or "let's-wing-it" approach to making decisions. These warnings, which are not ill-founded, along with the references in the trade press about the encroachments of government regulation and the severe sanctions the FCC *may* impose, convince most broadcasters that it is wise to retain an experienced Washington attorney. Some free-enterprise-minded buccaneers who choose to scorn FCC regulations wind up paying horrendous fees to lawyers to defend them in license-renewal hearings (although this happens less frequently than the bulk of broadcasters may realize).

Of course, lawyers profit substantially from the FCC's murky procedures and fuzzy standards. One lawyer wisecracked to the Kentucky Association of Broadcasters that "our job is to keep the FCC confused."

In *Washington Monthly* (May 1970) Elizabeth Drew discussed the reaction of some FCBA members to one of the maiden speeches of Chairman Burch. He stated his intention to clarify agency procedures and to establish "clear and definite standards." Drew noted that such a pledge "has become something of a tradition for new FCC Chairmen." She continued:

> A committee has now been established, made up of FCC staff and communications lawyers, the very groups that brought the procedures to their present state. "Those procedures put the lawyers' children through college," said one Washington communications lawyer. "I've been down this road so many times," said [another lawyer]. (Washington lawyers usually decline to have statements attributed to them; they say it interferes with the lawyer-client relationship.) "It's old hat," he said. "It's the old cry of the administrator saying, 'Please forget your clients and make my administration more effective.' Utter nonsense. I'm not skeptical about the committee. It's laughable. But it's an almost foreordained speech. I have news for Dean Burch: I'm going to try a case in a way that's best for my client and take advantage of every rule that's there."

During Cole's tenure at the Commission, members and staffers encouraged broadcasters to come directly to the FCC for help on relatively routine matters—including how to fill out applications for license renewal. Such offers were directed primarily to the smaller operators, the broadcasters who had to pay a fee every time they consulted their lawyers, not to the group owners who had law firms on retainer. These smaller operators were precisely the ones most terrorized at the thought of dealing directly with the government. They seemed convinced that anything they said might be used against them.

Cole discovered that an element of wistfulness accompanied the small broadcaster's fear. As a former faculty member at the University of Texas, he attended a meeting of that state's broadcasters. The questions they posed often ran along the lines of "Do I really need a lawyer?" and "What would happen if I tried to operate without one?" Their other questions indicated they were thoroughly confused by the FCC's lack of clear guidelines and felt that lawyers might be (as they so often represented themselves) the broadcaster's only hope of cutting through the Commission's vague policies and inexact procedures.

The broadcaster's fear of dealing directly with the Commission instead of calling his lawyer was demonstrated again in 1972. The Commission had announced a comprehensive review of radio regulation with "deregulation" as the goal. Newly appointed Commissioner Richard Wiley spearheaded the program and was making speeches around the country to solicit recommendations from broadcasters as to which regulations should be revised.

In an editorial on Wiley's efforts, *Broadcasting* (August 7, 1972) stated, "Broadcasters will never be provided with a more attentive and open-minded audience. Many of them are missing that chance." *Broadcasting* noted that "only a couple of hundred letters have come in," which it characterized as "an unimpressive representation of 6,700 radio stations." *Broadcasting* continued:

> As Commissioner Wiley has pointed out, broadcasters have been ignoring the commission's invitation on the theory that no comment is wise, that anything they say may be interpreted as a disposition to fight city hall. If that attitude does indeed prevail, it bespeaks a servility that deserves all the regulation it gets.
>
> Broadcasters are being asked to invest a little thought and an eight-cent stamp—about the cheapest Washington representation they will ever be offered.

Despite this editorial and other "news items" in *Broadcasting*'s "Closed Circuit," few letters were sent by broadcasters.

Two weeks later, *Broadcasting* reported that some broadcasters had confided "they were told by Washington advisors, presumably attorneys, trade-association contacts and political factotums, to keep a low profile lest the bureaucrats let fly with investigations and threats of fines or other reprisals."

Cole had heard similar reactions directly from broadcasters. "It's like writing a draft board," one said, suggesting that once he wrote the FCC, his name might be placed in a special file or computer list to be singled out later for unwelcome attention. A television broadcaster (whom one would have expected to be more sophisticated) called an FCC staff member during the inquiry into children's programming and asked if requesting an extension of time to file comments could be used against him in some future Commission proceeding (like filing small claims against insurance companies, perhaps).

Considering the climate of fear, it is not surprising that communications lawyers have developed a mystique. Most of them are not eager to dispel the broadcaster's anxieties.

These attorneys are practicing administrative law, which was characterized by one FCBA attorney as "law by telephone involving little legal research and, in fact, very little law." Except for the rare instance (how rare will be demonstrated and discussed later in this book) in which a licensee must go into an actual legal proceeding, a licensee receives from his lawyer mainly advance and "inside" information or interpretation rather than legal knowledge.

On various occasions during Cole's five years at the FCC, he became "the source of the law," even though he is not a lawyer. Communications lawyers called him for his interpretation of what the Commission meant or what it might do regarding license renewal requirements. His opinions, which he told the lawyers were merely gut reactions based on what he knew about the Commission and the attitudes of staff and commissioners, would presumably be communicated to the clients of the lawyers making the inquiries. Such information would be regarded as Commission policy.

Commission staff considered it natural and proper for FCBA members to get advance information regarding Commission actions. In fact, the desire of members of the staff in the Renewal and Transfer Division of the Broadcast Bureau to reduce the backlog of pending matters, coupled with the desire of various lawyers to satisfy their clients by informing them quickly of favorable Commission decisions, sometimes resulted in a law firm's providing direct assistance to the Commission staff in order to speed up the process. This assistance might relate to a decision already made; for example, the lawyer might be permitted to compose a telegram to be sent by the staff announcing an action. This assistance was also given, however, with respect to decisions not yet made and to material supposedly confidential.

While at the Commission, Cole learned of law firms (who were "parties at interest") providing secretarial assistance, including typing, in the preparation of memoranda that were part of "agenda items" presented to the Commission for decision-making purposes. Members of the Commission later learned of these practices, which have apparently been stopped. As one lawyer remarked, "At least the Commission staff now composes the telegram and types the agenda item."

Why are the Commission staffers so cooperative with attorneys? Probably they feel, "Why not?" Most proceedings are uncontested and the lawyer is generally a pleasant person who simply is asking for information in which he has a legitimate interest. Letting a lawyer know that his client's license application, for example, has been approved before notifying the licensee of that fact is hardly evil or improper.

A more significant—and self-serving—reason for the cooperation of FCC staffers with attorneys may be that many staffers intend to become members of the communications bar and would want similar treatment. For this reason, many key FCC staff people attend receptions for a law firm's clients. As one commissioner's legal assistant put it, "Someday I will be out there."

The camaraderie between communications lawyers and FCC members and staff officials includes a certain amount of gift-giving and party-throwing. Although some observers may believe that only a particularly stuffy, post-Watergate morality condemns such hale and hearty (and above-board) activities, a case can be made that the benefactions contribute to an atmosphere of patronage.

It should be emphasized that there is nothing improper, let alone illegal, in FCC employees having casual contacts with communications lawyers. What is important, however, is the influence exerted on the attitudes of staff people, particularly when it causes differences between the treatment of lawyers and the treatment of "the public." One bright young Commission attorney expressed astonishment at the way a key Broadcast Bureau official reacted to the questions from lawyers as compared with questions from members of the public. "A lawyer comes in and he [the FCC staffer] will sit there indefinitely and tell him all he knows—what's happening, what's liable to happen, what he would like to have happen. On the other hand, he won't even give the public the time of day!"

This dual standard of treatment is not limited to decision-making personnel. Cole heard secretaries and clerks ask callers on the phone, visitors in the office or in the reference room, "Are you from a law firm, or are you just a member of the public?"

3
Lobbyists at Work

The corporations that do business in Washington seldom resort to anything so gross as bribing public officials. By a series of small favors, the influence artists seek to instill in the officials a feeling of personal obligation. The favors range from theater tickets and imported liquors to French perfumes and free transportation. It is the accumulation, rather than any single gift, that gradually obligates the courted officials.

Jack Anderson and Les Whitten syndicated column of July 5, 1976 (Reprinted by Permission of United Feature Syndicate)

A trade association is first and foremost a defensive operation. What you are in business for is to resist governmental inroads, and against that background it is sometimes difficult to convey positive successes.

Vincent Wasilewski
President, National Association of Broadcasters

Any commissioner who pays for his own lunch is a fool.

Dictum of an FCC member to Cole, 1972

3 Politicians, as standard rhetoric, employ the phrase, "There's no such thing as a free lunch." Anyone who spends a few weeks in Washington knows better. Old government hands explain loftily, "I'm not going to sell my integrity for an expense-account lunch," and indeed they believe that. But the problem goes deeper than simply a matter of appearances.

Many representatives of industries regulated by the FCC attempt to influence the agency's rules and policies. As a matter of course, so do the lawyers who practice before the Commission. As long as this lobbying is done in an ethical, reasonably open manner, providing it does not touch upon cases in which the commissioners are exercising their judicial responsibilities, it is legitimate.

In the late 1950s, when the FCC was awarding television licenses, lobbying that amounted to influence peddling and ex parte (off the record) contacts between commissioners, who were supposed to be acting as judges, and applicants for stations led to a string of nasty scandals. Courts remanded the cases involved to the Commission for further hearings and disqualified the applicants that had broken the rules. One chairman, John Doerfer, was forced to resign for accepting repeated hospitality on a yacht from a major broadcaster, George Storer.

In the past 17 years, the FCC has been free of scandal. Lobbying continues, however; and not surprisingly, the interests with the greatest financial stakes in what the FCC does try to employ the best and brightest representatives to deal with the commissioners. This fact of Washington life tends to exclude the representatives of citizen groups, minority councils, and undercapitalized regulated industries.

The problem of what constitutes undue influence is not new. In 1949 the Hoover Commission report on regulatory agencies noted:

> The industry has sought to influence the Commission's policies both by direct pressures and by more subtle means. The direct pressures are calculated to affect the Commission's judgment by instilling a fear of recriminations. They involve a play on the assured sensitivities of the Commission to public criticism and congressional reprisals. . . . [The industry] has also devoted much of its energies to the development of a Commission sense of sympathy for the industry and its problems.

Eleven years later, in 1960, Dean James M. Landis, once SEC Chairman, reported on the operation of the FCC to President-elect John Kennedy. He referred to the "daily machine-gun-like impact on both the agency and its staff of industry representation that makes for an industry orientation on the part of many honest and capable agency members as well as agency staffs."

On the television program *The Advocates*, a former Federal Power commissioner discussed how regulators are encouraged, through a campaign of ingratiation and flattery, to do things "for the guy you know—do it for Joe Blow." When the FCC was considering revamping or rescinding the prime-time access rule, one commissioner mentioned that a lobbyist had pleaded with him to vote against the rule, saying that the lobbyist would be fired if the vote went the wrong way.

The lobbying Cole observed at the FCC, both subtle and meat-ax lobbying, was conducted chiefly by representatives of the broadcasting and cable industries. Commission colleagues told him that these lobbying efforts were downright diffident compared with those of other regulated industries, particularly those of AT&T. One FCC staffer told *The Wall Street Journal*: "From what I've seen, AT&T seemed to be a public-relations company first and a communications company second." The official characterized AT&T's influence as "overwhelming."

Roger Noll, a noted economist and professor at Stanford, told Cole of an example of AT&T's widespread influence. Several years ago when Noll was associated with the Brookings Institution, a representative of a specialized common carrier seeking to compete with AT&T in that area invited Noll to testify on the company's behalf. Noll said that Brookings discouraged its staff from advocacy, but he offered a list of ten economists who might provide pertinent information. The next day the company's representative called Noll and asked if he could supply any additional names because nine of the ten suggested economists were affiliated with AT&T.

Influencing public servants with meals and gifts is common lobbying practice. A bureau chief once told Cole of an assistant bureau chief who was courted assiduously over the lunch table: "He gives $500 value for a $20 lunch." The value to the lunch-giver of having the luncher's full attention for perhaps two hours without interruption from phone calls, secretaries, or rival salesmen can be inestimable.

Ralph Nader's Public Interest Research Group takes the matter of small favors seriously enough to ask the Civil Service Commission to prohibit regulatory agency employees from accepting gifts or free lunches from anyone who "has or seeks business relations" with the agency. The petition said, "Meals and gifts lead to a sense of personal obligation as well as fraternizing and social exposures that can affect the way regulatory employees approach their duties." In 1977, former General Counsel Henry Geller and Citizens Communication Center's Charles Firestone petitioned the FCC, on behalf of the National Citizens Committee for Broadcasting, to prohibit formally commissioners or staff members from accepting meals from representatives of regulated industries, except at industry conferences or conventions.

Little gifts have become a ritual. At Christmas time lobbyists and lawyers drop off little "gifts for the office." ("It's a tradition, not a gift," one lawyer told a newly appointed commissioner.) The recipients of these gifts are secretaries, file clerks, and assistants, as well as commissioners.

What gifts are acceptable from an industry representative is a perpetual question, and answers become very arbitrary. Glen Robinson, during his first Christmas as commissioner, decided that cream sherry was too luxurious a gift and should be returned, but that a red wine was acceptable.

When a congressional committee questioned regulatory agency employees about gifts they had received, SEC employees owned up to the following items: a $10 thermometer, a $12 paperweight, a $5 pen, a $10 sketch of an employee, a $25 camera, and a pickle plucker valued at $3.75.

In return for such good-natured gestures as little gifts and lunches, lobbyists, like salesmen, ask for no more than time to make their pitches. One lobbyist admitted to Cole that the lobbyist timed his visits to a sympathetic assistant bureau chief to coincide with the chief's dental appointments.

Douglas Webbink, who as a Brookings Institution fellow spent a year observing the FCC, commented on lobbyists' access in a memo, "Casual observation on the eighth floor indicates to me that lobbyists of certain groups or companies appear at the door of one or more Commissioners every day of the week." Webbink continued:

> It is obvious that the president of a broadcasting station in a town of 25,000 will have no trouble seeing a Commissioner; whereas in some cases even a division chief or bureau chief may have to wait for several days to see a Commissioner. The current priorities of most of the commissioners seem to be: 1. Parties with direct economic interests; 2. Congress and the Administration; 3. The Commission staff; 4. Outside persons with public interest but no economic interest (outside public interest groups and individuals).
>
> The appropriate priority for an agency working in the public interest is: 1. The Commission staff; 2. Public interest groups and individuals; 3. Congress and the Administration; 4. Parties with direct economic interests. Clearly industry groups with economic interests should be allowed far less of the Commission's time than any of the other three groups.

The number of lobbyists who appear when an important decision is incubating can be staggering. Lawrence Secrest, when legal assistant to Chairman Wiley, expressed "astonishment" at the intensity of the lobbying efforts that took place just prior to the Commission's adoption of its statement on children's television. Secrest indicated that some network lobbyists called in or turned up at the chairman's office three or four times during a single day. (Leaks in the trade press, supplementing a published schedule of planned Commission meetings, inform any interested party of the dates on which certain important decisions will be made.)

Chairman Wiley instituted publication of a broad schedule of proposed meetings and matters to be discussed as part of what he termed "an open-door policy." He said, "People ought to be able to talk directly to their government officials." He listed his telephone number in the local directory and said he received calls from individuals who were not connected with regulated industries, and met with them in his office.

In 1973, Wiley spoke before the National Association of Manufacturers:

> The Commission needs and wants all of the expertise which it can obtain—and from any available source. And, in this connection, I want you to know that I am firmly committed to the proposition that a member of the regulated community *can* talk to his government without fear of punishment, that he *can* make constructive suggestions and criticisms without fear of regulatory reprisal and, finally and most importantly, that he and the Commission *can* work together to the end of a better and improved communications system.

Some commissioners, notably Chairman Wiley, made their daily appointment calendars available to anyone who wished to review them. Other commissioners have been somewhat reluctant to open their appointment calendars to public inspection. Wiley said, "I think it makes sense to let people know who sees you." But Commissioner Abbott Washburn stated, "I don't keep a regular calendar and I wouldn't want to do that." He said the Commission is so bogged down in making its procedures public—"that government-in-the-sunshine stuff"—that its work had been slowed by 50 percent.

The open-door policies apparently lead some broadcasters to feel that it is their duty to check in with the Commission when they visit Washington. Once Cole overheard the complaint of two broadcasters who, with their lawyers, had just left Chairman Burch's office after such a courtesy call: "It's like having to visit your grandmother every time you come to town." After hearing this exchange, Cole went to Burch's office as Burch was telling an assistant how much he disliked "the ritual visits" of some out-of-town broadcasters.

Although some broadcasters give the FCC a wide berth, doing their business entirely through their Washington lawyers or representatives, other station owners come to plead their cases in person when trouble arises.

Sometimes even a small broadcaster can lobby effectively by turning up at the FCC. In 1973 the owner of a radio station in Starkville, Mississippi, was found to have violated FCC rules on sponsor identification. He had telephoned the 23 local primary candidates and had offered to include them in a candidate list that would be broadcast on the station—provided they each paid $30 for the mention. The broadcast announcement didn't mention that fees had been paid. Following a complaint to the FCC, the Commission unanimously voted to send to the licensee a Notice of Apparent Liability for a $2000 fine.

On the day the Commission was to discuss the licensee's response to its notice, the station owner came to plead for mercy from the five commissioners then in office. Chairman Burch, who had not been contacted directly (the broadcaster spoke to Burch's special assistant Charles Lichenstein, who felt it was inappropriate to mention the visit to Burch), was surprised when Commissioner Charlotte Reid suggested cutting the fine in half. When Burch asked the staff if there were any reason to reduce the fine, they insisted that the station could well afford the full sanction, that the offense was a particularly "heinous" one because it misled the public, and that reducing the penalty would "knock precedents for a loop."

"Well," said Commissioner Robert E. Lee, "I can think of a thousand good reasons, each one worth one dollar." By a 4–1 vote, the fine was reduced. Burch (who apparently was never told of the lobbying that took place) filed a dissent, in which he noted, "Admittedly, the Commission has every right to review staff recommendations, but such review failed to disclose any rational basis for reduction of the fine."

The National Association of Broadcasters is the primary lobby on behalf of the industry at large. The 1977–78 budget for the NAB's government relations department was $785,100, including $559,800 for staff salaries.

One thrust of the NAB lobbying is a political action committee, established in 1972, to collect contributions from broadcasters and to disburse the funds to aid the reelection of key, cooperative members of Congress. The plan was modeled after the AFL-CIO Committee on Political Education (COPE). NAB President Vincent Wasilewski later exhorted the membership: "The name of the game in lobbying is money and don't forget it." In the 1976 elections the NAB's political action arm reported contributions, averaging $650 each, to 100 congressional candidates.

Formation of the political action committee had been triggered by what the NAB considered severe legislative setbacks—the loss of $225 million in cigarette advertising when Congress banned cigarette commercials, and a campaign spending bill limiting candidates' broadcast advertising. In 1972 the NAB saw potential trouble in the form of legislation to help the growth of cable television, congressional dissatisfaction with violence in television, and consumer opposition to legislation to provide longer license-renewal periods (and protection from license challenges).

In addition to collecting and distributing campaign contributions, the NAB encourages its members, local broadcasters, to contact their congressmen. In September 1975, for example, an NAB task force spent two days on the West Coast urging broadcasters to establish closer ties with their representatives and senators.

The real lobbying power of broadcasters does not lie in the amount of money they may contribute to campaigns, nor even in the power of their editorializing or formal endorsements. The power lies in the discretion of the broadcaster to report what a member of Congress is doing *when the member is not running for office.* Both the House and Senate are equipped with television and radio recording studios, where a member of Congress can prepare a report for home consumption at the taxpayers' expense, and provide the report free of charge to broadcasters in his or her district. The broadcaster is certainly under no obligation to air the reports, which might be described as self-serving. But the broadcaster who does choose to give listeners the benefit of their congressman's views may certainly expect that congressman to listen to the broadcaster's problems.

Even when an incumbent is running for reelection and the equal-time rules of the Communications Act and the rules governing payment for political advertising come into play, a broadcaster may choose to devote a great deal of free time to the campaign and thereby help or, more likely, harm the incumbent. In the news coverage, the broadcaster is free to characterize the nature of the local political race— what is said might be more persuasive than paid political ads. In a business built on compromise, an incumbent congressman is generally quick to forgive a station owner for opposing the congressman in the last election: the next one is less than two years away.

Major market TV operators may have influence with senators, who want to reach the most voters in the state; but a small-town radio operator may be of crucial importance to a House member. Congressmen usually know the station owners in their districts—in fact, may cultivate them. Because of this normally close relationship, the NAB often is represented before a congressional committee by a small broadcaster who complains of overregulation, burdensome paperwork, and the efforts of big government to drive the broadcaster out of business.

The small broadcaster is also trotted before the Commission in rule-makings and informal proceedings to illustrate the dangers of passing a new rule, the existing burdens that must be eliminated if the industry is to survive, and so forth. Through the last several years in the many attempts to slow the development of cable television, broadcasters have repeatedly paraded before the Commission a UHF broadcaster from Salisbury, Maryland. He points out to the FCC that not all broadcasters are fatcats, that he has run his station at a substantial loss.

According to *Television Digest* (February 23, 1976), some broadcasters became dissatisfied with this tactic. "Our biggest problem is that it's hard to go in there and cry poor mouth when TV is having its best

year ever," one said. Another broadcaster added, "It's time we had a
show of force to let them [commissioners] know that we won't stand
idly by any longer and watch them continue to nibble away at us."

In the same article, *Television Digest* reported the general reactions
of some connoisseurs of lobbying: "Commissioners agreed that NCTA
[National Cable Television Association] has out-lobbied NAB in recent
months, that many more cable people than broadcasters have pleaded
cases in person. 'The broadcasters were being out-lobbied all right and
I think they woke up to that fact,' Commissioner Quello said. 'It was
time for them to come in and state their case.' "

The NAB, like any lobbying organization, is continually confronted
by grumbling from those it represents. Lobbyists generally pride themselves more on the horrible things they prevented from happening than
on the actions they initiated. Wasilewski said that people must recognize that "a trade association is first and foremost a defensive operation. What you are in business for is to resist governmental inroads,
and against that background it is sometimes difficult to convey positive
successes." The NAB's biggest legislative and regulatory victory, he
said, is that "broadcasters still have the freedom to program as they
see fit."

That many things can go awry when the NAB is lobbying for "positive successes" is illustrated by what happened in 1974 to a license
renewal bill, which NAB officials had termed their number one legislative priority. The bill would have given preference to incumbent
licensees over challengers and would also have lengthened the license
term. Rep. Harley Staggers (D.–W. Va.), chairman of the House
Commerce Committee, wanted the term lengthened by only one year—
from three years to four years. He told the late Grover Cobb, NAB
executive vice-president, that if this provision was retained, Staggers
would not object to the bill's passage. Cobb agreed to support the
four-year term; but other lobbyists, particularly radio station owners,
ignorant of this agreement, persuaded enough members of the House
to vote for a five-year term that the five-year provision was approved
overwhelmingly by the House. Staggers was so furious at what he considered violation of an agreement that in the waning days of the 93rd
Congress, he refused to name House members to a conference to recon-
cile differences in the versions of the bill that had passed the House
and Senate. Staggers's maneuver effectively killed the bill.

NAB officials must contend with the wide diversity of members' interests. The concerns and needs of a radio broadcaster in a community
of 4000 persons differ greatly from those of a television station owner
in a major metropolitan market. If association officials spend less time
and energy on setting the hours a daytime radio station can remain on
the air than on fighting the broadcasting of new motion pictures by
cable systems, many small NAB members will be unhappy. When the
Commission is making rules about the operation of television stations,

the licensees of network-affiliated stations might take the opposite viewpoint from that of independent television station licensees.

As a consequence of this diversity, many splinter trade associations, each with its own lobbyists, have been established. To cite just a few, the Association of Maximum Service Telecasters represents primarily top-power VHF stations; UHF stations have formed the All-Channel Television Society; the Association of Independent Television Stations furthers the interests of nonaffiliates; the National Translator Association speaks for licensees with translators (auxiliary stations that increase coverage areas). Some other Washington groups include the Clear Channel Broadcasting Service (high-powered AM radio stations), the Daytime Broadcasters Association, and the National Religious Broadcasters.

Among the recent crises in NAB internal affairs was the establishment of the National Radio Broadcasters Association in September 1975. This group, previously known as the National Association of FM Broadcasters, was expanded to include all radio because members claimed NAB was "not doing enough to advance the causes of radio in Washington." NRBA had roughly 950 station members by May 1977 and was attempting to get congressional approval of radio-only renewal legislation.

Broadcast industry lobbying efforts have been hampered not only by contradictory demands within the industry but also by the growth of nonbroadcasting lobbyists, who argue for contrary positions. Organizations such as the National Cable Television Association help bring counterpressure (although not equal pressure) on legislators and FCC members on issues involving both cable and broadcasting. Counterpressure is sometimes exerted by other agencies of government; for example, the Justice Department has attempted to reduce concentration of media ownership.

Formerly, a broadcaster who opposed something and could not get satisfaction from the FCC could go to Congress and exert the necessary pressure. Now, however, Congress, as well as the FCC, is getting pressure from other sources. These other sources include citizen groups and nonbroadcasting industries, which with their political clout and financial resources are sometimes more influential.

When the NAB attempts to take the offensive in lobbying as, for example, when 160 broadcasters met with the Commission in February 1976 to protest relaxation of some restrictions on cable television, they are often no more successful than are citizen groups when they try to change existing rules and policies. It is much easier to persuade the commissioners and their staffs to preserve the status quo that they created than to effect change.

Even though the three networks play an important role on the NAB boards, their interests do not always coincide with those of the general membership so the networks have their own lobbyists—Washington vice-presidents. The network vice presidents deal with members of Congress and with the FCC. Understandably, the vice presidents tend to concentrate their efforts on the most sympathetic listeners. For example, in the early 1960s, the broadcast industry viewed the majority of commissioners as "tough regulators," but considered the ranking members of the House and Senate communications subcommittees to be generally pro-business. Thus, network lobbyists went to Congress to undo FCC actions they considered unreasonable. During the early 1970s, lobbyists felt the commissioners were friendlier to the industry, and important congressional committee members often seemed less compliant.

Lobbyists work both ends of the Washington axis as diligently as possible. Even a "friendly" FCC may be confronted at congressional hearings by questions planted by a lobbyist. Observers of these hearings enjoy speculating on which lobbyist gave which member of Congress a particularly vexatious question to ask.

Lobbyists face certain constraints at the FCC, however, largely because of the quasi-judicial nature of the commissioners' responsibilities. In adversary proceedings, agency employees are forbidden to listen privately to arguments from a single party. A recent court case raised the question of whether it is proper for FCC personnel to accept private representations even in rulemaking proceedings.

In 1975 the Commission issued rules limiting the kinds of movies and sports programs that cable operators or pay-television stations could offer. The rules, having been passed after a protracted rulemaking proceeding, were challenged in the court of appeals by program suppliers and pay-cable operators. Former FCC General Counsel Henry Geller filed an amicus brief asking the court to consider the extensive lobbying that had been part of the proceeding.

Geller argued that the Commission had committed a procedural error by permitting ex parte presentations in the pay cable proceeding. Geller cited a 1959 court ruling that in proceedings involving conflicting private claims to a valuable privilege, ex parte communications should not be permitted. The case cited by Geller was *Sangamon Valley Television Corp. v. U.S.* (269 F 2D D.C. Cir. 1959), which involved a rulemaking proceeding to reassign a television channel from Springfield, Illinois, to St. Louis, Missouri. The Supreme Court ordered a further hearing before the court of appeals because the Commission had permitted ex parte presentations.

As a result of the *Sangamon* decision, the Commission, in July 1959, proposed a set of rules to govern ex parte communications in rulemaking proceedings. In July 1965, however, the Commission terminated this proceeding without adopting any rules; the Commission decided instead to determine case by case whether *Sangamon* standards should apply. If the Commission decides (as it usually does) that *Sangamon* is not applicable, the notice of inquiry or rulemaking states,

"In reaching its decision in this proceeding, the Commission may also take into account other relevant information before it in addition to specific comments invited by this Notice." If, however, in the opinion of the Commission, a *Sangamon* or "closed" proceeding exists, the notice states, "All submissions by parties to this proceeding, or persons acting on behalf of such parties, must be made in written comments, reply comments, or other appropriate pleadings."

Geller claimed that *Sangamon* standards should have been applied to pay cable proceedings because the two criteria specified by the court existed. Conflicting private claims had been made by various industry groups—the broadcaster, the cable industry, the pay entrepreneur, the feature film owner, the sports entrepreneur—to valuable privileges, worth millions to the contestants. Geller noted that in the pay cable proceeding, the private claimants had been given several opportunities to advance their views, both written and oral.

Geller also cited a speech (delivered on April 30, 1974, before the Federal Communications Bar Association) in which Chairman Wiley expressed concern about lobbying that took place after the Commission had held an oral argument on some rulemaking. Wiley had said:

> There is one other lobbying technique which disturbs me although I would acknowledge that it is largely due to a somewhat unfortunate practice on the part of the FCC. I mention it today because I want to put you on notice of my intention to change this practice wherever possible. When the Commission holds an oral argument on some rulemaking matter, we carefully divvy up the advocacy time available among the various parties. When the argument is completed, the Commissioners should then be in the best position possible to make a tentative decision on the merits. Typically, however, such a decision is not made until long after the conclusion of the formal argument. During the delay until decision, oral argument often continues informally in the privacy of individual Commissioner and staff offices. I simply do not think that this is a good practice and, accordingly, and to the extent practicable, I hope to have the Commission making tentative judgments very quickly following oral argument, thus obviating the possibility of any further seriatim presentations. . . . Compromises, fall-back position and the so-called "real facts" are often reserved for supplemental filings and, perhaps, subsequent visits to Commission offices.

Geller referred to trade press reports that after oral argument, industry representatives had participated in several lobbying efforts during what Geller called "the final, crucial decisional stage." In fact, Geller was able to quote a speech (by Everett Erlich, senior vice president and general counsel of ABC, before the ABC television network affiliates on May 10, 1974), in which Erlich bragged about ABC's last-minute lobbying efforts to change the rules that the FCC was about to adopt.

Geller also cited press reports: "Word of last week's changes . . . got out during the week, and both broadcast and cable lobbyists rushed to the Commission, unhappy with some facets" (*Television Digest*, March 10, 1975); "Various [industry] groups lobbied the Commission, pressing for changes in the tentative decision" (*Television Digest*, March 17); and "[NAB] staff members met with [FCC] Broadcast Bureau staffers to present data backing up asserted need for [more restrictive] standards" (*Broadcasting*, March 17).

Geller asked the court to require the Commission to detail succinctly the ex parte presentations made by interested parties, to require the Commission to include in the official docket of the proceeding this detailing and any accompanying papers given the Commission at that time, and to provide three weeks for interested parties to examine and comment on these presentations. Geller emphasized that, although parties filing amicus and other public interest briefs had submitted comments and had appeared at the oral argument, they had not had the same opportunity as the industry lobbyists to participate in the "final, crucial decisional stage."

The court, while not granting all of Geller's requests, did require the Commission to supplement the record in the pay cable case by providing the court with a detailed list of all of the ex parte presentations members and staff had received between July 1972 and October 1975. The Commission, when it produced the list for the court in April 1976, emphasized that the list was "fragmentary" and "incomplete" and was based on "suspicion" and "recollection" (because no requirement for detailed records of such contacts had existed). The list was more than 60 pages long.

In reporting on the list on April 19, 1976, both *Broadcasting* and *Television Digest* said there were no surprises. For those familiar with lobbying efforts at the FCC, this was probably true. Others, however, might indeed have been surprised at the length of the list and at the number of times certain individuals had contacted Commission personnel. The list included some very important people, such as the presidents of CBS and ABC, the commissioner of baseball, the president of the Motion Picture Association of America (with Gina Lollobrigida and Sidney Poitier in tow), and the heads of the NAB and NCTA.

The lobbying efforts were not restricted to commissioners. William Johnson, chief of the Cable Television Bureau's policy review and development division, and a major drafter of the pay cable rules under discussion, listed more than 70 contacts. Moreover, Johnson reported receiving scores of communication reports and other written materials from interested parties, and some 100 letters from members of Congress—most of whom were passing on letters from constituents regarding pay cable proceedings or pay cable rules.

The Commission was clearly reluctant to supply the list. In fact, it preceded its list with a motion that the court reconsider the order. The Commission noted that no one had challenged its method of proceeding, that Geller hadn't raised his objection until two and one-half years after the proceeding had begun (Geller petitioned for revision of procedures or for issuance of notice of inquiry or proposed rulemaking in December 1974), and that Geller himself had made some ex parte presentations. Moreover, the Commission expressed concern that requiring written records of all relevant conversations with outsiders during a general rulemaking "will drastically reduce, if not destroy altogether, the efficacy of one means" of increasing the Commission's understanding of policy issues.

Commissioner Hooks did supply a list "out of an abundance of intimidated caution in the face of the contempt powers of the judiciary." He called his list "deceptive and valueless . . . through no design or intention." He warned that "submission of such selective data becomes almost frivolous." Nonetheless, Commissioner Hooks was able to remember enough names to fill five pages.

In March 1977 the court overturned the FCC's pay cable and pay TV rules. It also discussed Geller's objections to the conduct of the proceeding, largely agreeing with him:

> Although it is impossible to draw any firm conclusions about the effect of *ex parte* presentations upon the ultimate shape of the pay cable rules, the evidence is certainly consistent with often-voiced claims of undue industry influence over Commission proceedings, and we are particularly concerned that the final shaping of the rules we are reviewing here may have been by compromise among the contending industry forces, rather than by exercise of the independent discretion in the public interest the Communications Act vests in individual commissioners. . . . Our concern is heightened by the submission of the Commission's Broadcast Bureau to this court which states that in December 1974 broadcast representatives "described the kind of pay cable regulation that, in their view, broadcasters 'could live with.' "

> If actual positions were not revealed in public comments, as this statement would suggest, and, further, if the Commission relied on these apparently more candid private discussions in framing the final pay cable rules, then the elaborate public discussion in these dockets has been reduced to a sham.

> Even the possibility that there is here one administrative record for the public and this court and another for the Commission and those "in the know" is intolerable.

The court found that the FCC was inconsistent with the Freedom of Information Act in deciding whether or not to accept relevant information outside the official record. "Equally important is the inconsistency of secrecy with fundamental notions of fairness implicit in due process and with the ideal of reasoned decisionmaking on the merits which undergirds all of our administrative law," said the court. If ex parte contacts occur, the FCC official receiving them should submit any written documents or summaries of oral communications to the official file.

The FCC has appealed to the Supreme Court saying that banning ex parte contacts in informal rulemakings would "paralyze federal agencies." Judge George MacKinnon, one of the three appeals court judges, suggested a modification of the ex parte findings, restricting them to rulemakings "that will involve competing private claims to a valuable privilege or selective treatment of competing business interests of great monetary value. . . ." This would cover the pay cable proceeding, of course; but MacKinnon felt that some rulemakings on general subjects might appropriately be conducted under less stringent constraints.

Just a few months after the pay-cable decision, another three-judge appeals court panel underlined MacKinnon's warning (he was himself a member of the panel) in the case of *Action for Children's Television* v. *FCC* (July 1, 1977). This panel said the majority in the pay-cable decision had gone much too far in putting restrictions on ex parte contacts in rulemakings. With unusual sarcasm the court said:

> If we go as far as [the court in the pay-cable case] does in its ex parte ruling in ensuring a "whole record" for our review, why not go further to require the decision maker to summarize and make available for public comment every status inquiry from a Congressman or any germane material—say a newspaper editorial—that he or she reads or their evening-hour ruminations? . . . In the end, why not administer a lie-detector test to ascertain whether the required summary is an accurate and complete one? The problem is obviously a matter of degree, and the appropriate line must be drawn somewhere. In light of what must be presumed to be Congress' intent not to prohibit or require disclosure of all ex parte comments during or after the public comment stage . . . we would draw that line at the point where the rulemaking proceedings involve "competing claims to a valuable privilege" [as Judge MacKinnon suggested]. It is at that point where the potential for unfair advantage outweighs the practical burdens, which we imagine would not be insubstantial, that such a judicially-conceived rule would place upon administrators.

In 1975, as part of an "open government" act, Congress proposed certain restrictions on lobbyists, including those who dealt with regulatory agencies. The bill defined lobbyists as individuals or firms that receive $250 or more per quarter or $500 per year or more for lobbying, that spend those amounts in lobbying activities (excluding personal expenses), and that communicate orally with one or more employees of Congress or the Executive Branch on at least eight separate occasions. Such lobbyists would have to make full disclosure of their activities by filing an itemized, quarterly list of all expenses of $10 or more. *Broadcasting* interpreted the bill to include broadcasters or cable operators who made eight or more contacts with congressmen, commissioners or staff members. The bill was not passed into law because of extensive lobbying.

4
The Trade Press
Spreads the Word

Watch out for the trade press reporters. They read the papers on your desk upside down. . . .

Advice from a seasoned FCC official to Barry Cole when he became an FCC consultant in 1970

Basically, you can't get the word out. You have to rely on the press, the trade press . . . to pick it up. If they don't pick it up—or if it is *only* in the trade press, it doesn't get the distribution that all this stuff should get.

Leonard Weinles, chief of the FCC Office of Public Information. Testimony of House Committee on Government Operations, 1972

4 *Broadcasting* and *Television Digest*, the two Washington trade journals, are published each Monday. Copies are delivered to the homes of commissioners and influential broadcasting industry people over the weekend. At other Washington offices, the small groups gathered on Monday morning are probably discussing the fate of the Redskins; but at the FCC, they are talking about what appeared in the trade press. As the mail comes in, secretaries extract copies of *Broadcasting* and *Television Digest* from the huge mail pile and dispatch them to impatient bosses. Bureau chiefs, commissioners' legal assistants, and lawyers with rolled-up copies roam the halls.

Even though the FCC purchases many copies and the magazines provide other copies free, demand on the staff level far exceeds supply, and some Broadcast Bureau people don't see the trade magazines until late in the week. In fact, the pecking order parallels the order of distribution of trade magazines.

The arrival of the trade publications turns FCC offices into Sardi's, where producers, angels, and stars anxiously await the critics' verdict on their last extravaganza. But Commissioner Nicholas Johnson took a darker view of the trade press, accusing the publishers, editors, and reporters of belonging to a "subgovernment," which influenced the Commission to act favorably toward the broadcasting industry to the detriment of the general public.

Trade press influence was explained by a participant in a Brookings Institution conference on reforming regulation. He pointed out that a Commission appointee realizes soon after coming to Washington "that nobody ever heard of him or cares much what he does—except one group of very personable, reasonable, knowledgeable, delightful human beings who recognize his true worth. Obviously they might turn his head just a bit." This group comprises avid readers of the trade press, which reports the comings and goings, wit and wisdom of FCC commissioners in the same touching detail that the daily press devotes to Jimmy Carter, Farrah Fawcett-Majors, and Andy Capp.

The patriarch of the trade press, Sol Taishoff, has published *Broadcasting* for more than 45 years and has educated generations of commissioners in the same manner that Arthur Krock and James Reston tutored Presidents. *Broadcasting* reports and analyzes all major FCC actions and records the thousand routine actions the agency takes. The magazine's news stories are generally straightforward (with an occasional editorializing headline); but the editors' viewpoints are hammered home to even the dullest bureaucrats through the editorial page and a venerable page of inside dope, speculation, and gossip called "Closed Circuit," the first page insiders turn to.

Television Digest is a weekly newsletter printed on some dozen yellow pages, half of which are devoted to broadcasting and cable and half to consumer electronics. Unlike *Broadcasting*, this magazine carries no advertising but depends on the impact of its reporting and its concise, but comprehensive summary of the week's news.

In addition to *Broadcasting* and *Television Digest,* other publications cover FCC activities. *Variety,* the weekly show business newspaper, covers the FCC as part of the general entertainment scene. This publication traditionally encourages its reporters to write as they please, mixing analysis and news; but since one person is responsible for Washington coverage from movies to nightclubs and theater, the depth of *Variety*'s FCC coverage depends on the ability and the schedule of the correspondent of the moment. *Television/Radio Age,* a biweekly trade magazine, includes a regular FCC column, which emphasizes feature material and agency trends rather than spot news. To some extent, *Advertising Age* also reports on the FCC, particularly on how its actions affect advertisers and their agencies.

Coverage of the FCC occasionally appears in less specialized publications. Reporters from the wire services and the daily press may swoop down on the FCC for an exposé or for a story on an agency action of overriding general importance. Usually, however, these reporters cover several regulatory agencies at once and are seldom thrilled with that beat. The more talented reporters are assigned to greener pastures before they can cement the kinds of contacts that produce intelligent, influential articles.

Trade press reports on the FCC do have impact, not only on outsiders but also on insiders. Before joining the Commission, Cole realized the necessity of an outsider's reading the trade press to keep up with what the FCC was doing, but he had not reckoned on the importance of the trade press to the people within the FCC looking out on the world around them. He soon learned that his own perceptions of what he was doing and how well he was doing it—and what people thought of him—were influenced by trade press reporting. As an academic, he wanted to sound intelligent and informed. True to the academic's code, he wanted to stay above the fray, to appear objective— the reasoned, neutral observer. His ability to project these qualities depended on what the trade press said about him and his activities. Citations in the trade press molded his reputation in the minds of important people in the broadcasting industry, most of whom had never met him. A broadcaster would say "Oh, I know *you*!" and would invite Cole to come to the broadcaster's town 2000 miles away for a round of golf and "a chance to talk over some of your thinking and, if I may say so, misconceptions about broadcasting."

The trade press has an advantage over the daily press. With antennae always quivering, trade reporters like *Broadcasting*'s Len Zeidenberg or Dawson "Tack" Nail of *Television Digest* would question Cole on his work when he had been seen taking home large volumes of papers. On the other hand, the FCC reporter for a national news service, who called when Dean Burch left the FCC to serve as a special counselor to the President, apologized as he asked basic questions like how many commissioners there were and how long their terms lasted. Finally he admitted that he had never met the chairman or any of his staff—the reporter had never even been in the FCC building.

In the past, television critics like Jack Gould of *The New York Times*, Robert Lewis Shayon of *Saturday Review*, and Lawrence Laurent of *The Washington Post* devoted considerable column space to regulation of radio and television. Nowadays, television columns are devoted almost exclusively to programming. One reason for this change is revealed in a 1973 survey of newspaper TV columnists: only seven percent of those queried believed that anything they wrote might significantly affect FCC policy. The survey revealed also that of 58 writers, more than a third had been writing about television for only four years or less, and two-thirds had had no previous experience writing about mass media.

Les Brown, who for years was chief broadcasting reporter for *Variety* and more recently has been covering industry affairs for *The New York Times*, summarized the problems and shortcomings of daily newspaper TV critics in a 1975 speech:

> What every critic should know is how the trustees of the public airwaves are allowed to carry such small freight. . . . Newspapers are content to give television a perfunctory wink. [They still consider] TV one of those extras that serves as a come-on for readership instead of a part of the day's legitimate news. . . . Most TV columns are made up of network handouts and "gonna" stories—NBC is "gonna" do this or CBS is "gonna" do that. . . . Covering TV from Topeka must be like covering baseball from a scoreboard.

When a daily newspaper does do some digging at the Commission, the effect may be more explosive than the within-the-fraternity reports of the trade press. Stephen Aug of *The Washington Star* exploited a leak in November 1975 and reported on a confidential staff memo analyzing a recommendation to authorize certain clear-channel radio stations to operate on "superpower" (more than 50,000 watts). As a result of the publicity, the Commission directed the staff to rewrite the memorandum emphasizing the tentative nature and stressing counterproposals.

On rare occasions the daily press comes through with the kind of story the trade press doesn't dare touch. In a thoroughgoing "the empress is wearing no clothes" exposé, *Wall Street Journal* reporter Karen Elliot wrote that Commissioner Charlotte Reid "lacks apparent qualifications for the job, and she doesn't display much interest in the work." The story was there to be picked up, but there was no open season on Mrs. Reid like that of the trade press on Nicholas Johnson. The front-page story on October 25, 1974, could not have been written for a trade publication because the reporter, and to some degree the publication that printed the story, would have become persona non grata throughout the Commission. The Elliot article* said:

> Probably the most notable thing Mrs. Reid has done so far in her seven-year FCC term is to spend $4600 of government money installing in her office a private bathroom with a large gold-framed mirror. She has also distinguished herself by her absence; she's gone from the FCC more than any other Commissioner. . . .

> At the FCC, Mrs. Reid can best be described as uninterested. Although she says children's television is a favorite issue, she admits she hasn't given any speeches on the topic or pressed for any new Commission action in that area. Although she is the first woman on the Commission in 25 years, she says, "I'm not a women's advocate. I came here to represent everyone."

> Instead of zeroing in on complex issues, Mrs. Reid has turned more and more to travels and speeches. In fact, Commission insiders say, she appears to have given up on really grasping the narrow legal technical issues before the FCC, relying instead on her legal assistant or on Commission Chairman Richard Wiley to cue her votes.

The article reportedly shook up Mrs. Reid. She began defending her record of travels and speeches in her out-of-Washington addresses. Chairman Wiley came to her defense in speeches, referring to "that *Wall Street Journal* article." Such references made broadcasters in the audience look puzzled and ask, "What article?" If it had been in *Broadcasting,* everyone would have known about it. Nevertheless, observers at the FCC noted that Mrs. Reid's interest, participation at meetings, and knowledgeability increased between the time the article appeared in 1974 and her FCC retirement in 1976.

Television and radio, which, as the NAB likes to point out, are the main sources of news for the American people, present little coverage of issues affecting their own industry. Except for a brief flurry of panel shows on whether broadcasting news had a "liberal bias" after the attacks of Vice President Spiro Agnew, TV networks usually avoid trade stories altogether.

The handling of stories on regulatory agencies reflects caution. For example, in June 1973, *CBS Evening News* devoted time to the pending Senate confirmation vote on Robert H. Morris, an oil company lawyer named by President Nixon to a term on the Federal Power Commission. Senators opposed the Morris appointment on the grounds that he had been too close to the industry he would be called upon to regulate. During the Morris hearings, Sen. Warren Magnuson (D.–Wash.), chairman of the Commerce Committee, stated:

The public is legitimately skeptical toward regulatory agencies whose important positions are assumed from the industries to be regulated. . . . The Senate should serve notice on the President that it expects revision of his criteria for the selection of nominees to all regulatory agencies. Now, more than ever, the Senate should not be asked to confirm appointments to regulatory agencies which appear to have been designed as rewards for politically supportive industries or other special interest groups.

The Morris nomination was defeated after a close vote of the full Senate.

One of the next regulatory-agency appointments proposed by President Nixon was that of James Quello, a former Detroit TV station manager, to a term on the FCC. Quello whose association with the broadcasting industry had been severed only shortly before his nomination, was vigorously opposed by citizen groups. His hearing was the longest ever conducted on a regulatory-agency nominee; one senator noted, "We've spent more time on this hearing than on the hearing to confirm the Secretary of State." Despite the controversy engendered by the Quello appointment and the similarity to the Morris fight, neither CBS nor any other network gave the hearings any coverage.

During the past six or seven years, network TV has paid little or no attention to the critical issues affecting the industry such as pay cable, the FCC Fairness Doctrine, license renewal legislation, or network policy on children's programming. When the networks volunteered to devote the first hour of prime evening time to "family viewing," they did so with a minimum of promotion. Since networks claimed that the purpose of the family viewing hour was to benefit parents, this would have seemed an excellent opportunity to communicate with the audience and to solicit audience reactions. The concept was mentioned at least twice: on NBC's *Tomorrow* at 1:00 A.M., and in a CBS *60 Minutes* feature on Norman Lear; but no such attempt at two-way communication was undertaken.

The networks' let's-not-talk-shop attitude was once challenged by a Los Angeles citizen group that petitioned the FCC to require network coverage of license-renewal legislation that had passed both houses of Congress. Stern claimed that such legislation was a controversial issue of public importance and deserved coverage under the Fairness Doctrine. The FCC denied the petition.

Unlike housewives who wash their dirty linen incessantly on TV commercials, the networks generally manage to handle their internal affairs with the discretion becoming billion-dollar businesses. However, the networks' attitude toward coverage of industry news was illustrated in an exchange of letters reported in the trade press in December 1973. Richard Dudley, chairman of the Forward Communications television stations, asked the three television networks to cover the FCC's pay cable hearings. Dudley insisted that the hearings were "just as news-worthy as many of the routine government stories covered by the net-works and far more important from the average TV viewer's stand-point." He suggested that if a network was "too sensitive" to put this coverage on the national news, "let's automatically put it on the station program feed and leave it to the discretion of the local news directors to use."

NBC President Julian Goodman offered a rationale for what Dudley called "meek silence":

> Most issues of concern about TV are controversial, in the sense that there are opposing views about them. To the extent that we used our facilities to argue our own case, we would be required under the fair-ness doctrine to give a free national platform to our detractors—one that they would certainly exploit—and I don't think that would ad-vance the cause in which we all believe. . . . In addition, it is probably true that most of the audience prefers to enjoy broadcast programs rather than to watch or listen to broadcast arguments about TV. If this is true, the use of the medium to advance its interests may be addressing the wrong audience—the people who rely heavily on broadcasting, like it, and are not very much influenced in their viewing and listen-ing by its detractors.

Similar considerations may well have prompted NAB executives to use the newspapers, instead of broadcasting, to lobby Congress regard-ing pay television. The association spent $25,000 putting forth its posi-tion in the Washington newspapers—avoiding any Fairness Doctrine responsibilities and any risk of stirring up the animals. Some broad-casters resented this advertising strategy.

Because coverage of FCC regulatory functions by the general media—newspapers, magazines, and broadcasting—is inadequate, the coverage that counts is invariably that of the trade press. The general media fail to bring issues of "public importance," as described in the Communica-tions Act mandate that the FCC operate in "the public interest, con-venience and necessity," to the attention of the very public that has shown such general interest in broadcasting, its programs, and its com-mercials.

The trade press sometimes manipulates the FCC by getting word of a contemplated action to the readership before the FCC is prepared to make a final decision. This is simply enterprising journalism, of course, whatever the motivation of the person who leaks the information. *Broadcasting* magazine, through a combination of reporting and editori-alizing, consciously attempts to affect the FCC's actions.

A classic case of an FCC staffer's incurring *Broadcasting*'s wrath oc-curred in 1962 when Kenneth Cox (later a commissioner) was chief of the Broadcast Bureau. Following a somewhat vague Commission policy requiring television stations to present live, local programming in prime time, Cox asked all stations that devoted less than 5 percent of their prime time to this kind of programming why they had so little. Remember that partly on the strength of their promises to present just such programming, broadcasters had obtained valuable licenses for TV stations a decade earlier. *Broadcasting* reported the Cox procedure in December 1962, and editorialized against it as a form of censorship and regulation by raised eyebrow. Broadcasters and their representatives complained to the commissioners, who promptly ordered Cox to desist. The whole episode constituted a notorious "horrible example" that is still occasionally cited by staff members who are disinclined by nature and training to stick their necks out.

Broadcasting struck again in September 1971 when Dean Burch established a special unit on children's television and hired an economist, Dr. Alan Pearce, to study the economic impact various alternatives would have on the networks. *Broadcasting* moved quickly to put Pearce and his mentor on the defensive. A snide "Closed Circuit" noted that Pearce was a former British broadcaster, and that in 1946 another British broadcaster had helped prepare an FCC policy pronouncement that was the "agency's first large-scale foray into area of program surveillance. . . . FCC watchers with long memories wonder whether history will repeat itself. . . ." An editorial in the same *Broadcasting* said: "We would have more confidence in an impartial resolution [of] that 'core issue'—whether commercial television and television that is good for children can be compatible—if Mr. Burch had not confirmed in the same speech that one of the FCC's two new employees had been assigned to investigate the 'economics of children's programming.' That can mean only one thing: the employee, an Englishman with a recent Ph.D. from Indiana University, is to judge whether broadcasters can afford to spend more money than they have been spending on children's fare."

In addition to attacking suspect people and programs, *Broadcasting* occasionally campaigns for rapid action on individual cases. During FCC deliberations over a $137-million sale of broadcast properties from Corinthian Broadcasting and Dun & Bradstreet, *Broadcasting* reported that the commissioners had tied 3–3 in a closed meeting vote and named the commissioner who held the deciding vote. Of course, such a leak could put the swing vote under considerable pressure. The next week the transfer was approved 4–3.

The trade press serves industry lobbyists as an early warning system in the appointment of commissioners. As Graham and Kramer stated, "There are very few trade journals which are more politically potent than *Broadcasting* magazine; the number of FCC aspirants who have had their ambitions either assisted or quashed as a result of this magazine's coverage defies estimation."

Competition between trade publications is sharp when it comes to getting the scoop on an FCC appointment although such scoops may

affect the candidacy. Being listed as a front-runner can be just as dangerous for an FCC candidate as for a presidential candidate: once designated the leading contender, you wait for everyone to take a crack at
you. *Broadcasting,* like every other Washington-based publication,
knew that predicting appointments by Lyndon Johnson was giving the
candidates the kiss of death. Reportedly Johnson failed at the last minute to make an appointment simply because *Broadcasting* had predicted that he would.

Throughout the years publisher Taishoff has been able to command
an audience with commissioners to supplement the advice he gives them
in the pages of *Broadcasting.* During the Eisenhower administration,
Taishoff met regularly with FCC members, more or less in rotation, at
a Colony restaurant table, which became known in the trade as the
"Confessional Booth." He still lunches regularly with some commissioners. For years Taishoff's advertisers learned inside news long before
it was published and sometimes gleaned information that was never
printed.

Broadcasters are not always pleased by trade press coverage, however.
At an NAB regional meeting in 1971, NAB board chairman Richard
Chapin was criticized by local broadcasters for not doing enough to
gain passage of renewal legislation. Chapin replied that NAB had invited the powerful chairman of the House Communications Subcommittee, Torbert Macdonald (D.–Mass.), to speak at another NAB regional meeting "not just because we like the way he parts his hair."
Dawson Nail reported the remark in *Television Digest* despite NAB officials' pleas. Some NAB members later said they thought the report
seriously alienated Macdonald.

Since 1974, the trade press has been getting some competition from
Access magazine, which calls itself the "first public interest 'trade journal.'" Its avowed goal is to "provide communication within the communications reform movement." Staffed primarily by volunteer students, *Access* handles FCC news differently, emphasizing actions (or inaction) that the regular trade press considers unimportant; but *Access*
seldom gets the scoops that are commonplace for trade reporters who've
been covering the FCC for 20 years or more. FCC staff members don't
compete for the monthly copies of *Access,* but the magazine has developed readership.

Access, spearheaded by former Commissioner Nicholas Johnson and
his National Citizens Committee for Broadcasting, editorializes about
FCC actions in a vein very different from that of *Broadcasting.*

When President Ford was about to nominate former FCC Commissioner Robert Wells as director of the Office of Telecommunications
Policy in August 1975, *Access* documented Wells' stock interests and
the hiring practices (minorities and women) of stations in which Wells
had an interest. It is impossible to measure what effect the article had

(or who used it as ammunition) as it is to measure *Broadcasting's* influence on FCC nominations. However, Wells withdrew his name from consideration for the OTP position.

In the tight little community of broadcasters, cable operators, and regulators, *Broadcasting, Television Digest,* and other trade publications serve the functions of community bulletin board, gossip fence, and volunteer fire brigade. They report such minutiae as commissioners' golfing feats, vacation plans, quips, and quirks.

Before FCC meetings were opened to the public, trade reporters relied on their FCC sources to tell the reporters what happened in the closed meetings. So much important business is still discussed outside the official agenda meetings that reporters need inside sources despite "government in the sunshine." Usually the reason that participants in closed discussions are willing to tell reporters what happened is that the participants believe the leak will further their objectives. In this symbiotic relationship, reporters and news sources "use" each other.

Often an FCC source will reveal information to a reporter to make the source's own actions appear more acceptable to others on the Commission or within the regulated industry. Sources may leak information to try to force a colleague's hand on a matter they consider important —or to scold or punish someone in the agency. Sometimes a commissioner or staff member feeds a story to a reporter simply to earn goodwill, to ingratiate the source with the press.

Not all leaks to the trade press are "plants" by an FCC player jockeying for position. Sometimes leaks result from a sincere effort to be helpful in informing interested parties about what is going on. When a *Television Digest* reporter asked newly appointed Commissioner Quello what he thought of a pending decision on a Commission Fairness Doctrine report, Quello simply handed the reporter his concurring statement and said, "Here's what I think." The reporter asked if he could take the statement, tucked it in his briefcase, and was out the door. After pondering a while, Quello decided out of fairness to give the statement to *Broadcasting,* too. As a result, both publications would be able to print direct quotations from a concurring statement to an important decision, which—officially—had not yet been made. When Quello told Chairman Wiley, Wiley considered "calling in some of the chips" by asking that the publications not print the statement until the decision had been issued; but Wiley decided to save the chips for more serious matters.

The most serious leakages involve adjudicatory matters—cases in which the Commission is acting as a court to review the opinions of administrative law judges. Any case may be appealed to the full Commission if a party disagrees with the law judge's "initial decision." Oral argument before the commissioners follows such an appeal; then the Commission votes on a tentative conclusion and directs the FCC Office of Opinions and Review to draft its decision.

Such a decision is patently news for the trade press, but premature disclosure can have serious consequences. For example, in January 1975 *Television Digest* revealed that the Commission had reached a tentative 4–3 decision to disqualify Teleprompter, a cable systems operator, from owning systems in Johnstown, Pennsylvania, and Trenton, New Jersey, because the president of Teleprompter, Irving Kahn, had been convicted of bribing a Johnstown city official. When the tentative decision was published, Teleprompter's counsel claimed that publicity had "irreparably impaired" the Commission's ability to continue consideration of the merits of the case and that the article would rush the commissioners and perhaps "lock in" their decisions. The lawyer asked that the staff prepare two opinions—one of which would favor Teleprompter—so that both opinions could be "fully considered."

The Commission responded to this request by issuing a special statement on February 4, 1975:

> The Commission disapproves of and greatly regrets the unauthorized reports concerning our deliberations in Teleprompter Cable Systems, Inc. . . . which have appeared in recent trade publications. The Commission confirms that it has given instructions to the staff to prepare a decision in this matter under the supervision of a designated Commissioner. Consistent with normal practice, the Commission's instructions are tentative and each member reserves the right to make a final determination upon review of the draft decision. The Commission plans no further consideration of this case until the draft decision is prepared.

Despite lawyers' cries of foul and the Commission's apparent anguish, the Teleprompter leak was not the last adjudicatory decision published before FCC's final action. In late 1975 *Television Digest* revealed that the commissioners were narrowly divided on whether to renew the license held by Cowles Communications for Channel 2 Daytona Beach–Orlando, Florida. The publication stated that the commissioners had asked for alternative decisions—rare at the FCC—one granting renewal, the other licensing a competing applicant. "If decision goes against Cowles, added impetus will be provided in industry's drive for renewal bill in Congress," the magazine predicted, adding that a "top broadcast lobbyist [said] 'if something like that happens, it certainly would show the need for stability.' "

Although the effect such comments might have had on the commissioners' eventual decision is impossible to determine (they voted 4–3 to renew the license), such a leak unquestionably applies to the decision-making process a pressure that is incompatible with a judicial posture.

Sometimes leaks help abort FCC actions. In such cases the source of the leak may be calling for reinforcements to bolster what he or she fears is a minority position within the Commission. In late 1972, Chairman Burch, after consulting the Justice Department, directed a member of his staff to draft a notice of inquiry into whether networks should be forbidden to own production facilities and to produce their own entertainment programs. Before the notice was even discussed by the Commission, leaks had activated network lobbyists, who had issued press releases and launched crusades on the eighth floor in visits to commissioners' offices. The vote was 4–2 against the proposal.

An ironic case in favor of leaks is sometimes made by media reformers. They argue that the primary beneficiary of leaks published by the trade press is the public because the principals in the regulated industries, their lobbyists, and lawyers inevitably know what the Commission has done shortly thereafter—and sometimes what the outcome will be well before the official vote.

5
The Public Comes on the Scene

A broadcaster seeks and is granted the free and exclusive use of a limited and valuable part of the public domain; when he accepts that franchise it is burdened by enforceable public obligations. A newspaper can be operated at the whim or caprice of its owners; a broadcast station cannot. After nearly five decades of operation the broadcast industry does not seem to have grasped the simple fact that a broadcast license is a public trust subject to termination for breach of duty. . . . The Commission of course represents and indeed is the prime arbiter of the public interest, but its duties and jurisdiction are vast, and it acknowledges that it cannot begin to monitor or oversee the performance of every one of thousands of licensees. Moreover, the Commission has always viewed its regulatory duties as guided if not limited by our national tradition that public response is the most reliable test of ideas and performance in broadcasting as in most areas of life. . . .

Judge Warren Burger
Court of Appeals decision on WLBT Jackson, Miss., March 1966
Office of Communications of United Church of Christ v. *FCC*

I have never understood the basic legally governing concept of "the people's airways." So far as I know there is only the atmosphere and space. There can be no airway, in any practical sense, until somebody accumulates the capital, know-how, and enterprise to put a signal into the atmosphere and space.

Eric Sevareid, CBS commentator
NAB convention, 1977

5 Broadcast regulators face a dilemma. Legally broadcasters are trustees of the airwaves, which belong to the public; broadcasters are also businessmen who have made substantial investments; in a capitalistic society, broadcasters are entitled to profit from these investments. Often commissioners have shown more concern for the broadcasters' economic health than for the service audiences receive.

For many years the public, which Alexander Hamilton once called a "great beast," remained a great abstraction to the commissioners. Commissioners knew broadcasters and their lawyers, many on a first-name basis, but commissioners' contacts with radio listeners and television viewers were coincidental and inconsequential.

Parties in FCC licensing proceedings must have legal standing—and until 1966 the FCC granted standing to only those parties who alleged economic injury or electronic interference from the outcome of a proceeding. The broadcast audience could complain—it's a free country—but these complaints had no legal weight. Commissioners, who were constantly besieged by broadcasters, members of Congress, and judges with their own conceptions of the public interest, didn't have time to listen to complaints if they didn't have to.

Only in the past decade has the FCC been compelled to consider the pleadings of the broadcast audience. The commissioners still hear a great deal more from, say, a network lobbyist than from any single media reformer, but have made efforts to adjust to a new climate.

During this decade commissioners have heard from a wide variety of citizen groups, media reformers, nonprofit law firms, representatives of racial minority groups, consumer organizations, and crusaders for myriad causes. The FCC has been petitioned by groups that want "morality in media," and groups that want uncensored access to the "public airwaves." The agency has been challenged in courts (successfully) by groups that do not want a radio station to stop broadcasting classical music and (unsuccessfully) by a group that wants television time to deplore Polish jokes.

Individuals and groups whose arguments would have been ignored by past Commissions have profoundly affected the course of recent regulation. Often these groups have not achieved all they attempted, but they have become a factor in many decisions they once would not have affected at all.

Albert Kramer, former head of Citizens Communications Center, explained that his firm and other "public interest" law firms were not representing the public—they represent private interests that were not heard formerly. "The public interest is a concept which results from the interaction of private interests." His goal, he said, was to open processes that those with a narrow, financial interest wished to keep closed.

WHO SPEAKS FOR THE PUBLIC?

In the 1940s and 1950s citizen groups concentrated on sending complaints about violence in programming or about offensive commercials to sponsors, networks, and stations. Groups like the National Association for Better Broadcasting and the American Council for Better Broadcasts evaluated programs and cited superior efforts in newsletters and reading lists sent to members, to industry and nonindustry groups, and to the FCC. These citizen groups occasionally submitted comments in general FCC rulemakings, but they took no part in the licensing procedure.

In 1959, Consumers Union asked the FCC to establish a radio and television consumer council with full power to review all FCC licensing decisions, obtain additional data (if necessary) about licensees' performances, and publicize its findings. Consumers Union proposed also that mandatory hearings, prior to all license renewals and transfers (sales), be conducted in the station's locality after extensive public notice. The proposal was not adopted by the FCC in 1959; nor would it be today.

It was in the 1960s—that turbulent decade of civil rights confrontations, women's liberation, and antiwar demonstrations, that decade when activism and militancy were dominant—that citizens entered the FCC's quasi-judicial hearing rooms. Four parties with no economic interest asked the FCC in 1964 for permission to intervene in the licensing of WLBT–TV, Jackson, Mississippi. They alleged that station management had consistently discriminated against black viewers, who constituted about 45 percent of the station's potential audience. Individual viewers and black groups had been complaining to the Commission since 1955 about the biased coverage of racial matters on the station. The four parties who sought to intervene in 1964 were two residents of Mississippi (one from Jackson), the local United Church of Christ, and its national Office of Communications in New York City. Everett Parker, director of the office, had been concerned with religious broadcasting for many years. In the 1960s, he was disturbed by the failure of some broadcast stations in the South to give adequate coverage to the civil rights movement. In WLBT, he found a test case.

Parker's plan was to persuade the station to provide fair coverage, not to strip the owner's license. However, Parker was eager to establish a legal precedent for the right of minorities and citizen groups to be heard in FCC proceedings. Because of the firm resistance to change by WLBT management and the Commission's unwillingness to hold a hearing on the station's renewal application, the case proceeded to the U.S. Court of Appeals, where a panel headed by Judge Warren Burger ordered the FCC to hold a hearing and allow the citizen complainants to participate. After the hearing, the FCC decided that the complaints did not justify denial of a new license. Parker's group, now granted standing, appealed again, and this time the court overturned the FCC altogether.

Parker remained active before the FCC in cases that alleged discrimination against minorities in programming and employment. He also crusaded for enforcement of the FCC's Fairness Doctrine in cases where stations presented solely "extremist propaganda" on subjects of public importance. Under the direction of Parker's deputy, Ralph Jennings, United Church of Christ published booklets and conducted regional workshops to encourage citizen action to improve broadcasting.

Because Parker is not a lawyer, his office was represented in the WLBT case by New York attorney Earle K. Moore, whose main practice is not in communications cases. Following their victory in the WLBT case, which gave the public the legal standing to intervene in renewal cases, Parker and Moore were unable to spend full time on cases involving similar principles; but in the early 1970s, a few Washington-based, nonprofit law firms took up the standard.

Albert Kramer, a 30-year-old Stanford law graduate who had been working for the eminent Washington firm of Covington & Burling, set up the Citizens Communication Center in 1969, after a chance conversation with Ralph Nader aroused Kramer's interest in the media reform movement. With a grant from the Midas International Foundation and an office converted from a supply closet at the Robert F. Kennedy Memorial Foundation, Kramer began accepting clients. Within seven months, Citizens was handling 30 to 40 cases, mainly representing black civil rights and antipoverty groups, the primary constituency of the RFK foundation.

Encouraged by citizen interest in the work he was doing and by the presence of consumer-oriented Nicholas Johnson on the FCC, Kramer was soon putting in as much as 17 hours a day on his caseload. He attracted additional funding from small foundations like the Stern Fund and the Playboy Foundation. In 1971 with the aid of officers of the RFK Memorial, Kramer obtained a Ford Foundation two-year grant of $200,000 per year, which permitted him to recruit other lawyers and to expand the scope of the center's legal interests.

The Ford Foundation continues to provide 80 percent of Citizens' $300,000 budget even though, as Kramer noted, some of the Citizens' program "has been a bitter pill for Ford to swallow." As examples, Kramer cited Citizens' attacking employment opportunity practices at public broadcasting stations, long-time Ford Foundation beneficiaries, and Citizens' charging public stations with unresponsiveness to community needs.

Citizens' present staff of four lawyers including its first black director, Nolan Bowie, who was appointed in May 1977, now has its own offices, which are far from luxurious. Although the firm handles more cases than it handled five years ago, it also turns away more.

Citizens' workload is heavy and staff turnover, large. Frank Lloyd, Kramer's successor as executive director, now a consultant to the Office of Telecommunications Policy in the Executive Branch, joked with FCC lawyers that the Commission could put Citizens out of business by designating a few of their cases for full evidentiary hearings. As it is, the ordinary workload, Lloyd told *Access* (October 1, 1976), "puts too much of a strain on marriage." The firm experiences turnover, he said, because "the people who go into this work are people who like kicks. As soon as they get competent and it's no longer a challenge, they move on." Young lawyers, however, know that at Citizens they can practice law immediately, instead of researching for and assisting senior partners, as in most other law firms.

On behalf of community groups, Citizens has filed petitions to deny license renewals to more than 200 stations. It has participated in almost all major broadcast-related FCC rulemaking proceedings, as well as in numerous congressional hearings. The firm will represent only those groups with no financial interest in the proceeding's outcome.

Citizens' first client, Black Efforts for Soul in Television (BEST), a Washington, D.C. group, was led by William D. Wright. When Cole first went to the Commission in 1970, Wright was *the* spokesman for the blacks in FCC matters—whether or not blacks realized it. Wright got along well with the commissioners and Chairman Burch, and had easy entrée to most FCC offices. Wright lobbied tirelessly with Congress and was instrumental in the appointment of the first black commissioner. In 1969, Wright and a few other blacks sat in the back of the room during Senate hearings on a license-renewal bill, and shouted, "Racist! Racist!" after testimony of which they disapproved. Their actions helped cause the bill to be shelved.

In 1973, when BEST folded and Wright went to California for a research project, funded by the National Science Foundation, on blacks and media, a new organization to carry on the work was formed—the National Black Media Coalition (NBMC). Like BEST, the new organization has its agenda largely set by one person, the executive director, currently Pluria Marshall. Despite difficulties in obtaining funds and tax-exempt status from IRS and though he says "very few black organizations rank communications as one of their top priorities," Marshall commutes from Houston for communications proceedings.

In the early 1970s, the Stern Community Law Firm, financed by the Stern Fund, specialized first in broadcasting's First Amendment cases and later in promoting counteradvertising (seeking air time for rebuttals to advertisements dealing with controversial issues of public importance). The firm was headed by Tracy Westen, another young Covington & Burling alumnus and a former aide to Commissioner Johnson. Since 1974, when Westen moved to California to direct the communications law program at UCLA, the Stern Firm has been inactive. Another nonprofit Washington firm is the Media Access Project. Originally headed by Thomas Asher, an attorney specializing in entertainment law, it is now led by Harvey Shulman. Although the Media Access Project has represented some groups seeking denial of license renewal, it has specialized in litigation involving the FCC's Fairness Doctrine and in urging requirements governing the broadcasting of public service announcements.

The National Citizens Committee for Broadcasting aspires to be like Common Cause. The group's roots go back to 1967 when a New York organization was formed to crusade for better programming. In 1974, Nicholas Johnson became chairperson of the now Washington-based organization; and Albert Kramer, having left Citizens Communication Center, became NCCB's executive director. Johnson is still at NCCB while Kramer, after a stint back in "the Establishment" practicing non-communications law at the firm of Arnold and Porter, became chief of the Consumer Protection Bureau of the Federal Trade Commission in 1977. Kramer appointed Tracy Westen as his deputy and Charles Shepherd, first editor of NCCB's *Access* magazine, as his assistant. Kramer's replacement as NCCB director is Theodore Carpenter.

In addition to *Access,* a pulpit for the media reform movement, NCCB has initiated the National Citizens Communications Lobby to promote legislation and express opinions on presidential appointments to important communications policy positions. Kramer had long urged public groups to lobby because "effective advocacy requires the ability to prevent hard-fought victories from being legislated away."

NCCB has attempted to become increasingly active in FCC proceedings and in congressional hearings. Represented by Citizens, NCCB successfully appealed the FCC's permitting newspapers to own broadcast properties in the same market. NCCB compiled a study of violence in television programming and included a list of sponsors of "violent" programs.

Minority group coalitions, formed primarily to crusade for civil rights, sometimes participate in individual license renewal proceedings. On various occasions these coalitions have petitioned the Commission to redress grievances in broadcasting employment practices, stereotypes in programming, and lack of programming directed to minority needs and interests.

Other special interest groups represent segments of the public. National Organization for Women (NOW) participates in FCC rulemakings and licensing cases where employment of women is at issue. NOW local chapters have frequently petitioned local stations to improve their hiring practices and to present more women's programming. Kathleen Bonk has been NOW's national media co-ordinator since 1973 and, at age 24, is one of the deans of the Washington-based media reformers. The Gay Media Task Force has presented to the FCC its case for unbiased presentations of homosexuals on television, but most of its activities have focused on protests to and discussions with networks and syndicated film producers.

In a *TV Guide* article (February 9, 1974), Max Gunther said, "It is probably safe to say that since the late 1960s, nearly every major religious group in the country has tried to get some offending TV material altered or banned. So has every racial minority group and almost every important national-ethnic group."

Citizen groups are not the creations of political liberals solely. Accuracy in Media, a conservative group, which seeks to combat "liberal bias" in all media, persuaded the FCC that an NBC documentary on pension plans violated the Fairness Doctrine, but an appeals court reversed the FCC's finding. A group called Happiness of Women (HOW) combats the proposals and aims of NOW.

Many public groups have come before the FCC to crusade on a single issue with varying degrees of success. For example, John Banzhaf, a law professor who formed Action on Smoking and Health (ASH) in 1968, persuaded the FCC that antismoking ads must be carried by broadcasters who aired cigarette commercials. (Later, Congress banned all cigarette commercials from the airwaves.) Action for Children's Television (ACT) was formed by a group of mothers in the Boston area who believed that their children were subjected to excessive and unfair commercials; their efforts are recounted in the case study that concludes this book.

Sometimes those crusading on a single issue are official representatives of the public. In 1975 twelve state attorneys-general asked the Commission to adopt rules prohibiting over-the-counter drug advertisements on television before 9:00 P.M. At the same time, the New Jersey Coalition for Fair Broadcasting—a group including New Jersey's two United States senators, the state senate president, and the mayor of New Jersey's largest city—asked the FCC to provide New Jersey with more local television coverage, preferably by allocating the state its own commercial VHF television station.

Public groups reacting to broadcasting are as varied as the causes they serve.

• The United States Humane Society asked the FCC to prohibit broadcasting of rodeos, which encourage cruelty to animals and which employ artificial devices to make the animals seem wild.

• Some 9000 Jackson, Wisconsin, residents opposed the sale of a station broadcasting German and Polish language programs to a new owner who would program religious shows exclusively; the new format would allegedly reduce public affairs programming and eliminate commercials, the businessmen's only local radio advertising outlet.

• The Energy Action Committee seeks opportunities to answer oil-industry commercials.

• The 6.6 million member Parent Teachers Association (PTA) has launched a multipronged attack against televised violence. Mass letter-writing campaigns, workshops to train parents in program-monitoring techniques, and instructions in how to participate in license renewal proceedings are among the basic strategies that the organization plans to use. According to *Television Digest* (May 23, 1977), PTA National Secretary Ann Kahn told delegates at the 1977 national convention: "This is not just a three or six month project . . . . We are not going to walk away from this until we really see a change."

In addition to these, dozens of other groups, both regional and national, take stands on single issues, such as abortion, the Equal Rights Amendment, gun control, and school busing. The media committees of these groups ask for and sometimes demand broadcasting time under the Fairness Doctrine.

Aside from groups campaigning on a single issue or concept, the ranks of full-time media reformers are thin. Because of the financial and other personal sacrifices required, some pioneers have been unable to hold on for more than a few years; but often their organizations continue to grow under new leadership. Some noted crusaders, like Everett Parker, remain active; and some media activists pursue their causes at their own expense. For example, Philip Jacklin, professor of philosophy at San Jose State University, has headed the successful Committee for Open Media in northern California.

FCC STEPS TOWARD PUBLIC PARTICIPATION

In an effort to increase their effectiveness, citizen groups have been trying to learn more about the day-to-day functioning of the FCC. For a number of reasons, they have found it hard work. Commissioners and FCC staff members complain that members of the public or citizen groups or consumer activists—whatever the term used—simply do not understand how the Commission works. They are usually right. What the FCC insider doesn't acknowledge, however, is that the public's ignorance is perpetuated by the agency's stubbornness. The bureaucrat, who knows in his heart that he's doing right by the people, also knows that the more individuals who mess in his work, the more complicated and difficult the work will become. Consequently, when public groups petition the FCC to open its inner workings to their view and to enable them to participate in the policy and rulemaking process, which is supposedly open to all comers, the majority of commissioners and staffers instinctively balk.

Most public interest groups lack the money to pay the large sums that many companies or individuals with a financial interest in FCC proceedings pay to lobbyists and lawyers. Public interest groups often can't afford to keep up with the dozens of minor FCC actions that might affect their interests. It's not that the FCC consciously discriminates against the smaller entities; it's simply that the processes are so confusing that anyone would have trouble following date changes for filing comments, the FCC's opening matters to comment, and the court decisions that force FCC reconsideration of matters that some parties thought settled.

When public interest groups have asked the FCC for help, the FCC has responded somewhat reluctantly. Some of the ways in which the Commission has tried to accommodate public groups may eventually truly aid their participation in FCC actions and decision making; others were initiated disingenuously and probably will make no great difference. In any case, the problems the FCC addressed under public urging are real problems—and the agency's response may sooner or later provide a key to the solution. Let's examine some of the responses the FCC has made to the public's calls for help.

FCC "Actions Alert"

The FCC's Public Information Office (PIO) has for years noted the agency's every action in twice-daily press releases. Copies of these releases, placed on a table in the anteroom of the office, are faithfully picked up and distributed by messenger services to their clients. *Broadcasting* sends a copyboy to pick up the releases and prints the gist of all actions pertaining to the industry. Only rarely, however, are the releases mailed. Mailing all the hundreds of releases on actions of varying importance would be prohibitively expensive. Thus the information, laboriously collected and duly made available, reaches only a small, self-selecting group of people.

The initial prod for wider dissemination of information came from the court of appeals (in New York), which in 1974 remanded the FCC's second version of the prime-time access rule, partly on the grounds that the FCC had not made sufficient efforts to get opinions from the public. In three days of oral argument about the rule, representatives of more than 60 industry groups came to speak, but only three consumer groups (ACLU, ACT, and NCCB) appeared. The industry spokesmen's concern was primarily the rule's economic impact on broadcasters. The consumer groups' concern was not economic: they wanted the FCC to require local television stations to program fare of local interest (instead of syndicated entertainment) in the time slot the networks would be relinquishing to their affiliates.

The court told the FCC not to act merely as a referee between competing economic interests. The FCC must consider "the various facets of the public interest"; and, furthermore, the Commission must "take the initiative to seek out such parties."

Frank Lloyd, then director of Citizens Communications Center, crusaded to persuade the FCC to summarize proceedings of general interest in the broadcasting field and to mail the summaries regularly to a broad spectrum of public interest and citizen groups. He held up the example of the Federal Trade Commission's information bulletin, "Call for

Comment." Mailed to many consumer groups, the FTC bulletin summarized the proposed action or rule, explained what the FTC hoped to accomplish by implementing it, and suggested the areas for respondents' focus. The outstanding feature of "Call for Comment" was its clarity —you needn't have been an expert to understand what was involved.

In 1975, over a year after the court's urging the Commission to seek out the views of the public, Chairman Wiley set up a task force to establish mailing lists of consumer and citizen communications organizations, determine the costs, and learn how other agencies informed the public. In August 1975, the task force made its final recommendations —"[a] weekly summary will be a one-page self-mailer and may be legal size, if required, to avoid two-page releases." Information would have to be compressed to fit the format. The mailing list was to be restricted to 500 names because of budgetary limitations.

The first "Actions Alert," sent to only 270 groups, was one page of truncated descriptions of all kinds of items the FCC was working on. These were typical items:

Overall revision of Part 18—Industrial, Scientific and Medical (ISM) equipment. Comments May 18.

Use of certain ship-to-coast channels for intership communications. Comments May 13; replies May 24.

Amendment of noncommercial FM broadcast rules. Comments July 1; replies August 18.

Review of Commission rules and regulatory policies concerning network broadcasting by standard (AM) and FM broadcast stations. Comments May 10; replies June 7.

Citizen groups were less than enthusiastic about the summary. Frank Lloyd, for example, asked, "Is this what we've been waiting for?" Even those items that could be expected to interest citizen groups were given short shrift. "Inquiry to explore what role, if any, FCC should play in proposed changes in entertainment formats of broadcast stations" was the only information supplied community groups that had been crusading for format changes. The groups would have to seek fuller information.

After receiving "Actions Alert," Cole went to the FCC's Public Information Office for a copy of the inquiry documents, but none was left. If he waited a week or more, he realized, he might find the text in the *Federal Register,* which Ralph Nader said is as hard to read as a seed catalogue and which is hard to come by, outside Washington. Eventually Cole went to a friend at the Commission and asked for one of the Broadcast Bureau's extra copies. Cole's circuitous route would be hard for a member of the general public to duplicate.

When the FCC later extended the date to file reply comments on the format change inquiry, "Actions Alert" failed to mention the date change. If the FCC had been truly solicitous of the interest of public groups in such a proceeding, the original notice of inquiry could have been mailed to everyone on the list just as certain notices of inquiry have been sent to all broadcasters. Citizen group representatives, particularly Frank Lloyd, expressed their dissatisfaction with the uninformative "Actions Alert" and with the lapses of notification on matters of special interest to them.

On December 13, 1976, some 17 months after the summary was initiated, the FCC issued its first "Special Feedback Edition" of the bulletin. This edition included a straightforward explanation of a rulemaking proceeding and of how, when, and where to file comments. It was ironic that this particular rulemaking—on standards governing franchise contracts between local authorities and cable companies, a subject of interest to several citizen groups—was one where the FCC had previously indicated it would not weaken existing standards.

By June 30, 1977, only one other "Special Feedback Edition" had been issued, devoted to the Commission's inquiry on underwriting and fundraising practices in public broadcasting. The FCC's Consumer Assistance Office had suggested a special edition be drafted on the Commission's network inquiry and sent to a special list of agencies and groups (four times as many as Action Alert). But Broadcast Bureau and chairman's office staff members squelched the suggestion by saying the issues involved were "too complex" for the public to grasp.

Office of Public Counsel

There was a time, back in 1971, when that fondest dream of citizen groups, an in-house office of FCC lawyers to help prepare cases before the Commission, almost came true. A blue-ribbon committee on procedural review, established by Chairman Burch, urged creation of such an office:

> As the Commission will appreciate, substantial and increasing efforts are being made by public interest groups to participate actively in administrative proceedings. The Commission has repeatedly stated that it encourages such participation but has had to concede that effective participation by such groups is rare and that their inability to obtain expert professional assistance is an important contributing factor.

The committee pointed out that communications law firms were "almost universally unwilling to represent public interest groups against any broadcast station," that most groups couldn't afford attorneys' fees anyway, and that those few firms that specialized in public interest cases couldn't handle more than their present caseloads. The public needed the FCC office which, the committee suggested, could be staffed by junior lawyers to hold down its payroll costs.

As the proposal took shape, staff members and commissioners split on whether an office of public counsel should be restricted solely to advising on procedures or whether it should serve as an advocate for its clients' interests. *Broadcasting* (August 16, 1971) editorialized against even the first alternative:

> The watered-down version may sound harmless enough in the modern context of consumerism and efforts to make the government more responsive to public needs. If implemented, however, it could lead only to the ends the original staff work-up prescribed. In the immutable traditions of the civil service, the advice would get less general and more specific, and more and more of it would be offered. Before the process could be stopped, lines of citizens would have been recruited to protest anything any citizen didn't like.

Despite broadcasters' opposition, the four votes needed to establish the office were on the Commission if Dean Burch stuck to his original position favoring the idea. It was Burch who suggested that the "watered-down version" be drafted after the other six commissioners split evenly on establishing any office at all. Although other regulatory agencies, the Civil Aeronautics Board and the Interstate Commerce Commission, did establish such offices, Burch failed to call the proposal to a vote. After he left the agency in 1974, it was too late; support for the office had evaporated.

Consumer Assistance Office

Although citizen groups failed to bring about an Office of Public Counsel, they did have an effect in the creation of the FCC's Consumer Assistance Office (CAO). In congressional hearings, public groups testified in favor of such an office; and some members of Congress prodded the commissioners to establish it. When the question was raised during a November 1975 Senate oversight hearing on the FCC's reregulation policies, public groups complained: Since you are doing all this for the broadcasters, why don't you make some move to accommodate the public?

Wiley moved on the plan rapidly—but failed to consult some of the other commissioners. The chairman had mentioned in several speeches that he was studying the idea of a CAO; but when the concept of the office appeared for a vote on the FCC March 18, 1976, agenda, the full commission saw for the first time exactly what was involved. Months later, Hooks recommended transforming the CAO into a more potent entity to advise the Commission on what impact its actions or proposals would have on consumers and to recommend to the Commission what actions should be taken on the consumers' behalf. But the March 18 proposal had specified that the CAO would not play an advocate role in proceedings before the FCC, that the office would serve as an information conduit to the public "to help assist them in becoming involved in the regulatory process." The item was passed 6–1, with Robert E. Lee, who had served 23 years without a consumer assistance office, dissenting.

The commissioners' comments on the action were mixed. In a concurring statement released with the announcement of the new office, Commissioner Hooks said:

> I suppose that if this office did no more than to decipher the bureaucratic maze and translate arcane rules and regulations to an overwhelmed public, it can be said to have accomplished a great deal. However, after its initial struggles, I believe there are other areas of consumer assistance it can tackle and become a responsible advocate of the consumer viewpoint.
>
> Let us, thus, hope it will exceed its embryonic mission and not develop into a glorified Information Office with a Dale Carnegie diploma. If that should happen, my support will certainly erode.

Commissioner Robinson also issued a concurring statement. He wrote:

> In the days before economic waste became an important item of public concern, the automobile companies in Detroit used to introduce their new models much as we have introduced our new Consumer Affairs Office. Following a period of dark secrecy about what is in store, the curtains are drawn, and Lo! some new sheet metal and a hood ornament that hums the first bar of *The Star Spangled Banner*. I concur in this item because in the present age, consumer consciousness has become the premier public virtue of the good bureaucrat, and I do want to seem au courant. However, I think I detect a hint of public relations trompe l'oeil about this new office. For the most part, the outline of tasks and responsibilities of this office appears to describe responsibilities of existing offices (though there seems to be a question of whether the responsibilities are being met). I hope experience proves this perception to be erroneous, however, and that the office will make a meaningful contribution to consumer interest in our work; but for that to happen will require more than a new name, some additional chrome, and a racing stripe.

Speaking to the American Bar Association Bicentennial Institute, Wiley said:

> Perhaps our most important action in the field of public oversight is our formation, just this morning, of a Consumer Assistance Office. The primary purpose of this new office is to establish a point of contact within the Commission for the average citizen who may phone or visit us—a means by which the public can cut through the bureaucratic maze to secure the right information from the right person

within the FCC. Further, it will provide procedural assistance to facilitate greater public participation in our processes. Finally, the office will help to educate the public about our policies by producing simple, unbureaucratic informational material.

One might have expected the Public Information Office to perform many of the functions Wiley listed. However, the 13 members of that office, created and staffed years before, had their own specified, time-consuming tasks to perform. The CAO, with a staff of three professionals, could concentrate on queries and problems posed by persons or groups with no financial interest in broadcasting.

During its first year of operations, the CAO, reading narrowly its mandate to be an information conduit, has acted primarily as a referral system; but the very existence of the CAO could prove important in the future if a majority of commissioners decides to confer broader powers on the office. Creating a new office with clout is always hard in a bureaucracy—such an office is certain to poach on someone else's preserve, and it does take time for the office to establish practical procedures. But it is easier to broaden the responsibility and scope of an existing office. The CAO may turn out to be, as Chairman Wiley predicted, his most significant contribution "in the field of public oversight."

Reimbursement of Public Participants

The need for public participation in the FCC is clear: courts have remanded cases to the FCC because the agency failed to seek public views; Congress has repeatedly pushed the FCC to broaden public participation in its processes. Citizen law firms and media activists, who provide some of the public views the FCC is supposed to be seeking, have asked the FCC to reimburse the expenses incurred in that effort.

There is precedent for reimbursement. The Federal Trade Commission has specific statutory authorization and an appropriation to pay expenses of persons or groups who otherwise would be unrepresented in rulemaking proceedings.

An example of the kind of proceeding in which the FCC could properly reimburse public participants occurred in 1973, when the Commission considered requiring television licensees to make their program logs available for public inspection. In its written filing the NAB claimed that this requirement would impose "excessive, needless and costly new burdens on broadcast licensees without any measurable benefit to the public." Citizen groups, however, maintained that they needed access to program logs to substantiate complaints against stations—if the citizen group charged that there was a lack of locally originated programming or an excessive number of commercials, for example, the evidence could be found only in a station's logs because the group couldn't monitor all the broadcasts.

Broadcasting interests persuaded the FCC to conclude tentatively that the burden of proof that public inspection of program logs was necessary should fall on the public groups. When the FCC announced an oral argument on the rule, lawyers representing the NAB or television station owners opposed to the rule had only to walk a few blocks to the Commission; but the public interest group representatives, who were not all located in Washington, had to come from as far away as California, Michigan, and Massachusetts. After the first hour of argument, Dean Burch was so impressed that the burden of proof was shifted to the broadcasters.

The outcome of the oral argument was a classic example of what informed, articulate, well-prepared public representatives can accomplish when they address the Commission in a respectful, businesslike manner. They cited many examples of why they needed access to program logs to form a clear picture of licensee performance and to document shortcomings. On January 4, 1974, exactly a year after the rulemaking announcement and four years after the rulemaking request, the FCC made program logs of television stations available for public inspection. The public representatives won their point, but they weren't reimbursed for their trips.

In November 1976, the FCC did agree to provide indigent groups involved in adjudicatory proceedings some relief in the form of free copies of transcripts and other information about the case. The commissioners did not agree even to explore the question of reimbursing expenses in prosecuting administrative matters, however. Commissioners Hooks and Fogarty contended that "given the important role of the public in monitoring licensee compliance with our broadcast rules and policies, we should consider whether financial assistance, including some form of reimbursement, would be desirable for citizen participants in petition-to-deny and rulemaking, as well as adjudicatory proceedings; and, if so, what standards should govern."

Hooks and Fogarty referred to the May 1976 opinion of the Comptroller General that indicated that the FCC and a number of other federal agencies had the legal authority to provide reimbursement to members of the public. In House oversight hearings in May 1977, Chairman Wiley was asked if the FCC were going to follow the lead of those other agencies that were in the process of investigating means of establishing reimbursement procedures for public participation. Wiley responded that he was "not philosophically opposed" to the concept, but "if Congress wants us to act it should provide the funds and give us the standards."

A bill to do just that was introduced in 1977 by Senator Edward M. Kennedy (D.–Mass.) and Representative Peter Rodino (D.–N.J.). The Public Participation in Federal Agency Proceedings Act, sponsored by

20 senators and 90 representatives, and endorsed by the Carter administration, would provide funds for public groups whose opinions might
not otherwise be heard in administrative proceedings such as rulemakings and inquiries. The bill would also provide funds for public
groups to participate in judicial proceedings before federal agencies.

Open Meetings and "The Sunshine Act"

Perhaps because some commissioners compared themselves to Supreme
Court justices when the commissioners retired behind closed doors for
weekly deliberations on the weightier communications issues, the majority consistently opposed opening these meetings to the public. Having
sat in dozens of FCC meetings, Cole wasn't sure how enlightening the
public would have found the often informal, sometimes desultory
disposition of matters. The meetings were frequently relaxed affairs:
Cole once counted four commissioners—a majority—asleep at the same
time.

After Congress voted in 1974 to open its own committee meetings to
the public, it was clearly just a matter of time before Congress would
require the FCC, "an arm of the Congress," to open its meetings; but
the commissioners fought the best delaying action they could. Testify-
ing before the House Communications Subcommittee on March 2, 1976,
Commissioner Abbott Washburn said of open meetings:

> Now I am convinced that if we do this we will be cutting back our
> effectiveness by about 50 percent. You will slow down this agency
> by 50 percent. The people in the audience at meetings will not be
> the public hoping to be educated as to how these matters are done.
> It is a semijudicial body. The people in the audience will be parties
> at interest. You cannot discuss these quasi-judicial cases out in the
> open the same way that you do amongst yourselves.
>
> What does this mean? It means that Commissioners, instead of
> having a free flow of exchange in that meeting amongst themselves
> and with the staff in a candid, frank way, will be meeting outside
> the meeting room. This will be time consuming.

Passed by a House vote of 384–0 and a Senate voice vote in September 1976, the law required some 50 agencies to open all proceedings
within 180 days—with a few exceptions. The FCC has noted that meetings may be closed if the subjects to be discussed involve national security, internal personnel matters, trade secrets, accusations of crime, invasion of privacy, or law enforcement, or if premature disclosure would be
"likely to significantly frustrate" implementation of proposed FCC
actions or formal adjudication. Some cynics believe that the law provides a rug large enough for the reluctant commissioners to sweep
whatever they want under it.

Perhaps the handling of the first major broadcasting matter to come before the Commission after the law's passage is indicative of the future. The commissioners were polled separately and privately on whether to consider immediately the Westinghouse request to require networks to provide advance program screening to their affiliates; the Commission's vote (no) was announced; but no discussion of the matter was introduced in the newly open Commission meetings. Whether the law will mean anything in the long run will depend upon the spirit in which it is implemented.

II
COMMUNICATING WITH THE FCC

6

The Commissioners
on the Sawdust Trail

Talking before broadcaster groups is no problem.
You know what they want to hear and that's what
you tell them.

A senior FCC staffer much in demand on the broadcast
lecture circuit, circa 1973

Q. Why do commissioners and staff members appear so much more frequently before broadcasting
groups than before other FCC-regulated groups,
such as the common carrier associations or the state
utility regulators?

A. It's simple. Other conventions are boring. Everybody there is an engineer or a bureaucrat or a corporation bigwig. Broadcasters, on the other hand,
are basically entertainers. They are much more
interesting people to be with.

A commissioner's engineering assistant, to
Barry Cole, in conversation

From 1971 through 1975, FCC commissioners and high-level staff (GS-15 and above) took 781 trips to visit industry groups and only seven trips to consumer groups. It took hundreds of pages to provide basic information about FCC speaking engagements for the House Subcommittee on Oversight and Investigations.

How can one explain the disproportion between the two kinds of trips? Of course, broadcasting associations hold many more meetings and conventions than citizen groups do. Most industry gatherings are scheduled at resorts or other amenable watering spots and invariably include a wholesome mixture of fun along with the working sessions. It's a rare citizen group that can afford to hire even the Bonanza Room of a midtown motel for a meeting. Furthermore, citizen groups often don't invite certain FCC commissioners or staff members who have no sympathy with the groups' aims. In fact, several commissioners admitted to Cole that they did not encourage invitations from citizen groups; and, after past negative experiences with such groups, some commissioners simply avoided them altogether.

During those same five years (1971–1975), $89,206 was spent to enable FCC commissioners and high-level staff to appear as invited speakers or guests at various conventions and conferences. This total exceeded that of other regulatory agencies for the same purpose: the Interstate Commerce Commission spent $77,626; the Securities and Exchange Commission, $61,989; the Federal Trade Commission, $38,145; and the Federal Power Commission, $34,326. The SEC figure was understated, however, because SEC members and employees *were* allowed to accept payment from private groups; the $61,989 represented only the government's share of trip expenses. The FCC, however, can accept private expense money only when speaking before a noncommunications audience on a noncommunications subject. More than a decade ago, according to the Graham–Kramer Study, some commissioners double-billed: that is, they took the money from the host and the reimbursement from the government.

Despite continued increases in travel budgets, some commissioners found themselves short of funds for trips they wished to take. For example, on February 3, 1975, *Television Digest* reported that Commissioner James Quello's travel money would be exhausted following his next trip to a broadcasters' convention, even though commissioners' annual travel allowances had been raised to $4250 from the preceding fiscal year's $3500. (In 1977, the allowance was $4500 for a commissioner, $9000 for the chairman.)

At the request of the chairman, Quello made his first speech in May 1974, after only one week on the job. Quello, a former broadcaster, began: "Tonight I'm breaking my pledge. I pledged that I would not accept any speaking assignments until at least 60 days in office." Quello continued, "However, I couldn't pick a better place to break that pledge than (1) a state broadcasting association, and (2) particularly the Oregon State Broadcasting Association." (Quello's father-in-law was a famous track coach at the University of Oregon.)

Some of the commissioners were making so many speeches before industry associations that Chairman Burch asked the commissioners to restrict their speeches to Mondays and Fridays to encourage full attendance at scheduled meetings on Tuesdays, Wednesdays, and Thursdays. Since the fall of 1972, most commissioners have complied.

On Mondays and Fridays, however, the commissioners are often out of Washington. For example, on Monday, September 30, 1974, Commissioner Robert E. Lee was addressing the Nevada Broadcasters Association Convention in Las Vegas; Commissioner Charlotte Reid was speaking to the American Association of Advertising Agencies in Vancouver, British Columbia; Commissioner Benjamin Hooks was addressing the Institute of Broadcasting Financial Management in St. Louis; and Commissioner James Quello was a speaker at the Pacific Northwest Cable Communications Convention in Boise, Idaho.

Extensive travel to industries' association meetings is not restricted to commissioners. During a period of 18 months, General Counsel John Pettit spoke to 16 state or national broadcasters association meetings as well as to meetings of nonbroadcasting industry groups. Warren Braren, associate director of Consumers Union, appearing before the Senate Communications Subcommittee in opposition to the FCC appointment of Quello, noted that on no occasion during that period did Pettit speak before a group "representing citizen interests." Braren also quoted Pettit's speech before the Kansas Broadcasting Convention on May 18, 1973:

> I am confronted by the friendly and familiar faces I have seen— including Charlie Jones of the NAB's radio information office (you know, Charlie and I have appeared on so many programs together that we now refer to the "Jack and Charlie Road Show"). If we occasionally sound the same, it's not because we rehearse but because we both happen to believe in a strong, viable, and vibrant commercial broadcast system which should not be saddled with outdated, inconsistent, and wholly unnecessary regulations.

Braren characterized these remarks as "an example of how vested interests walk hand-in-hand with key staff members of the FCC. . . ."

At one point, between trips to state broadcasting associations, Pettit told several FCC people that he'd heard so many complaints from broadcasters regarding overregulation and onerous burdens imposed by the Commission that he was beginning to dream about them. Commissioner Wiley, who was part of the group, asked Pettit, "You don't really believe *all* that stuff they've been telling you?"

While Pettit's successor as FCC general counsel, Ashton Hardy, made fewer trips to broadcasters associations, his speeches usually followed a similar line. For example, Hardy told the Broadcasters Association of Puerto Rico on August 15, 1975:

> While some regulation to protect the public interest may be necessary, we must not forget that commercial broadcasting is a private enterprise. I cannot and do not accept the philosophy of some who would state that you should have no quarrel with undue government intrusion into your business affairs because you are "public trustees." To those who maintain that, I would say "hogwash."

Congress has vacillated in its attitude toward the extent of Commission travels. Newton Minow, in his book *Equal Time* (Atheneum, 1964), complained of congressmen's criticizing commissioners for trying to regulate without understanding the broadcasters' problems and, in the next hearing, criticizing commissioners for getting too close to the industry.

During Cole's years at the Commission, members of Congress objected periodically to the extent of Commission travel. At the confirmation hearings for Wiley and Hooks in May 1972, for example, Senator Pastore said: "If they [commissioners] stayed home they could take care of the backlog." Pastore claimed that, "Every time broadcasters have a meeting in Chicago or Honolulu you have a commissioner there.... I don't think they ought to go." Pastore said he would discuss the matter with Chairman Burch. Nonetheless, the following year the commissioners established an all-time record for money spent on travel; and Commissioners Wiley and Hooks soon became the most peripatetic commissioners.

When asked on May 14, 1976 by the House Subcommittee on Oversight and Investigations about the Commission's many trips to industry meetings, Wiley said that travel "is part of our job." He and other commissioners said they addressed any group that invited them. Wiley, who prided himself on being able to travel widely without missing Commission meetings, added:

> If Congress has a view on this, if they don't want us to make these trips, if they prefer that we don't speak to industry groups, I would like to have the Appropriations Committee tell us that, because I am trying to carry out the mandate of Congress as I understand it, and, believe me, if someone wants to tell me I shouldn't take these trips, it would save me a lot of problems and a lot of time writing these speeches which I write until very late in the morning; that is, late in the evening, early morning, and on trains, planes, and all the rest of it. It is quite a burden.

Broadcasters have been quick to react to any hint of congressional criticism regarding Commission trips to meet with representatives of their industry. For example, following a report that a House committee would conduct an inquiry into the nature and extent of Commission travel, Bert Hatch, executive director of the Georgia Association of Broadcasters, wrote *Broadcasting* (November 27, 1972):

> It would be tragic if the general public were to classify these trips as "junkets" for they are extremely productive and have contributed greatly to the recently improved relationship between the Commission and the average broadcaster. The typical Commissioner and FCC department head is not a broadcaster by trade and it is only through these periodic face-to-face contacts with broadcasters that the isolation of the "ivory tower" can be avoided . . . and the unrealistic regulations which stem from such isolation can be avoided as well. It would be sad—and a classic example of being "penny wise and pound foolish"—if pressure from the [congressional committee] were to curtail these trips by FCC staffers into the field they regulate.

Usually, a commissioner or Commission staff member is treated very well on these trips. The broadcasters are almost always pleasant, respectful, and eager to hear the Word from Washington. Sometimes he or she gets an award or honorary membership. Commissioners get used to this kind of attention. *Broadcasting* noted some changes in "Closed Circuit" (February 2, 1976):

> Whether it's backwash of Watergate and political cleanups or simply lower political sensitivities of new generation, government officials, including those at FCC, are complaining of disappearance of amenities they used to get when travelling. Recent complaint came from Commissioner who wasn't met at airport by car from [broadcast] station on which he had agreed to do interview, wasn't fed dinner he'd expected. Going it alone on government travel allowances could keep officials home.

On various occasions, the Commission has timed major actions to precede meetings of regulated industry groups. Sometimes an item had to be hurried through the agenda before all the commissioners had time to consider the issue thoroughly. Other times, an item would be delayed so its disposition, if it was what the industry was seeking, could be announced at an industry convention.

Commissioner Robert E. Lee called items that cropped up with urgency just before the NAB convention "NAB specials"—crowd pleasers that would assure applause for a chairman who announced them and smiles for the other commissioners who supported them. The 1976 NAB convention was so garlanded that *Broadcasting* reported a "grab-bag of FCC favors greet NAB in Chicago," along with a headline referring to "The Week That Was: FCC Has Something for Everyone at NAB Chicago."

Although the NAB was certainly the key group eligible for these "specials," other industry groups, including the National Association of Educational Broadcasters, also received carefully timed good tidings at their annual conventions. The main problem with "convention specials" is that a commissioner is tempted to rush to judgment on matters that might merit more consideration.

Audiences tend to expect "specials" and commissioners want to deliver them. Late one evening in September 1975, Chairman Wiley told Cole that Wiley could think of "nothing to say" in his speech to the National Association of FM Broadcasters the next day. Earlier that week, when Wiley made a "policy address" to the International Radio and Television Society (IRTS), one of the major annual speeches a chairman delivers, he dangled before them such goodies as an experimental plan to excuse some radio stations from Fairness Doctrine obligations and another proposal to give broadcasters greater discretion in covering political debates. He had nothing comparable for the next day's speech.

By the time Wiley spoke to the FM broadcasters, less than 24 hours after he had "nothing to say," he could tell them to expect *further* simplification of the new "short form" renewal application for commercial radio stations. The proposal, which had been the subject of 131 formal comments, including strong opposition by citizen groups, was not to be acted upon for another six months.

The prospect of being bathed in applause by an industry group brings out the philanthropist in some FCC officials. In March 1974, *Broadcasting* commented: "The most popular person at last week's NAB Convention was Richard E. Wiley, the new Chairman of the FCC. Wherever he went he was applauded. His formal address evoked standing applause." At the April 1975 NAB Convention, according to *Television Digest,* Wiley brought down the house when he said: "Broadcasters should be spending their time in programming to serve the American public and not in filling out government forms or complying with unnecessary regulations. You are, after all, responsible men and women—and it is about time that we started treating you as such." By September 1976, the habit was fully ingrained. "Wiley's Happy News for IRTS" headlined a *Television Digest* story, which said his speech "pleased just about everyone in the broadcaster-dominated audience." His most popular remark was, "The last thing we need in this country is more federal controls on programming." And in October 1976, after Wiley's luncheon address to broadcasters gathered in Kansas City, Cole overheard one station owner tell a colleague, "Well, now that we don't have to worry about the FCC, let's go out and make some more money."

Occasionally a commissioner may use a speech to the industry to do a little lobbying of his own to stir up industry reaction to some course of action the FCC is pursuing. In November 1975, a Senate committee was holding hearings, instigated by complaints from citizen groups, on whether the FCC's actions in deregulating broadcasting were detrimental to the public interest. The day the hearings began, Commissioner Robinson, speaking to an NAB regional conference in New Orleans, exhorted broadcasters to tell Congress how pleased they were with the FCC's efforts on their behalf. Comparing himself to Galileo about to be burned at the stake in defense of truth, Robinson complained, "how vociferous broadcasters have not been in cheering us." He continued: "Now that we were out on a limb, with unruly crowds gathered below yelling at us to 'Jump! Jump!' it would be comforting to think that those who stand to profit by our sudden seizure of sensibleness would be more encouraging than has been the case." By releasing the text of his speech to the trade press the preceding week, Robinson ensured maximum exposure for his views in time for the hearings and annoyed the committee chairman, Senator Pastore.

In the course of the Pastore hearings, citizen advocate Everett Parker submitted speeches commissioners had made before industry groups as evidence of how FCC officials committed themselves to a position in pending proceedings before they had the opportunity to digest relevant comments and filed pleadings. Once having stated their positions, Parker charged, commissioners close their minds to legal arguments concerning the issues.

Sometimes commissioners or senior FCC staff members are so carried away by the heady atmosphere of an industry meeting that they make on-the-spot policy decisions on matters the Commission hasn't thrashed out officially. In response to a question at a broadcasters' meeting in Atlanta, Richard Shiben, chief of the Renewal and Transfer Division, said a broadcaster would meet the needs and problems of his community if he dealt with only three such problems in a year's broadcasts. The official forms called for treatment of up to ten problems—and the magic number three had never been mentioned in Commission meetings. A broadcast lawyer told Cole, "When I heard Shiben say that, I almost fell off my chair in surprise."

Citizen groups, too, have benefited from this tendency of FCC officials to tell audiences what they want to hear. Speaking before a Ralph Nader forum in 1975, Chairman Wiley made commitments to establish an office of consumer assistance and to make his appointments calendar public. Unfortunately for them, citizen groups, by the nature of their organizations, rarely hold large meetings that are addressed by commissioners. Cole heard citizen advocates joke that if they could hold one giant, annual, national citizens' convention and invite the FCC chairman to speak, they could reap greater benefits than from all their petitions, pleadings, and appearances before the FCC and Congress.

Commissioner Hooks defended commissioners' trips to broadcasting meetings: "I don't just tell them what they want to hear." Indeed, his many admonitions to broadcasters to improve their minority hiring practices and to increase programming for blacks and Spanish-speaking Americans were not the messages that pleased industry members the most. But commissioners known to view the industry with suspicion aren't often invited. Nicholas Johnson, for example, was not in great demand to speak before broadcasters associations.

Even commissioners who hold generally favorable views about commercial broadcasting sometimes use speaking engagements as an opportunity to mount the pulpit. Chairman Wiley frequently spoke of the need for imposing sanctions against the industry's "rotten apples," the broadcasters who lie and cheat. Commissioner Robert Wells, a former broadcaster himself, did not hesitate to tell industry audiences that regulation is a price they must pay for the glamour, profits, and power derived from their businesses. He suggested that no one forced them to go into broadcasting; they were free to dispose of their licenses at any time. In fact, next to Nicholas Johnson, Wells appeared to be the commissioner most skeptical about the FCC's policy of deregulation. He expressed fears that broadcasters would seize upon relaxation of standards as an invitation to ignore them completely; and he warned that this attitude might lead the Commission to assess more severe penalties for all types of violations.

Certainly the case has been made by FCC officials and by broadcasters that meetings provide a forum in which the broadcasters can get a better idea of what is expected of them and the bureaucrat can learn of the industry's problems. The question is this: Does all this attention turn an official's head?

7
The FCC Tangles with the Citizenry

FCC and its silver-tongued writers must stop
hiding behind the smoke screen of legal forni-
cation. There is no need for the institution
of racism of the Federal Communications
Commission to be perpetually fed and maintained by unnecessary legal entanglements.
James McCuller
NBMC chairman, FCC en banc meeting, November 12, 1973

One of the major weaknesses in our Federal
regulatory scheme is that the regulators are
always hearing the views of the broadcasters
they regulate and of their Washington lawyers.
They rarely hear the opinions of the people in
whose interests they presumably are regulating. This Washington meeting was organized
to let the FCC hear from you about what you
think of the decisions they are contemplating.
If the FCC is the conscience of the national
community in broadcasting, you are the conscience of the people you represent. It's up to
you to make that conscience informed and
articulate at the meeting.
Rev. Everett C. Parker, director, Office of Communications,
United Church of Christ, letter to citizen groups attending
FCC en banc meeting, January 14, 1974

7 Meetings with industry are nothing new to the FCC. Over the years, the full Commission has held periodic, closed meetings with various industry groups. Sometimes, these meetings were very successful from the industry's viewpoint. For example, a special meeting with television broadcasters from the Rocky Mountain area was followed by the Commission's unanimously granting their request to specify the hours of 6:00 P.M. to 10:00 P.M. (rather than 7:00 P.M. to 11:00 P.M.) as prime time in all Rocky Mountain states.

Sometimes the outcome of such a special meeting disappointed the broadcasters. Commissioner Robert Lee told Cole that in 1963 the Commission was proposing to prohibit the practice of network option time; that is, of a network's requiring an affiliate to carry a specified amount of network programming. CBS asked to meet with the commissioners to plead that option time be retained. Armed with charts and statistics, chalk talks and audiovisual presentations, CBS economists tried to persuade the FCC members that if option time were banned, the television network system would collapse. The commissioners went ahead and eliminated the practice anyway; and, Lee recalls, "Nothing more was heard from CBS—not a court appeal, not even a petition asking us to reconsider." Disappointed or not, the industry had had its meeting with the FCC.

An FCC meeting with a citizen group, on the other hand, was a very rare occurrence prior to 1970. In January of that year, Action for Children's Television (ACT) requested a meeting with the Commission and was invited to Washington. ACT's president, Peggy Charren, recalls, "When we got on the plane we didn't know who we were going to see— just Chairman Burch, members of the staff. . . ." ACT representatives were happily surprised when they arrived at the chairman's office; their audience included six of the commissioners.

A full three years passed before the Commission held another en banc meeting with a public group. In the interim, Charlotte Reid had been appointed as only the second woman commissioner in FCC history (the first was Frieda Hennock, 1948–1955). Although Mrs. Reid considered herself a conservative and "not a woman's advocate," it was through her office that the National Organization for Women (NOW) sought a meeting with the full Commission to air some grievances.

The meeting with NOW took place on January 3, 1973, in the early afternoon. When Cole walked into the meeting room just before the session, he overheard Chairman Burch talking with Wilma Scott Heide, NOW's president. Chairman Burch was telling Ms. Heide, "Remember, you have our undivided attention for almost an hour and a half. I suggest you take best advantage of it." Cole noticed that Burch seemed somewhat annoyed.

The meeting began with Ms. Heide's chastising the Commission. First, she announced that she wished to get several things on the record.

The chairman told her that there would be no written record of this closed meeting; but Ms. Heide responded, "I want to say these things anyway."

Ms. Heide then expressed some objections about the meeting itself. First, she complained about the seating arrangements—the Commission was sitting "on the bench" on a dais, and the representatives from NOW (and about 15 Commission staffers) were sitting below. Ms. Heide exclaimed, "We're equals! I don't look up to you, and I don't want to have to sit here looking up to you."

Ms. Heide then explained that because the meeting was being held in the afternoon, one NOW member could not be present; and Ms. Heide asked why the meeting could not have been held in the morning. When Chairman Burch explained that Wednesday morning was the normal time for Commission agenda meetings, and that later that afternoon the entire Commission was going to New Jersey to tour the Bell Laboratories installation, the explanation did not satisfy Ms. Heide. She suggested things still could have been arranged—including, if necessary, postponing the Commission's agenda discussions—to have the meeting in the morning when all the NOW people could attend.

After Ms. Heide enumerated objections to Commission policies that she would raise during the meeting, and introduced some colleagues, who would be addressing the Commission later, Ms. Heide told the Commission she was about to read an essay that would provide an "awareness experience." She did not want to be interrupted while reading the essay; she would tell the commissioners when it was appropriate for them to speak. To the utter bemusement of the commissioners, Ms. Heide proceeded to read her essay, which *Television Digest* (January 8, 1973) quoted in its brisk, truncated style:

> Feel further into the obvious biological explanation for woman as the ideal—her genital construction. By design, female genitals are compact and internal, protected by her body. Male genitals are so exposed that he must be protected from outside attack to assure the perpetuation of the race. . . . Males are more passive than females and have a desire in sexual relations to be symbolically engulfed by the protective body of the woman. . . . A man experiences himself as a "whole man" when thus engulfed. . . . He remembers his sister's jeering at his primitive genitals that "flop around foolishly. . . ." Because of his vagina-envy, he learns to bind his genitals, and learns to feel ashamed and unclean because of his nocturnal emissions." Commissioners couldn't be reached for comment. . . .

Cole wished he had had a camera to record for posterity the expressions on the faces of the commissioners as they listened or tried to avoid listening to Ms. Heide's presentation. Chairman Burch, when bored, angry, or uncomfortable, had a habit of scratching on paper with a pencil; by the time Ms. Heide had finished speaking, Cole wondered whether the pencil had gone through the note pad or even through the table. Another commissioner seemed to be reading a piece of paper, which, Cole was certain, was blank; one commissioner was looking out the window through drawn blinds. Most commissioners seemed acutely embarrassed.

Following her essay, Ms. Heide remarked on how inaccurately women were portrayed by the media: "Day by day, the media is anti-women, anti-feminist, anti-change." She cited a *Redbook* survey of 120,000 readers, 75 percent of whom thought women were portrayed as sex objects or mad dogs on the media.

By this time, the tone of the meeting had been so well established that it would have made no difference what followed. That was unfortunate because several important and useful suggestions were offered by Ms. Heide's colleagues; for example, some methods by which the Commission should select stations for further examination of their compliance with equal employment opportunity requirements.

As the meeting was ending, one of the NOW representatives—the only male (a black) on the panel—had not yet had the opportunity to speak. Chairman Burch addressed this man by name and apologized for the need to close the meeting. Ms. Heide was furious: "If I had wanted him to speak, he would have spoken." Her outburst triggered indignation from Commissioner Reid, who had been particularly cordial. Mrs. Reid expressed disappointment with the meeting, which she'd hoped would be constructive, and dismay at Ms. Heide's negative attitude.

Ms. Heide's colleagues had been courteous enough, but the milk was spoiled. The experience provided ammunition for those in the FCC who believed that meetings with public groups were a waste of time, a hairshirt. A month after the meeting, Ms. Heide, reelected president of NOW (unopposed), said, in her keynote address to the convention, that if petitions to the FCC to deny license renewal were not granted, "Then we must educate by station and network takeover actions to assure them we are in earnest." This statement didn't strengthen her position with the commissioners or encourage them to schedule further meetings.

As the NOW meeting with the commissioners was arranged through the sole woman member of the FCC, so a meeting of blacks and other minority group members was arranged by the first black commissioner, Benjamin L. Hooks, two months later. Under the auspices of Black Efforts for Soul in Television (BEST), which had been instrumental in a black's appointment to the FCC, a meeting was held between all the commissioners and some 50 representatives of minorities, including Orientals, Spanish-speaking Americans, and American Indians, who travelled long distances to Washington at their own expense.

In his opening statement, William D. Wright said he hoped the meeting would convey "something of the depth of frustration, the despair with the performance of the broadcast media, which afflicts the peoples of color." Wright emphasized that such feelings were not conveyed adequately in the written pleadings that had been filed with the Commission on behalf of citizen groups.

This meeting, unlike the NOW meeting, was low key. Wright set the tone when, in his opening statement, he expressed the hope of establishing a relationship with the Commission based on a "mutual desire" to solve the problems troubling minority groups. These problems included Commission decision-making and administrative processes as well as the broadcast industry's employment and programming practices.

Some of this group's grievances represented themes that would be reiterated by citizen groups during the coming years with varying degrees of success. Speakers criticized broadcasters, specifically television licensees, for "extreme racism and sexism" in programming, news reporting, editorial policies, and hiring practices; for abusing public service time; for keeping negative racial stereotypes alive; and for an imbalance between commercials and program material. The groups criticized the FCC for being insensitive to citizen complaints, for lackadaisical enforcement of equal opportunity employment regulations, and for cavalier handling of petitions and complaints submitted by minority groups.

Additionally, the spokesmen for various groups offered proposals: decentralization of the Commission through development of regional offices; more field investigations of complaints of discrimination in employment; legal assistance for groups unable to pursue petitions to deny licenses; and clear-cut rules governing agreements between broadcasters and citizen groups on hiring or programming.

Reactions to the meeting were mixed. William Wright, generally satisfied with the meeting, said, "If not all of the commissioners, a majority indicated a definite concern to identify problems in specific areas." Commissioner Johnson said, "Hopefully, they will come back later this year with a detailed list of very specific recommendations on which the FCC can act." *Broadcasting* (March 12, 1973) quoted negative reactions from two unidentified commissioners. One said the group's spokesmen were unrealistic in their refusal to acknowledge any progress by the Commission in the areas they cited. Another "resented a group's spokesman's demanding that each member of the Commission participate in the dialogue with questions or comment." Hooks was pleased with the session; he told *The New York Times* (March 19, 1973): "For the first time in its 39-year history the FCC talked to some black folks, and it will never be the same again." Said another commissioner, Robert Lee, to *Broadcasting:* "I'll tell you one thing—

broadcasters are in for a lot of trouble. They're [minority groups] well organized and they're putting the heat on is."

Broadcasting blasted the entire proceeding in an editorial (March 26, 1973):

> The hundred-odd broadcasters whose license renewals are hanging in suspension while the FCC considers protests by local activists may be excused for wondering why their adversaries have been given a private audience with the seven FCC members who are to vote those renewals up and down. As reported here March 12, some 50 blacks, Chicanos, Orientals, and Indians, accompanied by the professional and foundation-supported organizers of petitions to deny, met in closed session with the FCC to recite their grievances and aspirations.

> At the very least the challenged broadcasters deserve equal time. . . . This is not to say that minorities are without claim to a larger place in radio and television programming and employment. The point is that reverse discrimination is now at work and will only be accentuated by such questionable developments as secret sessions that exclude principal parties to adversary actions. . . .

The Commission responded in a press release four days later: the FCC intended to continue holding informal meetings on "a fair rotating basis." It accepted the suggestions of the trade journal that such meetings should be open to public attendance, if not free-for-all participation.

The first of these scheduled open meetings was held on May 21, 1973, with the Latino Media Coalition, which had been established as a permanent organization just a week before the meeting. Some 50 representatives from eight states appeared before five of the seven commissioners. The coalition represented Spanish-speaking Americans of different national origins, mainly Mexican-Americans and Puerto Ricans, but also persons from Cuba, the Dominican Republic, and South America.

The coalition complained of employment practices in the broadcasting industry and in the FCC itself, where of the FCC's 1620 employees, only 11 had Spanish surnames. The coalition cited examples of "exploitation" of employees by managers of Spanish-language radio stations, the difficulty of negotiating for greater orientation toward Spanish speakers on stations serving large Latino populations, and the laxity of FCC enforcement of equal opportunity employment rules.

The coalition requested the establishment of a task force composed of five FCC members (two of whom would be commissioners) and five coalition members to discuss and resolve the issues raised at the meeting. In a press conference after the meeting, one coalition spokesman said he regretted the FCC's lack of enthusiasm for the proposal: "The

Commission has formed task forces in other areas—in cable and common carrier. I see no reason why it should not establish a task force with our group. . . . It responds to the people it regulates, but not those for whom it regulates."

Although the Commission said it would take the proposal under advisement, nothing was done about the coalition's suggestion. Nor was anything done about a coalition report on "The Employment and Programming Practices of the Federal Communications Commission." In May 1974, one year after the meeting with the coalition, the president of Raza Association of Spanish-Surnamed Americans sent a letter to Chairman Wiley asking the status of the report. Wiley bucked the letter along to several staff members with a note that "This should be discussed prior to Atlanta." "Atlanta" referred to a planned public meeting where people could "speak directly to the Commission." Wiley recognized that the Spanish-speakers' problems were another area that the Commission had ignored and where the agency was vulnerable to criticism. The decision not to form a task force was consistent with later decisions not to become involved in any type of advisory committee relationship with any minority groups.

It was almost six months after the Latino meeting before another citizen group meeting—a second meeting with blacks agreed to at the March meeting—was held. Because Wright was in the process of obtaining a research grant from the National Science Foundation and thus was phasing out of advocacy, the black media movement needed new leadership, and because William Wright *was* BEST, a new organization as well.

On the weekend before the meeting, scheduled November 12, 1973, a group of blacks met to prepare their testimony; and according to *Access* (September 1975), the National Black Media Coalition (NBMC) was "hastily" formed. James McCuller, executive director of Rochester's (N.Y.) Action for a Better Community, became chairman of the new organization. While the Citizens Communication Center (including its new head, Frank Lloyd) was helping NBMC draw up its grievances and recommendations, preparations for the meeting and the funding for NBMC were in the hands of McCuller and the other black representatives. McCuller and his Rochester staff carried much of the financial as well as the physical burden of the organization for the first 18 months of its existence.

The November 12 meeting was a memorable one; and, in the opinion of many people Cole talked with, it had an important effect upon the Commission's thinking about NBMC and the black media reform movement generally. Even before the meeting, some commissioners were apprehensive. As he was about to walk into the room one commissioner commented to Cole, "This is going to be painful." The commissioner couldn't have anticipated just how volatile the meeting would be.

With membership from more than 40 local and regional organizations in more than 30 communities, and with the blessings of William Wright, NBMC had great potential strength. The group, in a 45-page petition for rulemaking and notice of inquiry, had outlined approximately 30 proposed rule changes and additions for Commission consideration. Unfortunately, the group's potential influence was probably severely damaged by the November 12 meeting. (The following quotes are from the FCC's transcript of that meeting.)

McCuller opened the meeting by stating that the history and experiences of black people made them special, that their needs deserved to be considered as "immediate priorities" for Commission action. McCuller contrasted the commissioners' interest in and willingness to visit small-market radio stations with its unwillingness to visit black communities.

> [The message to blacks] is specific, loud, and direct. It says if you are white, you are right; if you are brown, stick around; if you are black, get back. As I say this some Commissioners recoil in anger, even though the truth of my statement is only overshadowed by your record of faithful and positive service to white broadcasters. . . .

> FCC and its silver-tongued writers must stop hiding behind the smoke screen of legal fornication. There is no need for the institution of racism of the Federal Communications Commission to be perpetually fed and maintained by unnecessary legal entanglements. . . . If FCC is to be perceived as an objective, legitimate instrument for the transaction of the communications business of black people, the Commission must formally act on our concerns in an official manner at a specified time and place.

> FCC knows this is the second meeting it has held with a group of black people in the 39 years of the Commission's existence. This is fantastic, incredible, and contemptible. It is also an unforgivable insult to black people.

At this point the chairman interjected: "Mr. McCuller, you are doing your best to make this the last meeting, I might say." When McCuller asked to finish his statement, the chairman continued, "Well, Mr. McCuller, this has been billed as a meeting between the Commission and your group to construct a dialogue, not a diatribe. And very candidly, however strongly you feel some of these things, I feel that the simple bounds of civility require that this be carried on at that kind of level, and I would hope that you would."

Burch's comments sent McCuller into a rage. As he paced up and down and around the room, his voice grew louder and louder.

> . . . You have been saying behave; be quiet. The whole history of black people is white people saying, "Black people, be quiet." Now, stop me, Mr. Burch.

For 36 hours we have worked like dogs to come here organized. Wrote every damn thing you asked for. I came here in the morning, and you say, "Boy, behave." I ain't no god-damned boy. "Or be civilized." I am civilized. . . .

Tell us what you're going to do, Mr. Burch. You are the boss here. This is your facility. Nixon gave you that when he gave you your charter. Tell us. Tell us. You are master, Mr. Chairman. Tell us. You have been telling us all our god-damned lives.

You told my mama and my daddy on the shores of Africa. From the West Coast in the bottomless ships in cargoes, stacked with chains, and rode four months across the god-damned ocean on bread, salt, and water. Tell us. "Don't tell me that, man. Don't do that." God-damn it. Given time we will be what we are.

I don't apologize to America for being born out of a black womb from intercourse between a black man and a black woman. And I am proud. And I am not going to stand up here and let a Burch call me down. I will call Burch down. He is the only god-damned person who is wrong. . . .

This meeting is over. But I assure you, Mr. Burch, when you write it, when you write it this time, all you did was transfer it back. You transferred it into a battle you don't have no use for, and that will be a battle in every local station, that will be a battle in every newspaper, that will be a battle with the advertisers that is financing those god-damned stations that we pay for.

Now how do you want it followed, Mr. Burch? Do you want it constructed according to agenda, according to specific rules, according to Hoyle or would you rather have it jungle style? I like either. I prefer jungle style. I am more comfortable with that. Name it, Mr. Burch. Do you really want a fair and constructive atmosphere for discussing this issue? Name it. Name it. Name it, Mr. Burch. You're the boss. Master Mister Tom Communications, suh.

Tell us poor downtrodden black people, how can a nigger [be] walking around like I own the Commission—tell the uppity nigger to sit down. They've been telling me that all my life and I refused. And I'm not going to sit down until God stops my heart; and if He wants to call me, Mr. Burch. . . .

Tell us. Don't stop me, just tell us. My name is Jim McCuller. Come on, Dean. Tell us. If you're going to throw me out, be nice, do what you usually do. When we act unruly and you don't like it, throw us out. Stop them, Dean. Tell them to sit down. Tell them:

"Now I want you to sit down. I want you to be dignified. I want you to be quiet."

When McCuller sat down, the chairman asked, "Have you concluded your statement, Mr. McCuller?" Throughout McCuller's rage Burch had remained calm and expressionless, in sharp contrast to some of his colleagues, whose facial expressions ranged from fright to bewilderment. Had the chairman done anything other than sit quietly while McCuller shouted and paced across the room, Cole was not sure what would have happened. Even at the point at which McCuller paused, Cole couldn't guess what might happen next. Judging from the faces of those around him and the tenseness in the room, neither could anyone else.

Burch had already urged McCuller to discuss his petition for rule-making and notice of inquiry, to get to the purpose of the meeting. McCuller, however, wanted to continue with his statement. He told Burch, "If I go back up there to the rostrum, I will finish the statement like you agreed, or not at all." Burch replied:

> Mr. McCuller, you can make any statement that you like. But I would like to point out to you that we are here, as I understand it, by mutual agreement. And if the whole idea of your opening statement is to abuse the Commission, and accuse them of wrongdoing, evil motives, and the rest, I fail to see how it can be constructive.

> It seems to me that your purpose was to improve the situation, and if abusing me gives you personal satisfaction, I imagine you have had a great deal this morning. But if you would like to get to the material that is contained in your agenda, I would suggest that you do so; and if the condition precedent to that is to finish your statement, I would suggest that you do that. But I would also hope that it could be done on a relatively simple basis. That is all I have to say.

McCuller asked for and received a vote of confidence from the members of his organization. After he had argued further with Burch, the chairman reminded him that the meeting had already gone on for 30 minutes and that little had been accomplished. He suggested that McCuller "Get on with your business." McCuller replied:

> Okay. I will take that. I see that 30 minutes is so important. For 39 years—for 37 years you did not have a black Commissioner. For 37 years there did not appear to be any urgent reason to act, and now 30 minutes compared to 37 years, "get along with your business." I will. I will.

Ironically, in later portions of McCuller's prepared statement, he praised Burch as "the finest manager in the history of the Commission. . . . The first Commission Chairman with the guts and integrity to open the doors of this room to the public. . . ." McCuller also indicated that if recent reports about the chairman's leaving the FCC were accurate, "He will be missed by all of us who know what it means to see a man make a decision and then stick by it." McCuller praised Commissioners Johnson and Hooks, too.

There was such a dramatic difference between the first part of the meeting and the two hours or so that followed that it was as if two script-writers—one a Brechtian polemicist and the other a pedestrian, but sincere documentarian—had collaborated in patching together a happening. The NBMC speakers made cogent presentations concerning a wide range of problems; the commissioners, relieved that the storm was over, listened with interest.

Nonetheless, much damage had been done by that time. The apprehension that the NOW meeting had molded in the minds of many commissioners was cast in concrete. For years after the meeting, Cole heard broadcasters, commissioners, and FCC staff members refer to McCuller's outburst as an example of what broadcasters faced in negotiations with citizen groups.

The substance of the NBMC complaints and requests was far more quickly forgotten. The coalition's oral presentation, in which various speakers expressed their constituents' complaints, made no distinction between the significance of narrow questions—are black colleges discriminated against because network television doesn't regularly carry their football games?—and the significance of more sweeping questions —is black ownership of licenses precluded because all television frequencies have been assigned? A complaint that radio stations demand that a soul artist appear at their record hops before they play the musician's recordings was followed by complaints that stations' persistent hiring patterns close out blacks at all but the most menial levels.

At the end of the meeting, the coalition presented a petition asking for FCC study and adoption of certain rules and policies. In this petition, the polemic had been eliminated. NBMC asked the FCC to change its rules governing such areas as these:

- The FCC's decision-making process—to make it more responsive to all citizens;

- Equal employment opportunity in the cable and broadcasting industries, and at the Commission itself—to codify and enforce FCC policies;

- Agreements between community groups and broadcasters or cable operators—to legitimize and enforce such pacts;

- Ownership of broadcast facilities—to give preference in comparative hearings to applicants from racial minorities and to establish an FCC office to aid and encourage minority ownership;

- Monopolization of broadcast frequencies—to restrict the number of stations certain licensees may have and to reduce or eliminate clear channel radio stations;

• Broadcast programming—to make it responsive to all the community elements a station is licensed to serve;

• Challenges to existing licenses—to make the process easier by making station data more available, staggering renewal dates within a city, and providing legal assistance to challengers;

• Cable television—to permit black participation in an industry in which the rules are still evolving.

When the FCC was planning its first regional public meeting in May 1974, Cole reminded Chairman Wiley that nothing had been done in response to the NBMC November 1973 petition and suggested that someone at the Atlanta meeti   might ask about the document. Wiley asked Cole to write him a memo summarizing the NBMC requests. When Wiley asked the Broadcast Bureau the status of the petition, it took them nearly a full day even to find it. The lawyer who found it in the files expressed no regrets from the bureau that no one had read it —just finding it was considered an achievement.

Not until July 21, 1976, had the wheels of FCC justice ground fine enough to produce a decision on the 1973 NBMC petition. Some of the proposals, including those to make the FCC's processes more penetrable for citizen groups, to eliminate payola, and to prohibit cable cross-ownership, were "transferred to other Commission proceedings"; but many of these proceedings had been pending for so many years and entailed so many considerations that the specific NBMC requests are likely to be lost in the shuffle. Fifteen other NBMC requests were denied: some of these asked for special FCC offices or studies that would have required special appropriations; others, such as permitting a citizen group to amend a petition to deny license renewal if the broadcaster has amended the renewal application, could have been settled easily. An additional eleven NBMC proposals were dismissed because the questions raised had been settled (and in most cases denied) previously. In short, the National Black Media Coalition was granted not a single point.

In petitions like the NBMC request for rulemaking, lawyers traditionally ask for more than they expect to get. Had the FCC staff and the commissioners wrestled with the problems the petition raised, and had the commissioners decided after thorough debate that they could not conscientiously grant the requests, the NBMC might have questioned the reasonableness of its own petition. But in fact the FCC rejected most of the pleadings in a disingenuous manner. Many of the NBMC items that were consolidated into other proceedings were simply lumped with previous proposals, such as revealing broadcasters' financial reports, that the commissioners patently avoided acting on. Other NBMC proposals were said to have been already considered: one such, a proposal to amend the renewal form to require statistics on past programming service to minorities, was dismissed by the FCC's re-referring to a proceeding that had dealt with radio only, not with television. What interpretation could the NBMC give to the FCC's cavalier treatment of minorities' requests?

The next Washington meeting between the commissioners and public groups took place in January 1974, when a group organized by Everett Parker and consisting of representatives from 160 organizations, including the American Association of University Women, Consumers Union, the International Ladies' Garment Workers Union, the American Jewish Committee, and the NAACP, met with the Commission. The main item on the agenda was the FCC's policy of deregulation (or reregulation, as Wiley preferred to call it). Parker had informed prospective representatives that the policies "would dismantle FCC rules which provide access by the public to the air waves and insure that broadcast programming represents community interests and needs." Parker claimed the reregulation would lead to elimination of the Fairness Doctrine and to relaxation of the FCC's rules requiring that a station ascertain community needs.

The meeting had barely begun before Dean Burch revealed the FCC strategy: counterattack. He referred to a position paper that Parker had distributed to all at the meeting and said, "It [the position paper] is not factual in alleging a grand conspiracy between the FCC and the Congress to wipe out all public-interest protection." He objected to the paper's "shotgun approach."

The FCC continued its strategy. When Parker's group raised equal employment opportunity questions, Commissioner Hooks' legal assistant read a prepared statement asserting that the FCC had made progress in employing minorities. When reregulation was challenged, Commissioner Wiley called the program "government regulation at its finest," and turned the floor over to Broadcast Bureau Chief Wallace Johnson, who read a lengthy paper explaining the engineering aspects of the program in elaborate detail. During the recitation, participants in the meeting began to file out; and after about ten minutes, Dr. Parker interrupted to say, "Most of us don't understand all these technical things." As *Broadcasting* said, "Dr. Parker, in effect, hollered 'Uncle!' "

During this meeting the commissioners heard a new note they would hear often again in their public meetings. In addition to minority groups, labor groups, and consumer activists, a number of conservative ministers and church members were in attendance. The conservatives complained that the FCC had been "consistently biased in favor of the liberal point of view." In a way they provided counterattacks in the midst of the commissioners' own offensive.

For 20 months after the Parker meeting, the Commission held no general public meetings of that type, and no group demanded that such meetings be resumed. Participants in earlier sessions realized that some of the representatives' rhetoric reinforced the negative impressions that

FCC members and staffers already had of the groups, their missions, and techniques. Furthermore, the citizen advocates learned a lesson broadcast lobbyists had learned years before: occasional visits to commissioners in their offices to discuss specific grievances were more effective.

On September 5, 1975, the Commission abruptly announced it was scheduling a series of open en banc meetings as one of "a number of steps to insure greater public input into its work." Another reason, not revealed in the public notice, was that the Commission was about to vote down a congressional suggestion that all regular Commission meetings be open to the public, and wanted to offer the en banc meetings with all comers as a sop to the concept of "government in the sunshine." Congress eventually passed a law requiring all FCC meetings to be open.

The eight en banc meetings held between December 3, 1975, and May 31, 1977, were different in tone and substance from the earlier meetings. Representatives of the broadcasting, cable, and common carrier industries appeared along with those of citizen groups—not for the purposes of rebuttal but to explain their positions on various matters to the Commission. NBMC was represented by Pluria Marshall at half the meetings. He, too, spoke to specific issues, rather than issuing blanket requests. Marshall was accompanied by just a few colleagues, compared with the 75 NBMC members who attended the first en banc session. It was broadcasters who made a show of strength at a February 17, 1976, meeting when 160 of them turned up to protest relaxation of rules restricting programming on cable.

NOW and the Latino coalition attended no more of the FCC's en banc sessions; however, their members were active in filing petitions to deny specific license renewals. The groups had apparently decided that legal actions under existing FCC rules are more effective than requesting broader new regulations.

The National Gay Task Force, the only other national group to attend a scheduled en banc meeting, told the FCC on November 15, 1976, that broadcasters were not serving the "interest, convenience, and necessity of gay people, who represent at least 10 percent of every broadcaster's audience. . . . If the criteria for broadcast licenses were actually being enforced, there is certainly no television station and virtually no radio station in the United States which would qualify for license renewal." The task force also asked that the Commission's EEO requirements affecting broadcasters be extended to protect homosexuals. According to *Access* (December 1, 1976), Commissioner Quello refuted the complaint about lack of media coverage of homosexuals by saying, "Every time I turn on the television, I see Truman Capote."

8

The FCC Grants an Audience to the Audience

Indians, conservatives, ham operators, blacks, Chicanos, and other minorities demanded and got the panel's attention in the course of the evening. By now the overall tone of the replies became evident—the FCC is set up to license broadcasters, not to regulate specific programs; complaints are answered, but not all of them and not as quickly as the complainers would like. Action occasionally is taken—but only when inaction is impossible.

Los Angeles Times
November 24, 1975

If the FCC meetings with the public have given the commissioners a firsthand view of what we face all the time, the meetings will have served a good purpose.

Vincent Wasilewski, NAB President
speaking at a luncheon, January 8, 1975

8 When the Commission agreed to hold meetings with public groups in the FCC meeting room in Washington, with all commissioners hearing specific grievances of organized citizen groups, the commissioners dipped their toes into the pool of public opinion about broadcasting. As we have seen, they found the waters turbulent and cold.

FCC exposure to public opinion was only partial in those meetings. Only those citizen group representatives who could afford the time and money to come to Washington were heard. Furthermore, the agendas of the meetings were limited by the somewhat narrow interests of the groups that came: understandably, the black coalition wanted to discuss employment problems and programming of particular interest to the black community; the National Organization for Women was interested exclusively in sexist discrimination and the image of women that broadcasters presented. The wide spectrum of complaints represented in letters to the FCC was not necessarily expressed in these sessions. Although they heard angry voices and experienced confrontation, commissioners could not be certain that the voices they heard were, in fact, speaking for large numbers of that nebulous entity "the public."

When Richard Wiley became chairman, the FCC instituted a series of meetings "in the field." Open to all comers, these meetings theoretically allowed airing of every grievance. By his own admission, Wiley sort of backed into the project; but once committed, he pursued the project with characteristic energy.

Wiley's initial concern was for those broadcasters who felt the FCC was a monolithic combine of ogres, dangerous and unapproachable. To overcome this image of the FCC as a remote bureaucracy, Wiley proposed in 1972, when he was a commissioner but not chairman, that the agency institute a series of regional meetings and workshops for broadcasters. "I would even propose this question to kick off these candid and informal sessions: 'What is it about us that bugs you?' and vice versa." At a meeting of Mutual network affiliates, he expressed distress that the relationship between broadcasters and regulators was "marked by feelings of suspicion and distrust," a mood he called "negative and counterproductive." He called for a new relationship "based not on fear, isolation and distrust . . . but one in which the spirit of partnership and cooperation in serving the public can flourish and prosper."

In his first speech as chairman, Wiley informed the 1974 NAB convention that the regional meetings he had been advocating for almost two years would include sessions with members of the public as well as with broadcasters. Shortly thereafter in a Senate oversight hearing, Wiley conceded that the meetings with the public were an afterthought he had tacked on to his proposed regional meetings with broadcasters. Senator Marlow Cook (R.–Ky.) asked Wiley if he thought the public meetings would accomplish anything. Wiley replied:

Senator, let me say the whole idea of the regional meetings was conceived in the program of reregulation which would attempt to try to make our policies and regulations clear to the broadcaster because we think that will bring about better public interest programming service. I felt in setting up that regional meeting concept, which we think is a very appropriate thing to do for the government in and of itself—I thought as long as we are going to Atlanta and we're going to try this out, we would also have the FCC available in a major area, a major urban area, in that five-state region to discuss with citizen groups, who often have representatives from an area come in. Now that may not work out, but we are going to try. And obviously the Commission does not have the resources to go to every major area in the country, but I think this is the first step, at least, to see whether you can make the government more open, more responsive, on a regionalized basis.

Broadcasting (March 25, 1974) chided Wiley in an editorial:

Who does Mr. Wiley think will show up to represent the "public"? The same self-appointed speakers for special interests who are already on file a mile high at the FCC.

A decade ago the FCC went through something like this exercise with formal hearings on programming in Chicago and Omaha. The principal effect in both communities was antibroadcasting publicity in the local press. It's hard to think of a way to keep Atlanta from being a rerun.

Heads of three citizen groups defended Wiley in a letter to *Broadcasting* (April 29):

Good leaders react to stature by rising to statesmanship. From a chairman whose past record gave citizens every reason to doubt his evenhandedness, the regional meetings represent a first indication that the public interest counts for something [at FCC headquarters] . . . . If broadcasters treated communications issues in detail on their own stations, FCC Commissioners wouldn't have to go to Atlanta to hear what citizens think about broadcasting. They could sit home and watch the dialogue on TV instead.

The earlier hearings on programming mentioned in *Broadcasting*'s editorial took place in Chicago in 1962 and in Omaha in 1963. Four days of hearings had been held in Chicago after some individuals, religious groups, and labor unions complained to the FCC about the lack of local live programming, a problem exacerbated by network ownership of three of the city's five TV stations. The complainants claimed that local stations' managements were more responsive to network officials in New York than to the needs of entertainers, ministers, amateur performers, and news personnel in Chicago. Deferring renewal of the Chicago TV stations' licenses until the staff could investigate the complaints, the FCC sent Commissioner Robert E. Lee to conduct hearings. The stations called "defense witnesses," who praised the management of the network-owned Chicago stations; and the complainants mourned for the days of radio when Chicago had been a major center for program origination. In Omaha, more open-ended hearings, conducted by Commissioner E. William Henry in 1963, primarily showed citizen satisfaction with the extent of local live programming their TV stations offered. Both the Chicago and the Omaha hearings irritated members of Congress, who accused the FCC of meddling in program content; with very little public support for the concept, the FCC abandoned the practice.

The meetings envisioned by Wiley were different because they embraced multistate areas instead of specific cities; complaints about station operations were not being solicited though complaints wouldn't be precluded; the subjects to be discussed at the meetings were not even limited to broadcasting matters. Wiley wanted commissioners and staffers and all comers from the public to participate in a give-and-take for their mutual enlightenment. No station licenses had been deferred pending the outcome. In this spirit, the first meeting was scheduled for May 23, 1974, in Atlanta. Chairman Wiley, Commissioner Hooks, and a number of senior staff members would meet the public from a five-state area and then would meet with broadcasters from the same area the following day.

An immediate and unanticipated problem was who would attend this public party the agency was throwing. With arrangements handled by the Broadcast Bureau reregulation task force and by Bert Hatch, executive director of the Georgia Association of Broadcasters, the FCC simply issued a press release announcing its plans for a meeting and mailed it to newspapers in the five-state area. When Commissioner Hooks learned that the release hadn't been sent to black or Spanish-language newspapers, he tried to notify minority organizations.

To radio stations in the Atlanta area, Bert Hatch sent tapes, which he said "have been tailor-made for your station" to publicize the regional meeting. The tapes identified Hatch as the speaker, gave the call letters of the station, set forth the time and location of the meeting, and added, "Naturally, we hope there will be many who will come to speak kindly of the job being done by [call letters] and other area broadcasters in the fields of public service, information and entertainment . . . but if it is your desire to 'accentuate the negative,' then we will defend to the limit your right to do just that."

With the tapes, Hatch included a memo:

Having spent quite a lot of time recently with Chairman Wiley, I know him to be concerned that the FCC meeting for "citizens" on

> Thursday, May 23, will be dominated by organized groups of one kind or another . . . and that there are not likely to be many "just plain average citizens, speaking as individuals."
>
> You may rest assured that the organized groups will be, for the most part, anti-broadcasting in their remarks.
>
> Therefore, I assured the Chairman that I would make every honest effort to get metro area stations to promote attendance at the meeting by "average listeners."

Wiley claimed that Hatch had misrepresented their discussion, that Wiley had never sought nor received a promise such as Hatch mentioned. When WSB–TV Atlanta volunteered to videotape a television spot of Wiley urging citizen participation, Wiley accepted the offer.

The Atlanta meeting began at 8:30 A.M. on the Georgia Tech campus with time and location both a source of protest: a black media group claimed the location was inconvenient for the black community; and other citizens let the FCC know they couldn't attend a meeting during weekday working hours. Although the Broadcast Bureau organizers expected perhaps 1000 persons to attend, the actual count never exceeded 200.

When the FCC contingent arrived at the science and space building, they encountered pickets, marching outside the auditorium with signs proclaiming, "God gave us our rights." The pickets were followers of the Rev. Dr. Carl McIntire, a conservative evangelist who had been preaching on as many as 500 radio stations for almost 50 years. McIntire had had previous quarrels with the FCC. After McIntire's own station in Media, Pennsylvania, was licensed in 1965, the station was soon charged with violating the FCC's Fairness Doctrine and its personal-attack rules. In 1970, the Commission by a 6–0 vote unanimously refused to renew McIntire's license, a refusal upheld by the court of appeals in 1972. Nonetheless, on his radio program McIntire continued to crusade against the FCC and the Fairness Doctrine, and he enlisted the support of numerous conservative organizations. McIntire's supporters were out in force at several of the FCC's regional meetings and sometimes came close to dominating the proceedings.

No orderly system for members of the public to gain the floor (that is, the microphone) had been devised. In Atlanta, two McIntire supporters held the floor for 75 minutes; but the audience was so small that most people who wanted to be heard were. At the next regional meeting, in Chicago, 1000 persons attended the session, which was held at night in a downtown location, and the recognition process broke down. The crowd was so unruly, some staffers admitted later they were scared.

After their first fumbling efforts to publicize the Atlanta-area meeting, Wiley and his staff learned quickly how to attract an audience for the meetings. As with so many other Commission actions, their attempts to ensure a turnout were criticized by *Broadcasting*, and the rebuke triggered a typically confused FCC reaction about what was proper and appropriate.

For the Chicago meeting of October 30, 1974, the FCC task force members made certain they informed both minority and broad-circulation newspapers well in advance of the meeting. An assistant chief of the Broadcast Bureau asked NBC through its Washington office if the network's Chicago affiliate, which was owned by NBC, would prepare spot announcements to promote the meeting. When the station, WMAQ–TV, taped audio and video spots, and offered them at cost to other stations in the five-state area, *Broadcasting* snorted in an editorial (November 11, 1974):

> Mind you, it has all been very informal—no threats to WSB–TV Atlanta, which did the first promotional spots, or to WMAQ–TV; no pressure put on other stations to broadcast Mr. Wiley's solicitation. Nothing more than a good turn done for a worthy cause.

> Baloney. There is something cozy about an arrangement that puts broadcasting facilities and time at the disposal of an FCC that is out soliciting criticism of broadcasting. Broadcasters would lay larger claim to their souls if they reject the next booking.

"The next booking" was, as it happened, in the FCC's own backyard—from five states in the Washington, D.C., vicinity. FCC staff members responsible for publicizing the public meeting were so terrified that they would be identified by *Broadcasting* as agents of coercion that they avoided their previously successful request for assistance.

Instead, the assistant chief of the Broadcast Bureau boldly called a friend at a Washington station, identified himself as "John Smith," and started talking about the planned meeting in hopes that his friend at the station would recognize the voice, understand what was really wanted, and *volunteer* to tape promotional spots for the Commission. Instead, the totally confused friend complained to his boss, "Someone from the Commission is calling me up, saying he's John Smith, and talking about promotion for the meeting." The boss called Wiley, who knew nothing about the call and disowned it. Of course, the plot failed.

Another well-meaning attempt to generate interest in the Washington meeting was also rebuffed by Wiley. Tack Nail, *Television Digest*'s managing editor, mentioned to the chairman that the meeting—four days away—was "the best kept secret in Washington." Nail contacted a TV station and an AM station to suggest they might want to volunteer help. When the stations called Wiley, he, with the *Broadcasting* scolding fresh in his mind, quickly divorced himself from the idea.

By Friday, January 3, 1975, however, Wiley and his task force bowed to the inevitable. The meeting was slated for the sixth of January and no broadcasters had stepped forward to spread the word. Wallace Johnson, chief of the Broadcast Bureau, was given permission to make the request: he called WMAL–AM–TV; station management agreed; and a spot was taped. The results were astonishing. The five TV stations and 15 radio stations in Washington used the promotional spots on a saturation basis. Over the weekend, one could hardly switch on a TV set in Washington without seeing Wiley's face and hearing about the meeting. When all seven commissioners turned up at the Departmental Auditorium on the evening of January 6, they were greeted by 800 members of the public.

From then on, promotional help was more available in areas where meetings were planned. Attendance varied, of course, but it remained fairly high. In Denver (where the audience applauded at the end of the evening) the public meeting drew between 400 and 500 persons; and in Los Angeles, 700. Only at the last of the regional meetings, in Kansas City in October 1976, did the size of the audience drop to the level of the Atlanta meeting.

In San Francisco, Wiley agreed to an experiment: he accepted the invitation of station KTVU and Cox Broadcasting to hold a televised meeting with a call-in format from 8:00 to 10:00 P.M. (prime time).

The screening of calls by representatives of the League of Women Voters solved the problem, encountered in other public meetings, of a stacked audience's repeating the same question again and again. During the two hours, almost 1000 calls came in to the station; of these, some 40 queries were handled on the air by the FCC staff, Hooks, or Wiley. In addition, according to the Bay Area telephone company, 47,404 calls never got through to the station's switchboard, where twelve phone lines were in constant use. Besides the customary complaints about children's programming, citizen access to the airwaves, and equal employment opportunities in broadcasting, questions about citizens band radio and the telephone company were answered.

The television call-in format displeased organized citizen groups, which charged before the program that the FCC was afraid of direct confrontation with San Francisco media-reform activists. The groups claimed that the limited range of the TV signal, which couldn't be received even in Sacramento, made a farce of the FCC's intention to cover a five-state region. Others objected to the prescreening of questions, and they accused Cox Broadcasting of trying to curry favor with the Commission.

To appease the angry citizens, Wiley scheduled a meeting on the afternoon before the evening's telecast, but many of the 100 representatives who came were not mollified. Some complained further that the meeting room was too small, that the meeting was scheduled on short notice with little advance publicity, and that Wiley passed too many questions to staff members and to Commissioner Hooks.

Except for relatively minor sectional variations, similar themes were struck repeatedly in regional meetings whether in Houston or Boston, Los Angeles or Washington. For example, at many meetings, followers of Dr. McIntire complained about FCC treatment of him and about the Fairness Doctrine. They even criticized the commissioners' alleged lack of patriotism—as demonstrated by the American flag's position on the platform and by the failure to open the meeting with the Pledge of Allegiance.

At regional meetings everywhere, many members of the public rose to complain about sex, smut, vulgar language, double entendres, and nudity on the airwaves. In response, FCC personnel suggested they send their complaints to the networks, the stations, and the advertisers because the FCC had no power to censor programs. Commissioners and staff members gave similar replies to complaints about violence in programs, alleged bias in news reporting, programs said to insult the viewer's intelligence, and "good programs all scheduled in the same time period on different stations."

The FCC had no right to get involved in any program decisions, William Ray, chief of the Complaints and Compliance Division, re-iterated, unless evidence was offered that a licensee had deliberately distorted news stories, for example. Ray told audiences that they should be glad that this is the FCC's policy, and that the situation would be much worse if seven bureaucrats in Washington were deciding what should go on the air. Sometimes audiences applauded Ray's answer, but in Boston an angry complainant screamed that Ray was just filibustering.

At most meetings, representatives of citizen groups of blacks, women, and Latinos complained about the inadequacy of the FCC's equal employment opportunity rules and the laxity of their enforcement. When the complaint was directed against a specific area station, the FCC panel members told the speaker the proper procedure for filing written EEO complaints. When the complaint was more general—"Why aren't there more black newsmen on the air on local newscasts?"—the FCC officials explained that Commission rules requiring the employment of minorities in responsible positions in communities with substantial minority populations don't specify which categories of jobs.

Many complained about the television depiction of minorities (Italian-Americans objected to TV gangsters and movies like *The Godfather*; Polish-Americans deplored Polish jokes) or about the lack of local programming of specific interest to minorities. At two meetings, the latter point was dramatically demonstrated. In Washington a speaker, after delivering a lengthy presentation in Spanish, concluded in English: "If you could not understand what I was saying, you just got some indication of the frustration that we who speak no English go through when we are not able to find any programs in Spanish." In Kansas City, a representative of an organization for the deaf, who was urging the use of program captions, persuaded the panel members to put their fingers in their ears during part of his talk to experience how the deaf encounter television. When a man in Chicago complained that Hindus and Buddhists, who constitute a religious majority in the world, received no coverage or services in Chicago, Commissioner Hooks responded, "Black folks raised hell for 35 years, and others are just going to have to do the same."

At the meetings almost all the issues debated in this country found spokespeople—antiabortionists, gun collectors, senior citizens, gay rights advocates, opponents of drug lyrics in songs, and opponents and proponents of Women's Liberation. The Commission was denounced as an instrument of the Rockefeller interests and as part of the Communist conspiracy. Individuals complained about television sets spying on them in their homes or secretly giving them LSD.

Sometimes Cole felt that FCC panel members gave perfunctory or unresponsive answers to questions that deserved more consideration. One man asked why public service announcements were clustered between two and three in the morning. A graduate student asked why the FCC was supporting the extension of the license renewal period from three to five years. A member of a minority group asked what recourse he and others had when a radio station that called itself the city's leading ethnic station cancelled ethnic programs. Why did the Commission take so long to respond to employment discrimination complaints? How can quality programming get on the air if it is not particularly profitable and the FCC won't deal with programming? These questions got short shrift.

The intensity of the give-and-take within the meetings was impressive. Even though the issues raised were often not the kind the FCC could deal with, even though what was on the public's mind was not what the FCC calls "the public interest, convenience and necessity," the commissioners and staff learned how strongly individuals felt about what came over their radio and TV sets. For example, in Houston, a man identifying himself as a spokesman for the Gay Political Caucus asked that broadcasters be required to ascertain the needs and interests of the homosexual community. Immediately after he had spoken, a woman said, "I was raised by the Bible," and expressed shock that the FCC would permit such a man to speak in public.

In one exchange in Chicago, a woman objected to advertisements for personal products such as douches and sanitary napkins because she considered such advertising an invasion of her privacy and her children's in her own home. When Charlotte Reid suggested writing to the NAB code office, the woman replied, "I have and they told me they 'appreciate my comments.' " Commissioner Reid said if enough people wrote, the NAB would pay attention—"This is the era of the consumer."

Staff members were not enthusiastic about the public meetings. Many staffers told Cole that they were frustrated by the simplistic attitude of most speakers. Some angry citizens spoke as though the FCC had dictatorial powers to compel broadcasters to present or, more often, suppress certain program material—and as though the Washington bureau-crats were simply refusing to exercise those powers to do what the citizens wanted. Often staff members were acutely bored when members of the public filibustered on pet grievances.

Compared with the public roastings, the FCC meetings with broad-casters in nine cities were love feasts. The head of a local broadcasters' association would introduce the visiting regulators in fulsome terms; for example, in Kansas City, "Dick Wiley, a man endeared to us all." The broadcasters, on the whole, seemed grateful that FCC people were there in a spirit of cooperation; and the broadcasters tried to clarify interpretations of Fairness Doctrine requirements, equal employment opportunity regulations, and engineering problems. At these sessions, the commissioners met with broadcasters for several hours of individual consultations. "We're available for private confessionals," Wiley told the broadcasters.

The staff was more relaxed (relieved might be the word) when meet-ing the broadcasters than when meeting the public. Richard Shiben, chief of the Renewal and Transfer Division, assured the broadcasters at the Kansas City meeting that they could conduct their ascertainment of community problems and needs "anywhere—in the john, on the john, whatever." Later, he joked, "If you use toilet paper for writing notes, just make sure you don't flush it down the john." The audience laughed.

The regional meetings were Wiley's project and he stuck to his schedule tenaciously. At first, partly because all meetings were in con-junction with broadcast group sessions, Wiley took with him only those staff members who dealt with broadcasting; but he encountered ques-tions about telephone rates and citizens band radio. In a two-hour, radio, call-in show in Dallas (following the Houston meeting), all but three questions concerned CB. Wiley then added to the retinue per-sonnel equipped to deal with this and other subjects. Wiley worked his staff hard. Before the Kansas City meeting, Wiley and the staff members appeared on KMOX St. Louis for a scheduled two-hour program, between 9:00 and 11:00 P.M.; but listener response was so heavy that the station encouraged the FCC crew to remain on the air an extra hour.

The only good thing that staff members or commissioners, aside from Wiley, had to say about the regional meetings with the public was that at least the meetings let the people vent their frustrations. Curiously enough, however, it may be that the meetings actually served to in-crease some public frustration. The organized groups that did present their grievances to the FCC were frustrated by the panel's unrespon-siveness—and by the fact that their presentations were constantly interrupted by speakers on subjects the organized groups considered irrelevant.

Speaking for these organized groups, *Access* magazine (January 27, 1975) complained about the regulators' "rapidly building skill at evasiveness," and said: "The problem is not with the concept of public meetings. The Commission is on the right track in trying to educate the people to its functions and procedures and in allowing critics to ventilate their objections—especially on emotional issues like 'sex and violence,' racist programming, and the First Amendment rights of religious broadcasters." The problem, said *Access,* is that those questions are too easy for the FCC to duck by referring to the noncensorship provisions of the Communications Act. "The real questions that can be answered—or sidestepped only at great embarrassment—are likely to be asked only by organized groups with expertise at jockeying with the FCC. (For example, what happened to the Equal Employment Opportunity Policy Report promised by December 1973 by Dean Burch?)"

If organized groups were frustrated by the public meetings, imagine the feelings of the individuals—the citizen with a moral cause, the mother concerned about violent programming, the club chairman unable to get publicity on the air for his worthy cause, or the citizen badgered by repetitive commercials—when told quite truthfully by the FCC panel that the agency could do nothing to remedy his or her complaint. Some of those individuals no doubt complained to their congressmen about an unresponsive FCC, and started in motion the kind of pressure that often moves the agency members to do something —anything—to get Congress off their backs. Not infrequently, what the FCC does in such situations is found unconstitutional by the courts. In some cases where the FCC's power to act is unquestioned, the broadcasting industry would be so appalled if the Commission did take action that broadcasting lobbyists would rush to undo the action through federal legislation.

The public meetings provided a baptism of fire for Washburn, Robinson and Quello, who had not been members of the agency when representatives of the National Organization for Women and the National Black Media Coalition made their scathing presentations to the FCC. These commissioners subsequently indicated that the one public meeting they attended, the Washington meeting, had left them with negative opinions of what happens in such gatherings. Washburn, in speeches to broadcasters, called the public meeting "a refined and exquisite form of torture," in which a commissioner had no choice but to listen to a speaker drone on and on. Robinson was moved to interject in a congressional hearing: "I think you have to say, Mr. Congressman, with regard to the regional meetings, it is not the average citizen you have. . . . By and large, it is the average screamer. But my perception is that the people who turn out at those open public meetings are not the average citizen." As a broadcaster, Quello had not been favorably impressed by some Detroit citizens who complained about media performance; and as a commissioner, he had already spoken out against attempts at "program dictatorship by a small group of activists." The Washington meeting confirmed Quello's views.

One image from those tumultuous regional meetings sticks in Cole's mind. A group of angry Bostonians stomped out of a meeting, one member yelling, "Shit! Shit! This meeting stinks." And poor Wiley nodded and with admirable irony said, "Thank you for coming. Thank you for coming."

Wiley, who dreamed up the program, must be credited with great patience and perseverance. When he ventured forth (in the company of Commissioner Hooks), Wiley knew he was in for a roasting. The other commissioners were not demanding that the meetings be held, far from it; and since there was no long-range schedule, Wiley could have quietly abandoned the meetings after learning how unpleasant they could be. To his credit, he hung in there. Perhaps he was influenced by Broadcast Bureau Chief Wallace Johnson's evaluation. After a particularly fearsome meeting, Johnson said simply, "That was democracy in action."

9

Those Cards and Letters Keep A-Coming

The Commission receives roughly 75,000 complaints each year, so you will understand why you are receiving a form letter in response to your inquiry. Not only are we better able to handle more letters, but we are also better able to save money for you taxpayers, the guts, so to speak, of our democratic system.

We will try to answer your complaint in the best way that we can. If your letter remains unattended, nothing will happen; therefore, we will try to keep to the adage that something is better than nothing. In response to your message:

___ The Commission does not deal with such issues.

___ We would like to refer you to _____ for an answer.

___ Please write to the _____ network for a response.

___ Wrestling is an acceptable sport for telecast.

___ I'm sorry that _____ will not be seen next season.

___ Other:

P.S. If you are the obstreperous sort of citizen who demands a personal reply to every meretricious bitch, we suggest that you recopy your letter and address it to one of your senators here in Washington, who, of course, will never see it but his staff will send it along to us with all the damn formality of a congressional inquiry, whereupon we shall be forced to answer both you and the senator with dispatch. But don't you realize what a waste this is causing to *your* government? So why don't you forget it and read a book?

Modest proposal for all-purpose FCC complaint response, written by commissioner's assistant

Dear FCC—Please make Walter Cronkite stop saying "That's the way it is" at the end of his news programs. He don't know how it is. He just thinks he does!

Letter in FCC Complaints and Compliance Division files

9 The people who write letters are different from you and me. Long ago, professional pollsters learned that letter campaigns do not necessarily reflect the opinions of the majority. Networks have cancelled programs despite a blizzard of enthusiastic letters because the program chiefs believed the "right" kind of consumers were not watching. The FCC has learned to process letters, after a fashion, but the agency has never attempted to analyze what the people who write letters are trying to say. Of course the commissioners cannot set policy solely on the basis of correspondence from the broadcast audience; but if they read their mail more closely, they might learn when something is seriously wrong.

In theory, the public is supposed to be an important partner in the FCC's watchdog function. Chairman Burch said as much in a colloquy with the skeptical Senator John O. Pastore (D.–R.I.) during 1973 oversight hearings:

Pastore: What kinds of monitoring do you do? Do you monitor at all?

Burch: We do not monitor program content, Senator, not unless we have reason to. If we have had a specific complaint. . . .

Pastore: Well, that brings me to the point. The only time you have a reason is when someone makes a complaint, isn't it?

Burch: Yes.

Pastore: You have to rely pretty much on the public, don't you?

Burch: That is right.

Pastore: You have no other way of investigating? I mean, you don't monitor anything?

Burch: We could presumably monitor, Senator, but I think, frankly, I would rather rely on the public to complain than to have the FCC indulging in great monitoring effort.

Pastore: My experience has been when people are dissatisfied and write a letter to the station, they get sort of a courteous reply that really doesn't tell them much. And nothing ever changes. . . . And then they write to me, and I send it down to you. If it is a complaint from my state, you are about 450 miles away from where the complaint is. Usually I get a very polite answer from the FCC, too, and nothing happens. The only time these things really surface, to any extent, is at renewal time.

Although many of the public's complaints or comments are worthwhile, not all deserve government attention. At times, the tone of the letters that pour into the FCC may sound like fan mail to Don Rickles or petitions to the Wizard of Oz for miracle cures for society's ills. In an earlier appropriations hearing, Burch had told Pastore: "Many of those [letters], to be very candid, Senator, are the kinds of things you would not know how to handle, even if you had all the money in the world. You would not know what to do with them because there are people who write and say they just don't like commercials." "There is an easy answer to that," Pastore said, "just write back and say, 'Neither do we.' "

In fiscal 1976, the FCC received some 75,000 complaints about broadcasting matters, excluding letters to individual agency members and complaints transmitted through congressmen. One cause célèbre had been skewing the customary figures so much that the public responses to that matter were tabulated separately: a petition filed by two Californians in December 1974, asking the FCC to withhold grants of educational TV or FM stations to religious broadcasters, precipitated an evangelical letter-writing campaign that brought 5.5 million letters and postcards to the FCC by May 1977. The FCC denied the original petition in August 1975; but that denial did little to stanch the flood of letters from complainants convinced that a plot (led by Madalyn Murray O'Hair) was under way to banish all forms of religious broadcasting.

The Commission has never found a middle ground on which frivolous public objections would be turned aside politely and serious derelictions of broadcasters' public trusteeship would be investigated and corrected. On the inadequacy of the complaint procedures, Commissioner Quello has frequently commented that "we may simply demonstrate to concerned citizens that the complaint process is unproductive" and thus leave them "the costly and time-consuming petition to deny [license renewal] as an alternative."

The FCC established the Complaints and Compliance Division of the Broadcast Bureau in 1960, after Congress had held publicized hearings about fraudulent television quiz shows and payola to radio disc jockeys and program directors. Congress insisted that the FCC ensure such atrocities would cease. Frederick Ford, FCC chairman when the division was established, foresaw a unit with as many as 25 field investigators who would not only look into specific public complaints but also determine if alleged practices were industrywide.

In an FCC notice of May 20, 1960, Ford said:

Now we propose to undertake an audit in detail of a limited number of selected stations so that we can have a much more penetrating and more rounded view of how effectively stations discharge their stewardship in the public interest. We intend, among other items, to check on program logs, Sec. 317 [sponsorship identification] compliance, political broadcast records, . . . and other pertinent station controls, records, and procedures related to the Commission's nontechnical rules and regulations . . . ; to examine the extent, nature and disposition of complaints coming directly to the stations; to ascertain whether representations made in connection with license applications are reasonably complied with. . . .

Ford outlined a program of regular station audits, checking on programming as well as technical violations. He noted that some 5000 broadcast stations were operating in 2000 communities throughout the nation. "We would do well with the proposed staff if we could reach as many as 100 communities for full audit." He said the FCC would "develop means of effectively screening various types of situations" and "focus our resources where they will do the most good." In 1977, the FCC administered almost 9300 broadcast stations—but the surveillance Ford envisioned has not come to be.

Periodically a charade is played out in Commission meetings: a commissioner charges the division with failing to handle a complaint and a staffer responds that the division is understaffed and overworked—and there the matter lies. By May 1977, the division had only 48 employees, of whom 17 were investigators. The volume of correspondence has increased ninefold from 1962 to 1976. No commissioner has crusaded for the funding necessary for adequate division staffing nor has the FCC analyzed how to handle the most critical problems within the division's purview.

Most complaints, of necessity, are answered with form letters; some complaints alleging serious breaches of FCC rules or callous disregard of the public are forwarded to the stations involved for explanations. In any case, the division is often months behind in its responses. The Commission has had as many as 5000 form letters waiting to be addressed, but there is insufficient secretarial help to process them.

Significantly, the Federal Office of Consumer Affairs, in a 1975 study of 15 agencies, listed the FCC as one of four agencies that replied too slowly to public complaints. The same study rated the FCC satisfactory in speed and manner of responding to congressional queries. While correspondence from the public may languish for weeks, even months, the FCC has an expedited system to ensure prompt action on congressional mail.

The nature of the complaints sent to the FCC varies from year to year—often in response to organized efforts. For example, complaints about crime, violence, and horror in television programming rose to 8897 in fiscal 1975, from 895 the previous year, then sank to 3448 in 1976. Of the 24,344 complaints about obscene and indecent programs the FCC received in 1974, more than 20,000 were identical printed letters, distributed to its members by Morality in Media, headquartered in Warrenton, Virginia.

Of the 74,761 complaints in fiscal 1976, 62,724 concerned television. Two national letter-writing campaigns increased the number of Fairness Doctrine complaints to 41,861 (from 3590 the previous year): *The Guns of Autumn,* a documentary critical of hunters and gun owners, was opposed by the National Rifle Association and other sports groups (and CBS voluntarily ran a program replying to the documentary); the other campaign consisted of letters calling for invoking of the Fairness Doctrine to enable spokesmen for decency and morality to counteract programming on television.

A wide range of human pathology is exhibited in letters to the FCC. Each year women complain that Johnny Carson is watching them undress at night, and men complain that certain programs are being broadcast solely to render them impotent. Some people inveigh against Communist propaganda on regularly scheduled news programs, and others suspect that TV characters are "saying things about me."

Other letters are thoughtful and well composed, but they seek remedies beyond the FCC's powers. For example, a New York viewer complained about sportscaster Dick Schaap's referring to racehorses Secretariat and Riva Ridge as "the most famous pair of stablemates since Joseph and Mary." Many listeners complain about disc jockeys' making flip references to drugs or nudity. The FCC is empowered to levy penalties against licensees who broadcast obscenity, and the agency has occasionally fined stations on this ground, but many viewer complaints treat matters of taste, which would not come under any legal definition of obscenity.

Almost every ethnic, racial, and religious group has found occasion to complain about something programmed on television. Indian groups have complained about the showing of westerns; Japanese-Americans and German-Americans have deplored the reruns of war movies of the 1940s; and some Chinese-Americans resent Charlie Chan films. After complaints to the FCC had been unavailing, Spanish-American civil rights groups persuaded Pepsico to banish the "Frito Bandito" from commercials. A group of Polish-Americans took their complaint about Polish jokes all the way to the Supreme Court, which refused to hear the case. The National Black Feminist Organization protested that the program *That's My Mama* perpetuated racist and sexist stereotypes.

About 72 percent of the FCC replies are form letters. Often the reply includes a short mimeographed pamphlet about legal restrictions on the FCC on such matters as "Broadcasts That Demean Certain Groups," or "Obscenity, Indecency, and Profanity in Broadcasting." A covering form letter explains the Commission is sending preprinted material because "we believe the taxpayer will appreciate the economy" involved. Stephen Sewell, chief of the complaints branch, says the pamphlets were prepared as "part of a continuing effort to be more clear and more responsive," but he acknowledges that most complainants will not be satisfied. (At regional meetings commissioners were told that letter writers who had put time and effort into composing complaints believed they deserved thoughtful responses, not form letters.) "We've got to live with the fact that we can't do much with most of the letters. The public is mainly interested in programming—understandably so—and our authority in the programming area is limited."

If the complaint seeks station time for a reply, the Complaints and Compliance Division sends instructions about how to file an official Fairness Doctrine complaint:

> The Commission expects a complainant to submit specific information indicating: (1) the station or network involved; (2) the specific issue or issues of a controversial nature of public importance presented by the station; (3) the date and time when the issue or issues were broadcast; (4) the basis for the claim that the issue or issues were controversial issues of public importance, either nationally or in the station's locality at the time of the broadcast; (5) the basis for the claim that the station or network broadcast only one side of the issue or issues in its overall programming (complainant should include accurate summary of the view or views broadcast or presented by the station); and (6) whether the station or network has afforded, or has expressed an intention to afford, reasonable opportunity for the presentation of contrasting viewpoints on that issue or issues.

The FCC acknowledges its wish to afford a broadcaster latitude in choice of programming. In many cases, complainants have a nearly impossible task to establish that the issue with which they are concerned is a controversial issue of public importance. And once they have passed that threshold, they still have their work cut out for them.

To get a clear picture of the odds against the complainant, consider the statistics. In fiscal 1973 and 1974 the FCC received 4300 complaints dealing with fairness; complainants included politicians who claimed they weren't given equal time under Section 315, persons who claimed they'd been given no chance to reply to personal attacks, and persons who were turned down when they asked to reply to a broadcast editorial. More than 97 percent of these 4300 complaints were rejected by the FCC because of "improper filing or misunderstanding of the Doctrine." Of 138 complaints forwarded to the stations for an explanation, only 19 (0.4 percent of the total 4300) were eventually resolved against the station—14 of these involved violations of the personal attack rule or political editorializing, and five were general fairness violations.

One reason so few complaints are investigated is lack of staff and travel funds. In an internal budget review memorandum, the Complaints and Compliance Division stated that it was "presently able to conduct field inquiries into *less than 5 percent* of the complaints requiring some kind of investigation." The division estimated also that approximately 20 percent of the complaints that did require some kind of investigation would involve field inquiries (visits to the stations).

Usually after complaining to the Commission about a station's conduct, the complainant is not fully apprised of such developments as correspondence between the Commission and the station. Often the complainant is not even told whether the complaint will lead to the FCC's querying the station. Sometimes the complainant receives the following form letter:

Thank you for your recent letter about the above station.

Your complaint is being brought to the station's attention, and upon receipt of a response the Commission will take whatever action is deemed appropriate.

According to a senior member of the division, however, if the complaint alleges mistreatment of an individual—for example, a charge of a broadcast "personal attack"—the complainant is more likely to be kept informed of developments.

Often, when the Commission decides to investigate complaints, even the station is not fully apprised of developments. In April 1976, for example, the president and general manager of a South Carolina station claimed that the Commission had not disclosed the nature of the complaint that triggered an investigation being conducted at the station. The Commission, citing statutory authority for refusing the request for information, maintained that disclosure of who complained and why would "interfere with and prejudice" the investigation. The Commission claimed that disclosing the identity of a confidential source during an investigation might enable a licensee to "harass and to intimidate complainants and informants." The station manager thereupon filed a complaint of his own against a member of the Complaints and Compliance Division who had been investigating the matter and who, the manager claimed, had telephoned individuals in search of "detrimental" information.

Licensee indignation regarding investigations and their burdens helps explain the FCC's reluctance to forward public complaints. In a 1971 Senate oversight hearing, Senator Roman Hruska (R.–Neb.) insisted that the Commission evaluate the complaint and the complainant before putting a broadcaster to the trouble of responding.

In answer to a 1975 questionnaire from the House Investigations Subcommittee, the Commission put forth a somewhat idealized picture of the complaints process:

The Commission itself is given a monthly report on all complaints, comments, and inquiries received, separated into subject categories, for its own information on the current reaction of the public to various broadcast practices. Complaints which prove to be valid are, of course, widely used in the regulatory process—not only as the basis for imposition of sanctions on licensees or denial of license renewal, but in determining which of two competing applicants at renewal time should be granted preference, whether a transfer application should be granted, and whether an application for a major change in facilities should be granted. Commission personnel other than members of the Complaints and Compliance Division staff consult the C & C complaint folders and investigatory records regularly before determining what recommendation should be made to the Commission in other proceedings.

This procedure is similar to that proposed by Chairman Ford in 1960; it incorporates a close coordination between complaints against a station and consideration of license renewal. In practice, it works differently.

A monthly report *is* sent by Complaints and Compliance to all commissioners, and is accompanied by sample complaints that might raise policy questions for commissioners' consideration. The problem is that the members consider the C&C reports and the attached letters as mere "information items," which need not be discussed or acted upon or, from every indication, even read. Only once during seven years did a commissioner ask if C&C was investigating the complaint; invariably the commissioners offer no guidance and recommend no reprimands.

Two examples of lack of coordination stand out: a man in Kimball, Nebraska, complained that during snowstorms, the local radio station demanded two dollars for each announcement informing employees not to report to work at the area's missile sites. A Sitka, Alaska, lawyer wrote the FCC about various problems with the service being provided by the local TV station. One major allegation was that the station started programs on a haphazard, unannounced basis and often neglected to run the entire program or ran some portions more than once or out of sequence. (All programs were on a delayed basis because of the station's inaccessible location.) Both letters were circulated to the commissioners, but the complaints were not even discussed. Perhaps the members felt these were exceptional cases; whatever the reason, the Commission did nothing to help citizens in Kimball or Sitka.

The FCC did respond to the letter writers. The man from Kimball was told the station had violated no rule. No staff member chose to ask the station whether its policy was to broadcast only paid public service announcements nor were the station's logs checked to see if such paid announcements were properly recorded. In the Sitka case, the complainant was told the station had violated no rule nor policy, but that the letter was being sent to the station for its information—no response was expected. The complainant was also notified how to file a formal petition to deny renewal. Neither letter was forwarded to the renewal branch.

The FCC's assertion to the House Investigations Subcommittee that personnel outside the C&C Division routinely read complaint folders as an aid to making recommendations is rather farfetched. It could happen; but as a matter of practice, it doesn't. If a full investigation on a serious matter is under way when a renewal or transfer is pending, C&C notifies the renewal branch and the approval is deferred; but complaints are not checked automatically like parking tickets at auto license renewal time.

Even when the Commission decides that a complaint against a station is entirely valid—which is rare—nothing seems to happen if the complainant has no financial interest in the outcome. One such case was decided while Cole was at the FCC. Although not altogether typical because of various nuances and complexities, the case exemplifies how the Commission deals with such matters.

The case began in September 1971, when a caller to Detroit radio station WWJ *Speak-Out* launched what the Commission later judged to be a personal attack on Professor Leonard Moss of Wayne State University. The FCC noted: "The remarks in question accuse Professors Moss and Covensky of promoting the Russian form of government, described as one under which millions were butchered, and of trying to destroy the American form of government. Such statements reflect on the integrity and character of the named professors and fall within the purview of the Commission's personal attack rules."

The station never informed Moss of these remarks; but when he learned about them and complained, he was offered time to respond, which he refused. WWJ failed to give Moss a transcript of the remarks for 22 days. He complained to the FCC.

FCC's rules about stations' offering individuals an opportunity to respond to personal attacks are unusually plain. The Complaints and Compliance Division pointed out to the Commission that the station failed (a) to notify Moss of the personal attack within seven days of broadcast, (b) to provide a transcript or summary of the attack within the allotted time, and (c) to offer him a *timely* opportunity to reply.

By a unanimous vote (although three commissioners were absent), the FCC voted to fine WWJ $1000 and ordered a letter notifying the station of its apparent liability sent February 9, 1972. In the letter, the Commission rejected the station's responses to the complaint: whether Moss availed himself of the right to respond when he was furnished a transcript of the attack, or whether he would have, had he been notified within seven days "is immaterial to a determination that you violated the terms of the Rules." The station's assertion that another professor had expressed contrasting views to those of the anonymous caller did not relieve the station of its obligation to observe the provisions of the rule in respect to Professor Moss, the person who had been attacked.

Not until June 26, 1974, after receiving further station defenses did the Commission consider whether the $1000 fine should finally be imposed. By that time, a different set of commissioners was considering the matter: Burch and Johnson, both of whom had voted to send WWJ the notice of apparent liability, had left the FCC; Quello, Robinson, Washburn, and Hooks had joined the Commission. Wiley had been absent for the 1972 vote. Reid and Robert E. Lee, who approved the original notification, were still commissioners.

When the matter of the fine arose, Quello vigorously defended the station and opposed the fine. Several staff members, including commissioners' legal aides, privately expressed astonishment at Quello's participation in the decision: he had been a Detroit broadcaster when the program was aired; and as he said, "I know these people [WWJ's management] well," and knew that they were "very upset about the whole thing—to fine them is just putting a larger black mark on them." Quello's defense raised the same points that the FCC had previously rejected when WWJ made them. When Quello added that management had been unaware of the incident when it happened, Wiley responded that if the Commission could not hold management responsible for the actions of its staff, the Commission could not regulate.

Commissioner Reid, accustomed to "congressional courtesy"—if something is really important to one's colleague, one goes along—suggested reducing the fine from $1000 to $500; but William Ray, chief of the C&C Division, said that reducing the fine for a major station in a large market would make the FCC "look ridiculous." Ray urged the commissioners to either stick with the $1000 fine or rescind it completely; it was clear that he did not favor the latter course. Nonetheless, the Commission voted without dissent to rescind the fine and instead to send WWJ a letter of admonition. The letter said that although the Commission still believed the station had violated the personal attack rule, the violation "was not so flagrant as to warrant the imposition of a forfeiture."

Staff members who had worked on the case were outraged. One senior member told Cole that the decision "gutted" the personal attack rule. A lawyer said that if the station had been a small one, "the fine would have been imposed like that. . . . There's no equal justice at the FCC. They just are afraid of punishing the big guy." In a meeting a few months later, Ray wryly told the commissioners that the personal attack rule "is difficult to enforce and maybe we'd all be better off forgetting about the whole thing."

On some occasions the FCC decides to take no action on complaints that raise broad questions of policy. In April 1974, an Albany, Oregon, undertaker complained to the FCC that the licensee of the local radio station was broadcasting without charge the Sunday services of the licensee's church, but was requiring other churches to pay for air time. Ten months later, the Broadcast Bureau suggested to the Commission that the licensee was failing to give a "fair break" to other religious groups in the community, and that "by providing free time consistently each week to only one church, KRKT practiced a type of religious discrimination contrary to Commission policy." According to the bureau the station's practice, which had already lasted over a year and a half, "raises a novel question of Commission policy."

The general counsel, however, recommended that the FCC not admonish the licensee or conduct a further investigation because the case was de minimus—peanuts—from the legal point of view; the FCC should wait for a more "egregious" case before "moving in this sensitive area." Wiley, who seemed generally to support the Broadcast Bureau position, asked, "Supposing a Protestant, as station policy, gave free time only to Protestants, and the rest had to pay?" A staffer replied, "I'm a Catholic and I'd take up a collection and buy time." A commissioner said, "I'm a Catholic and I'd complain to beat hell." Another staffer quipped, "I'm a Jew and I'd buy the station."

The commissioners decided in January 1975 to leave the matter to the licensee's discretion, but this decision was not transmitted to the licensee or the renewal branch. In June 1975 and again in December, the licensee wrote the FCC asking about the status of his February 1975 renewal application. In his second letter, the licensee said he was attending another church, and as of 1976 would no longer broadcast free the services of First Baptist Church. Richard Shiben, head of renewals and transfer, replied: "The problem was not so much one of discrimination against other religions as it was a question of your use—out of essentially personal motives and private purpose—of a public trust. We remained concerned about the appearance of religious discrimination. By eliminating the practice, you appear to have eliminated the source of the instant complaint." Shiben told the licensee that if no other problem arose, the license would be renewed; but that a copy of the letter would be placed in the station's complaint file, the renewal file—and that the broadcaster should put a copy in the public inspection file. Shiben had himself done inadvertantly what the FCC chose not to do, but no precedent was set about how to deal with such matters. The entire process had been improvised.

In other complaint areas of major importance to the broadcast audience, the commissioners seemed unable to take action—and showed neither ingenuity nor perseverance in coping with the problems. An outstanding example is the FCC's long failure to respond to thousands of complaints about loud commercials. This is *not* a delicate First Amendment area—the issue is not the content of the commercials, merely whether they are purposely made louder than surrounding program material. A typical letter of complaint to the FCC concludes: "Commercial TV is a part of our lives, and we should pay a price for it, but couldn't you regulate the noise pollution we are asked to accept in our homes?"

In 1965, after a two-year study, the Commission issued a public notice regarding loud commercials. The six-page notice detailed the practices that result in loud commercials and told licensees that, to the extent that it was within their control, they had an "affirmative obligation" to prevent broadcast of objectionably loud commercials. The Commission told licensees to adopt adequate control-room procedures and take "appropriate steps to provide for pre-screening recorded commercials for loudness." The public notice announced that "the Commission, through its complaint procedure or by spot checks at renewal time, will determine whether licensees are carrying out their obligation in this respect, and will take whatever action is appropriate on the basis of such review." By June 1975, almost exactly 10 years after the release of that public notice, the Commission still had not spot-checked licensees at renewal time nor used its "complaint procedure" to enforce its policy on loud commercials.

In a 1975 FCC agenda meeting, Commissioner Washburn asked if the Commission had any rule regarding loud commercials. William Ray replied that no such rule existed because the Commission had concluded there was no objective standard by which to judge how loud is too loud. Commissioner Robert Lee joked, "We once said, if you wake up during a program, it's too loud," and noted that, "Years ago, there was going to be a machine to measure loud commercials." Lee asked Broadcast Bureau Chief Wallace Johnson, "What happened?" Johnson responded, "It didn't work." Chairman Wiley then noted that Senator Howard Baker (R.–Tenn.), ranking minority member of the Senate Communications Subcommittee, had been complaining about loud commercials. Wiley suggested, "Why not send out another reminder? We'll just change the date."

The new reminder on loud commercials appeared on the agenda of July 22, 1975. In a cover memorandum to that agenda item, a legal assistant to one of the commissioners wrote the following:

> This item is a public notice advising licensees of their continuing obligation concerning loud commercials. The basic Commission policy was stated in a public notice dated July 12, 1965, which is attached.

> Considering that recurring violations and complaints continue to occur after 10 years' notice, this seems like a fairly weak method of dealing with the problem. Is there any precedent for fines, sanctions, or admonitions to violating stations?

The new public notice, which contained only two paragraphs, was adopted with little discussion: the notice simply said that "complaints in this area still persist," and reminded "all licensees that they have an affirmative obligation to see that objectionably loud commercials are not broadcast." The public notice was sent along with a copy of the 1965 statement.

In an editorial on September 27, 1975, *TV Guide* commented on the Commission's latest notice regarding loud commercials and noted that the *Guide* had editorialized against loud commercials on June 11, 1955, ten years before the Commission had issued its first policy statement:

Well, the scene changes again. *Another* 10 years go by. Now it is 1975. And history prepares to repeat itself. The FCC, noting that it still receives complaints from the public about loud commercials, has just reissued its 1965 directive. But since the directive lacks a penalty provision, there is no reason to assume that it will be any more successful this time than it was last. . . .

TV Guide's assumption was solid. No penalties have been imposed for loud commercials, despite the fact that the appeals court suggested that the broadcasting of loud commercials should be considered in FCC evaluation of renewal applications. The Commission has not investigated other ways to control loud commercials. The simple statement that the loudness machine, tried years before, hadn't worked was enough to convince the Commission not to try again.

No one has to listen to commercials—and too many commissioners believe they do not have to listen to complaints from the audience.

III

REGULATORY FUNCTIONS

10
The Renewal Game

If I were to pose the question, what are the FCC's renewal policies and what are the controlling guidelines, everyone in this room would be on equal footing. You couldn't tell me, I couldn't tell you—and no one else at the Commission could do any better (least of all the long-suffering renewals staff).

Dean Burch, FCC chairman
International Radio and Television Society
September 14, 1973

10 According to the Communications Act, every broadcast licensee must apply to the FCC every three years for renewal of the license. The FCC is supposed to study the application to decide whether the licensee's service to the public has earned the right to license renewal. As a practical matter, the Commission cannot determine the quality of performance of the thousands of renewal applicants; but by studying renewal applications, the agency can tell if a licensee may be violating FCC policies.

The primary gauge of whether a licensee is serving the public is the licensee's programming, which the Commission has long considered the "essence of broadcast service." The FCC's program policies give a licensee broad discretion as to what may be aired, but the Commission has set guidelines in certain areas. A major portion of the radio and television renewal forms is devoted to questions about what programs have been aired and what programs are proposed in these guidelined areas.

Regardless of how important programming is and regardless of which renewal form is used, answers to the programming questions and to related inquiries have *never* by themselves resulted in a denial of renewal. A renewal application has never been denied solely because of a failure to meet community needs and problems, an excess of commercials, a lack of public service announcements, or an inadequate amount of news, public affairs, or other nonentertainment material. Nor has a combination of these misdeeds ever resulted in denial of a renewal application. No renewal has ever been denied solely for failing to live up to programming promises made previously.

Renewal tends to be automatic, provided the applicant's papers are in order. Any consideration of program matter in renewing a license has usually been raised by an outside complaint, not by the FCC's renewal branch. The staff follows the commissioners' lead; and the commissioners, with few exceptions, have simply not wanted to become involved in the renewal process. This attitude encourages the staff to grind out the renewal grants under delegated authority and to bring as little as possible to the commissioners' attention.

In fiscal year 1976, the renewals were ground out at a typical rate. Of 2995 processed renewal applications, 2964 were granted, 23 (16 AM, six FM, and one TV) were designated for hearing, and eight were denied. Less than one percent (.0077) of processed applications went into hearing, and only one-quarter of one percent (.0027) of applications was denied. Most licensees who went into hearing or had their renewal applications denied had problems not reflected in the applications. For example, a station may have been guilty of fraudulent billing, or may have failed to answer satisfactorily the allegations in a petition to deny. None of the 23 licensees went into hearing because the renewal branch itself, without outside suggestion, had recommended the action.

To understand the renewal process, it is helpful to examine three general points about the forms used and procedures: the composite week and the annual programming report for commercial television licensees, differences between radio renewal forms and television renewal forms, and rules for processing renewal forms.

THE COMPOSITE WEEK AND
THE ANNUAL PROGRAMMING REPORT

The composite week is the Commission's main tool for determining what commercial radio or television stations are actually programming. For all commercial stations, the FCC selects seven days and announces this composite week to the licensees, who then prepare programming statistics using the composite week. Licensees don't know beforehand which days will comprise the composite week; therefore the statistics presumably reflect the stations' typical programming.

Noncommercial (public broadcasting) licensees have a much easier task because their programming has not interested the commissioners much. The FCC does not assign a composite week to these stations, nor is their programming evaluated by the renewal staff. Public broadcasting stations themselves choose seven consecutive days from the last year of the license period and submit programming statistics for these days. Because the choice of days is not mandated, the noncommercial licensee can preselect the days to be used and program accordingly.

When the Commission originally adopted the composite week concept in 1946, the idea was that each commercial licensee would submit information covering seven days chosen *each year* so that at the end of the renewal period, the FCC would have "data concerning the actual program structure of the station during a sample week in each year under the existing license," and industrywide "statistical summaries and trends" could be "published annually." The original plan was not carried out. Instead, until 1973 both television and radio licensees submitted statistics for one composite week every three years.

One of Cole's first recommendations to the Commission was that it institute the original concept of the composite week—a composite week for every year, at least for TV licensees—a concept with clear advantages. An annual composite week would certainly be more representative of a station's performance than would seven days over three years. The licensees could keep checking their own performances annually and could upgrade their programming if they consistently fell below the promised percentages. All commercial television stations would prepare annual statistics for the same seven-day period, and these statistics would provide a base for FCC measurement of industry performance from year to year. Commissioners could, for example, tell quickly if the amount of local programming had risen, fallen, or remained the same as in previous years.

Although Cole considered his proposal of an annual composite week as a modest, though essential, step, the proposal met with considerable opposition—from FCC staff members and the broadcasters. General Counsel John Pettit told *Broadcasting* that such an annual report would give citizen groups "more ammunition" to use in filing petitions to deny renewal of broadcast licenses. An annual composite week would, indeed, permit media critics or reformers to rank comparatively the performances of all commercial TV stations. When Commissioner Nicholas Johnson had attempted such nationwide comparisons, he had had to rely on renewal forms that reflected programming during different composite weeks. For example, the comparison between a New York station and a Los Angeles station was based on performances during two different seven-day periods because New York and California license renewals came up in different years.

In 1973, the Commission finally did adopt an annual programming report, based on the concept of an annual composite week, for commercial television licensees. Each licensee now prepares an annual report with two copies, one for the Commission and one for the station's local public inspection file. (An annual programming report form is included in Appendix B.)

For commercial television, the composite week is now selected from the first 42 weeks of every year, which are divided into seven consecutive six-week groups. Cards are prepared as follows: (1) one card for each of the seven groups, (2) one card for each of the six weeks, and (3) one card for each day of the week. The days of the composite week are drawn from a container holding the various cards. Once a card is picked representing the first six weeks of the year, no more days from that group can be picked. Once a card representing a Monday is selected, no more Mondays are eligible. If the process results in the selection of a legal holiday or a day during which something unique happens, such as a space shot, that day is *supposed to be disregarded* and a substitute day selected. The FCC announces the composite week for television as early in the fall as possible so that the licensees will have ample time to prepare their composite-week statistics, which must be turned into the FCC in February of the following year. Consequently, television licensees know that the last ten weeks of the year will not be covered by the composite week.

The Commission showed no interest in requiring a comparable annual report for commercial radio licensees. Their composite week is still made up of seven days from the three-year license period. Actually, the FCC selects the composite week in the same way as for television: seven days are picked from a 49-week period divided into seven consecutive groups. The commercial radio licensees, therefore, can rest assured that approximately 24 months of their renewal terms will not be scrutinized by the FCC. Furthermore, because the composite week is normally chosen from the months June to June, the licensee can estimate ahead of time which 24 months are ineligible (for example, all licensees up for renewal in 1978 will have a composite week selected from June 1976 to June 1977).

The choice of a composite week for commercial licensees is not sufficiently careful to ensure truly representative statistics. The 1975 composite week for television stations included a day when NBC aired a three-hour (8:00 P.M. to 11:00 P.M., EST) public affairs special in prime time. In an explanatory note to its annual compilation of programming statistics, the FCC blandly pointed out that "stations carrying that program show a percentage of public affairs higher than normal for that station." In fact, such a burst of prime-time public affairs programming is extremely atypical and distorts any examination of the regularity with which a station is devoting time to public affairs.

DIFFERENCES BETWEEN RADIO RENEWAL FORMS AND TELEVISION RENEWAL FORMS FOR COMMERCIAL STATIONS

Renewal forms (copies of which are in Appendix B) require a much greater amount of detailed information from TV licensees than from radio licensees. Both renewal forms require information on programming of news, public affairs, and all other nonentertainment or nonsports (that is, religious, instructional, educational, or agricultural programming); but for television the categories are broken down by time of day and source. Also, the TV renewal form contains a separate category of local programming. The radio form asks merely the number of public service announcements; the television form distinguishes public service announcements by time of day and nature of the beneficiary (for example, local or nonlocal). In the television form, questions on commercial practices also specify time of day and differentiate children's programs from all other programs.

The differences between the two forms can be explained largely by the differences in thinking that influenced the drafting of the forms. When Cole first went to the Commission, the radio and television forms were identical; but after making a lengthy presentation to the commissioners, Cole was instructed in 1970 to coordinate the drafting of a revised form for television. Chairman Burch decided that the television form should be revised first because TV was "where the action is" and did not involve the problems of special formats, such as radio's all-news and all-classical-music formats.

Cole recommended the deletion of fifteen questions that were useless in making the public interest determination, questions that could not be evaluated fairly. For example, to the question, "How do you keep informed of FCC regulations?" one licensee could answer, "I read *Broadcasting* magazine," and another applicant provide a long list of legal sources and staff briefings. However, Cole also suggested expanding and refining information solicited for those areas in programming the Commission *did* think important, at least officially. As a result, questions in these seven programming areas—news, public affairs, all other nonentertainment, local, public service announcements, commercial practices, and programming to meet problems and needs—were revised. In addition, under pressure from public groups and Congress, the Commission, for the first time, added questions on programming for children.

The new commercial radio renewal form was drafted by the Broadcast Bureau in 1975 and adopted in 1976, after Cole had left the Commission. From the beginning, the Commission was eager to develop a "short form" to lessen the load on what was considered an already overburdened radio operator. When the proposed new form was announced as a 1975 "NAB special," Chairman Wiley told broadcasters, "We believe that this form will help to make the renewal process for radio licensees—and for the FCC—simpler, quicker, and cheaper."

The result was a one-page form, with questions on both sides. The brevity of the form caused some problems for the presumed beneficiaries. *Broadcasting* (May 10, 1976) reported that "some communications attorneys said spaces in which answers were to be written are so small that renewal applicants will be obliged to use separate sheets to complete some answers." Renewal and Transfer Chief Richard Shiben disagreed and proudly told a regional NAB conference that, except for the program logs, the answers to the questions on the form would fit inside a regular envelope. A major reason Shiben was pleased with a shorter form was that many license renewals were being deferred simply because applicants weren't filling out the existing form properly. Much of the information wasn't being used by the FCC anyway; and the staff was under pressure to reduce the backlog, which often reached 40 percent of pending applications.

Bent on brevity, the Commission deleted from the radio form the same fifteen questions previously deleted from the television form. Of the remaining questions relating to programming, except for one about programming to meet problems and needs which was revised in another proceeding, none was expanded or revised. Requiring an annual programming report was not even considered because of the Commission's passion for reducing the radio licensee's burdens.

RULES FOR PROCESSING RENEWAL FORMS

There are two fundamental guidelines for efficient renewal procedures: first, everyone should know the rules by which applications are processed; and second, license applications that raise problems should be the ones scrutinized. Cole emphasized these points in his presentation to the Commission before he was hired as a consultant, and in numerous later staff briefings and Commission meetings. Even if the Commission wants merely to spar with renewal applicants, not to "knock a station down" by designating its application for a hearing, nor to "knock a station out" by denying renewal, the Commission should choose the right sparring partners.

A thorough examination of every renewal application from each broadcast licensee is logistically impractical. Like the Internal Revenue Service, the FCC cannot audit every station. The FCC could, however, use information collected on categories and percentages of programming and commercials to identify stations suspected of not performing in the public interest, much as the IRS questions taxpayers who take unusually large deductions in certain categories.

Cole urged the Commission to set up a system to isolate those licensees whose records demanded further scrutiny and to expedite renewal of the other licenses. The staff could review those applications singled out for further questioning, and apply well publicized and relevant criteria established by the Commission. Only those licenses that could not be renewed by the staff would be brought to the Commission's attention. All interested parties, including the public, would know on what basis the Commission's decision would be made.

Soon after Cole's arrival, the staff studied the fifty largest television markets and placed stations in homogeneous groupings: e.g., VHF network affiliates in markets ranked by population size, 11–25. A major purpose of the study was to answer two questions: Were certain stations consistent low-enders in the number of programs in various categories on the renewal form? Was there substantial quantitative difference between low-enders and high-enders in the same group?

When the results of the study were presented to the Commission, the answer to both questions was yes. One VHF affiliate in markets 11–25 was in the bottom ten percent of its group of stations in the following categories: total news, local news, public affairs and all other non-entertainment combined, and local prime-time programming. Nor could the station in question use finances as an excuse: it had revenues of $7.9 million and pretax profits of $4.1 million. The performance range from high-enders to low-enders was substantial, sometimes staggering, in all groupings. In that same grouping of VHF affiliates, total news ranged from 18 hours, 25 minutes down to 4 hours, 45 minutes; total public affairs, from 7 hours, 28 minutes to *zero;* and prime-time (6:00 P.M. to 11:00 P.M. EST) local programming, from 8 hours to 4 minutes.

Although stations were then still using different composite weeks, the study demonstrated that the staff could process renewal applications by a bottom-ten-percent approach: that is, the staff could, under delegated authority, renew licenses of stations with performances above the bottom 10 percent; and those stations requiring further scrutiny could easily be weeded out. Opponents of the approach might argue that there is always someone in the bottom ten percent, and that stations a decimal point below their colleagues would be unfairly penalized; but this study revealed far more than a decimal point's difference. That some stations in the bottom 10 percent were low-enders in several categories suggested the direction staff efforts should take when processing television renewal applications. In the unlikely event that the performances of all licensees in the bottom 10 percent were so high that their applications did not require further scrutiny, so much the better.

When the presentation was made and during the next three years, the commissioners did not debate nor even discuss the bottom-10-percent approach; they discussed *no* approach. The Commission had previously rejected the suggestion of Commissioners Cox and Johnson to scrutinize licensees proposing less than prescribed minimum levels: 5 percent news, 1 percent public affairs, and 5 percent all other nonentertainment (or a combination of public affairs and all other). The Commission was simply not interested in discussing how the detailed quantitative information or any other programming information on the new form would be examined, if at all.

By 1973, the new television renewal form and annual programming report, both proposed in February 1971, seemed finally to be on the Commission's front burner. When redrafting the notice of rulemaking adopting the form, Cole didn't have to be told to be vague as to how the information on the form was to be processed and evaluated. When he defended the new form before the Office of Management and Budget (OMB), which had to approve all government forms sent to ten or more people, Cole had to fudge answers to some questions: What are you going to do with the information? What happens if the licensee puts zero news hours or one hundred hours? Cole's answers were appropriately nonspecific: The question solicits information regarding performance or promises in one of the eight areas the Commission considers relevant to programming in the public interest; this information will contribute to a composite picture of the licensee's past efforts and future proposals. After such circumspection, the form was approved by OMB in the summer of 1973 and ratified by the Commission later that year to take effect in December 1974.

Between the February 1971 proposal of the new TV renewal form and annual programming report and their final ratification in October 1973, the Commission was attempting to lighten its heavy workload. In 1972, the FCC's executive director was instructed to make a Commission-wide study of the delegations of authority to the various bureaus. In September 1972 and again in March and April 1973, the Commission's agenda meetings were swamped with bulky agenda items that listed the existing delegations of authority to the individual bureaus.

At the April meeting, Commissioner H. Rex Lee, a veteran of government, suggested that the Commission's concept of delegating authority was outmoded, and he recommended that the Commission adopt the approach of other agencies: rather than keep all authority except that specifically delegated to the staff, delegate all authority except that which the Commission wishes to keep. Consequently, the lists concerning delegations would contain only those matters the Commission didn't wish to delegate and would be much shorter because most Commission actions are performed by the staff.

The Commission readily agreed to Lee's recommendation and instructed the Broadcast Bureau and all other bureaus to decide which matters the commissioners might wish to reserve for themselves. Because the renewal branch was already processing all renewal applications on its own, and the commissioners had given no indication of wanting to see *any* applications, no guidance was available on what types of renewal applications the Commission should see.

In October 1973, a very large agenda item detailing all Broadcast Bureau matters that would now be presented to the Commission included some rules for processing renewal applications. Basically, the processing rules provided automatic license renewal unless stations fell below certain performance levels. Many of the figures were arbitrary —"picked out of thin air," according to Shiben. The renewal branch understood the significance of the new processing rules: "If the delegations [of authority] are restructured in the manner proposed, it must be recognized that the industry and its legal representatives will, for the first time, gain a clear insight into the general benchmarks used in determining whether a particular matter is to be referred by the staff to the Commission."

This statement should have alerted the commissioners to a change they'd resisted for years. Cox and Johnson hadn't been able to get the third supporting vote for commissioners' seeing all renewal applications promising less than a certain percentage of news, public affairs, and all other nonentertainment programming. Later, when Cole was drafting the notice adopting the new commercial TV renewal form, the commissioners had repeatedly declined to discuss plans for processing renewal applications. Now, almost by accident, the commissioners were about to adopt processing rules by which they would automatically view some of the weakest renewal applications.

Much to the staff's surprise, the commissioners didn't even discuss the proposed processing rules before accepting the whole item. Apparently, because of the bulk of the Broadcast Bureau item and the lengthy list of other agenda items, some of the commissioners didn't fully realize what was happening. Months after the rules had been adopted, Chairman Wiley, who was usually thoroughly conversant with material in agenda items, asked Shiben, "Where did some of the figures [in the processing rules] come from?"

Word that now the commissioners would automatically see certain renewal applications was slow to spread to the outside. Even the trade press didn't hear about the new processing rules until some law firms discovered them in a standard listing of FCC actions. Caught unprepared, the NAB soon sent the FCC chairman a copy of an internal NAB memo expressing surprise and concern over the Commission's action.

In November 1973, the new processing rules were to take effect and the commissioners would see for the first time some of the rotten apples in the three-year barrel of over 9000 renewal applications. Ever optimistic, Cole hoped that the exposure would raise the commissioners' consciousness and result in the establishment of new processing rules, not "picked out of thin air" by the staff, but thoroughly discussed and considered by the commissioners. Moreover, Cole expected that when the new renewal form and the annual programming report both took effect in December 1974, the processing rules for television renewals would be revised to reflect the significant amount of new information solicited by the new forms.

None of what Cole hoped for happened. Instead, the commissioners, exposed to some renewal applications that raised problems, responded with no interest. Things soon returned to normal: the staff ground out renewal grants, commissioners remained uninvolved, and the processing rules were ignored.

The processing rules have had their uses, however: the FCC refers to them when explaining and defending its renewal policies. In October 1976, the Commission used the processing rules to buttress a special report to Congress advocating amendment of the Communications Act to eliminate comparative renewal hearings.

Under the existing Communications Act, after a renewal application has been filed, any party may file a competing, mutually exclusive application for that same frequency. The competing applicant is entitled to a full, consolidated, comparative hearing, during which the merits of each application are presented, and after which the Commission selects the applicant best qualified to serve the public interest. Because the incumbent almost always wins, few competing applications are filed; but recent decisions in favor of the incumbent were difficult for the Commission to justify. Consequently, many commissioners favored eliminating the comparative hearings; and the broadcast industry agreed.

In its special report the FCC told Congress: "In advocating that the comparative renewal process be eliminated, the Commission believes that the existing criteria for evaluating overall licensee performance are adequate to assure that its licensees continue to adhere to the public interest standard of the Communications Act. In this regard, each broadcast licensee must undergo an extensive review every three years when it files its renewal application with the Commission. The Commission believes that the scrutiny which each licensee receives at renewal time provides it with a great deal of information regarding ascertainment, programming, commercial practices, technical operations and equal opportunities in employment."

The renewal processing rules were cited repeatedly to support the Commission's contention that "extensive review" was given renewal applications. For example:

> Uncontested renewal applications, i.e., those not subject to either a petition to deny or a competing application, receive close scrutiny by the Commission staff. If the licensee's application and past record meet certain processing standards, the staff may grant renewal under delegated authority. Applications that do not meet the delegation standards and those which are subject to petitions to deny are acted upon by the [commissioners].

> Quantitative processing standards are helpful to the Commission in the noncomparative renewal process because they, along with other information received from the licensee, provide the Commission with direction on where to concentrate its limited resources.

> In other areas, where station performance is measured against general Commission policies rather than specific standards, the Commission has set processing standards for use by the staff. Applications that do not meet these processing standards are not precluded from grant, but rather must be referred to the [commissioners] for consideration.

The FCC October 1976 Report to Congress is the most recent and "complete" outline of license renewal policies and procedures the Commission has given Congress in years.

11
The FCC Paints Congress a Rosy Picture

As I read the Communications Act, broadcasting—rightly or wrongly—is an industry invested with the public trust, and the Commission—again rightly or wrongly—is invested with the responsibility to judge the fulfillment of that trust by its licensees. How should this responsibility be exercised? What is the basis for our judgment that a broadcaster's license to operate should be renewed? It seems to me that the answer to these questions lies in what this industry told Congress last year: a broadcaster at renewal time must run primarily on his record of service. And it is self-evident that programming is the primary factor in that record.

Richard Wiley, FCC chairman
NAB Annual Convention
April 1975

11 Commission policies, when viewed in a vacuum and as portrayed in the October 1976 Report to Congress, seem to be responsible and fair-minded. However, the rules of the renewal game reported to Congress and those actually observed are not always the same. There are several programming areas in which discrepancies occur between what the Commission says and what it does.

PROMISE VERSUS PERFORMANCE

In its report to Congress, the FCC stated, "the licensee's actual performance during a cross section 'composite week' is compared with the proposals made in the previous license application. If there are substantial differences between the two, the application must be considered by the [commissioners]." Later in the report, the FCC offered a somewhat different description: "In evaluating a licensee's quantitative performance in the promise vs. performance area, the Commission looks at licensee's prior renewal promises regarding news, public affairs, and [all other] programming and compares these past projections with the licensee's actual performance as reflected in the most recent renewal application. . . . *If the licensee's explanation is not satisfactory*, the matter must be submitted to the [commissioners for their] consideration." The second statement reflects the 1976 revision of the processing rule for promise versus performance; the first reflects the original 1973 rule. But neither statement accurately reflects the Commission's handling of and attitude toward renewal applicants with promise-versus-performance problems.

Many broadcasters and most television licensees got their stations in the first place by following the old Arpège slogan—"Promise her anything. . . ." In the 1950s, when the FCC was allocating VHF television licenses, and several applicants were competing for a valuable frequency, their programming promises were positively utopian. Applicants vied to see who could promise the most uplifting and enlightening programs: each vowed to educate the community's children; provide local, live church services for shut-ins; and offer hours to develop the talents of local artists and actors. Drama? Sure, Shakespeare and O'Neill. Comedy? Aristophanes. Commercials? Only if we can squeeze them in between the city council meetings and the help-for-handicapped-veterans show.

The applicants with the greatest imagination for extravagant benevolence won the channels from their just slightly more realistic rivals, and then promptly threw the switch to get whatever programs were offered by ABC, NBC, CBS, or Dumont, according to their affiliations. On the rare occasions when the successful applicants were asked at renewal time what had happened to all the magnificent eleemosynary programs, the broadcasters would blandly reply that they had found these programs unprofitable. One station, when challenged, replied typically, "It was the judgment of the licensee not to present the proposed programs." Of course, that license was renewed.

The FCC once calculated that a sample of 35 successful television-license applicants, between 1952 and 1965, had promised an average of 31.5 percent of broadcast time to be devoted to local, live programming; but such programming was actually broadcast on an average of 11.8 percent of the time. With many stations ignoring their original promises, the FCC simply backed off from requiring local, live programming —and from demanding that applicants fulfill their commitments.

The art of making and then ignoring promises had been mastered years earlier by some of the same people with respect to radio. For example, in 1938, a Toledo, Ohio, station, authorized to broadcast during the days only, applied for permission to operate at night in order to serve local community organizations and to utilize abundant local talent. Toward these ends, the station would devote 84 percent of its nighttime hours to local, live-talent broadcasts and would donate evening time to the Toledo civic opera, the Toledo Council of Churches, The American Legion, the Boy Scouts, and "other worthwhile organizations." After obtaining its authorization, the station ignored its end of the bargain. When the station was monitored by the FCC for one week in 1944, local, live programming accounted for only 13.7 percent of the evening hours; nearly half of it was "rip and read" (wire service) newscasts with the news announcer as the only local talent. The only other local, live, nonsponsored programs of a public service nature were ten minutes of bowling scores and ten minutes of general sports news. Nothing was presented by *any* of the local organizations that the petition had said desired and deserved free evening broadcast time. Commercials, however, were plentiful in the evening hours: in one *Music Hall* program, ten commercial announcements, seven of them one-minute spots, were presented during a ten-minute interval.

Periodically, the Commission threatens to get tough with licensees who ignore the promises made in their last renewal applications. In its first comprehensive programming policy statement, the *Blue Book,* in 1946, the Commission called attention to "the need for trustworthiness . . . with respect to representations concerning program service" and warned that henceforth the promises in the last renewal application would be readily available to those examining the next application. In July 1961, the Commission notified all stations that "proposals versus actual operation" vitally concerned the Commission and "those stations which have not been making good faith efforts to meet their promises should take immediate steps to do so." To show its seriousness of purpose, the Commission in July 1961 granted only a short-term renewal to KORD–AM, Pasco, Washington, for not fulfilling its promises.

By 1970, when Cole first went to the Commission, these warnings about promise versus performance were distant memories; few commissioners or staffers knew about the 1961 public notice or the precedent of the short-term renewal. Nonetheless, the renewal form still divided programming and commercial practices into past and proposed; and the Commission had never publicly disavowed its interest in promise versus performance. As a result, the bureau's draft of the processing rules included a provision that renewal applications "which vary substantially from prior representations with respect to nonentertainment programming and commercial practices" would be brought to the commissioners for disposition.

Not all substantial variations in the programming area merited scrutiny as broken promises. The Commission has allowed licensees not "to adhere inflexibly in their day-to-day station operations" to the promises made in their previous renewal applications: "We have long recognized the licensee's discretionary and permissible adjustment of programming and other aspects of station operation to meet changing needs and circumstances." Substantial changes in licensees' proposals must be reported to the FCC whenever the changes occur; in circumstances where licensees know they will not fulfill their promises, they are not only permitted but encouraged to change those promises during the license period. Stations that notified the Commission of the changes did not have to worry about promise-versus-performance scrutiny, which was reserved for those who deviated from their promises and never amended their applications.

However, the commissioners did see some substantial variations in the programming area. In the first agenda items under the new processing rules, from the Iowa and Missouri February 1974 renewal groups, the staff listed 70 stations that deviated substantially. Some deviations were enormous and in more than one category. Each of a Missouri station's deviations met the bureau's definition of substantial: the station promised 29.5 percent nonentertainment and broadcast 12.2 percent in the composite week, promised 14.5 percent news and broadcast 9.5 percent, promised 3.4 percent public affairs and broadcast 1.3 percent, promised 11.6 percent all other nonentertainment and broadcast 1.4 percent. Similarly, an Iowa station promised 4.6 percent public affairs and broadcast 0.5 percent; it promised 15.3 percent all other nonentertainment and broadcast 0.5 percent.

The bureau stated that, "Except for those cases where the licensees have yet to respond or the staff has been unable to review their responses, the Bureau believes that further action with respect to the stations listed . . . is not necessary. Generally speaking, the licensees have offered adequate explanations for their variances." These "adequate explanations" included: "Operating losses required curtailment of certain programs," "Certain program service was discontinued by supplier and several months elapsed before suitable replacement was found," and "New competition caused re-evaluation of program service." The bureau then added its own catchall as to why some applicants should be renewed: "The renewal applications otherwise indicate that each station has broadcast programming servicing the problems, needs, and interests of their respective communities."

Because the commissioners didn't even discuss the promise-versus-performance portion of that agenda item, the staff understandably assumed that all was well and prepared an agenda item covering the next renewal group of five states. This time 84 stations were found to have substantial promise-versus-performance deviations. The bureau indicated that additional information had been requested from 43 stations, and answers had been received from only two. The bureau was awaiting answers from the other 41 stations: "Upon receipt of the responses . . . if the staff believes that the explanations are inadequate, an agenda item will be submitted to the Commission with appropriate recommendations." The bureau requested, however, that "if it is determined that a station's response is adequate," the staff be authorized to grant the renewal under delegated authority.

To list all 84 stations with substantial deviations required seven pages. Chairman Wiley just shook his head from side to side when he started thumbing through the list while the staff explained that there really was no serious problem. After the Commission meeting, Wiley called Cole into his office and said he was very distressed at the number of stations who were disregarding their promises. The staff was told to "hold tight" on granting renewals for the stations listed on the agenda item.

When the next renewal group—licenses in Kansas, Nebraska, and Oklahoma—came up on June 1, 1974, Wiley was ready to act. The bureau was instructed to send three types of letters to licensees who appeared in agenda items for deviating from promises. The toughest letter required additional information about the variance, an explanation of controls planned by the licensee to eliminate future variance, and an explanation of how the station's past programming met the problems and needs of the community. A second, weaker letter questioned what controls the licensee would use to prevent future promise-versus-performance deviations. A third letter, weaker still, admonished the licensee for the variance and warned against future deviations.

The staff was not very discriminating in dispensing its letters. For example, these stations did *not* receive the most severe letter: one station promised 21.2 percent nonentertainment programs and broadcast only 3.1 percent—its deviations included 15 percent news promised and 2.7 percent broadcast, 1.2 percent public affairs promised and 0.2 percent broadcast, 5 percent all other promised and 0.2 percent broadcast; one station promised 3.8 percent public affairs and broadcast 0.6 percent; one station promised 25.2 percent total nonentertainment and broadcast 3.4 percent. A Minnesota FM station got the weakest letter although it promised 8.4 percent nonentertainment and broadcast only 4.0 percent and performed below its promises in all nonentertainment categories. In contrast, a Montana station got the toughest letter because it promised 6 percent public affairs and broadcast 2.8 percent, although it exceeded its promise of total nonentertainment programming, 25.6 percent broadcast and 25.0 promised, and in news, 13 percent promised and 17.5 percent broadcast. The sending of the letters in June 1974 was the high-water mark of the Commission's latest attempt to get licensees to live up to their promises.

In reporting on the Commission's decision to instruct the staff to send out these letters, *Television Digest* (June 3, 1974) quoted Chairman Wiley as saying, "I've always been a strong promise-versus-performance man. . . . If a licensee fails to fulfill his promises, it's the same as misrepresentation, a lack of candor." Wiley indicated it would be "ludicrous" to sift out licensees who violated their promises "and then just wave them through" for renewal. *Television Digest* noted that the chairman had the unanimous support of the other commissioners at the meeting.

Some of the commissioners, however, didn't seem very concerned about promise versus performance. *Access* magazine reported that Commissioner Quello told an August 1974 meeting of the Virginia Association of Broadcasters that the best way to avoid the problem of meeting their promises was just not to promise anything at renewal time. Quello wrote *Access* (October 1974) that he was misquoted and enclosed an excerpt from the prepared text of his speech: "The obvious message to broadcasters is—'Don't let your zeal for public service at renewal time exceed your ability or desire to perform after the renewal has been granted.' "

For the August 1974 renewal group (Texas) of stations with substantial deviations between promises and performance, the staff provided more details: one-paragraph discussions of 23 license applications that the staff felt should be renewed; and a list of 76 other stations from which the staff had requested explanations for the variances, and which the staff considered the real problem cases. When the staff requested authority to handle as it saw fit all 99 renewal applications in question, the commissioners didn't even discuss the request. Nor was there inquiry into the status of those past applicants, now on deferral, who had been sent letters in June; even the responses from those stations that had received the toughest letter failed to interest the commissioners.

The commissioners' silence on the entire matter told the bureau all it needed to know: the commissioners didn't want to be involved. In the next agenda item for renewal applications of the October 1, 1974, group, the bureau didn't even list stations with promise-versus-performance deviations, let alone provide paragraph descriptions of the problems. Moreover, the staff no longer even spoke of "substantial variance." Instead, the agenda item referred to ten stations with "*the most extensive variance* from their previous proposals" that had been written letters. Only if their responses did not satisfy the staff, would the Commission become involved.

The Commission's desire to "hear no evil, see no evil" was made official in a 1976 revision of the renewal processing rules. Henceforth, only variations for which "there is lacking, in the judgment of the Broadcast Bureau, adequate justification in the public interest" would be brought to the Commission's attention. The unofficial definition of substantial deviations was now more strict: more than 20 percent deviation in combined nonentertainment programming, and 15 percent in either news, public affairs, or all other nonentertainment. The Commission still refused to define substantial in its official rules. Given the Commission's lack of interest, the staff's subsequent actions were predictable: no more promise-versus-performance-problem cases have been referred to the commissioners since 1974, unless a petition to deny or some other special problem was involved.

NONENTERTAINMENT PROGRAMMING

The Commission reported to Congress that the renewal applicant's proposals for nonentertainment programming "are reviewed," and "if they fall short of specific processing standards, again the Commission itself must consider the application." This statement is consistent with the Commission's renewal processing rules but does not describe what really has happened. Stations whose nonentertainment programming proposals fall below the specific processing standards have, in fact, been renewed without the commissioners' being involved. Moreover, the "specific" processing standards seem not very specific when one considers the information available and the importance the Commission has attributed to nonentertainment programming and its scheduling.

The Commission's stated policy is to strike a balance between "the preservation of a free competitive broadcast system, on the one hand, and the reasonable restriction of that freedom inherent in the public interest standard provided in the Communications Act, on the other, [by] requiring licensees to conduct formal surveys to ascertain the need for certain types of nonentertainment programming, while allowing licensees wide discretion in the area of entertainment programming." The Commission's *Primer on Ascertainment of Community Problems by Broadcast Applicants* refers specifically to the licensee's "nonentertainment programming obligations," which apply to all broadcasters without exception, inasmuch as the Communications Act makes no distinctions among broadcast licensees regarding their responsibilities.

Either standardizing or not standardizing this type of requirement would create problems. Good arguments can be made for not requiring specialty stations—e.g., classical-music, easy-listening, or country-and-western-music formats—to interrupt their programming with news broadcasts that could be heard on other stations. However, if certain stations were exempted from having to provide nonentertainment programming when other local stations were already providing a sufficient amount, who determines what is sufficient and by what criteria? What happens when the other stations no longer want to provide as much nonentertainment programming? Should they be forced to continue it anyway? At what point does the Commission reimpose the nonentertainment obligation on stations previously exempt? Because not standardizing creates these and other problems, the Commission took the path of least resistance: it imposed nonentertainment obligations on all stations.

For years, renewal forms have divided nonentertainment programming into three major categories: news, public affairs, and "all other," which includes religion, instruction, education, and agriculture. Public affairs is defined by the Commission as "programs dealing with local, state, regional, national or international issues or problems. . . ."

In 1974, the Commission, in a policy statement on the Fairness Doctrine, emphasized the importance of public affairs programming by all broadcast licensees:

> In the context of the scarcity of broadcast frequencies and the regulating necessity for governmental licensing, the First Amendment implies, rather than prohibits, governmental promotion of a system which will insure that the public will be informed of the important issues which confront it and of the competing viewpoints on those issues which may differ from the views held by a particular licensee. . . .

> In reviewing the adequacy of the amount of the licensee's public issue programming, we will, of course, limit our inquiry to a determination of its reasonableness. We wish to make it plain, however, that we have allocated a very large share of the electromagnetic spectrum to broadcasting chiefly because of our belief that this medium can make a great contribution to an informed public opinion.

When the Broadcast Bureau drafted the processing rules, the necessity for a provision on nonentertainment programming was obvious, but the bureau decided to have just one category for nonentertainment, including news, public affairs, and all other nonentertainment. The minimum requirements the bureau settled on, those Shiben described as "picked out of thin air," were as follows: less than 6 percent (for FM), 8 percent (AM), and 10 percent (TV) of broadcast time proposed for nonentertainment programming would automatically refer the renewal application to the commissioners.

The failure of the processing rule to distinguish types of nonentertainment programming allows a radio broadcaster to avoid Commission scrutiny by broadcasting, say, commercially sponsored, religious programs at 3:00 A.M. Religious programs at 3:00 A.M. might serve those people who are awake; but, by themselves, such programs obviously do not "insure that the public will be informed of the important issues which confront it."

Many radio stations broadcast little, if any, public affairs. A *Television/Radio Age* survey (December 6, 1976) showed that of the respondents, mainly leading stations in the 100 most populated radio markets, only one in seven programmed public affairs on a daily basis; one in two concentrated public affairs programming on weekends; and of these, seven out of ten confined public affairs to Sundays. Of all the respondents, one out of eight limited public affairs programming to public service announcements, a dubious practice according to the Commission's policies. The *Television/Radio Age* report on the survey said that, though no tally was made of the actual volume of public service programs, a wide spread clearly existed between the most active and the least active; and "there is no obvious correlation between money and the volume of such programming." Cole's examination of Commission records, including annual financial reports, revealed the same two things were true of both radio and television stations in other markets.

The Commission continues to insist that all radio stations should provide public affairs and informational programs, but doesn't specify what amount of such programming, broadcast or proposed, demands staff investigation and commissioner attention. Thus, Commissioner Quello told an NAB regional meeting in Las Vegas (November 1974) that FM stations should broadcast news and public affairs programs, but "I hasten to add that I am not prescribing the amount of time devoted to the information portions of FM broadcasting nor am I suggesting ratios of news to entertainment. However, I do expect the public service effort of any licensee to be more than perfunctory since his opportunity for public service is great."

What happens to radio stations that refuse to propose even 6 percent or 8 percent nonentertainment? In theory, such cases should go to the commissioners. In fact, they rarely have. At the outset, when the 1974 processing rules first took effect, the staff did list in the agenda items stations not promising the minimum nonentertainment. Most of these were FM stations. If the FM station was an independent—without an AM station in the same community—the staff suggested that the struggling independent be given a break; if the FM station was owned in common with an AM station that promised at least 8 percent nonentertainment, the staff suggested the FM station be given a break. When the commissioners showed little interest in the subject, the staff soon got the message: future reports, prepared every two months for the current group of renewal applicants, did not list any station by call letters, nor indicate what percentage of nonentertainment programs was being proposed. These future reports merely indicated the number of stations sent letters of inquiry, and promised, "Upon receipt of the explanations, the stations' responses will be reviewed to determine appropriate action on their renewal applications." In short, the staff had unofficially been given the authority to renew all applications regardless of the nonentertainment programming promises.

In late 1975, Renewal Chief James Hobson, abjuring responsibility for renewing licenses of those who refused to amend their nonentertainment programming proposals, brought 14 renewal applications to the commissioners' attention in a special agenda item and specifically asked for guidance. The result was that, henceforth, AM licensees were expected to propose at least 8 percent nonentertainment; if not, the staff would hassle and implore and, when necessary, strongly suggest the need for a full explanation of how the licensee would meet community problems; what happened next was left up to the staff. Any justification would suffice for renewal of FM licensees unless they proposed under 2 percent nonentertainment. These instructions to the staff were not publicized.

Although some FM licenses were approved despite very low proposals (just over 2 percent in one case), licensees were warned that they might well be vulnerable if a formal complaint, petition to deny, or competing application were filed against the station: "Our decision to accept your programming proposal is based solely upon the information now before us and should not be interpreted as guaranteeing Commission approval of a similar future proposal should information be submitted to the Commission which indicates that your FM station may not be serving the needs and interests of its service area."

Henry Baumann, the 1976 successor to Renewal Branch Chief Hobson, also decided, by early 1977, that the commissioners should see some FM license renewal applications with less than 6 percent proposed nonentertainment programming. Baumann originally considered recommending a 4 percent cut-off point for renewal, with those below, some as low as 1.6 percent, being asked for more information; but he decided that a 4 percent cut-off in 1977 made no more sense than had the 2 percent cut-off in 1975. Unless a station had some good reason to be treated differently, it should, Baumann felt, promise at least the 6 percent nonentertainment programming specified in the processing rules. With the support of his colleagues, Baumann recommended that these stations be sent a letter warning that the application had been referred to the commissioners, and that renewal could not be granted until the licensee either amended his nonentertainment proposals or provided a "sufficient" explanation of how the station planned to meet the needs of its service area during the up-coming renewal period. The commissioners agreed to the recommendation.

Letters were sent in March 1977, and response was immediate. Both FM licensees and program syndicators, who felt the "good music," syndicated program package supplied to FM stations should not be interrupted by nonentertainment, started lobbying individual commissioners. Baumann, in turn, soon heard from several commissioners their reservations about forcing stations to amend nonentertainment proposals and disrupt existing programming formats.

The bureau's recommendation that renewal depend on a station's justification of its low percentage of nonentertainment programming "does not intend to establish a minimum acceptable percentage of proposed nonentertainment programming for FM licensees. However, a licensee's proposals, if below the delegation [processing rules] threshold, should be supported by public interest justifications. We find the explanations less than adequate and are of the view that further explanations regarding the adequacy and responsiveness of the proposals are required."

The bureau summarized the justifications and indicated why they were inadequate: 6 percent nonentertainment did not destroy the uniqueness or effectiveness of a station's format; programming on a co-owned station in the same market could not fulfill the requirement of the station in question; the presence of a large number of other stations in the area, regardless of their programming, doesn't relieve the licensee of its responsibility; high audience-acceptance doesn't mean ascertained needs are being met with nonentertainment programming; a low number of commercials does not justify a low amount of non-entertainment.

By June 1977, some stations had amended their proposals after receiving the letters; others had not and were trying to enlist the support of individual commissioners for exemptions from the rule. Baumann told Cole that Baumann wouldn't be surprised or upset if some of these stations were renewed despite their low nonentertainment proposals. Because the Commission has, until now, never officially indicated what would sufficiently justify the proposal of less than the prescribed levels in nonentertainment programming, one wonders what

Although promising less than 6 or 8 percent nonentertainment has not automatically brought the application to the commissioners' attention, and has not resulted in any renewal hearing or conditional renewal, the mere inclusion of percentages in the processing rules has brought complaints from radio broadcasters. At its 1976 convention, the National Radio Broadcasters Association met with FCC staff members for two and one-half hours to complain about the 8 and 6 percent "guidelines," which, even if they weren't ironclad rules, were "intimidating." *Broadcasting* (September 27, 1976) quoted a broadcaster: "I never got any letter saying, 'Thank you for your six hours of public affairs.'" And, according to *Broadcasting*, another broadcaster drew "loud applause" when he said, "We would like to be free to do our own thing."

Not all at the NRBA convention agreed with those comments, however. In a letter to *Broadcasting* (October 11, 1976), Cliff Gill of Cliff Gill Enterprises stated:

Nearly everyone, including the Association officials, grumbled at FCC procedures, which establish some criteria for an absolute minimum program service. Only one of the long string of participants, whose questions often became speeches, expressed any recognition of the fact that broadcasters are not the owners of a wired music service but are licensees of the people of the United States. . . . One speaker thought just one percent of public-affairs programming was an intrusion on his rights as a broadcaster to protect his ratings. Hats off to Bill Ray, Chief of FCC Complaints and Compliance, who with a wry smile and dry humor advised the complainers in these approximate words: "As long as you are in broadcasting, you are going to have some regulation by the government. If you want an industry without any regulation I suggest you open a peanut stand."

While radio broadcasters complain publicly about the (not totally enforced) processing rule for nonentertainment programming, their television counterparts are not all that unhappy about the rule. Most television stations have no trouble meeting their 10 percent nonentertainment programming, and most of those who might have trouble are now exempt.

According to the 1974 processing rule, TV applications proposing less than 10 percent total nonentertainment programming would be referred to the commissioners. By 1975, when the annual programming report and the new renewal forms were in effect, the Commission was receiving information about past and proposed nonentertainment programming in eighteen separate categories—36 specific percentages. Twelve of the percentages related to nonentertainment programming during prime time; these were ignored. Of all the percentages, only one figure—total proposed nonentertainment—was considered relevant to the licensee's nonentertainment programming obligations.

In 1975, revision of the nonentertainment processing rule was being discussed by Chairman Wiley and the staff. The Broadcast Bureau strongly opposed any changes, especially specific categories and percentages for news and public affairs, and requirements for time of day (that is, prime time). And the bureau expressed this opposition in a memo to Chairman Wiley:

> The staff members who favor retaining that standard [10 percent nonentertainment] view the adoption of other numerical standards as a substantial intrusion into an area where heretofore the Commission has been reluctant to tread. They believe that the Commission should continue to defer to the licensee's good faith judgment, predicated upon its awareness of the local scene, and rely in the first instance on the public to inform the licensee or the Commission if they feel their significant needs are not being adequately or equitably served. It should be left to the individual licensee, they submit, to determine how and when it will present programming to inform the electorate and to give voice to local expression.

In May 1976 (after Cole had left the FCC), the Commission finally revised the 10 percent total nonentertainment processing rule for television. The rule still requires ten percent nonentertainment programming, but it must be broadcast between 6:00 A.M. and midnight. A new rule was added: television applications proposing less than 5 percent informational (news and public affairs combined) programming between 6:00 A.M. and midnight would automatically be referred to the commissioners. Exempted from both rules were UHF stations not affiliated with a network: stations which theoretically had been subject to the 10 percent minimum, but whose licenses had sometimes been renewed without it.

The five-percent rule for informational programming will present no more problems than the original 10 percent rule for nonentertainment, either to licensees or to commissioners. Just as before, the Commission can easily avoid dealing with stations that may have problems because the new rule was called "procedural rather than substantive." In announcing the revised processing rules in a May 6, 1976 order, the Commission emphasized: "The amount and kind of programming to be broadcast in serving the interest of the public is left largely to the reasonable, good-faith judgment of the individual licensee."

Even with the 1976 revisions, the processing rules still fail to specify news and public affairs. Moreover, no processing rules refer specifically to prime-time television although six separate categories of prime-time nonentertainment programming appear in the annual programming report and the renewal form, and the number of households watching television during prime time is four times the number in the morning and twice the number in the afternoon.

Because prime-time news and public affairs programming is left totally to the discretion of the licensee and the networks without fear of the commissioners' review, ratings become the dominating consideration. A season's network rating point is equivalent to an extra $36 million lost or gained, and it should be no surprise that not all networks run a prime-time public affairs show weekly. Similarly, many local stations avoid broadcasting local, prime-time public affairs regularly because ratings would suffer. Each year, stations' annual program reports show blanks in the prime-time public affairs column despite the Commission's general pronouncements on the importance of public affairs programming during peak viewing hours.

The FCC's inaction has provoked a campaign by the National Conference of Parents and Teachers, the League of Women Voters, the National Council of Senior Citizens, the Consumer Federation of America, the National Association for the Advancement of Colored People, and others. The coalition has two specific goals: (1) all stations must provide one hour per week of regularly scheduled, prime-time, locally originated, public affairs programming; and (2) each network must provide one hour per week of regularly scheduled, prime-time public affairs. Any affiliate choosing not to carry the network public affairs program must provide a second hour of public affairs—either produced locally or acquired elsewhere. The campaign is coordinated by the National Citizens Committee for Broadcasting.

Westinghouse Broadcasting (Group W) and its president, Donald McGannon, joined the coalition. In December 1976, McGannon told a Philadelphia audience that news programming does an excellent job of bringing people the hard news, the facts. For example, "People are aware of prejudice," said McGannon, but public affairs programming is important because "what we do not see or hear enough of over the broadcast media are the causes of the problems we face, the reason the prejudice exists, how it could be alleviated."

The coalition's campaign aims for direct discussions with local stations and the networks. "Because Congress and the FCC won't act," reads an NCCB statement, "the time has come for citizens to create their own 'public interest standard' and take it directly to their local broadcasters."

PROGRAMMING TO MEET COMMUNITY PROBLEMS AND NEEDS

In the FCC report to Congress, the Commission declared:

> A broadcast analyst checks the licensee's efforts to ascertain the problems, needs, and interests of its community, and the programs it broadcasts in response to them. Substantial ascertainment defects that cannot be resolved by the staff require referral of the application for Commission action.... The Commission has long been of the opinion that one of the principal ingredients of a licensee's service in the public interest is his obligation "to make a positive, diligent and continuing effort, in good faith, to determine the tastes, needs and desires of the public in his community and to provide programming to meet those needs and interests." Thus, the Commission pays particular attention to the areas of ascertainment and programming at renewal time.

Because the Commission has repeatedly emphasized the importance of ascertainment of community needs and programming resulting from it (for example, in the 1960 Programming Policy Statement), the Broadcast Bureau thought the 1974 renewal processing rules ought to include something relating to community needs. Consequently, the new rules provided that the commissioners would see all renewal applications containing "substantial ascertainment defects which, for any reason, cannot be resolved by further staff inquiry or action." In reality, all substantial ascertainment defects were and are resolved by the staff, not the commissioners; and little attention is paid to ascertainment and programming to meet community problems and needs.

For years, the staff had been handling any problems relating to ascertainment and programming to meet community problems and needs; and no applications went to the commissioners although some stations did have their renewals deferred for a time. The problems were eventually resolved; and as long as no petition to deny renewal had been filed, licenses were renewed.

The new processing rules certainly had to suggest that the commissioners would see the really serious problems regarding ascertainment. The staff anticipated that the commissioners would not be very interested, but felt that something should be said in the first agenda items (January 1974 and March 1974) that followed the institution of the new processing rules: "During the processing of the renewal applications . . . several stations were written staff letters concerning their ascertainment efforts. . . . However, all of these problems have been (or are being) resolved by the staff."

Predictably, the commissioners paid no attention to these statements. By the time the third agenda item (May 1974) under the new rules was drafted, the staff felt even this vague statement to be unnecessary. So the commissioners have heard no more about applicants with "ascertainment defects" in their proposals.

Since 1976, stations place information about ascertainment efforts in their local public inspection files instead of sending it to Washington. Chairman Wiley told the House Communications Subcommittee, "We are not looking at the ascertainments any more; we are putting those in the public file and allowing the citizens to look at that."

The Commission still gets limited information about ascertainment. The first item, an annual "community leader checklist," submitted by 80 percent of licensees (those in communities with populations over 10,000), indicates merely the number of community leaders interviewed each year in various categories "representing institutions and elements commonly found in a community (such as business, government, religion)." (Checklist examples are included in Appendix B.) Assistant Renewal and Transfer Chief James Brown acknowledged to a 1977 NAB convention workshop that the staff had no standards for processing these checklists, and no limits to trigger an automatic investigation. Instead, Brown indicated, the staff felt "the local citizenry" would bring to the FCC's attention deficiencies associated with the annual checklists.

The second item of information, received from all licensees, is an annual listing of up to ten significant community problems and needs, together with typical and illustrative programs broadcast to deal with each. No method to determine the significance of listed problems and the validity of remedial programs has been established; no standards for investigation have been set. By simultaneous examination of the quantitative information on informational programming and the annual listings, the staff might be able to isolate applications for further investigation.

The commissioners give neither the staff nor the licensee much guidance on criteria for meeting community needs. For example, when to air the programs dealing with community problems is left solely to the licensee's "good-faith judgment," which may dictate the hours after 1:00 A.M.

When asked for guidance, Shiben sometimes gave broadcasters instant, on-the-spot policy pronouncements, never thoroughly discussed with the commissioners. Shiben gave ad-lib advice on the nature and frequency of ascertainment interviews and of programming to meet community problems.

In Cole's opinion, Shiben wasn't trying to establish any shortcuts in his division's work—and he certainly wasn't trying to sabotage policy handed down by the commissioners—he was simply filling a vacuum. Shiben was being asked questions that the commissioners had refused to grapple with by people who were trying to follow the FCC's instructions. Shiben judged the need from his past experience: he had taken glaring violations of FCC policy to the seven commissioners on the eighth floor; at best, they ignored the problems laid at their doors— and at worst, they made it plain that they didn't want to be forced to decide knotty questions about which they themselves might be second-guessed (by Congress and the courts).

Meanwhile, the Commission still talks of ascertainment and programming to meet community problems and needs as the "principal ingredient of a licensee's obligation to operate in the public interest." And, although the commissioners have yet to see a renewal application with deficiencies in this area (barring a petition to deny), the Commission's processing rules and its report to Congress both suggest that problem cases are being brought to the commissioners' attention.

COMMERCIAL PRACTICES

The FCC's report to Congress stated that a renewal applicant's commercial practices are examined "from two perspectives." First, performance during the composite week is compared with proposals in the last renewal application, and "substantial differences" between the two mean "the application must be considered by the Commission." Second, the applicant's commercial proposals for the new license period are reviewed, and "if they fall short of specified processing standards, again the Commission itself must consider the application."

In actuality, unless a petition to deny renewal for excesses in commercial practices has been filed, the commissioners never see applications with promise-versus-performance deviations in commercial practices and rarely see applications with proposed commercial policies exceeding the Commission's guidelines (that is, the "specified processing standards"). Such applications are granted on the staff level. Although there is a processing rule to cover commercials, the rule is not strictly enforced. A full understanding of how the guidelines came about and why the commissioners are unwilling to establish specific rules limiting the number of commercials requires some history.

Concern about the amount of commercials broadcasters would present began in the early days of radio and never really ceased. Even in 1922, Herbert Hoover, then Secretary of Commerce in charge of what radio regulation there was, told radio broadcasters, "It is inconceivable that we should allow so great a possibility for service, for news, for entertainment, for education and for vital commercial purposes to be drowned in advertising chatter." In 1928, the first formal statement of the Federal Radio Commission about the "broad underlying principles" that would govern its decisions on who should obtain a frequency declared that "the amount and character of advertising must be rigidly confined within the limits consistent with the public service expected of the station. . . . Advertising must be accepted for the present as the sole means of support of broadcasting, and regulation must be relied upon to prevent the abuse and overabuse of that privilege."

The broadcasting industry adopted a self-regulatory code of commercial standards in 1929: commercial announcements were banned between 7:00 P.M. and 11:00 P.M. Needless to say, not all broadcasters were willing to abide by the code, and there was a gradual relaxation of its provisions. The provisions became so relaxed that the FCC's first major policy statement on programming, in the 1946 *Blue Book,* noted the tremendous number of commercials then appearing on many stations and the "abundant evidence" that the NAB standards were being flouted. Of four program service factors relevant to the public interest, factors to which the Commission had promised particular attention in the future, two concerned commercials: encouraging nonsponsored or sustaining programs to ensure a well-balanced program structure, and eliminating advertising excesses. A revised renewal application form would request applicants to indicate the amount of time per hour they proposed to devote to advertising matter.

By the early 1960s, station logs submitted to the FCC indicated that 40 percent of renewal applicants exceeded the NAB commercial standards during the composite week. In 1962, Commissioner Robert Lee proposed that the existing NAB standards be adopted and enforced as FCC policy. By May 1963, Lee had three supporters and the Commission proposed to adopt rules governing the amount of commercials.

Broadcasters quickly pounced on the Commission's proposal. Many liked the flexibility of the NAB commercial guidelines, which could be followed or ignored, and which couldn't be enforced except through NAB membership. If the Commission adopted as rules this portion of the NAB code, where might it all end? The entire code might become fair game. The broadcasters formed committees in each state to contact congressmen and lobby against the FCC initiative.

By January 1964, the departure of Chairman Newton Minow and the arrival of Commissioner Lee Loevinger meant that there were no longer four votes for the Commission's proposal. Moreover, the lobbying efforts of the broadcasters were working. Largely through the efforts of House Communications Subcommittee Chairman Walter Rogers (D.–Tex.), the House Commerce Committee had passed a bill prohibiting the Commission from adopting any rule governing the length or frequency of commercials. In these circumstances, the Commission unanimously decided to terminate the rulemaking proceeding.

The NAB, however, wanted to make sure that the message came from the full House. On February 24, 1964, the NAB dispatched memos to all member stations marked *"URGENT URGENT URGENT"*: phone or write your Congressman that "a vote for the bill is a vote of confidence in the broadcasting in his district. A vote against the bill would open the door to unlimited governmental control of broadcasting." Three days later the full House passed the bill, 317–43.

Broadcast historians still debate what the Senate would have done had the Commission not terminated its rulemaking, and what the Commission might have done had its composition not changed at a crucial time. What is certain is that this experience patently discouraged the Commission from attempting to adopt rules regarding overcommercialization.

During the late 1960s, the Commission did adopt a policy of questioning renewal applicants whose proposed commercial policies exceeded 18 minutes per hour on radio and 16 minutes per hour on television—not coincidentally, the NAB limits. Gradually exceptions were added: by 1970 radio stations could exceed the limit as often as 10 percent of the time, up to 20 minutes per hour, or 22 minutes per hour "during periods of high demand for political advertising"; moreover, these guidelines applied only to "nonseasonal markets"; in "seasonal markets" (a term never clearly defined), radio stations would not be checked. Television stations could raise their normal commercial ceiling of 16 minutes to 18 minutes, or even 20 minutes in political campaign periods as long as the increases did not exceed 10 percent of the station's total weekly hours of operation.

When proposed commercial policies exceeded Commission guidelines, the staff was supposed to investigate. Instructions at one point required violators to submit midterm reports detailing their actual commercial practices for the past 18 months and proposals for the next 18 months. However, the Commission was not really interested in such reports, and the staff itself was lukewarm about questioning violators. George Smith, Broadcast Bureau chief when this policy was first adopted, told Cole that there should be no limitations on commercials, especially in one-station communities, where reduction of commercials might prevent advertisers' exposure of their goods and services to the public. Renewal and Transfer Chief Robert Rawson, who became deputy chief of the bureau after Smith left, believed that a station with a great deal of advertising must be serving the public interest because its audience was obviously large enough to attract many sponsors. Despite staffers' feelings, the commercial guidelines were still on the books in 1973 and were included in the processing rules.

Renewal applications from Iowa and Missouri (for the license term beginning February 1, 1974) were the first to be processed under the new procedures. In an agenda item to the commissioners, the staff noted that 14 radio stations were proposing to broadcast more than 20 minutes of commercials per hour. The bureau stated that, "where appropriate, further inquiry into the proposed commercial practices was made of the station to clarify its policy. It appears, however, that in all instances none of the proposals for commercial practices are *so excessive* [emphasis added] as to warrant deferral of action on the renewal applications."

In listing the 14 stations and the normal commercial limits proposed, the bureau included proposed "special" limits and summarized, in a column headed "circumstances," when these limits would prevail. One station claimed special limits of 21 to 30 minutes per hour "not over 10 percent of the time"; another proposed a 22-minute commercial policy during the month of December; another proposed a 27-minute limit during "short broadcast days"; and yet another proposed a 25-minute ceiling during emergencies.

When Commissioner Hooks questioned why no rules governed the amount of commercial matter, he was told of the events in 1963 and 1964, and he responded, "How about trying it again? Maybe Congress feels differently now." Other commissioners brushed this aside as a radical suggestion. General Counsel John Pettit suggested that the FCC could bring the matter up at an oversight hearing. Richard Shiben, however, repeated the claim that was echoed again and again during Cole's five years at the Commission: because relatively few stations are involved, "we have no problems with overcommercialization." Commissioner Wiley said, "For all practical purposes, our policy constitutes a rule." No further discussion took place.

Two months later, however, with Commissioner Wiley now Chairman Wiley, and a new group of renewal applicants (all the stations in Colorado, Minnesota, Montana, North Dakota, and South Dakota), 21 more stations exceeded Commission guidelines for commercial proposals. A Minnesota station proposed a commercial ceiling of 30 minutes per hour and estimated that the limit would probably be reached no more than 15 percent of the time. A North Dakota station proposed a policy of 25 minutes of commercials during "drive time" (7:00 A.M. to 9:00 A.M.) each weekday morning and again between 12 noon and 1:00 P.M. daily. A Montana station listed its policy of a 21-minute limit not over 20 percent of the weekly hours broadcast. Wiley expressed shock at the commercial proposals and surprise at the bureau's statement that "none of the proposals for commercial practices are so excessive as to warrant deferral of action on the renewal applications." What, Wiley wondered, might be sufficiently excessive to hold up renewal? The bureau did not respond.

Wiley instructed the bureau to provide more details regarding the commercial policies of stations in the next renewal group. He wanted to know how stations could justify such practices—practices he later told Cole were "inexcusable." Wiley suggested that it would be inconsistent with his announced principles to permit some stations to violate a policy that was well known and adhered to by most stations.

The May 30, 1974, agenda item for the next renewal group contained some additional information on five stations whose commercial proposals violated Commission guidelines, but whose explanations in the renewal applications satisfied the bureau. In 11 other cases, the bureau hadn't considered the explanations satisfactory, and additional inquiries had been sent; but the inquiries were still unanswered when the agenda item was drafted.

The commissioners' lack of interest in the explanations to be received from the 11 stations, as well as in the additional information provided about the five stations, prompted the staff to revert in its next agenda item (July 31, 1974) to the earlier format of simply listing call letters, giving commercial limits, and indicating in a word or two the circumstances governing these limits. By September 1974, the agenda items didn't include even that limited information: without giving any station call letters, the bureau merely announced that 17 stations proposed commercial excesses and that "each of these stations has been requested either to conform to the Commission's guidelines on commercialization or to furnish public interest justification for their policies."

Some of the offenders fell in line; others did not. The case of a South Carolina AM station illustrates how showdowns are avoided. For the renewal period beginning December 1, 1975, the licensee proposed a normal commercial policy of 20 minutes per hour with exceptions up to 24 minutes per hour. In spite of several letters from the renewal branch, the licensee, whose proposals had been excessive since 1966, refused to lower the current proposal to the guideline limit of 18 minutes per hour. The staff, knowing the commissioners really didn't want to force the issue, eventually wrote the licensee that he could promise whatever he wanted, but the FCC would hold him to the Commission's commercial guidelines. The station was then granted an ordinary, unconditional renewal. If the staff were really serious, they could hold a station to the guidelines by asking for reports during the license period (as the Commission used to do at the end of 18 months), or by periodically checking the station's program logs. Actually, in the South Carolina case, the staff will simply wait for the next renewal application and hope that the licensee doesn't exceed the guidelines during the composite week: if he does, the staff will find other means of avoiding the issue for at least another three years.

The commissioners' failure to discuss problems of commercial limits underlies the staff's laxity. When stations might reasonably be allowed to exceed the guidelines was never discussed. Instead, the licensees permitted to propose more are those daring to insist on more. Nor is the Commission interested in determining which stations fall under the guidelines. For example, theoretically only "nonseasonal market" stations are bound by the guidelines, but the definitions of seasonal and nonseasonal markets have not been discussed at any Commission meeting since at least October 1970.

The commissioners' lack of involvement in commercial problems is even more striking when one remembers that they are to see only *proposed* violations, not actual violations, which are supposedly covered by the promise-versus-performance rule. Under the 1974 processing rule requirement that applications "which vary substantially from prior representations with respect to . . . commercial practices" be brought to the commissioners, none was brought. The 1976 revised processing rule, officially reflecting the Commission's lack of interest, limited still further the applications to be brought to the commissioners: only those with deviations "for which variation there is lacking in the judgment of the Broadcast Bureau adequate justification in the public interest." Thus far "adequate justification" has been found for every renewal application unless a petition to deny renewal was filed.

Whether or not Congress would now be as quick to resist Commission attempts to adopt commercialization rules is academic: the Commission is reluctant even to admit the existence of a policy on commercialization, let alone enforce it or suggest its adoption as a rule. In June 1976, for example, *Broadcasting* (June 14) reported that, at a banquet of Mutual Broadcasting's affiliate advisory board, Wiley "brushed off" a question on the Commission's guidelines, saying the standards were in the NAB code, not in FCC rules. According to *Broadcasting*, some of the audience left "wondering whether lawyers had misled them into believing 18 minutes per hour of commercial time was an FCC standard."

Actually, the NAB code is tougher on amounts of commercials than the FCC is. Those radio stations that belong to the code adhere strictly to 18 minutes of commercials per hour with no exceptions. In June 1977, the NAB radio code board was directed to consider amending the time standards to permit more flexibility consistent with the FCC processing rules that allow exceeding the 18-minute limit 10 percent of the time, or to consider having no time limitations at all.

Television, too, has a code stricter than the FCC's guidelines. Television stations that are NAB code members (roughly two-thirds of all stations) must abide by a 16-minute-per-hour limit with no exceptions. Moreover, the NAB code contains separate commercial standards for prime time: 9½ minutes per hour for network affiliates, and 12 minutes per hour for independents. Prime-time commercial practices and policies fall under no special FCC guidelines and are not mentioned in the processing rule despite the specific questions on past and proposed, prime-time commercial practices in the renewal form. The Commission has, however, officially expressed interest in commercial practices in programs designed for children. (This matter will be discussed in the case study on children's television.)

EQUAL EMPLOYMENT OPPORTUNITY (EEO)

The FCC told Congress: "An EEO specialist checks the [EEO] program for compliance with Commission rules, and determines whether the EEO program, any complaints, and the station's annual employment reports indicate that the station's employment practices are compatible with its public interest responsibilities. As in other areas, deficiencies result in submission of the application for Commission action."

In fact, between 1970, when the EEO rule took effect, and spring 1977, only a small portion of those stations with EEO deficiencies was brought to the commissioners for review. Moreover, the EEO forms used by the FCC are inadequate.

Of all regulatory agencies, only the FCC has adopted rules against discrimination in employment by its licensees. The Commission considers the licensee's employment practices to the extent that they raise questions about the licensee's character qualifications and affect his obligation to provide programming that fairly reflects the tastes and viewpoints of minority groups.

The FCC rule was adopted after some reluctance. In 1967, the United Church of Christ petitioned the Commission to end discrimination in employment by broadcast stations. In 1968 the Commission announced a policy against discrimination. However, not until the expert agencies, like the Equal Employment Opportunity Committee (EEOC) and the U.S. Commission on Civil Rights, told the Commission that policies and complaint-oriented procedures wouldn't work, did the FCC adopt compliance-oriented procedures and rules.

In May 1970, with only four commissioners in favor, the Commission decided to require licensees with five or more full-time employees to file annual employment reports listing the number of blacks, Orientals, American Indians, and Spanish-surnamed Americans in nine job categories, which were taken from an EEOC form. In 1971, because of pressure from feminist organizations, especially the National Organization for Women, women were added to the list. Moreover, stations had to submit, as part of their renewal applications, written equal employment opportunity programs, which detailed efforts to recruit minorities and women. The annual reports and the EEO programs are central to the limited scrutiny that equal employment practices receive from the Commission.

In 1976, the Commission eased EEO requirements by limiting the filing of EEO programs at renewal time to about one-third of all licensees (those with ten or more full-time employees). This action caused the citizen groups interested in EEO to complain to Congress. These groups have now taken their appeal to the U.S. Court of Appeals (New York district).

Although the equal employment programs required from the stations have been less than illuminating, citizen groups insist on the potential value of such information. Everett Parker told Senator Pastore, "Candor compels me to admit that most of these programs are not worth reading, because they simply parrot the general language in the FCC regulations." Parker added, however, that the programs "could become meaningful" with the adoption of the recommendations in the November 1974 report of the U.S. Commission on Civil Rights. These recommendations would require the FCC to orient its policies toward achieving results and to demand more specific and relevant information from licensees.

The job categories on licensees' annual reports were the focus of the Civil Rights Commission's recommendations. Borrowed from EEOC, these categories, including skilled craftsman, semiskilled operative, and unskilled laborer, are not relevant to broadcasting. Consequently, as the Civil Rights Commission said, it is "extremely difficult to determine from the forms the nature of the positions occupied by minorities and women." The Civil Rights Commission's analysis of eight stations showed these problems: stations failed to agree on the category for job titles; each of eight job titles was classified under three different categories; and one job title was listed under four categories. In the officials and managers category, male minority employees were given titles like "Supervisor of News Graphics" and "Manager of Building Services"; and women, "Supervisor of Word Processing" and "Administrator of Motion Picture Scheduling."

The inadequacy of the categories was recognized from the beginning, even by the Broadcast Bureau, which had opposed the adoption of EEO rules. The Broadcast Bureau and others, including the National Association of Educational Broadcasters, recommended that the Commission design a statistical report more relevant to the broadcasting industry if a report was going to be required. However, stations with more than 100 employees were already filling out forms for the EEOC; and the Commission majority, in 1970, expressed its reluctance to overburden these stations by requiring them to provide additional, parallel information for the FCC. The Commission, in its 1976 clarification of EEO policies, declined to change the categories. Citizen groups believe that this action is indicative of the low priority most commissioners place on equal employment opportunity in broadcasting.

Initially the Commission ignored the annual statistical reports. Procedures for processing the information were not developed until the

United Church of Christ used the statistics to request a Commission inquiry into certain stations' EEO practices, and Commissioner Johnson did his own study of similar data.

In 1972, the Commission instructed the staff to request further information from stations that had ten or more employees, were located in markets with at least 5 percent minority population, and showed one or more of the following shortcomings: (1) zero blacks or other minorities, (2) zero women, (3) a reduction in the number of blacks and minorities from the previous years, or (4) a similar reduction in the number of women. These four criteria were, according to the Civil Rights Commission's report, "severely restrictive and inadequate for analyzing minority and female underutilization . . . [and] tend to focus on small stations and ignore a number of relevant factors," such as the variation in cities' percentages of minority populations. In Philadelphia, where minority percentages are high, a station need employ only one black and one woman (or even one black woman) to satisfy FCC standards. Moreover, the FCC "completely ignores the occupational segregation facing females and minorities in the broadcasting industry"; stations need employ them only in office and clerical jobs and in stable numbers to avoid FCC inquiry.

The Broadcast Bureau, too, disapproved of the criteria. When the first agenda item that included stations failing to meet the criteria was presented, the staff stated, "We suggest that the Commission refrain from instituting further such inquiries pending the establishment of a more effective EEO compliance program."

The FCC had planned to send letters to all stations that failed to meet the criteria, but the list was so long that the Commission instructed the staff to "make the list more manageable" before sending letters. In some renewal groups, as many as a third of the stations failed to meet the four criteria, but most were not asked for further information.

The Commission agreed that, to isolate stations that should be investigated, it should adopt a "zone of reasonableness standard"—the court's term for an appropriate criterion for determining satisfactory EEO efforts. The courts do not expect that percentages of blacks and women in a community will equate exactly with percentages employed by the local station; the ratio should be in a zone of reasonableness, which takes account of the number of blacks and women in the service area and in the labor force.

In March 1977, nearly five years after the court had presented the concept of zone of reasonableness standard, the Commission finally decided to act. The staff was instructed to henceforth examine the EEO policies of renewal applicants whose hiring practices failed to meet two criteria: (1) minorities and women employees should represent at least one-half of their respective percentages of the market's work force, and (2) at least one-fourth of these percentages should be in the top four job categories (officials, professionals, technicians, and salesworkers). How many of these stations will receive a detailed FCC investigation of EEO practices remains to be seen; the number of stations below the zone of reasonableness is too great to permit all the investigations that may be warranted.

Under new EEO processing standards, the renewal applications from stations with five to nine full-time employees (almost one-third of all stations) and with "an absence" of minorities were also to be checked. Previously the staff hadn't been looking at the employment reports filed by this size station unless a complaint had been raised. The June 1, 1977, Texas renewal applicants were the first stations affected by the new policy. The staff interpreted "an absence" of minorities to mean that no minority employees were indicated in any of the licensee's latest three annual employment reports. Thirty-two Texas stations with five to nine full-time employees fell into this category, a figure far higher than many expected. In all, more than 100 Texas applications were deferred because of the new processing standards.

The Commission has said that its EEO approach "is prospective, seeking to lead a licensee who has not possessed an adequate affirmative action program in the past to adopt policies ensuring an active recruitment program and genuine equal employment opportunity in the future." The FCC is reluctant to punish stations for past wrongs as long as the stations' future policies will be adequate.

In the meantime, EEO-related problems consume the great bulk of the time of Renewal Branch Chief Henry Baumann, and the number of conditional renewals is increasing because of EEO employment statistics and responses to staff inquiry. By June 1976, the Commission had issued conditional license renewals to 202 stations, 155 on the Commission's own motion rather than because of a petition to deny. A conditional renewal generally means that the station must provide specific updated information about its efforts to improve its EEO profile during the course of the new renewal period.

In rare instances, the Commission has issued a short-term renewal because of EEO deficiencies. A station owner in Rochester, N.Y., received a short-term renewal because no blacks had been employed full time at *either* his AM or his FM stations in the past five years—since the annual EEO reporting requirement was instituted. The number of such short-term renewals may increase in the future, following a May 1977 court decision (discussed in Chapter 14) about an EEO-related petition to deny.

Employment of blacks and women has certainly risen since the Commission adopted its EEO rules and reporting requirements, but the extent of the improvement is open to debate. In January 1977, the FCC published the results of the 1976 annual statistical reports from stations with five or more full-time employees: women represented 26.2 percent (41,527) of the total number of employees (150,783);

blacks, 8.3 percent (12,654); Spanish-surnamed, 3.7 percent (5660); Orientals, 0.8 percent (1259); and American Indians, 0.4 percent (706). The FCC said that each of these percentages, except the American Indian percentage, which remained the same, was higher than in the previous year. The first annual statistics, compiled in 1971 by the United Church of Christ from FCC reports, showed minorities were only 9 percent of the total employees and women were 22 percent.

Citizen groups are not satisfied with the FCC statistics. United Church's own calculation of the year's annual employment reports suggests that stations misclassify job categories, especially higher-level categories: 78 percent of the full-time jobs in television are listed as managerial, professional, technical, or sales. Moreover, "paper promotions" have taken place: since 1971, 6122 upper-level jobs have been created while 3024 lower-level posts have disappeared.

Citizen groups maintain also that the rate of improvement has decreased and that the decrease began when the industry first realized (in 1974) that renewals would not be threatened by EEO deficiencies. An April 1976 Citizens Communication Center (CCC) study of 1975 annual employment reports revealed that 378 commercial stations with ten or more employees in areas with at least five-percent minority population employed *no* minority, full-time employees. An August 1976 CCC study on employment shows the situation in public broadcasting was no better and in some ways worse: 27.9 percent of all public radio and television stations receiving federal funds and submitting EEO reports in 1975 failed to employ any minority group members full-time.

ENGINEERING REVIEW

The FCC told Congress:

> An engineer reviews the technical portion of the application to ensure that the applicant's operation conforms with the terms of the station license and that it does not violate the Commission's technical rules. More detailed information is considered for those stations with recent histories of technical problems, those selected to submit additional information under a sampling program, and those inspected by engineers of the Commission's Field Operations Bureau.

The Commission's single-paragraph description of its engineering review is incomplete, omitting some important facts. Moreover, it suggests the information available and examined is the same for radio and television stations, which it is not.

The FCC's Field Operations Bureau inspects approximately 40 percent of the stations during each three-year period; stations found to have numerous, serious, technical violations are normally visited once during every renewal period; other stations are not inspected for many years. The results of these inspections were reported by the FCC to the

Senate Appropriations Subcommittee in 1972: 70 percent of the stations inspected violated some technical rule; 50 percent were guilty of technical violations serious enough to affect the quality of their broadcast signals; and approximately the same percentages occurred every year during a five-year period. General Counsel Pettit, in a September 1972 speech to the Nevada Broadcasters Association, cited the 70 percent and suggested that this demonstrated the need for simpler rules, not for stricter regulation.

A technical inspection is conducted usually without advance warning to the licensee. An FCC representative appears at the station's front door one day and tells whoever is there that the station is about to be the privileged recipient of an inspection. Periodically, the NAB's Radio Reregulation Committee, established to work with the FCC Reregulation Task Force to update and simplify FCC regulations, disapproves of this lack of warning. The committee told the Commission in December 1976 that stations should receive advance notice of technical inspections because an inspection should be *educational* in nature, not punitive.

As part of the deregulation program advocated by Chairman Wiley, the FCC, in amending 375 of its technical rules in the broadcast services, had by May 1976 dropped requirements that licensees submit technical information and claimed that greater reliance would be placed on spot checks of stations. In September 1975, Wiley publicly cautioned the Field Operations Bureau not to be overzealous in monitoring broadcasters' technical operations. He told a Washington IEEE audience that he was not suggesting that the integrity of the rules be compromised, but rather that there be a "modicum of understanding of the licensee's good faith efforts to bring operations into compliance."

What happens to a station found in violation of a number of technical rules? Usually very little. In one case where the licensee was found guilty of 87 technical violations at three stations during a three-year period, all three stations were renewed. Stations may be fined for technical violations; but if they have not misrepresented the facts to the Commission, by falsifying technical logs for example, and if they promise to mend their ways, normally nothing else will happen. Nonetheless, in the short list of stations denied renewal there is a high percentage of those whose crime was originally associated with technical violations and who attempted to avoid penalties by lying.

In theory, the FCC could help bring stations up to snuff technically by inspecting operating logs submitted with renewal applications; in practice, this was too great a burden for FCC personnel. During some of Cole's years at the Commission, as many as 25 to 30 percent of the applications placed on deferral could not be renewed because of problems associated with the transmitter logs. The Commission solved the problem in May 1976; the FCC decided to stop asking radio licensees to submit the logs:

While analysis of logs has revealed some technical deficiencies, the number has been small compared with the vast amount of time required to review the hundreds of logs submitted each renewal period. We think it will be a better use of our engineering staff to devote less time to reviewing these logs and more time to those stations with problems.

Other technical exhibits were also eliminated in the new radio renewal form. The Commission acknowledged that "analysis of more detailed technical data may reveal problems not otherwise discoverable" and said, "For this reason, we will conduct a sampling program, periodically asking selected licensees to submit operating and maintenance logs and other required technical reports for Commission review." It is too soon to determine how serious the Commission is about asking selected licensees to file such information.

In the meantime, the Commission's approval of automatic transmitter systems for most stations will mean elimination of the requirement to make periodic transmitter readings. This elimination should reduce the number of technical violations and make it easier for the licensee to be technically qualified for renewal.

In the matter of engineering review, as elsewhere, what the FCC reported to Congress was the theory of renewal, not the actual process of renewal.

12
Policies Swept under the Rug

I think it would be in the public interest for the Commission to spend less time processing what now amounts to 3000 renewal applications each year and to focus more thorough attention on those few licensees whose failure to meet their responsibilities also is a disservice to the vast majority of conscientious broadcasters.

Commissioner Margita White
American Women in Radio and Television
1977 convention

12

In outlining the rules for renewal to Congress in October 1976, the Federal Communications Commission failed to cite certain areas as part of the renewal process. It is instructive to note what areas were omitted and why.

LOCAL PROGRAMMING

At one point in its report to Congress, talking about comparative renewal proceedings (involving more than one applicant), the Commission cited local and informational programming as "the two important areas to focus on in evaluating a renewal application." However, in the discussion of processing ordinary renewal applications, local programming was not mentioned. The reason is that only network affiliates and VHF, independent, commercial television stations are subject to a processing rule on local programming. The limited provisions of that rule are such that the FCC may have felt better off not referring to it, even in passing.

From the start, Congress has been committed to local broadcasting: both the 1927 Radio Act and the Communications Act of 1934 stressed the concept of locally based broadcasting. In 1962, Congress enacted the all-channel law, which requires television receivers to be capable of receiving both VHF and UHF. To quote the report of the House Committee on Interstate and Foreign Commerce on the all-channel bill, "The goal is a commercial television system which will be not only truly competitive on a national scale in all large centers of population, but would permit all communities of appreciable size to have at least one television station as an outlet for local self-expression."

The Commission, following the lead of Congress, theoretically maintains the importance of local broadcasting. Section 307(b) of the Communications Act requires the FCC to allocate licenses so as "to provide a fair, efficient, and equitable distribution of radio service." On this authority, the Commission devised a table for allocating TV and FM stations that places a higher priority on every community's having a station than on how many signals even the largest communities receive. The Commission has chosen not to establish national or regional, high-power, clear channel TV or FM stations, which could have simultaneously covered large areas, ensured more people a larger number of stations, and saved valuable frequency space.

The Commission's emphasis on the importance of local service to meet local problems gives preference to local applicants who are involved in the station's day-to-day operations. By 1946, the Commission was already referring to "the consistent Commission policy of encouraging a reasonable proportion of local programs as part of a well-balanced program service." In the 1960 policy statement, the Commission's current, basic, programming policy pronouncement, opportunity for local self-expression and development of local talent were the first two "major elements usually necessary to meet the public interest, needs and desires of the community in which the station is located."

Furthermore, the Commission emphasized that local programming should be broadcast during hours when listeners are most likely to be tuned in. By 1941, when defending its attempts to reduce the amount of network control in radio, the Commission was referring to its "consistent intention . . . to assure that an adequate amount of time during the good listening hours shall be made available to meet the needs of the community in terms of public expression and of local interest." Thirty-three years later, in 1974, when amending the prime-time access rule, which restricts the amount of network programming carried by local television stations in prime time, the Commission indicated that it expected some local programming to be presented during prime-time hours.

When cable TV was developed, the importance of local programming became the primary justification for protecting local television and radio broadcasters from the unregulated growth of cable. In 1977, the NAB is attempting to prevent the importing of distant radio signals by cable systems and asserting that cable systems should be required to carry local radio signals, if the systems choose to carry radio signals at all. The main rationale is that local radio service is unique and important; its preservation is jeopardized because cable's carrying distant radio signals further fractionalizes the audience and results in revenue loss for local radio stations.

Cable development is not the only technological change that threatens existing over-the-air broadcasting and causes defenders of the status quo to call for a rally to the flag of localism. Chairman Wiley and Commissioner Quello, along with other commissioners, have warned broadcasters of the need to improve local service because of the satellite-to-home broadcasting "threat on the horizon." Quello told his audience at an NAB Regional Conference in November 1976, "Local service might well emerge as the sole justification for the continued existence of our present system for broadcasting."

The continuing theoretical importance of local broadcast service is shown in a recent court decision about the reassignment of the AM frequency originally allocated to KRLA in Pasadena, California. KRLA lost its license in 1962 because of fraudulent contests and misrepresentations to the FCC.

When twenty applicants filed for the frequency, a comparative hearing began and, typically, dragged on for years. As Cornell Law Professor Robert Anthony, chairman of the Administrative Conference of the United States, said:

The process of comparative decision has been widely and continuingly assailed as unpredictable, excessively discretionary, complex and

baffling, deficiently consonant with the rule of law, and producing results that seem inconsistent from case to case. There is truth in all
of these charges.

Anthony could also have said that an FCC comparative hearing can
last for years, especially when many applicants are involved, as in the
KRLA case. Eleven years later, in December 1973 (an interim operator
for KRLA had been approved), the Commission finally decided to
award the frequency to Western Broadcasting because the company
would make the "most efficient use" of the frequency, by operating a
full-time station in Pasadena with authorized power of 50,000 watts (the
maximum for AM) during the day and 10,000 watts at night.

When three of the remaining applicants appealed the decision, the
court remanded the case to the FCC in May 1977. The remand noted
that while the Communications Act does refer to "most efficient use"
of frequencies, it also calls for "equitable distribution of radio service."
The court indicated that preference should have been given to an applicant who wanted to locate in Newport, which is 50 miles south of Pasadena, because, unlike Pasadena, Newport did not already have another
station. Because the Newport applicant would provide a daytime service
only and would operate with 1000 watts of power, his station would
reach only 3 million people compared with the 5 million Western
Broadcasting would have reached. However, a station in Newport would
be providing the first *local* service to the people of that community.

Local programming, for all its theoretical importance, was not included in the 1974 renewal processing rules. Finally, in 1976, the Commission added a processing rule relating to the amount of local service
provided by television licensees. In explaining this belated action, the
FCC said simply, "We have long recognized, of course, the importance
of any broadcast facility's function as a locally oriented transmission
service, not only with respect to nonentertainment but also sports and
entertainment programming."

The new processing rule provides that commercial television renewal
applicants, except UHF independents, who propose less than five-percent local programs between 6:00 A.M. and midnight be automatically
referred to the commissioners. Thus far the commissioners have seen no
such applications, largely because the five-percent figure can be easily
met by most stations. Furthermore, the processing rule has several important limitations that should be noted.

First, the rule does not apply to radio. The Commission eliminated
the category of local programming from the new, short-form, radio
renewal application; no reason was given for the action, but it certainly
precluded any processing rule governing local programming. And the
NAB's argument for protection of local radio from the growth of cable

can be neither supported nor contested by information gathered by the Commission's renewal form. Radio broadcasters argue that all radio programming is local; cable operators counter that the only thing local about most radio service is the announcer's location. Cable operators also refer to the increasing number of fully automated stations (about one-fifth of all radio stations in the United States), using syndicated pre-taped programming services.

Second, the processing rule on local programming refers only to the *total* proposed and makes irrelevant detailed information on the television renewal form regarding proposed *types* of local programs, including proposed amounts of local news, local public affairs, and so forth. Moreover, with such a low percentage (only 5 percent) involved, a station's total local output could be unrelated to the kind of local informational programs both Congress and the FCC intended to deal with community problems and needs.

Third, despite the FCC's lip service to the general subject, the processing rule has no reference to prime-time local programming. A station may or may not choose to put on a local newscast in the evening, depending on the profitability. Examination of the Commission's annual programming reports suggests that if the Commission did have a processing rule for prime-time local programming, even one as low as 5 percent, a number of applications would theoretically have been headed for review by the commissioners.

Fourth, like the nonentertainment and commercialization processing rules, this rule refers only to proposed programming, not to actual programming. Therefore, all annual programming report information on local programming presented during the license period is irrelevant to the local programming processing rule. True, the Commission's promise-versus-performance processing rule could catch some delinquent stations; but variations between promise and performance are permitted, provided there is "adequate justification." Unless the Commission gives the staff new signals, the Commission will continue not to see stations with inadequate local programming.

Fifth, UHF independents are exempted from possible review by the commissioners. Staffers were directed not to worry about the UHF independents because of their "special situation": 1976 financial statistics showed 63.9 percent of independent UHF stations were profitable, as compared with 68.4 percent of affiliated UHF stations and 90.9 percent of all VHF stations. The Commission's reluctance to put UHF independent stations out of business is understandable, but a growing number of these stations are now profitable. In obtaining their licenses, most UHF independents made a number of local programming promises far in excess of 5 percent between 6:00 A.M. and midnight. It may be time for the Commission to reconsider and for at least the profitable UHF independents to make good on their promises.

PUBLIC SERVICE ANNOUNCEMENTS

A public service announcement (PSA) is an announcement broadcast free of charge for a governmental, nonprofit, or community organization. *Access* (May 17, 1976) succinctly states the importance of PSAs: "Public service announcements offer nonprofit organizations the opportunity to use the techniques of their commercial counterparts to increase their visibility and to present new messages and ideas to the public."

In its report, the FCC did not tell Congress about the importance of public service announcements in the evaluation of renewal applications because PSAs are not mentioned in any of the processing rules. Although the renewal forms for commercial radio and television stations solicit information on the broadcasting of PSAs, and the Commission makes periodic public statements about PSAs' importance, the answers to the PSAs' questions are normally ignored completely by the processing staff.

The Commission has said through the years that PSAs are important but has never established any guidelines regarding their frequency and scheduling. Because the commissioners have never shown any interest in including PSAs in the processing rules for renewals, large discrepancies exist in the PSA policies of stations throughout the country. In the study of network affiliates in the top 50 television markets, done soon after Cole arrived at the Commission, the PSA frequency range among stations in the same groupings was staggering: in markets 26–50, one network affiliate broadcast 503 PSAs during its composite week while another broadcast only 37; a UHF independent station broadcast only six PSAs during the same week.

The Commission did adopt Cole's suggestion that the new television renewal form divide PSA promise and performance into different time periods and different categories. Now, although television licensees still needn't state the number of prime-time PSAs, PSAs broadcast between 8:00 A.M. and 11:00 P.M. are separated from those broadcast at other hours. Licensees must indicate also whether the PSA benefits a local organization, a nonlocal organization, or an organization in a third, mixed category.

Lack of FCC guidance leads to licensees' arbitrary choice of the number of PSAs and often to a minimum of PSAs. A November 1976 study by the Association of National Advertisers revealed that of the total programming broadcast by the three network-owned-and-operated television stations in New York City, only 0.76 percent of air time between 7:00 A.M. and 3:00 A.M. was devoted to PSAs. Of course these are three of the most lucrative stations in the country; less prosperous stations often donate even less time to PSAs, unless they cannot sell the time.

Because PSAs on television aren't scheduled for optimum impact but often are inserted wherever time is unsold, a PSA may have little relevance for its audience. Robert Choate, Director of the Council on Children's Media and Merchandising, monitored broadcasting by network affiliates on a Saturday morning in January 1973, when toy manufacturers had withdrawn their Christmas advertising, and a lull in commercial demand increased the number of PSAs: children watching their favorite cartoon shows were advised, among other things, that the National Alliance of Businessmen wants to get all men working; the Army wants young men in ROTC; and religion keeps marriages together. Conversely, Choate has documented that PSAs directed at children frequently are broadcast after 11:00 P.M. or during the school day.

Although the Commission has shown no interest in setting guidelines, let alone rules, governing PSAs, at least the television renewal form now provides some specific information about scheduling and type of PSAs. The new radio renewal form, however, retains the old questions on the total number of PSAs broadcast during the composite week and the number proposed during a typical week in the new renewal period. The Commission's explanation was this:

> We recognize that the number of such announcements broadcast, standing by itself, does not give a complete indication of the licensee's efforts in this regard. . . . We would stress, however, that we expect licensees to make a good faith effort to tailor and schedule PSAs so as to enhance their effectiveness and to provide a meaningful service to the public. That is, exclusive scheduling of PSAs in "grave-yard" hours or perfunctory treatment of such announcements could fall short of the reasonable effort we would encourage.

This pronouncement could have had a positive impact on diversifying the types and increasing the amount of PSAs broadcast on radio; but unfortunately, the licensees probably weren't aware of the statement. It was not sent out in a public notice; it was not even included in the renewal form's detailed, question-by-question explanation, sent to all radio licensees at renewal time. A sharp-eyed communications lawyer might have read the words in the *Federal Register* or on the Commission's press release table in its public information office. If the lawyer were exceptionally conscientious, he or she might have called the admonition to the attention of clients; but a sharp-eyed lawyer might also have read between the lines that the FCC really doesn't much care.

In the meantime, some radio stations that broadcast no public service announcements whatever during the composite week are routinely renewed. Cole saw renewal applications in which the applicant simply didn't bother to fill out the space for the number of PSAs proposed for the new renewal period. As Commissioner Quello told the Southern California Broadcasters Association in March 1976, "I am aware of the practice by some broadcasters of refining the form of the public service announcement to the point where the least possible amount of air time is consumed and the greatest possible amount of commercial availability time is preserved."

The importance of PSAs to nonprofit community organizations and citizen groups prompted 67 of them and five members of Congress to petition the Commission in June 1976 to impose PSB requirements on both radio and television. The proposed rules would require, among other things, that a station broadcast at least three PSAs (lasting a total of at least 90 seconds) during each two consecutive hours, including prime time in television and drive time in radio. In addition, a minimum of 25 percent of all PSAs must be either produced or sponsored by a local organization or chapter of a national group; and a substantial portion of these local PSAs would have to concern the community's ascertained problems and needs.

The petitioners documented some of the difficulties experienced in obtaining PSA time on local stations. Congressman Timothy Wirth (D.–Colo.), of the House Communications Subcommittee, suggested in a February 1977 letter to Wiley that the documentation was sufficient and, "What remains now is for the Commission to conduct its own study to determine how widespread these difficulties are and what is the most appropriate remedy."

The chances are remote, however, that the present Commission will take any action towards adopting specific rules or even policies regarding PSA practices. In August 1976, the Commission, by a 6 to 1 vote (Hooks dissenting), denied a request, which had been made in the November 1973 petition by the National Black Media Coalition, that 30 percent of PSAs be locally originated with at least 25 percent of these to be broadcast in prime time. The Commission said, "NBMC has not shown why PSA's should be given greater attention than it is [sic] presently accorded in order for the Commission to determine how well a licensee has satisfied its overall programming responsibilities during its license term." And, two months later, during a discussion of attempts to get the Commission to adopt policies regarding scheduling a minimum number of PSAs throughout the day, including prime time, Commissioner Washburn said he was "philosophically opposed" to requirements which "needlessly impinge" on the broadcaster's discretion to schedule the broadcast day as the licensee feels best serves community needs.

ENTERTAINMENT PROGRAMMING AND FORMAT CHANGE

Although the Commission's report discussed the importance of non-entertainment programming in the consideration of the renewal application, mention of entertainment programming was avoided for good reason. The Commission has tried to stay clear of prescribing entertainment programming, including entertainment formats of radio stations.

The audience's primary concern about radio is the local station's format. Citizen groups have objected to format changes by licensees, particularly when the station is the only one in the listening area with a particular format, such as classical music or all-news. Citizen groups have sought also to block station sales when format changes were proposed. The court of appeals has found listeners' objections justified although recent Commissions have said that program formats should not be an FCC concern.

On the radio license renewal form used prior to May 1976, applicants were asked what format they used and proposed to use during the next renewal period, and how the format contributed to the overall diversity of programming services. The FCC ignored both answers without exception. Not that licensees' answers would have helped much: one station described its format as "the only factual local news"; another, as "the only alive good music station." The commissioners were not interested in retaining any question about program format on the new renewal form because they were resisting court pressures to respond to petition to deny licenses on the same issue. Even so, the question of what format a radio broadcaster was following and what format he proposed for the next renewal period was kept on the new form; but the Commission made it clear that the question was retained only because of pending court decisions, and the answer would have no bearing on renewal.

Two months after adopting the new radio form with the format question, the FCC concluded an inquiry into changes in entertainment formats of broadcast stations. The FCC decided that:

> Our reflection, aided by extensive public comment on virtually every aspect of this matter, has fortified our conviction that our regulation of entertainment formats as an aspect of the public interest would produce an unnecessary and menacing entanglement in matters that Congress meant to leave to private discretion. . . . Any such regulatory scheme would be flatly inconsistent with our understanding of congressional policy as manifested in the Communications Act, contraproductive in terms of maximizing the welfare of the radio-listening public, administratively a fearful and comprehensive nightmare, and unconstitutional as an impermissibly chilling innovation and experimentation in radio programming.

While the question of FCC regulation of radio program formats is unresolved in the courts, the Renewal and Transfer Division has advised licensees to say as little as possible in answering the renewal form questions about program format. Division Chief Richard Shiben told broadcasters at an NAB regional conference to "be vague" in their answers. Assistant Chief James Brown told an audience at the 1977 NAB annual convention that the small spaces for answers on the renewal form were designed specifically to avoid lengthy explanations;

one- or two-word responses, such as "rock" or "good music," were ideal. "Please don't bind yourself in and give yourself a greater headache down the road." Brown cautioned licensees especially against specifying what portion of the format might be devoted to a specific type of programming (such as 80 percent "country and western" and 20 percent "middle of the road"): "Whatever you do, don't give a percentage."

RENEWALS OF NONCOMMERCIAL (PUBLIC) STATIONS

The FCC report to Congress talks of "licensees" and "renewal applicants" as if all licensees filled out the same form and were subject to the same Commission review. In fact, noncommercial stations fill out a quite different form and are not subject to any of the various Commission processing rules.

The renewal form is identical for all noncommercial or public broadcasting stations (from a ten-watt FM station to a channel 13 in New York). The section on programming (included in Appendix B) is perfunctory. There have been three traditional questions. (1) For a seven-day period, selected at the licensee's discretion from the most recent school term (past year), the licensee is asked to list total percentages devoted to each of six categories of programming: educational, instructional, performing arts, news and public affairs, classical, and all other. (2) The licensee is asked to indicate whether any "material" changes in program service are anticipated during the next renewal period and, if so, what changes. (3) The licensee is asked whether the station is a member of a network and, if so, which network.

The licensee has great leeway because he or she can pick *any* consecutive seven-day period during the past year for the composite week, and because no processing rules are applied to noncommercial stations' applications. The programming percentages will be totally ignored by the renewal branch as long as the six percentages total 100 percent. In addition, the answer to question (2) does not reflect a promise to which the licensee may be held accountable: even though the renewal applicant answers question (2) with a "no," the licensee has not promised to continue to maintain the existing percentages and balance between the various program categories. As a result, the public broadcaster has no worry about promise versus performance, even if a petition to deny renewal has been filed.

In March 1976, the Commission acknowledged that educational stations really need not provide *any* educational or instructional programming. A petition for rulemaking filed in May 1972 by the Corporation for Public Broadcasting (CPB), seeking changes in FCC rules on educational FM stations, was used as a general framework when the Commission issued a notice four years later; under "Issues to be Resolved," the Commission stated:

As the Commission rules now describe the station's obligation, it is called upon to pursue an educational program and to describe the nature of that program when applying for a station. However, nowhere is the term "educational program" defined. As a result, there has been a confusion about whether this meant a station was necessarily obliged to offer educational programming, and if so, did it need to be educational in the instructional sense or was it meant to be broader. Also, what is the role of information and cultural programming in the schedule of these stations . . . . Thus, [the petition] raises the question of whether the current ambiguous situation should be allowed to continue. When spectrum space was not at a premium, the Commission did not have to address these questions. Now, circumstances have changed. Clear answers are needed about whether all these uses can still be accommodated now that spectrum space is so limited.

One of the things the 1972 CPB petition sought was the institution of ascertainment requirements more rigorous than those for commercial broadcasters. Because noncommercial stations enjoyed "relatively privileged status" under the act and were "afforded special treatment in reserved frequency allocations, higher expectations of applicants seeking to achieve or maintain this special status" were warranted, the CPB reasoned. Most other public broadcasting agencies disagreed, but Pluria Marshall, Chairman of the National Black Media Coalition, shared the CPB sentiments. Marshall told Senator Pastore in the April 1975 Senate Oversight Hearings:

On its record, the public broadcasting system desperately needs some kind of community ascertainment procedures, perhaps even more than commercial broadcasters. Public stations should be held to a higher degree of community responsiveness because they are publicly funded and can escape the normal commercial pressures of the regular broadcasters. Moreover, the public system was instituted specifically for the purpose of catering to those minority and specialized audiences which have been ignored by the commercial system. For this reason, the public broadcaster should be required to engage in an even more strenuous ascertainment in accordance with its special responsibilities.

When the FCC finally did promulgate ascertainment requirements in 1976, the role of noncommercial educational broadcasting was still not defined. Instead, the Commission notice repeated its earlier conclusion:

In establishing an ascertainment process for noncommercial broadcasters, we shall not attempt to relate the purpose of the ascertainment to the special "role" of the service as we might view it. Whatever the distinct role of public broadcasting may be, it should evolve as the service matures, and not be defined and imposed by the government.

Thus, while public broadcasters that operate with more than ten watts must ascertain and compile their annual listings of problems and needs and programs, the Commission will not, as this statement clearly indicates, evaluate the listings at renewal time.

One commissioner willing to define a clear role for public broadcast stations, especially public television stations, was Commissioner Hooks. Hooks was quoted in *Television/Radio Age* (September 13, 1976):

> When I look at public television—the great promises it made to serve all the people. Now they admit they're elitist. The president of PBS says, "Yes, we're elitists. What's wrong with that?" . . . What in hell is wrong with it is that you promised to serve all the people, including ethnic minorities. We can't get on commercial broadcasting because the time is too valuable. And we don't get on public TV because we can't buy it. So it's all the same. I think public television was established to serve minorities, ethnic minorities and those cultural minorities who were being deprived.

Commissioner Hooks said he was all in favor of *Masterpiece Theatre* and the Metropolitan Opera, but public television should also carry programs appealing to others, "like people in Appalachia who are interested in survival, not in French cooking."

Because none of Hooks' colleagues was eager to join the debate over public broadcasting's role, renewals of public radio and television stations continue to be granted routinely, without any processing rules. On various occasions, Cole suggested to the commissioners that it was about time to reevaluate the renewal form for public broadcasters and separate the 10-watt FM stations from large-city, VHF television stations. No commissioner ever disagreed. In fact, in one meeting, Commissioner Lee, the 24-year Commission veteran, responded to the suggestion by telling his colleagues that perhaps it no longer was good policy to ignore public broadcasting activities. "We meant well," said Lee, "and probably everyone benefitted from us just letting them alone. But the time has probably finally come when we should begin to treat them as first-class citizens." As yet, however, the Commission has indicated no plans to revise the renewal form or develop processing rules for noncommercial stations.

FINANCIAL QUALIFICATIONS

Although the Communications Act specifies that the Commission must find applicants to be financially qualified before renewing their licenses, the FCC report to Congress did not mention the procedure for ascertaining financial qualifications. The absence of a description of the procedure was not accidental. No review of a renewal applicant's financial qualifications normally takes place.

Only for new stations does the Commission review the financial qualifications of applicants, and their arrangements to construct the facilities and sustain operations for one year. Beyond that, the Commission has little interest in a licensee's financial condition unless a specific problem is called to the Commission's attention.

Until recently, the Commission had required radio and television renewal applicants to submit balance sheets, with detailed information current to the close of the third month prior to application. Since the May 1976 adoption of the new, short-form, renewal application, radio stations are no longer required to submit balance sheets.

When the short-form renewal for radio was first proposed, the Commission intended to retain an annual balance sheet and add a further question: if the licensees' current liabilities exceeded their current assets, they would be asked how they planned to finance the stations' continued operation and how they intended to liquidate the stations' liabilities. Several parties objected to the question. One broadcaster claimed such matters should be private and disclosed only on a confidential basis. Another opponent argued that as long as the station was on the air it should be presumed to be solvent, at least for purposes of the Commission's public interest determination. Another broadcaster suggested that either an unprofitable station would be cancelled or its facilities would be sold, and thus its financial problems would be resolved in due course without Commission interference.

The Commission accepted radio broadcasters' arguments and eliminated the balance sheet and the additional question in its order adopting the new short-form renewal. The elimination was justified on the grounds that Congress had given the FCC discretion regarding the need to determine financial qualifications (Section 308(b) of the Communications Act): the act directed the FCC to consider the applicant's financial ability but did not require that the Commission gather specific information; nor did the act require close scrutiny of an applicant's financial fitness. The Commission stated:

> The licensee's proven ability to maintain the broadcast operation of that station over a period of time affords the Commission reasonable assurance of the renewal applicant's financial qualifications. . . . Serious financial problems arising during the preceding license period term and persisting at renewal time have generally been resolved with the licensee, prompted by economic realities, refinancing its broadcast operation or, with Commission approval, assigning the station license to another who is fully able to sustain the station's continued operation.

Commercial television renewal applicants, the Commission added in a footnote, would still be required to submit balance sheets "since the balance sheets supplied at renewal time also provide the Commission with ready information that can be useful in solving disputes with CATV systems and others as to a particular commercial television licensee's present financial posture." In other words, the balance sheets required from commercial television licensees would not be used for purposes of license renewal any more than the annual financial reports, submitted by all radio and television licensees, which list expenses and revenues for the previous year. These financial reports for both radio and television are sent to another branch of the Broadcast Bureau and stored until used in compiling industry statistics or consulted in determining the amount of a fine for a violator of FCC rules.

In announcing that radio renewal applicants would no longer be required to make "an affirmative showing of their financial qualifications," the Commission promised to "fully explore the financial posture of any broadcast licensee in the unlikely event that its past stewardship is insufficient to support the likelihood of continued station operation. . . . We reaffirm our belief that prolonged suspension of station operation disserves the public interest and we stand committed to the expeditious restoration of broadcast service to the public."

Unfortunately, the Commission has often disregarded this commitment to expeditious restoration of broadcast service. Stations have remained silent for years without having their licenses taken away. In January 1974, at the request of the Commission, the staff prepared and circulated among the commissioners a status report on silent stations: 27 broadcast stations were silent because they lacked funds to keep them on the air; 12 additional stations that were to have been constructed remained silent and unbuilt after their construction permits expired.

In the discussion of the report in the form of an agenda item, Broadcast Bureau Chief Wallace Johnson told the commissioners: "We go along with stations as long as they are trying to do something or things are outside of their control." Trying to sell the station was an example of trying to do something. Martin Levy, chief of the bureau's Facilities Division, which had primary responsibility for monitoring the 27 cases, said that silent stations, individually according to circumstances, presented "a feel situation"; and if a station had been on the air for years, "we've even been more lenient." Levy indicated that as long as the station had something to sell, its transmitter for example, the staff would try to be patient; when asked by one commissioner, "How long do you wait?" Levy replied, "The key is when they've lost their equipment." With educational stations, "we give them as long as possible": one New York educational television station had been given from ten to 15 years.

One staff member pointed out that with only 27 stations involved, "When you consider the number of stations in the United States, this is really no problem." Judging by their reactions, most commissioners agreed. To listeners in Centerville, Mississippi, however, there was definitely a problem because their only station had been silent for three years. Finally, in March 1975, more than four years after that station had gone dark, the Commission dismissed the station's renewal application. In its letter, the FCC made the classic understatement that the licensee's continued silence without authorization was in violation of the Commission's rules and "cast doubt on your capacity to meet the licensee's minimal obligations of actually operating a station."

While many of the instances cited affect a small portion of the broadcast audience and few broadcasters, the cumulative effect of the FCC's unwillingness to set firm standards in the area of license renewal is indeed significant. The Commission has been accused of regulation by raised eyebrow; but when dealing with renewals, the FCC practices regulation by a nod and a wink. The unlucky broadcaster who runs afoul of the FCC's elastic standards may justifiably feel singled out. Members of the public are uncertain just what they have a right to expect from the licensee charged with serving their interests. Despite assurances to Congress from time to time, the FCC has left the questions of renewal murky and vague.

13

The Commission's Sanctions: From Wrist-Slappings to Death Sentences

Forfeitures were authorized to obtain greater compliance by licensees with the terms of their licenses and the Commission's Rules, and to deter noncompliance. If serious, repeated violations are excused without sanction, the sanction of forfeiture will not be the effective tool it was intended to be. Rather than being deterred, licensees would be encouraged to continue violating rules and to depend upon excuses and promises to avoid liability. We intend to use the forfeiture proceeding, as we believe it was intended to be used, to impel broadcast licensees to become familiar with the terms of their licenses and the applicable rules, and to adopt procedures, including periodic review of operations, which will insure that stations will be operated in substantial compliance with their licenses and the Commission's Rules.

Commission statement in one of the early forfeiture proceedings
Crowell-Collier Broadcasting Corporation, 1961

The "short-term renewal" has always struck me as a rather bizarre sanction under the best of circumstances. It generally carries no financial consequences whatsoever. The station is not off the air for an hour. The profits continue to roll in.

Commissioner Nicholas Johnson
dissenting in case of WWRL New York, May 19, 1971

13 Columnist George Will once observed that capital punishment may not be an effective deterrent to murder, but it certainly would discourage double parking. For many years the FCC had only one sanction at its disposal: to revoke a license and put a station operator out of business. Understandably, the Commission was extremely reluctant to take that draconian measure against licensees guilty of minor violations. And so the double parkers of the air, and even the reckless drivers and petty thieves went largely unpunished.

In the wake of the 1960 congressional hearings on payola and rigged TV quiz shows, Congress decided to give the FCC authority to impose fines on minor offenders or to renew their licenses for a short term, a form of probation, instead of for the regular three-year term. Previously, in 1952, Congress had set up a cumbersome formula for the Commission, like the Federal Trade Commission's, to issue cease-and-desist orders against licensees who violated rules; but the FCC has never used this power, largely because a hearing is required. The 1960 House bill would have permitted the FCC to levy fines against licensees who "negligently or intentionally" violated rules; but the Senate changed the wording to "willful or repeated violations" to be consistent with the revocation criteria of the Communications Act. The Commission was permitted to assess fines of $1000 per day of violation to a limit of $10,000. A statute of limitations confined issuing notices of apparent liability to offenses occurring within the past year.

Fines or short-term renewals could be levied for violations falling into one or more of the following categories: (1) failure to operate the station as set forth in the license; (2) failure to observe provisions of the act or rules or regulations of the Commission; (3) failure to observe any cease-and-desist order of the Commission; (4) violations of the sponsorship identification or "rigged" contests provisions of the act; and (5) violations of certain statutes of the United States Code, primarily lotteries, fraud by wire or radio or TV, or obscene language.

In 1976 a bill permitting the FCC to impose forfeitures up to $20,000 and lengthening the statute of limitations was passed by the Senate. Because of its other provisions, the bill never came to a House vote; but in light of inflation and the impracticality of the one-year-limitation statute, Congress is expected to eventually broaden the agency's power to levy fines.

FINES

If a licensee fails to pay, the FCC asks the Justice Department to sue him or her in a local court. Because of the cost of prosecuting such cases and the danger that a local court will be unfamiliar with broadcasting regulation, Justice has usually settled these cases out of court for about three-quarters the amount of the fine. All fines are paid to the U.S. Treasury.

The language of the congressional authorization to fine has been the subject of periodic debates and discussions in Commission meetings. William Ray, chief of the Complaints and Compliance Division since January 1963, suggests the Commission "could not prove willfulness in one of 100 cases." Most fines, therefore, are imposed for "repeated" violations of a rule, but the definition of "repeated" has led to arguments, too. Commissioner Quello, for example, questioned whether a station that runs an improperly identified commercial 18 times, but drops it when management learns it is in violation, is guilty of a repeated offense; he doubts that a court would sustain such a definition. The Commission continues to levy fines, sometimes in a markedly arbitrary manner; and what constitutes a "willful and repeated violation" has not been determined in court (but two cases are pending).

In 1975 the Commission wrestled with whether a licensee's financial condition should affect the amount of the fine. Until that time, FCC policy had been to increase the fine when the station was so large and profitable that the ordinary amount would make no impression. But Commissioner Robert Lee made the analogy that traffic ticket fines don't increase simply because a violator can afford to pay more. The Commission agreed that willfulness or gross negligence, but not a station's relative prosperity, was sufficient reason for increasing the fine; on the other hand, fines for stations that clearly can't afford to pay should be reduced because the fining power was not meant to have the same effect as license revocation.

The FCC usually levies fines in cases of technical violations: improper logkeeping, failure to measure equipment performance, unlicensed engineers, broadcasting during unauthorized hours or with too much power, or late filing of renewal applications. In half the cases, the licensee pays without protest when the FCC issues a notice of apparent liability. Over the years the major offenders have been commercial radio station operators in towns with populations less than 20,000. Fewer than 5 percent of the fines were levied against commercial TV stations, and hardly any against public broadcasters.

In fiscal 1976 the FCC issued 176 notices of apparent liability: 161 were staff-initiated and averaged fines of $656; the other 15 were directed by the commissioners and averaged $2850. In the same year the FCC issued 145 fining orders (of which 20 were reductions or remissions). The 124 staff-originated orders averaged $792; the 21 commissioner-directed orders, $2086.

Fines are reduced if the station's financial condition has deteriorated seriously, or if the licensee can persuade the Commission on other grounds. Because fining procedures don't fall under the ex parte prohibitions, a licensee is free to plead his case officially or informally.

A particularly strange example of the Commission's fluid policy on fines arose on April 15, 1974, when KLAS–TV Las Vegas had been found guilty of violating the equal-time provisions of the Communications Act during a political campaign. The station was licensed to the Summa Corporation, owned by Howard Hughes. (Legend has it that while living in Las Vegas, Hughes bought this station, which previously had signed off the air at 1:00 A.M., because he wanted to program all-night movies for his own entertainment.)

The Broadcast Bureau recommended a $1000 fine against the station for the equal-time violation. KLAS–TV had been fined twice before during the past six years: $1000 for violation of sponsor identification, and $2000 (reduced from $4000) for fraudulent billing. Although William Ray asked if the commissioners doubted Hughes's ability to pay $1000, the members agreed to Commissioner Reid's recommendation and reduced the third fine to $500. The upshot of the matter was that Hughes refused to pay, and the Justice Department has not prosecuted the case in Nevada for a mere $500.

William Ray told Cole that the amount of the fine isn't terribly significant for large, lucrative stations; having a fine on their records is what disturbs them. However, it's ridiculous for the FCC to go through prolonged procedures to levy a fine no larger than a salesman's weekly expense account. Since 1974 the commissioners have delegated to the Broadcast Bureau the authority to levy fines under $2000 (licensees have the right to appeal to the full Commission). Even for relatively serious offenses, the staff has at times preferred to keep fines under $2000 rather than face the hassle and the likelihood of a reduction if the commissioners had to review the recommendation for a higher fine. The staff must also keep the statute of limitations in mind.

Despite the designation of the FCC as a "quasi-judicial" agency, and despite the commissioners' judicial function in imposing sanctions against broadcasters, the Commission does not consider itself bound by precedent. (Of course, even the Supreme Court has been known to ignore the doctrine of stares decisis.) Ignoring precedent may be unintentional or intentional. The turnover of commissioners is so frequent that often they simply don't know what the agency has done in similar, past cases. Occasionally members prefer a different ideological viewpoint and a different result, with which they feel comfortable.

Sometimes beliefs clashed within the FCC. At some Commission meetings Ray indicated that the bureau's recommendation of a fine instead of designation for a hearing was based on his belief as a veteran staffer that the Commission wouldn't take the license away anyway and that a hearing would result only in a fine. Ray's remarks increasingly irritated Wiley, who cited Wiley's policy that the Commission would be stern and even rescind licenses for misrepresentations and cheating. In one agenda discussion, Wiley criticized Ray's cynical attitude, but

Ray cited his 12 years of experience as evidence he was being realistic rather than cynical.

By the time a hearing had been completed, there would be six new commissioners, who knew nothing about the case, Ray explained; and the defendant's lawyer would persuade them not to take the license away because "the licensee was good to his mother or something." If he believed a hearing might result in a license revocation, Ray claimed that he'd support a hearing.

This challenge motivated Wiley to gain the support of his colleagues for designating the particular application for hearing. The bureau had recommended a short-term renewal and a fine of $4000 for numerous violations, including technical violations, falsifications of logs, and, most important, lack of candor.

Traditionally lack of candor is what puts the Commission in a frame of mind to take away a license. Even when violations include prior falsifications, licensees can get away with a lot if they confess when caught. For example, a Guam station, fined $10,000 for a long series of falsified operating logs, quickly acknowledged its transgressions, paid the fine, and kept its license. Even if the violation is minor, a licensee who tries to get away with it and doesn't "fess up" may lose the license. Misrepresentation is an offense that merits a penalty more severe than a fine.

The attitudes of the commissioners who happen to be serving when a broadcaster gets caught crucially affect the penalty. The FCC first warned licensees in 1962 against fraudulent billing: false affidavits of performance or "double billing," furnishing to any contributor of broadcast advertising payment false information about the amount actually charged. For years punishment for this offense was a fine or a short-term renewal, provide the licensee didn't lie when discovered. After another warning in 1972, the FCC began taking away some licenses for this offense; in 1976 eight stations were so punished.

Customarily, Commission sanctions are exercised against licenses for "business offenses," such as fraudulent billing, not for practices that upset only the audience, where no clear rules exist.

SHORT-TERM RENEWALS

In 1960 Congress granted the Commission explicit authority to renew licenses for terms shorter than the customary three-year period. The FCC may have had the power previously, but it had not exercised it. In annual reports, the Commission describes short-term renewals as a form of probation for licensees whose violations did not justify revocation or nonrenewal of license. In theory, the FCC reviews the short-term licensee's performance more rapidly than it otherwise would and views the operation "in the light of past deficiencies."

During fiscal years 1972 through 1976, the FCC granted short-term renewals to 51 stations, of which 33 were AM, 13 FM and 5 TV.

The probationary nature of a short-term renewal was underlined by Judge Warren Burger, then on the Court of Appeals for the District of Columbia circuit, in the famous case of WLBT–TV Jackson, Mississippi. He referred to "a grant which by its nature assumes that the renewal licensee has been unable to persuade the Commission that it is presently in the public interest to grant a three-year renewal." The court indicated that for a renewal licensee applying for a full-term license after being sanctioned by a short-term renewal, the burden of proof is increased.

In practice, such scrutiny of short-term licensees seldom takes place. Sometimes, station owners guilty of fresh violations during this probationary period have been simply renewed for another short term instead of being ordered into hearing. Sometimes if a licensee's regular renewal is coming up soon, the FCC will grant a license for the remainder of the period and call it a short-term renewal—or will decide that there's no need to issue a short-term renewal. In the latter case, the licensee is not effectively sanctioned at all because the renewal branch is not notified that the application should be subjected to more thorough scrutiny.

In one case, which is not unique, a licensee had distorted listener survey results, but the FCC staff said (in July 1975): "The broadcast licenses for these stations will not expire until August 1, 1977. If the license terms were near completion, then short-term renewal would be seriously considered. However, the [Broadcast] Bureau believes that the licensee should be admonished presently, and that the possibility of a short-term renewal may be properly considered in deciding whether to grant the station's next license renewal." The logic of this seemed strange to Cole, but apparently it was based on the staff's belief that a short-term renewal would inconvenience the licensee and would, therefore, be too harsh a penalty.

Commissioner Johnson, never impressed by the deterrent effect of the short-term renewal, dissented with particular vigor to renewals that expired on the date when the three-year license would have expired anyway. He said, "Needless to say, if 'short-term' renewals are to have any effect whatsoever, the date when they expire must at least be earlier than it would otherwise have been."

From the very beginning, the Commission failed to institute any special review procedures or investigatory processes to ensure a really thorough inspection of short-term licensees when that term expires. Consider the example of WILD Boston, which received one of the first short-term renewals. In April 1960, the Commission renewed the station for only one year because of uncertainties regarding the station's financial condition and violations of some FCC rules. In July 1961, still not satisfied with the station's operation, the FCC granted WILD a second short-term renewal. But by the time the second grant expired the situation had worsened, so in 1962 the station's new application was designated for hearing. Basing its decision on the hearing record, the Commission concluded in July 1965 that WILD had been guilty of a lack of adequate control of its foreign language programming, had failed to file time-brokerage contracts, had made numerous misstatements to the Commission, had engaged in the broadcasting of lotteries (violating both FCC rules and the Criminal Code), and had demonstrated continued financial instability. The FCC acknowledged that "the station's virtually bankrupt condition from 1960 until about 1964 . . . prevented it from securing sufficiently competent personnel to operate the station in full compliance with the Communications Act and the Commission's rules." Yet despite all this, the Commission permitted the station to file another renewal application in 1966. Moreover, the Commission indicated it would take into account upgrading by the licensee since 1964, promises made in the new renewal application, and any other "new data" which became available. In June 1966, WILD was given a regular three-year renewal.

Another case in point is an Ohio station that repeatedly ignored FCC requests for information on its nonentertainment programming. After the licensee ignored all letters from the FCC for eight months, the commissioners finally dismissed the licensee's application for renewal; but the licensee asked for reconsideration on mitigating circumstances: new management, the heavy demand on the licensee by his law practice in another city, and other "chaotic" conditions. The commissioners agreed, in 1971 by a 5–2 vote, to reconsider and issue the licensee a short-term renewal because "despite the licensee's derelictions, the Commission cannot fail to take cognizance of the fact" that this was the only broadcast facility in that particular Ohio city and county, and because the licensee promised to present programs emphasizing local affairs and events. H. Rex Lee noted, "Certainly if I did not believe that the licensee would effectuate his promise of better performance in the future, I would be hard-pressed to permit even a short-term renewal." Yet, when the renewal came up again in January 1973, there was no evidence whether the licensee had, in fact, carried out the promises that won his reprieve; the brief staff statement that "there is no evidence of any of the misconduct for which the short-term was granted" could and probably did mean that the licensee had merely responded to recent inquiries.

Even where a major violation has been found during the short term, the sanction may be simply another short-term renewal. One of the most notorious of such cases involved WIFE–AM–FM Indianapolis, which, during short-term renewals, granted in 1964 because of deceptive practices about station ratings, falsified bills to advertisers. Although the law judge recommended that renewals not be granted, the Commission, in September 1969, overruled the finding and granted (by a 4–3 vote) additional short-term renewals instead of taking the licenses away.

In a blistering dissenting opinion, Nicholas Johnson (joined by Kenneth Cox) said:

> The result reached here is truly shocking. In an astonishing opinion, the majority has concluded that, although the licensee of WIFE fraudulently deceived its clients with respect to certain promotional contests and bilked its advertisers of more than $6000 advertising revenues (all during a one-year probationary license renewal period), the licensee's operation has nevertheless "minimally met the public interest standards" and its license should be renewed. If fraud and deception of more than $6000 are minimally in accordance with the public interest, then I think it must be apparent to all that the FCC's attempts at serving the public interest are themselves without even minimal standards.

Johnson noted that the majority "does not attempt to dispute the licensee's conduct in any respect." The majority held the licensee "fully responsible for the conduct of its officers" with respect to holding a fraudulent contest. Moreover, the majority found that the licensee on a number of occasions had furnished clients

> false and misleading information with respect to the times and dates purchased advertising was broadcast. . . . What is more, the licensee took no steps to insure that blatant frauds such as this could not happen. Indeed, it deliberately abandoned a control book used by an earlier manager to prevent just such fraud—again as the majority acknowledges.

Johnson referred to the majority statement that "this is a very difficult and close case" as a "cosmic non sequitur," which "can only be described as a pathetic equivocation." He also noted that on the same day the Commission imposed no fine on WIFE, the FCC had levied

> numerous fines on other stations for far less culpable behavior—$700 on WKVA Lewistown, Pennsylvania (failure to make field intensity measurements and excessive modulation) . . . $500 on KWMC Del Rio, Texas (unauthorized operator—logging violation), and $7500 on WVOZ Caroline, Puerto Rico (overmodulation, excessive power after sunset, and false logging).

Johnson accused the Commission of maintaining a double standard:

> Is there any doubt that this Commission too often reserves punitive action for smaller licensees? Is there any lingering doubt that the majority's marked disinclination to enforce its rules and policies by revocation of valuable broadcast properties simply enshrines the precept that the wealthier and more influential any broadcaster be-

comes the more immune he is to regulation? Can there be any doubt left that there is something very wrong with the will of this agency to discharge its responsibilities to the public?

Following these second short-term renewals, Congress raised questions while the FCC was investigating further. In 1970 the Commission designated all five stations owned by the licensee, Star Stations, for hearing on numerous charges including Fairness Doctrine violations, intentional slanting of news, and misrepresentations to the commission. In 1975 the FCC voted to take away all of the licensee's stations.

CONDITIONAL RENEWALS

Seldom faced with such a wealth of provocation as in the WIFE case, the FCC usually avoids such final actions and relies on lesser sanctions. It exercises these other options in a rather arbitrary fashion. If it questions whether renewal would be in the public interest, the Commission has the option of deferring a renewal; but this deferral is not considered a sanction, and the licensee continues to operate the station. Another option is conditioning a renewal on specific licensee behavior.

Although in 1973 the Commission's general counsel advised that "there is no question of the Commission's authority ... to attach such conditions as it deems necessary to assure operation in the public interest," the FCC lacks the *specific* authorization of such agencies as the Civil Aeronautics Board and Interstate Commerce Commission. Nonetheless, the FCC's authority to condition renewals hasn't been challenged in court.

The most common reason for a conditional renewal is that a licensee has an unsatisfactory record of employing minorities and women. Then renewal is conditioned on regular reporting of steps taken to ensure equal employment opportunities. Sometimes the FCC renews a violator's license on the condition that ownership of the station and license be transferred within a specified period of time.

Such conditions can be assumed to produce tangible results, but such an assumption can't necessarily be made when the condition is that the licensee must be found to have the necessary character qualifications. For example, for a licensee appealing a guilty verdict in a criminal or civil suit or for a licensee the Commission is investigating on charges of fraud or misrepresentation, what is the FCC going to do—possibly years later—if the judgment against the licensee is upheld? Unless the condition clearly states that licensees will *not* be renewed if, after exhausting their appeals, they are found to lack character qualifications, the FCC accomplishes very little by conditioning the grant on the vague phrase "pending the outcome."

During Commission discussions, Daniel Ohlbaum, then deputy general counsel, repeatedly raised strong objections to the FCC's permitting station purchases by those found guilty of offenses that reflected on the applicants' basic character. Ohlbaum subsequently drafted a public notice to all broadcast licensees that "action on applications to construct new facilities or to acquire, either by assignment or transfer of control, existing facilities will generally be deferred" when questions of the applicant's basic character qualifications were unresolved, when a license renewal or revocation proceeding was instituted following an FCC investigation, when a criminal proceeding was in progress, or when the seller was involved in "a pending renewal, revocation or investigative proceeding involving the particular station which he seeks to sell." In October 1973, the commissioners approved this deferral policy except for cases where the potential buyer was in proceedings with other government agencies, like the FTC or SEC, or where the seller was involved in criminal legal proceedings.

This public notice, of course, says nothing about whether licensees who own several stations will fail to have some licenses renewed if the licensees are involved in hearings on their other stations for violations that clearly reflect on the licensees' character. Richard Shiben pointed out this omission: "If we researched the records [of group owners], we'd find we have been all over the ballpark on this issue. In the past, we've given some unconditional renewals, some conditional, and some deferred renewals to depend on the outcome of the hearing." When Shiben asked the commissioners for a "commitment" that thereafter all renewal grants in such cases would be conditional grants, the commissioners declined to make a firm policy although the Communications Act requires their finding each renewal applicant to possess the necessary character qualifications.

The anomaly resulting from the FCC's putative policy and its practice of dispensing licenses in the least complicated fashion is illustrated by the case of George T. Hernreich, who was an FCC licensee since 1956. Hernreich owned a TV station in Jonesboro, Arkansas, and a construction permit for a TV station in Fort Smith, Arkansas, in addition to AM stations in Fort Smith and Hot Springs. In July 1971 his application for renewal of the Jonesboro TV was set for an FCC hearing to determine if he had bribed an ABC network employee to increase Hernreich's network compensation and if he had lied (made "misrepresentations" and showed "lack of candor") to the FCC. At the time, Hernreich had applied for an FM station in Fort Smith. While the hearing proceeded to determine if Hernreich should lose his Jonesboro TV, the Fort Smith TV was allowed to go on the air, conditional on the hearing outcome; and his other licenses were deferred.

In April 1973 an FCC administrative law judge recommended denial of Hernreich's licenses for *both* TV stations because Hernreich had on two occasions paid $3000 to an ABC employee to increase the amount of compensation the network would pay. The judge rejected Hernreich's defense that he was the victim of extortion; the judge ruled that

Hernreich knew the money was going to the individual, not the network, and that it wasn't "the natural way" to conduct such business. He said Hernreich had attempted to bribe the ABC employee and had "deliberately elected to attempt to conceal his complicity."

Traditionally in such cases, the commissioners are supposed to give great weight to a law judge's decision because the judge is the person who has observed witnesses' demeanor, heard their testimony, and ruled on admissibility of evidence. In this case, the commissioners, finding Hernreich's actions to be "wrongdoing pursued specifically to advance his financial interest as a licensee," ratified denial of the Jonesboro license; but the commissioners permitted Hernreich to retain the Fort Smith TV license because that station's operations had not been involved and because of the "unlikelihood" of the offense being repeated. The commissioners' decision was an obvious compromise. Commissioners Robert Lee and Benjamin Hooks didn't think Hernreich should lose either station. Hooks' dissent said that a short-term renewal "would have been the more proper sanction" because "denial of renewal or revocation is a draconian measure to be taken when there is no hope of penitence." As a result of the decision, Hernreich's AM licenses were also renewed, and he continued to be considered for the Fort Smith FM station.

In April 1975 the Commission approved Hernreich's application to buy yet another Arkansas TV station, a UHF in Fayetteville. At this time, because Hernreich was still appealing the decision to take away the Jonesboro TV station, the FCC conditioned the UHF purchase on the outcome of his appeal, despite the FCC's October 1973 public notice deferring transfers to applicants involved in proceedings on their character qualifications. Commissioners Reid, Wiley, and Robinson dissented to this transfer, pointing out that "the more prudent course" would be to await disposition of Hernreich's appeals before granting another license. Furthermore, the dissenters noted, Hernreich had informed the FCC that because of his age (72), he was planning to transfer his properties to his sons, in which case, his acquisition and sale of a broadcast property within three years would violate FCC rules designed to prevent "trafficking in licenses."

In July 1975, the commissioners granted still another unusual boon to Hernreich, who asked that the Jonesboro and Fort Smith TV applications, which had gone to hearing together, be separated. Hernreich feared that a court might find that the Fort Smith license as well should have been taken away, and he wanted to appeal the Jonesboro loss without risking the Fort Smith license. The commissioners stated that "without a strong, public interest showing," the FCC wouldn't ordinarily grant such a request, but that in this case the two applications had been simply "consolidated for administrative convenience."

As for the Fort Smith FM application, *another* FCC administrative law judge stated that "because of Hernreich's demonstrated propensity for wrongdoing," the application should be denied. This statement amounted to a rebuff of the Commission's decision to allow Hernreich to keep his Fort Smith TV station because his misconduct had been confined to the Jonesboro operation. The FCC Review Board overruled the law judge, citing the commissioners' reasoning in the television cases.

After five years, Hernreich had the same number of licenses he began with—plus another FM station. And this was a case of which veteran law judge Forest L. McClenning had said: "Whether such conduct be termed bribery or merely moral turpitude is of no materiality. It is conduct that must lead to denial of the license applications here in issue. To condone such conduct would be a disservice to the public, to the industry and to effectuation of the functions of this Commission."

REVOCATIONS

Over the years the Commission has been extremely reluctant to impose the "death penalty" of stripping a station owner of his license, either by refusing to renew his authority or by revoking it. Since 1934, the FCC has taken away fewer than 150 licenses, mostly small radio stations—and in some cases the licensees had Gary Gilmore's attitude— they were resigned to the loss.

The most common causes for revocation or failure to renew have been misrepresentations to the Commission, unauthorized transfer of control (selling without permission), technical violations, lack of character qualifications, default (simply turning in the license), financial disqualifications, and programming. The programming issues related to violations of the political broadcasting rules and/or violations of the Fairness Doctrine; and in each case, other violations—usually misrepresentations—were also involved.

Technical violations must be flagrant before the FCC will refuse to renew a license. In 1971 the Commission overruled a law judge's recommendation that two South Dakota TV stations licensed to the same owner be given short-term renewals and voted to take away the licenses. The stations had a ten-year history of repeated and serious violations of the rules: neither station had provided the public in their communities "with a picture of usable quality" since at least 1965; 2000 Rapid City viewers petitioned the FCC and NBC to improve service in 1967; and as late as July 1969, an FCC inspector had found the station broadcasting an unacceptable signal. The FCC allowed the owner to operate both stations until 1975 before granting construction permits to another party.

The commissioners' main excuse for not taking away a license when the incumbent has been found derelict is that the community will lose its local service. But except in cases where licensees have voluntarily surrendered their licenses (usually UHF TV stations or FM stations in small communities), eager applicants for the facility almost always come forward quickly. The Commission can then grant temporary operating authority to a consortium of applicants, and the community will suffer little loss of service. In some cases, such groups have operated stations for five or six years under temporary authority during the ponderous business of a comparative hearing. Chairman Wiley suggested to the NAB in 1976 that legislative reform might enable the FCC to choose equitably between license applicants where no incumbent is involved:

> If it can be conceded that we can only speculate concerning which applicant, among a group of qualified newcomers, is likely to provide the 'best' broadcast service, it seems to me that the selection process might be better based on some kind of an objective, non-discriminatory method of selection: for example, a lottery. Such a system would be both equitable and rapid.

A broadcaster who loses his license can make things difficult for his successor. One licensee set an exorbitant price on his transmitter site, the only high ground for miles around. A radio operator, during his appeals of license revocation, changed formats from rhythm-and-blues to Spanish-language programming. The prospective licensee, who won a comparative hearing, doesn't plan Spanish programming and worries about complaints from that substantial segment of the community about his future program format. This case presents a difficult problem, but it would seem an opportunity to employ the cease-and-desist authority the Commission has never chosen to use.

Sometimes the Commission has renewed the license of an unfit broadcaster on condition that the license be sold within a short specified time and without profit to the licensee. In one such case, although a competing application had been filed for the station, the FCC chose not to accept it and permitted a "no profit" sale. Wiley's dissent to this action pointed out that (because the unfit licensee would now have total discretion in choosing a successor) the competing applicant (who would probably have prevailed) had been frozen out.

No one loves a policeman. When the commissioners must dole out sanctions, they know that frequently their decisions will embroil them in controversy. Each licensee is the constituent of at least one congressman and two senators—and multiple owners with properties in several markets have considerable political clout. This consideration may partly explain the FCC's seeming reluctance to chastise the big operator: the big operator can make more trouble for the agency than the penalty is worth. Political consequences aside, commissioners hesitate to commit large numbers of staff attorneys to major cases that are certain to be appealed to the courts, where the legal underpinnings of the FCC's authority to impose penalties may be weakened.

When the Star station in Omaha (KOIL–AM) was finally shut down in September 1976, a feature on the *CBS Evening News* showed employees who were losing their jobs and noted that the public would lose service. By implication, the FCC was the villain in this death-of-a-newspaper-type story. One way or another, commissioners have found, levying penalties leads to complications. Many commissioners would sooner avoid the hassle.

14
Petition to Deny: Heavy Artillery

This is the age of the consumer. It's not as much fun being a broadcaster. If I were a broadcaster, I'd worry that someone might file against me and perhaps prevail.
Commissioner Robert E. Lee
Television/Radio Age
June 1972

Petitions to deny are the only tools broadcasters and the Commission give us. It is the one thing you can hold over stations. Your petition will almost always be rejected, but upgrading by the licensee often occurs.
Tracy Westen at 1976 Aspen Conference on Public Interest Communications Law

14 The most powerful weapon in the arsenal of a citizen group is the petition to the FCC asking the agency to deny renewal or transfer (sale) of a broadcast license. A petition to deny is to a simple letter of complaint as a declaration of war is to a foreign minister's protest. Under the Communications Act, any "party in interest" may file a petition to deny, which must contain specific allegations of fact that granting the renewal or transfer would not be in the public interest. Although the renewal or transfer branches process a petition, the commissioners must rule on it—it cannot be dismissed under delegated authority.

WHO PETITIONS AND HOW

Before the U.S. Court of Appeals' landmark decision in the case of WLBT Jackson, Mississippi, persons or groups with no financial interest in whether a license was renewed or transferred (or those with no proof of electronic interference) were not considered parties in interest. Beginning in 1966, the courts have held, in the words of then Judge Warren Burger, who wrote the decision: "Since the concept of standing is a practical and functional one designed to insure that only those with a genuine and legitimate interest can participate in the proceeding, we can see no reason to exclude those with such an obvious and acute concern as the listening audience."

The FCC doesn't have to grant every petition by ordering a hearing on the application, of course; but a petition can no longer be dismissed simply on the grounds that the licensing decision is none of the petitioner's business. Understandably, the applicant is permitted to reply to such a petition by filing an opposition—and the petitioner can respond to the applicant's defense. Petitioners themselves have had to develop the facts for allegations against applicants. The Commission has opposed providing prehearing discovery procedures, by which the petitioner could subpoena witnesses, take sworn depositions, and demand that the licensee supply certain information. Without such information, the petitioner is handicapped in justifying the complaint.

Furthermore, the applicant can amend the application at any time before it is designated for hearing by the FCC. For example, after a citizen group asks the FCC to deny a license renewal on the grounds that the station's programming promises were inadequate, the licensee can amend those promises and then tell the FCC that the allegations are not valid. The Commission need not and normally does not permit the citizen to comment upon the amendments.

If the FCC doesn't grant the petition, it must "issue a concise statement of the reasons . . . and dispose of all substantial issues raised by the petition." Otherwise, the FCC is supposed to designate the application for hearing and to specify the issues to be determined.

Appeals of the Commission's decisions on a petition to deny and a license application may be taken to the U.S. Court of Appeals for the District of Columbia Circuit, which has appellate jurisdiction for all broadcast licensing cases. Should the court uphold the Commission's denial of a license renewal, the frequency becomes vacant and the Commission begins the process of selecting a new applicant. Sometimes the Commission or the court allows the former licensee to remain on the air and compete for the new authorization. The scope of the court's review is limited, and generally the court will "defer to the experience and expertise of the Commission within its field of specialty." The primary reason given for the court's reversing the FCC is a finding that the Commission's action is "arbitrary, capricious or unreasonable."

Both groups and individuals were given standing by court decisions. When the court ruled in WLBT that a church group and members of the black community had standing to intervene in a license renewal proceeding, the court specified that the Commission "should be accorded broad discretion in establishing and applying rules for such public participation." In another case, in 1970, the appeals court ruled that a single individual could be granted legal standing as "a representative of the listening public."

In the WLBT case, the court dismissed as unfounded the FCC's fears that it would be inundated by similar proceedings. In fiscal 1969 (the year ending June 30, 1969), two petitions to deny were filed against the license renewals of two stations. The following year, 15 petitions were filed against 16 stations; in fiscal 1971, 38 petitions, against 84 stations; and in fiscal 1972, 68 petitions, against 108 stations. Between July 1, 1972, and May 15, 1977, various groups filed 237 petitions to deny the license renewals of 618 stations. Although the FCC does not issue official statistics on the number of petitions granted, inquiries revealed that as of May 15, 1977, no more than 20 of the 360 petitions filed since July 1, 1968, resulted in renewal hearings. Only one licensee (Alabama Educational Television Commission) designated for hearing because of a petition to deny has been refused renewal (for eight public TV stations and a construction permit). Of course, cases in hearing status as of May 1977 may result in other denials of renewal.

Petitions to deny transfer of licenses have been fewer than petitions to deny license renewals. An FCC official estimates some 20 petitions against transfers are received annually. The FCC has never, without a specific court order, conducted a hearing on a transfer after a citizen group petition to deny. Most of these petitions have been filed by citizen groups objecting to sales that will result in radio format changes by the new owner, most commonly changes from classical music to some other format.

By far the largest number of petitions to deny renewal has been filed by organizations representing blacks, Latinos, and women. As of September 1975, Richard Shiben, chief of the Renewal and Transfer Division, estimated that 80 percent of the challenges to renewals had been filed by black groups. By May 1977, Henry L. Baumann of the renewals branch said women's groups were filing an increasing number of petitions, almost as many as were filed by black groups.

In the 1960s, black groups were generally represented by white lawyers; but in the 1970s, more black lawyers have shown interest in the field, and black citizen groups have become far more sophisticated. In 1973, BEST's William Wright recommended to a Washington conference that petitions to deny were the most effective way for minorities to make progress in employment and to affect programming: "There's no getting around it. . . . The broadcaster's pocketbook is the only thing that's going to make him respond."

TESTING THE WATERS IN WMAL–TV

Between 1969, the time of the appeals court's final ruling on WLBT, and the middle of 1972, the Commission was confused and uncertain about how to handle petitions to deny. In effect, the FCC was "on hold," waiting to see whether the court would approve its handling of those petitions it had already processed. The commissioners' uncertainty centered on what facts and allegations by petitioners were "material and substantial" and gave sufficient cause for ordering a hearing on the applications. Although many commissioners and key staff members wanted to dismiss most of the petitions before them, they were anxious lest the courts find them to be improperly dismissing petitions to deny.

The court had been tough on the FCC in the WLBT case. In 1966, in granting standing to the petitioners, the court negated the Commission's short-term renewal grant and ordered a renewal hearing. In 1969, after the Commission had held the hearing and decided to give WLBT a full three-year renewal, the court, in effect, ordered the license to be vacated and new applications for the frequency invited. (WLBT was permitted to apply.) The court took over the case because according to Judge Burger, "The administrative conduct reflected in this record is beyond repair."

Until the court gave the Commission some further indication of how the agency was expected to handle petitions, the Broadcast Bureau was being cautious. More than 100 petitions to deny the renewal of twice that number of stations were being processed gingerly by the bureau in mid-1972.

The intent and the efficacy of all these petitions were questioned. General Counsel John Pettit told *Broadcasting* that he didn't believe the petitions represented "a positive good": "It's like saying the only time broadcasters do a good job is when they have a gun pointed at their heads." Commissioner Wiley suggested in a 1972 speech that constant license challenges would lead to exactly the opposite of what petitioners were seeking—that because broadcasters would want to play it safe, they would program blander and cheaper fare. The increase in the number of petitions to deny, said Wiley, "indicate[s] that either the industry has changed its practices radically or that someone is taking advantage of broadcasters."

The test case for which the FCC was waiting came in the appeals court decision on WMAL–TV Washington, one of the first petitions to deny license renewal filed by a citizen group after the WLBT decision, and the first to be appealed to the courts. The petition was filed on September 2, 1969, by sixteen Washington black community leaders—a veritable "Who's Who" of the black community—including Walter Fauntroy, later D.C.'s first representative to Congress; Marion Barry, Jr., Julius Hobson, Douglas Moore, and Channing Phillips, all members of the D.C. City Council. The petition raised the three most typical allegations found in that period's petitions to deny renewal: inadequate ascertainment of community needs, inadequate programming for the black community, and discrimination in employment. Citizen groups —and commission personnel—believed that precedent would be riding on the decision in WMAL–TV.

In some important ways, however, the case was not typical of the other petitions to deny renewal. WMAL was not among the most egregious offenders, even if all the allegations were accepted. The petitioners based their charges of discrimination, for example, on minority employment statistics for the city, not the entire service area, and specific cases of employment discrimination were not cited. The programming of WMAL, unlike that in most other cases, was familiar to the judges of the D.C. appeals court. Although the station's original ascertainment of needs might have been deficient, after the petition was filed, WMAL had amended its ascertainment, an act sanctioned by the FCC and later by the court. And although the station didn't program the requested number of shows of particular interest to blacks, the station could document its efforts to do some programming for blacks.

The court affirmed the FCC's decision not to set WMAL–TV's license renewal for hearing. Commissioners and key staff members expressed great relief: if the court had ruled a hearing was necessary in this case, the FCC would have had little choice but to set the majority of petitions for hearing. The decision on WMAL–TV did not stop the flow of petitions to deny, but it was interpreted by the FCC's general counsel as "allowing substantial Commission leeway in processing renewals." Citizen groups were generally disappointed and discouraged; and the original petitioners asked the court to reconsider.

Although it denied reconsideration, the court tried to placate the petitioners and to emphasize that representatives of the public were not engaged in "a meaningless exercise, or a never-ending battle for which they have insufficient resources." The court noted:

The participation of petitioners in this case was effective in forcing WMAL to conform its prospective ascertainment to current FCC standards, and in pointing out that future deviation will not be tolerated. We do not view this as defeat for petitioners, but as successful public intervention which this court has consistently welcomed as serving the public interest.

JUSTICE DELAYED IS JUSTICE DENIED

A major complaint about the FCC is the delay experienced in getting action on a petition to deny. The delay in processing petitions causes problems to both the public and the licensee. Although courts have allowed licensees to stay on the air while a petition is being processed, as the NAB told the Commission, delays in processing petitions to deny are extremely costly, demoralize the station's staff, and strain community relations.

Delays disturb petitioners, too. Public interest lawyers refer to the problem of the "disappearing client"—the person or group gets all "psyched up" in filing the petition and then gets frustrated when nothing happens. Moreover, since the Commission permits stations to upgrade—especially in employment—after the petition has been filed, the delay may allow the station to avoid the hearing by improving its practices. Although the improvement in station practices is what the citizen group has sought, these groups and their lawyers think that scoring a few victories (hearing designations) is important for morale and for the impression on future adversaries.

The problem of delay in processing petitions to deny was soon very apparent. One 1973 study showed that between June 1969 and January 1973, for those petitions which were finally processed, the average time required for resolution was 18 months—and all but one were denied. By early 1974, the situation was far worse: action on more than 200 petitions to deny renewals was still pending. Some petitions were more than three years old, and the licensee had to file a "supplemental" renewal application when the next renewal period came around again. Particularly frustrating to the renewal branch was that as quickly as petitions could be processed and sent to the commissioners, more petitions were being filed. Moreover, the tremendous staff turnover made Shiben complain that he had trained two and one-half staffs in two and one-half years.

Something had to be done to cope with the backlog. In December 1974, the deferred renewals list still included roughly 280 stations because of 180 petitions to deny. By themselves, petitions filed against 62 stations in Texas and California represented a year's work. As a result, a special six-lawyer task force, drawn from other branches of the Commission, was assigned to assist the ten renewal-branch lawyers who processed petitions.

In addition Chairman Wiley established a special "petition to deny day" on the FCC's regular calendar. On this day, Wiley explained to the 1975 NAB convention, "each new petition will be examined by the Commission to determine if an early, almost immediate, decision can be made as to whether it raises substantial and material questions concerning the licensee's performance. At the same time, we will expedite our efforts as to the older petitions in order to attack our backlog from two directions."

Wiley's concept of a special day for discussion of petitions was hailed by at least one public interest lawyer. This day would give the commissioners an opportunity to discuss, even debate, the kinds of station practices they found unacceptable. The commissioners could then give clear guidance to the staff about which allegations were serious and which were trivial. The renewal staff, charged with drafting tentative opinions on whether or not to grant a petition, would know the commissioner's views.

Unfortunately, petition-to-deny day didn't work out that way; it became what Commissioner Washburn inadvertently called "denial of petition day." On the first petition-to-deny day in May 1975, the staff asked the commissioners their feelings on an issue raised in one of the petitions—Was hiring news consultants an abdication of licensee responsibility? The commissioners quickly agreed it was not, looked at the other allegations in that particular petition, and ordered the petition denied. Before the citizen group could reply to the license applicant's opposition, before the due process of the pleading cycle had run its course, the commissioners had decided the case. *Broadcasting* noted this rapid shuffle—the petitioners were outraged, and the commissioners were embarrassed. The Commission decided that henceforth it would consider only completed draft recommendations from the staff.

With the aid of petition-to-deny day and the increased staff, the Commission began to reduce the backlog. As of January 1, 1975, 215 petitions were pending against 265 stations. Petitions were processed and turned down more quickly. On one petition-to-deny day in October, 21 petitions against 31 stations were discussed; but no stations were designated for hearing, although some received conditional renewals on EEO problems. By February 1976, only 60 petitions were outstanding against 70 stations. Citizens Communication Center Executive Director Frank Lloyd complained of the "disingenuous denial" of scores of petitions to deny.

The process was, indeed, speeding up. In March 1976, Wiley told the NAB convention that he hoped to provide 90-day service on renewals, even when a petition to deny had been filed. And in October, he told an NAB regional convention that by the end of 1976 there would be zero backlog; but subsequent findings would be acted upon within six months, not 90 days. As of May 15, 1977, the backlog was 26 petitions against 50 stations.

Sometimes delay in processing petitions or voting them up or down is the fault of the Commission. Sometimes it is the natural result of due process. In a few cases, when the petition to deny raises other legal questions with which the commissioners would prefer not to wrestle, they put off the evil day by not deciding whether to grant the petition.

Bureaucratic inefficiency is another cause of delay. A petition filed against a TV station in Madison, Wisconsin, in October 1970, was not decided for more than five years (at which time the FCC denied the petition on a 3–2 vote). When the item was brought before the Commission in early 1974 (after the next renewal period had already passed), the item was so badly drafted that the bureau, chagrined, asked to withdraw the item from the commissioners' consideration until the decision could be more elegantly expressed. The case, apparently forgotten or misplaced, languished in the renewal branch for well over a year until a thirty-paragraph item was redrafted.

The commissioners' reluctance to move expeditiously if the problem might go away is shown in a case involving a Greenwood, Mississippi, radio station. The licensee of a local FM station bought an AM station in 1969 and promised to provide "the only primarily Negro programmed station in the city or county," where more than half of the population was black. Eight months after the sale was approved and his license renewed in 1970, the owner discontinued all black programming on the station, fired all black employees, dropped public service programming geared to the black community, and began operating with a country-and-western-music format.

When Citizens Communications Center asked the FCC to issue either a cease-and-desist order or a revocation order, the Commission considered itself embattled in its position on format changes. The majority of commissioners had held that a radio station licensee should be able to change formats at will; the courts had disagreed. The FCC dispatched investigators to Greenwood, but for over a year took no action on Citizens' petitions until the law firm's request for a writ of mandamus in July 1972 got the FCC moving. After the commissioners had decided to approach the case on the grounds of misrepresentations to the FCC (after all, the allegations went far beyond a simple format change), the commissioners ordered the licensee to submit an early renewal application.

In April 1974, four years after the original complaint had been filed, the FCC set the renewal for hearing and also questioned the licensee's qualifications to operate the FM station. In August 1975, an FCC law judge recommended that neither license be renewed. In June 1977, the FCC was still considering the appeal by the licensee, who contends that surveys showed that problems of blacks and whites in the community were inseparable. If his appeals fail, this would be a highly unusual case of a station's losing its license without court intervention. Had the FCC been willing to use its cease-and-desist powers when Citizens made its initial request, the case might have been resolved far more quickly and at less loss to the licensee. And, of course, the black community might have been getting the service it was promised in 1969.

Even when the Commission grants a petition to deny and sets a license renewal for hearing, the process moves slowly. There are numerous occasions when roadblocks can be placed in the FCC's path. In 1967 citizens in Puyallup, a small town near Tacoma, Washington, complained to the FCC that the local AM station, KAYE, was violating the Fairness Doctrine and the FCC's rules on personal attacks. When the station's license came up for renewal in 1969, a committee of 69 community residents, including officers of the NAACP, the Urban League, the League of Women Voters, bankers, and lawyers, filed a petition to deny. After a year had passed, a group of 147 citizens with legal aid from the United Church of Christ again asked the FCC to act on the petition, and asserted that petitioners and potential witnesses were being harassed by KAYE management both by vilification on the air and by tactics such as late-night telephone calls. The FCC in July 1970 designated the renewal application for hearing.

About a year later, a law judge recommended that the renewal be denied for the reasons petitioners cited. The station reportedly continued to excoriate its enemies over the air and to plead for listeners to contribute money to fight the petitioners. KAYE appealed the law judge's decision and asked the FCC for a further hearing to present more evidence.

The matter went back to hearing, but the law judge terminated the proceeding on September 11, 1972, and, in a December 4 order, dismissed the renewal application. The judge found that the station was unprepared, and that it and its attorney had conducted themselves in a manner designed "to frustrate and prevent any semblance of an orderly evidentiary hearing." Relations between Judge Ernest Nash and the station's attorney, Benedict Cottone (a former FCC general counsel), were so strained that on September 8, the judge ordered the attorney out of the hearing room. When told to leave, the attorney, who had obviously expected this turn of events, said: "I have a prepared statement to make. I want to make this statement. 'Your mind, sir, is a cesspool of filth, venom, venality, bias, and prejudice. To call you a savage would cast aspersion on innocent savages. If I believed you had any semblance or vestige of rationality, I would call you a very, very evil man. . . .' "

KAYE appealed the judge's actions in dismissing the application and asked for renewal of its license. The Commission heard oral argument in September 1973. The Puget Sound Committee for Good Broadcasting, which had filed a petition to deny more than four years earlier, filed a pleading with the Commission asserting that (1) the proceeding should not have been remanded, (2) the initial June 1971 decision to deny license renewal should have been affirmed, and (3) there was no basis for the station's appeal. The Broadcast Bureau argued that while the judge had properly excluded the attorney from the hearing, the judge had erred in not affording the station an adequate opportunity to get a substitute lawyer and in dismissing the application. The commissioners agreed with this argument; and in April 1974, they remanded the proceeding for further hearings before a different law judge.

When the station said it wanted to be represented by Cottone, the attorney that the law judge had ordered out of the hearing, another hearing was begun to determine whether Cottone could represent KAYE. In 1977, the FCC decided he could not and suspended him from practice for one day—an action Cottone is appealing. In the meantime, the licensee said he could find no substitute.

KAYE's general manager raised $200,000 through his broadcast appeals for funds. He took these contributions as a sign of community support. The FCC interpreted the action as using a station for personal benefit instead of community service.

As of June 1977, the station (with different call letters and a new general manager) was still on the air although it has been operating without a license since 1969. It has been more than eight years since the citizens filed a petition to deny—and any action the FCC may take to put the licensee off the air can be appealed to the courts. Although the KAYE case is not typical—very few cases get so embroiled in personalities and technicalities—the case demonstrates the frustrations citizen groups may encounter even after persuading FCC staff members that the complaint is legitimate.

In the one case that resulted in the FCC's denying renewals, in response to a petition, the circumstances had changed significantly by the time the final act took place. In 1953 the state of Alabama created a five-person Alabama Educational Television Commission with members appointed by the governor to establish and maintain an educational TV network statewide. By 1970 AETC was the licensee of eight noncommercial TV stations and had a construction permit for a ninth station.

In 1970 the chairman of the faculty senate of the University of Alabama complained to the FCC that the AETC had discontinued the *Black Journal* series and had preempted several other public-TV network programs of interest to blacks; some 60 students also complained that the AETC was censoring black-oriented programs. The licensee responded that public network programs "containing lewd, vulgar, obscene, or repulsive material have no place in the crowded AETC schedule." Despite other complaints, the FCC renewed the eight licenses by a 4–3 vote in June 1970.

Alabama groups charged the AETC with conscious discrimination against black viewers, and engaged Citizens Comunications Center to ask the FCC to reconsider. Wiley, then general counsel, and Shiben

the renewal application, the staff makes a recommendation to the commissioners. Since the WMAL case, the commissioners have *never* been unwilling to support a staff recommendation for designation. If the staff says the petition to deny raises serious allegations which should be explored fully in a hearing, the commissioners have, without exception, ordered a hearing. Conversely, however, if the staff doesn't recommend a hearing, the commissioners, who don't have access to all of the facts, almost always go along with the bureau's recommendation to dismiss the petition.

Once the staff has determined what outcome it wishes to recommend to the commissioners, it is a simple matter—especially for veterans of the Commission—to cite some standard paragraphs and citations supporting that position. There are enough FCC policy pronouncements, specific statements made in various petitions-to-deny decisions, and statements made by the courts to support a variety of positions: if the staff wishes to deny the petition, it has ample precedent to cite; if the staff wishes to recommend a hearing, it can find legal support for that position, too.

The staff, therefore, is the gatekeeper of information and is the real decision maker. What Cole found particularly disturbing was that often the staff's internal disagreements on the proper disposition of certain cases were never reported to the commissioners; they were not told that a case was close, that it could go either way. The commissioners weren't told that one staff member believed the petition should be designated for these reasons, and another staff member disagreed for those. Instead, the staff-level decision maker had the staff item written to support his position; and the agenda item simply said "the bureau" recommends renewal be granted.

A classic example of how this system works took place in 1974. In late August, Cole returned from a vacation and was told by a renewal branch attorney that the Commission had "struck a new all-time low mark" in turning down petitions to deny. "The courts will definitely reverse this one," the attorney said, referring to a case he himself had not worked on. Cole learned that the original staff recommendation— the recommendation of the attorney who examined all the pleadings— was to designate the station for hearing; and an order to that effect had been drafted.

The petitioners, a coalition of Mexican-Americans, had for many years attempted to get stations in the Albuquerque, New Mexico, area to be more responsive to the problems of Mexican-Americans. As early as 1966 they had written local stations to request increased coverage for events of interest to the Mexican-American community. In May 1971, they petitioned the FCC for a public hearing to evaluate all the Albuquerque stations' performances. In denying the hearing, the Commission informed the petitioners they could file a formal petition to deny any Albuquerque station's license renewal, and would find all the necessary supporting information "by examining [the] stations' renewal applications." The petitioners' second informal protest to the Commission on June 17, 1971, alleged that the Albuquerque broadcast media had imposed a "blackout" on news of importance to the Mexican-American community. Once again the Commission rejected the request for a hearing.

On July 16, 1971, the petitioners filed a formal petition asking to inspect the annual financial reports of station KOB–TV for the calendar years 1968 through 1970. Petitioners, citing a recent court decision, contended that one principal test for measuring a station's performance for renewal should be, in the words of the court, "whether and to what extent the incumbent has reinvested the profit on its license to the service of the viewing and listening public."

With the request still pending and the deadline for filing petitions to deny upcoming, the petitioners in August filed a formal petition to deny the license renewal of KOB–TV. On September 2, 1971, the Commission denied their request for inspection of the station's financial statements because such access would broadly revise Commission policy, and broad revisions of Commission policy were more appropriately accomplished through rulemaking. Anticipating this reaction by the Commission, the petitioners had filed a formal petition for general rulemaking. In May 1977, the Commission had still not acted on the formal petition for rulemaking—neither sent it out for comment nor dismissed it.

In their petition to deny the renewal application of KOB–TV, the petitioners alleged that the licensee had failed during the past license term to provide adequate programming dealing with the problems of racial discrimination and had failed to propose future programs to deal with those problems. The licensee's 1968 renewal application had listed racial tensions between Mexican-Americans and Anglos as one of the community's significant problems; the 1971 renewal application revealed that "minority-related problems" were among the eight most important community problems ascertained in the community leader survey, and were, in fact, at the top of the station's list of problems.

The attorney assigned to the case thought a hearing was necessary, and proposed a draft order, which stated that, "taken as a whole, a significant question exists" as to the adequacy of the licensee's past and proposed programs to meet the Mexican-American community's ascertained needs and interests, particularly the problem of racial discrimination. To *support* the hearing designation, the lawyer cited the court's WMAL decision: while the court had said the manner in which the licensee responded to problems and needs was within his or her discretion, the licensee "may not flatly ignore" a matter of importance, such as racial discrimination. After discussing the programs the station listed as supposedly dealing with problems of racial discrimination, the lawyer concluded that the station's efforts were still in question and that a hearing was needed to determine whether the needs of the Mexican-Americans had been adequately addressed.

The draft order was passed up the line. The senior officials in the branch decided that the station should not be designated for hearing and that a new order should be drafted. By August 21, 1974 (three years after the petition to deny had been filed), the redrafted order, which granted renewal and denied the petition, was ready for the commissioners' agenda.

The redrafted order, which denied the petition, simply repeated the petitioners' charges and then quickly dismissed them. At one point the new order said, "It is, of course, entirely possible that [the station] has not broadcast the amount or types of programming on these problems as petitioners would prefer." Ironically, the order then quoted the same part of the WMAL decision which the original draft order used to designate the station for hearing: how stations had discretion to respond to community problems and needs, and how only flatly ignoring a strongly expressed need should cause a hearing. The item then cited the same programs cited in the earlier draft; in this case, however, rather than detailing why these programs were inadequate, the order simply said "It appears, therefore, that [the station's] public service programming has been responsive to the problems of the public which it serves, including Mexican-Americans."

Because none of the commissioners or their assistants was aware of what had happened on the staff level, the redrafted order was not discussed. The item, which granted renewal and denied the petition, passed "on consent"—in other words, at the beginning of the meeting, it was one of the items which none of the commissioners indicated an interest in discussing.

The attorney who predicted the court would overturn the FCC's decision was wrong. However, the court did say it was "troubled" by the petitioners' contentions and "by the issue whether the minimal amount of public interest programming serving the needs of a 40 percent minority does not create a disparity so significant as to amount to a difference in kind rather than degree." Tracy Westen, a public interest lawyer with more FCC experience than the attorneys who filed the original petition to deny, had entered the case on the appeal. Using the statistics that had been available to the FCC all along, Westen pointed out that, according to its renewal application, the station had devoted no more than .05 percent of one year's air time to the problems of 40 percent of the viewing audience. The court said that this "explicitly quantitative argument," because it had not been raised in the original petition the Commission considered, could not be introduced in court for the first time. Later, Shiben commented to Cole, "If Tracy Westen had filed the original petition, there would have been a hearing. They almost got one anyway. It was a toss-up." (This fact was totally unknown to the commissioners.)

PETITIONS ON GROUNDS OTHER THAN DISCRIMINATION

When petitioners allege a station hasn't been meeting its public service obligations in programming, but no question of racial discrimination has been raised, the Commission usually cites its philosophy of leaving program judgments to the licensee's discretion. The Commission has stated on many occasions, "The mere citation of what is deemed to be an insufficient amount of programming without any evidence to support the assertion that such performance would fail to serve the public interest, is insufficient to raise a substantial and material question of fact as to whether a station will serve the public interest."

When a petition claimed that a station scheduled all its informational programming between 6:00 A.M. and 9:00 A.M. on Sunday, the Commission responded:

> Here, petitioners have presented no specific allegations necessary to show an abuse of discretion by this licensee, other than the unsubstantiated assertion that "most people" are asleep when the majority of the station's programming designed to meet community needs is presented. There is no demonstration that programming presented at 6:00 to 9:00 A.M. on Sunday could not reasonably be expected to be effective.

Once a petitioner claimed—and the Commission acknowledged—that more than 80 percent of a station's public affairs programming was broadcast from 4:00 to 5:00 in the morning. The station was already involved in a renewal hearing because of possible "misrepresentation" in categorizing public affairs, but the Commission refused to add an issue regarding the scheduling of public affairs. This action resulted in a front-page *Variety* story, which began, "This should have broadcasters heating up those transmitters early in the morning. The FCC thinks the 4:00 to 5:00 A.M. time slot is fine for public affairs programming."

Even when community representatives file a petition to deny for stations that carry no news or public affairs, or far less than promised, the Commission tends to renew the license on the strength of the station's pledge to do better in the future. Sometimes such pledges have been amended to the license renewal application months after the petition to deny has been filed. In March 1975, for example, the renewal staff decided to deny a petition and to renew a license primarily on the basis of specific programs promised for the next renewal period; but since the renewal grant didn't mention this condition, the staff that analyzes the next renewal application (in 1978) won't know the importance of these programs, or have reason to check for their broadcast in the composite week.

The FCC has never designated a renewal for hearing solely for overcommercialization, although occasionally that issue has been added to cases set for hearing on other grounds. In one such case, the staff noted in passing that the licensee had, in the past two renewal periods, violated the FCC's generous rule of thumb (and his own proposals) regarding commercials by broadcasting as much as 30 minutes of commercials per hour. The FCC complained of the licensee's lack of compliance with his "self-selected commercial policies," but took no action for six years until a community group petitioned to deny the license renewal.

The second most common complaint, next to failure to meet equal employment standards, has been failure to program to meet the problems and needs of a segment of the community. The Commission used to require licensees to list problems and needs and programming responses both for the last year of the license period *and* for the future; but since January 1976, the FCC has required licensees to list only the past three years' problems and programming, not prospective ones.

Licensees who take the ascertainment-of-needs problem lightly have traditionally been renewed nonetheless. In a 1975 dissent to the commissioners' decision to dismiss a petition against various radio and TV licensees in Kansas, Commissioner Hooks expressed outrage. Hooks declared: "The licensees had asserted, and the commissioners had accepted, the proposition that local and minority needs were served by such programs as: *John Chancellor Commentary, Social Security, Governor's Energy Report,* and *Ann Landers*; that programs such as *Meet the Press, Pass It On, The Today Show, America, A Conversation with Senator Robert Dole* in particular catered to the black audience in Topeka." Hooks said, "While these programs have great appeal and do serve the general public, the assertion by the broadcasters that they specifically serve minority needs reeks of arrogance and shows an utter disdain for the minority population residing within their service area. I can only add that the Commission's acceptance of these assertions is incredulous at best."

In the rare cases where the Commission has called for a renewal hearing following a petition alleging ascertainment defects, it has simply been a case of the licensees' repeated failure to respond to FCC inquiries. Almost any answer would probably have been acceptable to the FCC; some licensees totally failed to list the community problems or completely neglected to link ascertainment with programming. One station manager, for example, listed the station's "sign on" and "sign off" as public affairs programming to meet community needs; because of other deficiencies, that station was designated for hearing.

Citizen groups that petition to deny licenses for noncommercial stations have been unsuccessful in persuading the Commission, except in a case involving racial discrimination (the Alabama Educational Commission stations). Educational stations aren't required to make the same promises of categorized service as those of commercial stations—thus educational stations cannot be accused of breaking promises. Until

1976, educational stations didn't have to list community problems and needs the stations proposed to meet; therefore, they could not be shown negligent. Even today, it is not clear to what extent the public broadcasting station's obligations to meet community needs resembles the obligations of commercial stations.

PETITIONS ALLEGING DISCRIMINATION IN EMPLOYMENT

Despite the hundreds of petitions to deny renewal alleging employment discrimination or equal employment opportunity (EEO) deficiencies, the Commission has never set a license renewal for hearing solely on employment-related issues. As of May 1977, the FCC had added an EEO issue to a dozen renewal or revocation cases already designated for hearing.

Petitioners have attempted to prove a licensee guilty of employment discrimination by citing the number of minority personnel or women at the station. This was one of the issues cited in the petition against WMAL Washington in 1969. The court's ruling has been cited by other petitioners and by the FCC as well:

> Finally, our opinion does not hold that statistical evidence of an extremely low rate of minority employment will never constitute a prima facie showing of discrimination or "pattern of substantial failure to accord equal employment opportunities." Petitioners' evidence was not an adequate showing in this case because their assertion that WMAL's record stood at 7% black employment in an area 70% black was somewhat misleading. In evidence before the FCC was data that approximately 24% of the entire Washington, D.C. metropolitan area is black. WMAL's employment of approximately 7% blacks out of this total metropolitan area is within the zone of reasonableness.

The concept of a "zone of reasonableness" has been relied upon by the FCC to justify its EEO decisions. As recently as April 1977, the appeals court affirmed the FCC's refusal to set WRC–TV Washington and WABC–TV New York licenses for hearing on 1972 NOW charges that they hired an insufficient number of women. But Judge Malcolm R. Wilkey, who had been on the three-judge panel in the WMAL case, said the zone of reasonableness is an evolving concept, not a static or concrete criterion, and "the Commission can be expected to adopt a more stringent view of the acceptable 'mode.' " The Commission has still not officially defined what the zone is in equal employment cases. However, as previously noted, in March 1977, the commissioners directed the Broadcast Bureau to examine a station's EEO program if its minority and/or female employment profile does not represent "at least one-half of their respective percentages of the market's work force

and at least one-fourth of their percentages in the top four job categories (officials, professionals, technicians and salesworkers)."

In a June 1976 order, clarifying its EEO policies, the Commission
said it had no "sweeping mandate" to advance the national policy
against discrimination. Although the Equal Employment Opportunity
Commission might conclude on the basis of statistical evidence that
there was "reasonable cause to believe" discrimination existed, the FCC
stated that this deficiency by itself is not justification for denying renewal although special reporting requirements were sometimes imposed as a condition of the renewal. "We do not believe that a licensee
is guilty of discrimination under the public interest of the Communications Act where adequate affirmative efforts are being undertaken to
correct . . . deficiencies and there is no evidence of intentional wrong
doing." The court agreed in essence in the case of *NOW* v. *FCC* (involving WRC–TV and WABC–TV), but in its April 11, 1977, ruling
warned the FCC to be diligent:

> As an agency with a different mission than the EEOC, the Commis-
> sion may properly employ different standards: a finding by the EEOC
> that a licensee's employment practices *may be* in violation of Title
> VII of the Civil Rights Act does not necessarily mean that the same
> finding raises an issue under the Communications Act. This is not
> to say, of course, that the Commission could safely ignore in its
> ultimate determination about renewal a clearly relevant finding by
> an expert agency. Rather the Commission must evaluate the finding
> carefully and *fully* in light of its own established standards.

In the NOW case, the appeals court dealt with an issue that had long
been a battleground for the Commission and citizen groups—prehearing discovery. Citizen groups and their lawyers complained about their
inability to view station records and take affidavits under oath to bolster
allegations against a licensee. In EEO cases particularly, petitioners
believed that they needed to question station employees about hiring
practices. Otherwise, to secure evidence, petitioners had to find a station employee willing to risk his or her own job by providing them
with information voluntarily. Previously, in 1976 the Commission (with
Hooks dissenting) stated its view:

> Predesignation discovery as envisioned by the petitioner could, in
> our view, have the undesirable result of amounting to nothing more
> than a fishing expedition for complainants who have nothing more
> than a mere suspicion that a broadcast licensee may have breached
> a Commission rule or policy.

In the NOW case, the court countered:

> If the Commission here, for example, had not itself sought out more
> detailed data from WRC about its hiring and promoting; it may

have been under some obligation to NOW to afford it some discovery from WRC so that the effectiveness of its EEO plan could be fairly assessed.

The courts continued to treat the matter of prehearing discovery in three other cases, which were decided in April 1977 and which involved FCC dismissals of petitions to deny. In cases where a Mexican-American group challenged a San Antonio station (*Bilingual Bicultural Coalition on Mass Media* v. *FCC*) and a Chinese group petitioned to deny a San Francisco station's license renewal (*Chinese for Affirmative Action* v. *FCC*), the court said the FCC "must afford those challenging renewal a reasonable opportunity for prehearing discovery through appropriate interrogatories," and petitioners should be given opportunity to probe a licensee's responses to a petition. Finally, in the EEO case involving WTVR–AM–FM–TV Richmond, Virginia (*Black Broadcasting Coalition of Richmond* v. *FCC*) the court said, "Had the Commission's rules provided for prehearing discovery in this instance, a far more adequate factual record (bearing on the failure of the stations to meet their license-term responsibilities to blacks) would have been before it at an earlier stage and post-term actions would have been better explicated and placed in proper context."

The most significant court judgment in the WTVR case was on another issue that had frustrated community groups in EEO cases—upgrading. If a licensee who had employed no blacks, for example, during his three-year license period hired some after a petition to deny was filed, the FCC customarily would renew the license. Sometimes the renewal was conditioned on the licensee's continuing to pursue an affirmative action program and reporting regularly on its progress. In February 1975 Commissioner Hooks recommended that "in the future, references to subsequent performance should not be cited" in recommendations to dismiss a petition in EEO matters. He said upgrading of a finite license-term record was contrary to the FCC's statutory scheme. "Although I can understand, from a practical standpoint, that reliance on later performance was helpful, as indicia of good faith application of our nondiscriminatory requirements when our EEO rules were first adopted, ample time has now passed so that each license term should stand on intrinsic merit."

The majority did not adopt Hooks's view, as in the case in which the Black Broadcasting Coalition of Richmond asked the FCC not to renew the WTVR licenses because of its hiring practices. During the 1969–1972 license period, WTVR–TV employed one black part time (out of 62 full-time and six part-time employees), and the radio stations had no blacks among their 26 employees. The coalition also alleged overt discrimination in hiring. When the Commission dismissed this petition in August 1975 and simply conditioned the stations' renewals to EEO reporting requirements, petitioners appealed to the courts. At the time a leading citizen-group lawyer predicted this case could be "the WLBT of the Seventies."

The court was highly critical of the Commission's handling of the WTVR case. "It did not require much analysis for the Commission to perceive that the situation highlighted by [the petition to deny] called for a 'hard look' and for prompt decisive action in the public interest. But the Commission delayed for three years and then looked only to post-license term statistics and ignored term-time performance which, as measured by the licensee's reports to the Commission, was clearly outside the 'zone of reasonableness.' " The court emphasized that "allegations of overt discrimination in hiring and firing remained contested and unsatisfied." In remanding the case to the Commission and ordering that a hearing take place, the court insisted that upgrading was not enough, because "when overt discrimination is responsibly claimed and a licensee's minority employment during the license term is below the 'zone of reasonableness,' a strong case for a hearing on the licensee's compliance with its obligation not to discriminate is made out." Moreover, the question of the adequacy of the station's affirmative action program was in itself sufficient reason for a hearing.

The court's language in the WTVR case is sufficiently unequivocal to ensure that the Commission will no longer be able to dismiss petitions and to renew licenses simply on conditions of future improvement in hiring minorities. It was the first case since WLBT, 11 years earlier, in which the court overturned a renewal grant made after a citizen group's petition to deny and ordered a hearing. The court said that if this "curious neutrality-in-favor-of-the-licensee"—Burger's phrase from the 1969 WLBT decision—is to end, "there must be a more meaningful accounting for conduct during the contested license period and more exacting standard established for the future."

Although the 1977 cases refer to EEO matters, the decisions may have an impact on other petition-to-deny cases as well, particularly with respect to prehearing discovery. The greatest significance may bear on the question of what constitutes a material and substantial question of fact that must be resolved (through a hearing or some sort of investigation) before renewal can be granted.

In light of court actions, the FCC may be more receptive to complaints that stop short of demanding that a broadcaster lose his license. Because of the long battle over petitions to deny, public groups may finally be gaining increased FCC attention.

15
Grassroots Regulation: Citizen-Licensee Agreements

Everyone wants cooperation rather than confrontation.
We want to negotiate agreements. We don't want to
have to challenge any license renewals. But if that's
necessary, we want to be as well-equipped as possible,
as aware and sophisticated as possible.

Janet Whittaker, northeast vice-chairperson
National Black Media Coalition
February 15, 1975

. . . Over recent years we have found enough reasonable
suggestions [during negotiations] that I honestly believe
our service to the entire community has broadened
and improved. This is impossible unless cooperation
replaces confrontation. And that can be achieved only
when both parties sincerely try to understand each other.
It's not always easy to come by. Sometimes it becomes
impossible. But for the broadcaster who wants to serve
the broadest interests of his service area, I believe it's
worth a real try.

Jack Harris, General Manager, KPRC–TV Houston
1977 NAB convention workshop

15 In many instances, citizen groups with complaints about the performance of broadcast licensees have not needed to make a federal case of it. The groups have sought specific, often rather narrow, improvements in station programming, increased broadcaster responsiveness to what the groups perceive as important community problems and needs, and increased job opportunities for minority groups. Sometimes these differences have been settled through negotiations between the community groups and the broadcasters, and the resulting agreement obviates FCC action. In some cases, the agreements simply bind the broadcaster to observing policies that should, under FCC rules, have been followed all along. In other cases, the agreements include sweeping changes in station practices.

Commissioners have shown ambivalence about agreements, however. Although many commissioners prefer to see regulation enforced by community dynamics rather than by official sanctions, some commissioners fear that licensees may be relinquishing too much control over what they program. Licensees, not citizen groups, are responsible to the FCC for what goes over the air; and reliance on the individual licensee's discretion and judgment has been a keystone of the FCC's regulatory philosophy.

The path of negotiation and agreement has advantages for citizen groups and for broadcasters. Usually (though not always) the citizen group is pursuing limited objectives. The high costs in money and time required to pursue a petition to deny before the FCC and the unlikelihood of the petition's leading to a hearing on the license renewal make citizen groups prefer negotiation. Denial of license renewal by the FCC accomplishes nothing directly for the citizen group, except for putting other broadcasters on notice.

Unless the citizen group's requests are outrageous, the broadcasters, too, have strong motives for reaching an agreement. The broadcaster may be forced to pay many thousands of dollars in research and legal fees to defend against a petition to deny, even if a hearing is not ordered by the FCC. If the sale of a station is involved, the buyer has even stronger reasons for reaching an agreement: the delay and uncertainty may cause the transaction to fall through; meeting citizens' demands may cost the potential licensee a mere fraction of the cost of a valuable broadcast property. Aside from costs, a station being besieged by a citizen group is under a cloud in the community; management is continually defending itself against charges of insensitivity (and may be making countercharges of moral blackmail). If the charges are being considered by the FCC, the broadcaster may have to wait years to learn whether or not the Commission will clear the license.

Broadcasters who do make agreements with community groups may face their fellow broadcasters' accusations of behaving like Neville Chamberlain. In June 1974 John Schneider, president of the CBS Broadcast Group, told the Georgia Association of Broadcasters that some licensees were too fearful of petitions to deny: "There are broad-casters who are willing to trade too much for too little ... simply to buy a little peace for today." In July 1971, Wayne Kearl, president of KENS–TV San Antonio, felt constrained to send the following letter to *Broadcasting*:

> In your June 28 report of the Bilingual Bicultural Coalition's broad-cast demands in San Antonio, you state that KENS–TV "accedes to the coalition's demands." I would appreciate the following clarifi-cation. The coalition presented a list of demands. Some were deleted because our attorney felt they raised legal problems, others because the station felt they were unworkable or not in the public interest. Other demands were felt to be in the legitimate interests of the Mexican-American community and consistent with good broadcast-ing practice, and it was upon this basis that an understanding was reached.

Agreements can lead to further problems. Not all citizen groups are representative of the entire community (nor do they necessarily purport to be). For example, WXYZ Detroit signed an agreement with NOW to broadcast a minimum of 90 minutes of women's programming each year during prime-time hours, and to accept a women's advisory council appointed by NOW. Antifeminist organizations, such as Happiness of Womanhood (HOW), Stop ERA, and the National Council of Catholic Women, objected strongly to the station's signing of the agreement. Elaine Donnelly, chairman of the Michigan Stop ERA Committee, wrote the FCC, "If feminists are allowed to tighten the screws on broad-casters every three years at license renewal time, there is every indication that TV stations could be turned into controlled public-relations tools of the women's liberation movement." The station's general manager observed, "We're damned if we do, and damned if we don't."

Agreements may hinge upon some minor reforms—or may require station management to undertake sweeping changes costing a substan-tial amount of money. The licensee who fears he may be vulnerable to FCC sanctions if he doesn't settle "out of court" usually grants the broadest concessions. For example, in June 1973 a Selma, Alabama, station agreed to the following terms with a local citizen group: estab-lishment of a community liaison committee of seven to 11 citizens, at least five black; group meetings with station officials at least four times a year to make recommendations regarding employment, programming, and ascertainment procedures; surveys, conducted by a team of "sur-veyors" prior to expiration of each license period, to ascertain commu-nity needs, particularly those of blacks; local production of at least 35 percent of nonmusical programming, featuring black input on a con-tinuing basis; devoting at least one hour per month to educational needs and problems of Dallas County; the same amount of time devoted to problems of black youths; another monthly hour devoted to "the full range of black life and values" and produced in conjunction with the liaison council; devoting at least one-third of the news stories broadcast to local issues, including those pertinent to blacks; hiring black "stringers" when possible and employing at least one full-time black newsman; production of at least 15 minidocumentaries per year on specific black needs and problems; at least three community-access editorials per week featuring presentations by local citizenry; black participation at all levels of station's administration; recruitment of and on-the-job training for minority personnel with the liaison advised of all forthcoming job openings; nondiscrimination in purchasing equipment and accepting advertising; refusal to do business with any firm that has practiced discrimination in employment or services to blacks or women.

The station that reached this agreement may seem to have made many concessions to placate the petitioner, The Dallas County Progressive Movement for Human Rights. But the group withdrew its petition against that station. The other two stations in Selma were designated for renewal hearing by the FCC on the strength of the group's petitions. One station turned in its license rather than undergo a hearing; the other reached a "consent agreement" with the group, asked the FCC to renew its license for only one year and then to consider if a hearing were still necessary. This novel approach had not been approved by the FCC by June 1977, and even citizen groups were in disagreement over whether the request should be approved. The station was not admitting guilt but was promising to refrain from specified practices in the future.

In April 1977 a group called Feminists for Media Rights reached a rather spectacular agreement with WGAL–TV Lancaster, Pennsylvania, a station owned by a family that also owns the only newspaper in town and part of a cable system in the area. FMR asked the FCC to deny license renewal because of the concentration of media control and because of discrimination against women in employment and programming. The discrimination charges were dismissed but the renewal was designated for hearing on some of the other charges. WGAL–TV, therefore, agreed to sell or trade its station license by 1981; and in the interim, it agreed to program a half-hour, prime-time, public affairs show; increase coverage of women's sports; upgrade its EEO program; and endow a $100,000 scholarship for training area women in broadcasting. The station agreed also to fund a $150,000 program to establish a nonprofit news service specializing in information of concern to women, to set up a women's advisory council, and to initiate "free speech messages" on the air. Significantly WGAL–TV agreed to reimburse the women's group for expenses incurred in challenging the license renewal and negotiating the agreement. Finally, the station promised to take steps to find a new owner who would continue to honor the provisions of the agreement; in return, if such a buyer were found,

FMR indicated it would not object to the sale "barring extraordinary circumstances." By June 1977, it was uncertain if the FCC would approve the agreement and call off the hearing.

A *Wall Street Journal* article* (January 2, 1975) sampled FCC sentiment about citizen–broadcaster agreements:

> We want to tell a broadcaster he must continue to meet with citizens, to hear them out but not to sell his soul.
> *Chairman Wiley*

> We license a broadcaster to serve the public—all of it. What we have now is program dictatorship by a small group of activists. . . . These groups come in and say, "Give us what we want or we'll file a petition to deny your license." Broadcasters have got to have enough guts to stand up and say no.
> *Commissioner Quello*

> We've left broadcasters in a dilemma. We say, "Go ascertain the needs of your community and meet them," but on the other hand, we say, "Don't delegate your responsibility."
> *Commissioner Robinson*

When the Commission was first introduced to the practice of agreements between citizen groups and broadcasters, special circumstances prevailed. Everett Parker, of the United Church of Christ, and Earle Moore, the organization's lawyer, seeking a test case to solidify the gains made in the WLBT Jackson case, coordinated community group complaints against KTAL–TV Texarkana, Texas. Some of these 12 groups represented minorities dissatisfied by the station's lack of programming to blacks; other groups, such as the Texarkana Junior Chamber of Commerce, were angry because the station had moved studio facilities to Shreveport, Louisiana, and was ignoring local public affairs. The groups, represented by Moore, filed a January 1969 petition to deny KTAL–TV's license renewal. Some five months later, the station and the groups negotiated an agreement: the groups would ask the Commission to dismiss their petition and renew KTAL–TV's license; and the station would agree to specific programming and employment practices. (The station had not denied many of the petition's allegations about programming for minorities.)

Some of the provisions of the KTAL–TV agreement would become commonplace in future agreements: hiring a minimum number of black reporters; a commitment not to preempt network programs of particular interest to minorities without consultation with minority groups; and agreement to present regular programs with black and white panelists discussing controversial issues. However, Parker and the

---

groups, to cover matters that were by assumption, though not in practice, the responsibility of all broadcast licensees, broadened the terms
of the agreement to include a monthly discussion program to explore
current religious issues; regular presentation of clergymen of all major
faiths and all races; regular meetings with community groups, and
prime-time announcements of the station's willingness for such meetings; and increased local programming, including news coverage of state
capitols in both Texas and Arkansas. The station promised also to
solicit PSAs from community groups and organizations, and to cover
their regular meetings on news programs.

Moore, who had an important role in drafting the agreement, talked
by phone to several commissioners and said that if the FCC approved
the KTAL–TV agreement and renewed its license, the agency would
be setting a positive precedent, which would assist in settling differences on the local level without the need for the heavy hand of the
federal government. Moore persuaded the commissioners to approve
the agreement in July 1969 and renew the license, despite a Broadcast
Bureau recommendation to hold a hearing. Commissioners Rex Lee
and Nicholas Johnson expressed reservations; Johnson said:

> License renewal proceeding is, in my judgment, a matter between
> the broadcast licensee and *all* the people in the community, a matter
> to be resolved by the FCC according to the statutory standard of
> the "public interest." The Commission can utilize the services of
> volunteer local groups. . . . But just as licenses should not wrong-
> fully be withheld, revoked or denied in response to unwarranted
> citizen protests, so they should not be granted automatically because
> a certain group of once-protesting citizens has for some reason with-
> drawn its objections. I am not fully convinced that any agreement
> could justify a finding that the KTAL past performance has been a
> service to "the public interest" of its service area.

The Commission's approval of the KTAL–TV agreement resulted in
a number of agreements in the next several years. While few were as
all-encompassing as KTAL's, concerns about programming, employment, community involvement in station policy-making, and improved
production facilities were common elements in most of these agreements. The Commission continued to endorse dialogue between citizen
groups and licensees; and by not voting to ratify or to disapprove various agreements being reached—or even to require that they be submitted to the Commission—the FCC encouraged agreements.

In August, 1971, the Commission went one step further. It was willing
not only to ignore a filed petition to deny after the petitioning party
and the licensee had resolved their differences through an agreement, it
was willing even to negate a hearing designation order simply because
the petitioners were now satisfied.

One agreement avoided FCC action even though the agreement was not kept. In March 1970, a petition to deny was filed against the renewal application of WSNT Sandersville, Georgia, the only broadcast facility licensed to a town of 5425 citizens (1960 census), 60 percent of whom were black. The allegations of racial discrimination in the station's overall policy were so devastating that the FCC designated the renewal for hearing—the first time the FCC had ever taken such an action after a petition. (In the WLBT case, the court had ordered the FCC to hold a hearing.) Before the hearing began, however, the parties reached an agreement and requested the Commission to renew the station's license. The agreement reached provided that WSNT would make its facilities available to blacks; broadcast news of local boycotts, marches, and demonstrations; meet monthly with representatives of the black community; broadcast a weekly 15-minute discussion on community problems by black and white community spokespeople; and maintain minority representation on its broadcast staff.

In fact, WSNT didn't live up to all the commitments in the agreement. In its next renewal application, the station admitted this failure and the reasons for it. The FCC had no mechanism to monitor the efficacy of agreements; and the petitioners chose not to ask for FCC enforcement, perhaps because the case involved potential reimbursement of $1,931.60 for the petitioners' legal expenses. The Commission had ruled no reimbursement; but the petitioners were in the midst of convincing the appeals court that their valuable contribution had saved the FCC the time and expense of holding a hearing, and that they should be reimbursed for this public service. Reimbursement was to become a major issue in agreement cases.

Citizen groups held a stronger hand in cases involving station sales than in renewal cases. A renewal applicant remains on the air while a petition to deny is decided by the FCC, and the applicant's odds of gaining renewal are great; a station buyer remains in limbo. Consequently, citizen groups achieved more spectacular agreements with potential station buyers.

For example in 1970, Capital Cities Broadcasting Corporation, a major group owner, wanted to buy from Triangle Publications stations in Philadelphia, New Haven, and Fresno, California. The deal, involving both television and radio properties, some of which CapCities would sell later, totaled $110 million. The companies involved were particularly anxious about quick FCC approval of the sales: if a hearing were ordered by the Commission, the agency would be obliged to scrutinize whether such a sale was compatible with FCC policy (not vigorously enforced) restricting group owners who had two or more VHF stations in the top 50 TV markets from acquiring other stations without a "compelling" public-interest showing.

After intensive, often round-the-clock negotiations with the areas' citizen groups, represented by Citizens Comunications Center, Cap-

Cities reached an agreement. The broadcaster agreed to earmark, over a three-year period following FCC approval of the sale, $1 million for the development of programming reflecting minority group views and aspirations in Philadelphia, New Haven, and Fresno; a third-of-a-million dollars deposited each July 1 in a minority-owned bank would be apportioned among the three cities. The company agreed to consult minority-group representatives before spending any of the program funds and to explain any rejection of programming suggestions from these representatives. The programs would be presented even if CapCities couldn't find sponsors for them. If the agreement seems extravagant, remember that it represented a minuscule fraction of the $110-million purchase price for the stations.

Broadcasting (January 11, 1971) called the agreement a "shakedown," but conceded it was "probably a prudent investment" for CapCities. Nicholas Johnson, in a statement attached to the unanimous FCC decision to approve the transfer, called the agreement

> an important breakthrough for public participation in the process of administration and governance of the public airwaves. . . . It may well be that FCC licensees have the responsibility under law to provide such programming—and more—already. But the fact remains that they don't do it, and the FCC doesn't insist upon it. At a time of mounting public outrage against the excesses and abuses of the corporate dominance of American broadcasting, it is at least heartening to see that humble citizens can extract *some* public service commitment from big broadcasters.

In general, the Commission continued to beam down upon the practice of citizen–broadcaster negotiations and the resultant agreements. In most cases, the commissioners never got to see the agreements—the petitions to deny were simply withdrawn and the station licenses were renewed. But in a few cases, the commissioners voted not to accept some provisions of some agreements that commissioners felt impinged upon the licensees' responsibility. Each of the cases had its own extenuating circumstances and regulatory history; but briefly, here is the kind of provision that was involved.

A Georgia radio station agreed to "make maximum use of all available network programming of special interest to the black community" and not to preempt such programs without the advance approval of the community group. Although consultation was acceptable, this provision, the FCC said, "would appear to curtail improperly the licensee's flexibility and discrimination in matters of programming and program scheduling."

In August 1973, the Commission disapproved of principles in two agreements. When an FM station in Sylvania, Ohio, was sold to a broadcaster who intended to change the station's format from "pro-

gressive rock" to "middle of the road," a community committee devoted to the former art form petitioned the FCC to deny the transfer.
After the FCC approved the transfer, the court overruled the agency
and demanded a hearing. Instead the broadcaster and the citizen group
negotiated an agreement, which would bind the broadcaster if the
only other area station with a progressive-rock format changed its
musical programming: then the broadcaster must survey the demand
and play progressive rock if the survey results warranted. The FCC
disapproved the agreement until it was revised: the station would
conduct a survey to determine interest in the music and would then
"exercise licensee discretion in determining whether . . . changes in its
programming practices would be consistent with its obligations as a
licensee."

The case that engendered the most controversy over agreements involved citizen groups' trying to reform children's programming. Agreement with Metromedia's KTTV (Channel 11) in Los Angeles was the
intended aim of several groups: the Mexican-American Political Association (MAPA), and the San Fernando Valley Fair Housing Council,
two California regional organizations; and Action for Children's Television (ACT) and the National Association for Better Broadcasting
(NABB), two national organizations. NABB, which was founded in
the late 1940s and which traditionally was concerned with violence
on children's programming, monitored KTTV's programming. The
citizen groups discussed with the station specific recommendations on
how the station could improve its programming and avoid a petition
to deny; but the station was unwilling to reach agreement with the
citizens, and they filed a petition to deny the station's license renewal.

Among other charges in the petition to deny was the allegation that
the station aired "a large quantity of old, outworn, and violence-ridden
programs for children which are, in part, harmful to the mental and
physical welfare of child audiences," and that the station was "using
violence and brutality as a pervasive element of the station's entertainment programming, in disregard of past and present scientific dis-
closures of the dangers of such a program policy to the children of
the community."

Moreover, the station had failed to "reinvest a significant proportion
of income in order to maintain acceptable program standards." The
petitioners alleged that Metromedia had been "siphoning" the profits
of KTTV even though Metromedia had assets of more than $192
million.

In its opposition to the petition, Metromedia made the mistake of
saying:

Petitioners made reference to the fact that Metromedia had assets
in excess of $192 million. This is meaningless, its liabilities are com-
pletely ignored. Since Petitioners have brought up the subject, the

Commission should also examine KTTV's performance in the light of its income picture compared to the huge profits of the three (3) network-owned stations [in Los Angeles].

Metromedia itself "opened the door" to the question of its profits. The petitioners seized on the chance to ask to see the station's annual financial forms, and the FCC had no choice but to agree. As a staff opinion stated, "Even though the degree of profit reinvestment in community-oriented programming is not ordinarily an issue in evaluating a renewal applicant's past performance, the licensee's assertions have made [this] information relevant and material to the review of the renewal application." After Metromedia exhausted its internal appeals of this FCC ruling, the company became amenable to the petitioners' suggestion that if an agreement could be reached, the groups would withdraw both the petition to deny and the request that the financial material be made public. (For competitive reasons, broadcasters are more modest than Victorian maidens about revealing their figures.)

The agreement, which was to last for three years, contained provisions to satisfy the minority community's complaints but differed from previous citizen–broadcaster agreements on children's programs. The station pledged to attempt to purchase and air "meaningful, integrated children's programs" and to blacklist programs NABB judged to be "unsuitable for younger children because of excessive violence and/or other possible harmful content." Among the 42 such prohibited program series cited were *Batman, Superman, Aquaman, Dr. Doolittle, Felix the Cat, Lone Ranger Cartoons, Mighty Mouse, Popeye* and *Tom and Jerry*. An additional 82 syndicated programs were graylisted. This list included a broad spectrum of Westerns, including Gene Autry and Roy Rogers shows, and a passel of cops-and-robbers series. The station promised to notify listeners whenever any of the graylisted shows was aired before 8:00 P.M. that the programs contain material "potentially harmful to children."

Citizen groups were delighted with the agreement. NABB referred to it as "a spectacular milestone," and stated:

> There is no doubt that the agreement constitutes the most far-reaching and fundamental revision of policy related to violence ever undertaken by a commercial broadcaster in the United States. . . . The agreement is unique in that it is based on major revisions in the presentation of *entertainment* programming. Most other petitions by citizen groups to deny license renewal applications have been centered on the failure of broadcasters to meet the special interests of minorities. In this instance the petition covered the entire program spectrum. . . . The result will also inevitably affect programming on a national level, even though the impact may spread

within a community-by-community or station-by-station pattern. As this success is followed by other successes, the momentum will increase.

Television columnists in many daily papers across the country noted the potential impact of the KTTV agreement in giving parents in other communities a method to deal with their concerns about televised violence. The program director of KTTV told *The Wall Street Journal*: "It was easier to agree. It finally seemed pointless for us to spend hundreds of thousands of dollars [fighting a petition to deny] to preserve a few unimportant cartoons."

The agreement was a distinctly unpleasant shock to program syndicators, who had paid millions of dollars to produce or syndicate program series. Kevin O'Sullivan, president of Worldvision Enterprises, which syndicated three of the blacklisted and five of the graylisted series, charged that KTTV "has abrogated its right and responsibility for programming the station and has placed a great deal of its responsibility into the hands of a group of people who have set themselves up as virtual censors of the television medium." Backed by other program syndicators, Worldvision filed an objection with the FCC to the KTTV agreement.

In July 1974 the Commission discussed what to do with the KTTV agreement and the informal objections filed by Worldvision Enterprises. The staff recommended that the Commission approve the agreement with specific reservations. The language in the agreement, while suggesting that licensee discretion and responsibility might be improperly limited, could be interpreted as not foreclosing Metromedia's exercising its discretion and responsibility for programming the station. The commissioners, leery of following the staff recommendation to accept the agreement with reservations or permit the parties to resubmit an amended agreement, continued to defer final action on the matter. At about the same time, Chairman Wiley was attempting to reach his own agreement with networks and independent TV stations about the "family viewing hour," the FCC's own approach to the problem of excessive violence in programming.

Frank Lloyd of Citizens Communications Center wrote the FCC:

In light of the nature of the criticism aimed at KTTV's commitments, it is ironic that you have chosen the "jawboning" approach to the televised violence problem. . . . It should be at least as legitimate —and even healthier—for the laudable goals shared by you and the NAAB to be achieved through community dialogue and individual licensee response to local needs. Surely that process is less of a threat to the proper exercise of licensee discretion and First Amendment principles than direct national pressure from the head of a Federal agency with the power to withhold broadcast licenses.

In September 1975, three months after a proposed general policy statement had been issued, the commissioners voted to negate the KTTV agreement. The FCC decision used much the same language as the staff's earlier recommendation that the agreement be approved; but where the staff said the agreement could be interpreted as leaving programming judgment to the licensee, the commissioners added, "We believe it will be more appropriate to refrain from doing so in this instance." They said they couldn't enforce any program aspects of the agreement without being censors. The Commission's decision left unanswered whether the FCC would distinguish between agreements promising to air specific programs and those promising to ban certain programs.

Reactions to the decision were predictable. *Variety* reported that broadcasters would still be slapped if they scheduled violent programs, but that syndicators would not have to cope with semiofficial, yet ironclad, blacklists or graylists: "Pressures on broadcasters aren't likely to ease, but syndicators can breathe a little easier." NABB complained that the FCC had frustrated its efforts to improve children's programs "by releasing this internally inconsistent, ambiguous, and patently illogical decision."

The Commission's final December 1975 version of its policy statement on agreements reflected the ambivalence the members felt on the subject. The statement was adopted unanimously after the commissioners reconciled some sharp differences on whether such agreements resulted from "blackmail" or "constructive dialogue between the broadcaster and his community." The commissioners didn't want to place a blanket prohibition on agreements, which were often the best and simplest way to resolve problems; but the members also didn't want to get involved in evaluating and approving every agreement. Basically, the Commission endorsed the concept of dialogue between licensee and citizen groups and refused either to encourage or to discourage agreements in principle. However, the FCC said it would sanction no agreement in which a licensee delegated programming responsibility and public service decisions, even voluntarily. Furthermore, agreements couldn't restrict licensees' flexibility to change their way of serving the public interest if they saw a need for change. The Commission would examine written agreements only if they were incorporated in a licensee's renewal application or other official forms, or if someone asked the FCC to review an agreement. Although they would consider the effect of an agreement that resulted in the withdrawal of a petition to deny, the commissioners would not agree to dismiss the allegations if they considered the initial complaints were serious enough. (Based on past history, they were unlikely to cavil.) Finding that licensees had abandoned their responsibilities in signing an agreement might raise questions in the commissioners' minds about the licensees' "basic fitness," the statement warned. As for enforcement of private agreements by the FCC, "The Commission will consider appropriate action if there is evidence any party abused the processes or acted in bad faith." The Commission's requirement of ascertainment of community needs and encouragement of "extensive local dialogue" with members of the public did not oblige licensees to negotiate with citizens to reach an agreement.

The FCC document had something in it to please everybody. Frank Lloyd said it was precisely what he wanted: "It reaffirms existing law." Lawyers representing broadcasters said that the FCC had clarified the licensee's ultimate responsibility to program in the broad public interest and to resist demands from special-interest groups.

The practical effect of the statement is hard to gauge. Some citizen groups believe that broadcasters are more hesitant to commit agreements to writing for fear the FCC will penalize them either for failing to live up to agreement promises or for delegating too much responsibility to citizen groups. Yet agreements are still being reached, many containing specific provisions regarding programming and station operation. In the past, submission of agreements to the Commission wasn't required; and the "master list" of agreements reached, which was used by the FCC staff in preparing the policy statement, was Cole's notes from trade press reports. Even today, not all agreements are in writing; but some renewal applications include promises, even if they aren't clearly identified as being part of an agreement.

One thing is certain, however: many agreements reached since the policy statement was first proposed require licensees to do things the Commission would have never required. For example, in Washington, D.C., where all the commissioners can see them, WMAL–TV (now WJLA–TV) is broadcasting up to three daily "speech messages," each repeated four times per week. Delivered by local citizens, these messages express a point of view on a matter of public concern. Broadcasting them was part of an agreement the station reached with several citizen groups.

The commissioners have delegated to the renewal staff the task of reviewing agreements between public groups and broadcasters. If some agreement provision, such as a licensee's ceding program control to a community group, violates the policy statement's principles, the staff sends the parties a letter explaining why the provision is not acceptable. Once the agreement is revised, the staff grants approval without the commissioners' becoming involved. Although the FCC has not established a procedure to monitor agreements, the citizen group with which the agreement had been reached could be expected to bring violations to the FCC's attention; and under the policy statement, the Commission would be bound to consider such complaints.

One aspect of agreements that has troubled the Commission is whether a licensee should reimburse a petitioner's legal costs incurred in helping the licensee see the light of reason. Those who consider agreements blackmail are particularly suspicious of agreements that include "consultancy fees" or other payments to the citizen group. Some citizen groups' law firms expend a large percentage of their resources on a single case when the FCC decides to set a license for hearing. If the FCC officially approves the agreement, the firm can be reimbursed and still retain IRS tax-exempt status.

In the KTAL Texarkana case, the Commission voted 4–3 to deny the local petitioners $15,137 for expenses leading up to the agreement. The four-man majority disapproved the voluntary reimbursement on the grounds that

> there are clearly detriments to the public interest, were we to allow the payment of expenses in these petitions to deny situations. First, there is the possibility of abuse—of overpayments (e.g., inflated fees) or even opportunists motivated to file insubstantial petitions in order to obtain substantial fees. . . . Second, there is the possibility that settlement of the merits of the dispute might be influenced by the ability to obtain reimbursement of expenses from the licensee.

The Commission noted that none of the "significant number" of agreements reached in 1970 involved a request for reimbursement of expenses, a situation that suggested that "not one of these groups had been discouraged by the fact that there would not be any reimbursement, either in the filing of its petition or the amicable settlement thereof."

The three-man minority included the only three lawyers then serving on the Commission—Chairman Burch and Commissioners Cox and Johnson. In one of the rare joint statements Burch and Johnson issued, they said that while there was "the very real possibility of abuse in this area," there were "strong countering considerations." They noted that the Commission allowed reimbursement of expenses in several situations; such as when one of the applicants in a comparative hearing for a new station withdraws, that applicant's expenses are paid by the remaining applicant or applicants. Moreover, the "public interest benefits" stemming from such payments were considerable. "It may facilitate the settlement of issues between the licensee and the petitioning groups, and, as the majority recognizes, that kind of amicable settlement generally markedly serves the public interest." Burch and Johnson went on to suggest guidelines for the payment of reimbursement: the petition to deny must be filed in good faith by responsible organizations; the petition must raise substantial issues; the settlement, too, must entail solid, substantial results; and a detailed accounting must document that the spending was legitimate and prudent.

When the United Church of Christ appealed the Commission's August 1970 decision regarding reimbursement, a three-judge panel in March 1972 unanimously overturned the FCC's decision and remanded it for further review. The court's reasoning resembled that of the Burch–Cox–Johnson minority dissent. Since that time, the Commission has considered voluntary reimbursement case by case and has permitted it in various instances.

However, the Commission has done nothing to encourage reimbursement. On the contrary, because its 1975 policy stated that the FCC didn't want to be in the business of approving agreements, the Commission has allowed some agreements to stand without taking steps that would allow tax-exempt law firms to collect fees. One example was the case where the FCC permitted the transfer of WNCN–FM New York in April 1976. Citizens Communications Center, representing classical music devotees opposed to the sale if the classical music format was to be changed by the new licensee, drew up an agreement that the new owner would continue to program classical music and the petitioners wouldn't seek to block the sale. The agreement called for $90,000 reimbursement to petitioners, $35,000 of which was to go to Citizens. Commissioner Hooks maintained that in approving the sale, the agreement "is de facto and de jure approved. Anyone doubting that result is wearing blinders." However, no clear precedent was set for reimbursing public law firms.

In cases such as WSNT Sandersville, where the licensee has not agreed voluntarily to reimburse citizen groups, the FCC felt it did not have the authority to *order* reimbursement. The court agreed with the FCC in this special instance.

Some agreements have contained provisions that would oblige the licensee to pay *future*, out-of-pocket expenses as a kind of consultancy fee. The commissioners, who weren't enthusiastic about the whole concept of reimbursement, made this special kind of agreement the subject of an official inquiry. No action was taken for almost four years, even though Burch, as chairman, had requested an expedited inquiry. In January 1976, the Commission issued a report and order terminating the inquiry and declaring that the issues involved were "essentially the same issues and the same concepts" treated in the FCC policy statement on agreements: "We do not believe that reimbursement for future expenses and consultancy agreements require the adoption of separate rules." In essence, the commissioners washed their hands of the matter, making it plain that they had no desire to determine whether the services provided and the fees involved were desirable, necessary, or reasonable. This is one of those questions that may someday rise to haunt the Commission—but in 1976 its members were content to evade the issues and leave them as a legacy for future, bolder Commissions.

IV
THE KIDVID CONTROVERSY

The following three-chapter case study is an instance of FCC response to specific suggestions of a citizen group. The odyssey of every major issue that comes before the Commission follows a different path; there are no typical cases. Nonetheless, the history of the children's programming inquiry and rulemaking contains many of the elements discussed in earlier chapters.

The case demonstrates the FCC chairman's important role as first among equals and the effect of turnover within the agency—commissioners' terms expire or the commissioners resign; key staff members work on a portion of a proceeding, then turn elsewhere. The case illustrates the FCC's lack of research capability, specifically on complex sociological questions. It shows also how some staff members become advocates of broadcast industry positions while other staff members, accustomed to the language of legal pleadings, tend to ignore letters from individual viewers. And other staffers champion the citizens' cause.

Citizen groups with a complaint the FCC can do something about can get a hearing and set wheels in motion. But the complex regulatory machinery makes it difficult for citizen groups to be in on crucial stages of decision making. Broadcasters, who have large sums at hazard, have established their own mechanisms for following a case closely and making their positions known effectively.

The history underlines the important role of the press. Articles in the general press helped keep the issue alive and forced action when the process was in danger of bogging down. Trade press articles served to keep broadcasters current with attitudes of key FCC decision makers and the timing of each step of the proceeding. And, of course, there was the dog that didn't bark; broadcast stations gave scant coverage to the controversy. Yet some broadcasters voluntarily went along with part of the citizens' program.

The children's proceeding was typical in taking a long time to wend its way through the FCC's processes. Citizen groups need staying power that they often cannot afford. They must be prepared for frustration as the Commission postpones decisions and waffles on issues that it has repeatedly said it wants resolved. The commissioners are not eager to stick their necks out on tough problems. Part of this reluctance is understandable: the commissioners prefer to persuade broadcasters to take action in the form of self-regulation rather than to impose rules and regulations. If the commissioners take the latter course, they know they can be overruled by Congress or the courts. Furthermore, commissioners recognize that the issue is complex, with valid points on each side, and that reaching a fair compromise is not easy.

When the hour of decision arrives, in most cases, the language upon which the commissioners agree will be open to varying interpretations. The guidelines are certain to be full of loopholes—some placed there intentionally as a result of compromise. This may not be simple pusillanimity on their part; it may be an attempt to give themelves and future commissioners what they consider to be desirable flexibility.

Finally, the children's proceeding demonstrates how open-ended the process is. In July 1977 the court affirmed the propriety of the FCC programming statement. At the same time, the court opened the door to further pleadings, meetings, and edicts on the subject. The question of the broadcaster's responsibility to the youth audience will be before the FCC for years to come.

16
ACT Gets Rolling

16 When Abraham Lincoln met Harriet Beecher Stowe, author of *Uncle Tom's Cabin,* he said, "So you're the little woman who started the big war." Broadcasters with an eye for history might remember the date February 5, 1970, when five Boston mothers boarded a plane for Washington to talk to the FCC about the sorry state of children's programming. They had called Dean Burch, who told them to come ahead.

They weren't sure to whom they would be presenting their case, but they weren't surprised that they'd been invited to Washington. "We were citizens who had a grievance and we expected that the representatives of government would hear it," Peggy Charren, one of the founders of Action for Childrens Television (ACT), said seven years later.

Ms. Charren by 1977 was a veteran of the Byzantine, labyrinthine processes of the FCC; she was by then party to a court of appeals suit that attempted to force the agency to take more positive action. But even on their initial trip, she and her colleagues were not babes in the wood. They had forged a grassroots citizen movement through willpower and study.

The Commission didn't have what could be called a policy towards children's programming in 1970. In 1960 the FCC had cited programs for children as one of fourteen elements "usually necessary to meet the public interest, needs and desires of the community"; but the Commission emphasized that these elements should not be regarded as a "rigid mold or fixed formula." Programming for children was a minor element in a lengthy litany of hollow promises that licensees would recite prior to acceptance of their stewardship of the airwaves. If broadcasters happened to win a prize for a certain children's program, they would boast about it; but if they simply took network offerings or ignored the category altogether, they had no fear of losing their licenses.

ACT was born of the mothers' indignation about the programs—and the incessant commercials—television offered their children. The group prospered because of its founders' savvy. Peggy Charren called the first meeting in her Newton, Massachusetts, living room in January 1968. She was head of the Newton Creative Arts Council and had worked for WPIX (TV) New York in television's early days. Her colleagues included Evelyn Sarson, ACT's first president, a free-lance journalist, and wife of a producer at Boston's public station WGBH–TV; Lillian Ambrosino, whose husband was assistant program manager of WGBH–TV; and Judy Chalfen, founder of Boston's experimental Everyman's Theatre. All had preschool children, and all were disgusted with the fare that television was feeding their children.

"When we first talked, we were most concerned with violence," Judy Chalfen recalls, "but we got off that. Violence is so hard to define and really, it's just part of the whole picture of poor quality—something we were all aware of." Charren adds, "We knew that if we got into violence alone, we would be treading into the area of censorship. That's not what we wanted. But after almost a year of discussion and argument, we could all agree that we didn't want our children to be dismissed by the medium simply as a market—a group of naive little consumers." Evelyn Sarson notes, "The only point of the television programs, as we saw them, was to sell things to kids. But it wasn't enough for us to say that. We decided we needed statistics to back us up. So the first thing we did was to sit and watch hours of television."

As they watched, they wrote. They started with letters to suburban Boston papers like the *Allston-Brighton Citizen* and the *Newton Graphic*. The women encouraged the TV critic of the *Boston Globe* to do a feature on the formation of ACT, its goals, and procedures for joining. The first story in the *Globe* was four sentences long, but other stories followed.

The membership of ACT grew slowly but steadily; the sophistication of its founders developed rapidly. Lillian Ambrosino recalls, "It became clear that the villain of the piece was not violence but commercialism." Even on shows that ACT members conceded were not violent or debasing, the hosts would win the young viewers' confidence and then switch to a commercial pitch. A "teacher" would encourage the young program participants to sit down at table and pray, "God is great. God is good. Let us thank Him for our food," and the teacher would respond, "And now you may have your Tropicana Orange Juice from the Pleasant Hill Dairy."

When a Boston station attempted to show only half of *Captain Kangaroo,* one of the few network programs that ACT believed entertained children without exploiting them, ACT sent out sample petitions to nursery schools and solicited protests to the station. After the station received some 2500 ACT-inspired letters, it agreed to restore *Captain Kangaroo* to his full 60-minute time slot.

In October 1969 the organization made its first foray outside Massachusetts. In a letter to *The New York Times,* Sarson sounded the theme on which ACT would make its stand: "What is really needed is some basic rethinking about children as viewers. They're special individuals who differ vastly at different ages, and programs for them should begin by considering these differences. . . . Children's TV is subject to exactly the same criteria as adult TV: will it get viewers, sell products, and make money?"

Ambrosino, at about the same time, appeared before the Senate committee considering the FCC appointments of Dean Burch and Robert Wells—not to oppose their appointments, but to ask "what they think the FCC can and should do in this field." She was rewarded by being termed by presiding Senator John Pastore, "a very, very alert, young girl," and being told that he shared her concern about the damaging effect of television upon children. Claiming a membership of 150 parents, educators, doctors, psychologists, and psychiatrists from 40 Massachusetts cities and towns and five northeastern states, Ambrosino said,

"ACT is here today because we see no hope for change without a strong FCC—one that will establish a code of ethics for children's television, enforce it, and hopefully even form a children's division." The code desired by ACT would (1) "recognize the special needs of children and encourage appropriate programs for children of various ages; (2) prohibit performers from promoting, advertising, or using brand-name products during children's programs; (3) specify the total separation of program content from sales messages, limiting the latter to only the beginning and/or ends of programs." Ambrosino stated, "This is not a new concept; it exists in many countries of the world."

Three months later, in January 1970, when the four charter members of ACT asked the networks to meet with them about children's programming, ABC and NBC declined; but CBS agreed. Peggy Charren recalls that network officials invited them into a plush screening room to see children's programming. "They thought we would ooh and aah, and that would be it. We told them we'd seen *hours* of children's programs. We weren't going to be snowed." The ACT requests to CBS were similar to those presented in the Senate hearing. Through persistence, the ACT members met with Mike Dann, CBS's program vice president, who listened to their views and later told *The New York Times* that the women were "among the most logical and constructive I have heard." In fact, according to Charren's recollection, CBS's giving a hearing to these Boston housewives with little national clout inspired the *Times* to do a full-scale story on ACT. "If we had talked to the *Times* before the meeting, it might not have been much of a story," Charren says.

Although Mike Dann told the *Times* he would be glad to have the ACT officials come back at any time, he told *Broadcasting* he would risk no changes that might lose CBS any of its youth audience while ABC and NBC weren't considering any changes. So the ACT officials decided it was time to turn to the federal government, and they asked for an audience at the FCC.

Again, the ACT officials had a stroke of luck. Dean Burch, who'd been ill the weekend before he met them on Monday, spent Saturday morning watching TV with his children. Consequently, he was even more receptive to the women's complaints than he might otherwise have been. After a two-hour meeting in Burch's office with all commissioners except Robert E. Lee, Burch said the ACT people were "very compelling [and] not a bunch of crybabies." He said he could make no promises about reforming children's programming; he wasn't certain that the FCC had the authority to make changes and, even if it did, he wasn't certain action by the FCC would be wise; "But I'm not against a dialogue on the matter."

The written proposal that ACT presented to the Commission was similar to that suggested to CBS, with the added requirement that the 14-hour-a-week minimum of children's programs be divided into age-specific categories broadcast during specified time periods. ACT urged the Commission to propose and adopt the following rules to govern all programming for children:

1. There shall be no sponsorship and no commercials on children's programs.

2. No performer shall be permitted to use or mention products, services or stores by brand name during children's programs, nor shall such names be included in any way during children's programs.

3. As part of its public service requirement, each station shall provide daily programming for children and in no case shall this be less than 14 hours a week. Provision shall be made for programming in each of the age groups specified below, and during the time periods specified below:

a. Pre-school (ages 2–5): 7:00 A.M.–6:00 P.M. daily; 7:00 A.M.–6:00 P.M. weekends

b. Primary (ages 6–9): 4:00 P.M.–8:00 P.M. daily; 8:00 A.M.–8:00 P.M. weekends

c. Elementary (ages 10–12): 5:00 P.M.–9:00 P.M. daily; 9:00 A.M.– 9:00 P.M. weekends

The four ACT officials were not presuming to recommend specific kinds of programs (ACT made no mention of violence, for example), but they maintained that quality would improve if commercials were eliminated. Commissioner Wells disagreed and told the women that the mere elimination of commercials wouldn't necessarily lead to good programming. "You may be right," said the women, but it would certainly provide a better climate for program improvement. Chairman Burch emphasized that the women were challenging the very structure of television and termed their proposal "radical." Nicholas Johnson and Kenneth Cox, whose term was to expire in a few months, were highly supportive of ACT's presentation while Robert Bartley indicated surprise at the amount of commercials permitted on *Romper Room*. The commissioners said that the ACT proposals would be discussed further and any conclusions would probably be reported to ACT at another meeting. Burch explained to the women that the Commission would have to vote on the question of even issuing the ACT proposal for comments to see whether rulemaking should be adopted. That vote might be taken after a staff study.

On February 12, 1970, the FCC did, in fact, issue a public notice setting forth the ACT proposal and asking for comments. Each day the Commission receives dozens of petitions, some of extremely limited interest, such as a request that a 500-watt radio station in a remote location be permitted to increase its power to 1-kilowatt in order to serve a larger area. Often the petitions are lumped together and put out in a notice that acknowledges their submission. In this case, however, the FCC reprinted the full text of ACT's short petition and asked for comments—but this action lacked the force of the FCC's initiating a rulemaking proceeding on the question or ordering an inquiry.

The officials of ACT were never informed by the FCC that ACT's petition had been issued publicly; Albert Kramer, director of Citizens Communications Center, brought the FCC public notice to their attention. Even so, they didn't realize that this was not an FCC rulemaking proceeding—but they did seek support for the ACT position. At the time, ACT had about 240 dues-paying members—mostly mothers—from 17 states. The ACT officials urged members and nonmembers to write the FCC and sought publicity for their cause. *The Christian Science Monitor* (March 24, 1970), Boston-based with a national circulation, editorialized: "A new movement is afoot which could lead to a crusade as decisive as the public action on auto safety and cigarette advertising. It has to do with the quality of children's programming on commercial television. This cause is every bit as critical as its two predecessors. After all, children watch TV more than they engage in anything else during their waking hours." Thousands of letters were submitted in favor of ACT's stand, but the only formal comments favoring it were from ACT itself.

Broadcasters, as expected, turned out long legal comments opposing ACT's proposition as a violation of the sanction prohibiting FCC censorship, an incursion into the licensee's responsibility for programming, and an unworkable plan calling for definition of children's programming. Above all, broadcasters claimed that a ban on advertising would destroy the necessary source of funding for children's programs and lead to such programs' vanishing from the airwaves. Candymakers and other heavy advertisers on children's programs also opposed the plan.

The controversy brought ACT to the attention of large numbers of concerned parents, generated informal pleadings to the FCC, and helped to increase ACT's membership. In speeches to broadcasters that focussed primarily on other subjects, Chairman Burch began interjecting comments about the defects of children's programming. At the NAB's annual convention, he asked whether broadcasters "operating on the public channels as public trustees" had fully met their responsibilities to children, "the nation's most valuable resource." He noted that before graduating from high school, the average student spent 15,000 hours watching television and only 11,000 hours in school. Burch commended networks for their *plans* to improve children's programming and reduce the violence level—and he sternly warned that not only the networks but also individual licensees bore responsibilities.

ACT engaged in attention-getting stunts worthy of a TV-station promotion manager. For example, the group sponsored a rally at the Plaza fountain in New York and gave away balloons to children and pens and envelopes to their parents with advice on how to write the FCC. In

The Oakland Tribune (March 31, 1970), columnist Bob MacKenzie wrote: "Like other activities of ACT, the balloon-in smacks of the crackpot. What is remarkable about ACT is that its crackpot ideas appear to be gaining momentum, and that they seem less crackpot at every hearing, and finally begin to make the most obvious kind of good sense."

Broadcasting's gossip column began complaining that perhaps Dean Burch was not the conservative's conservative, the "industry man" observers had expected him to be—especially on the issue of children's programming. *Broadcasting* characterized Burch's September 16, 1970, speech to top industry executives at the International Radio & Television Society in New York as "a formal expression of what the chairman had vented previously in interviews about children's programming—a concern given focus by a petition of ACT."

Combining cajolery and castigation, Burch put forward a plan of network cooperation in presenting "outstanding or experimental children's programming" between 4:30 P.M. and 6:00 P.M. on weekdays: each network would take responsibility for such programming on different days of the week; lest it violate federal antitrust laws, network cooperation would be "facilitated" by the FCC. Burch's ideas weren't novel: Newton Minow had suggested a similar plan to the same forum in 1961 (Henry Geller, FCC general counsel, had a hand in drafting both speeches); in 1959 FCC Chairman John Doerfer had suggested a similar network arrangement for prime-time documentaries and public affairs programs. Burch went a step further in recommending that group owners might want to cooperate in producing and sharing quality children's fare.

Burch continued to introduce recommendations on children's programming in other forums during the succeeding months, usually qualifying his remarks. In September 1970, he told a mass-media section of the White House Conference on Children and Youth: "[The ACT petition] is important because those ladies think it is important, but the Commission should be chary of entering into an area in which subjective judgments regarding program quality are involved—I don't think anyone can decide what is good children's programming and what is bad. The government is no more capable at it than anyone else." Broadcasters are making progress in the area, he said; after all, "Capitalists are human beings and have children of their own"; but he added, "Whether the networks have made sufficient progress remains to be seen."

Before the FCBA, in a speech on a different subject, Burch ad-libbed that children's programming is one of the problems "that are in the minds of the people," and that the FCC wouldn't "slough off" the problem on grounds that remedial action would violate the First Amendment. Burch expressed confidence that the FCC had the legal authority to make proposals on children's programming. His IRTS speech had sought to convey a mood; he asked the communications lawyers, "How many of you have reported that mood or perhaps made suggestions to your clients for joint action in this area?" *Broadcasting*'s "Closed Circuit" (November 2, 1970) warned that the ACT petition, "which once drew snickers from broadcasters and their attorneys, may become deadly serious business" because although Burch was undecided how to vote, the three Democrats, Johnson, Bartley, and H. Rex Lee, favored adoption.

Burch was more interested in pushing the networks to adopt a voluntary program of rotating quality children's programs on weekday afternoons than in adopting ACT's suggestion of restricting commercials. On December 11, 1970, he met with the three network presidents (Leonard Goldenson of ABC, Frank Stanton of CBS, and Julian Goodman of NBC) and got their reactions to his plan. Burch later told Cole that none of the network heads was interested in the plan; in effect, they told Burch to "give it your best shot," but not to expect the networks to agree voluntarily to much of anything.

Burch met also with FTC Chairman Miles Kirkpatrick to explore a plan for the two agencies to hold a joint hearing on children's television, with special emphasis on commercials. Kirkpatrick was active in pursuing what the FTC considered unfair advertising practices in commercials beamed to children—in late 1970, the FTC found three toy manufacturers airing deceptive spots. Kirkpatrick felt the FCC had primary jurisdiction over television and wanted a cooperative effort. However the majority of FCC commissioners didn't favor the proposal.

By January 11, 1971, Burch was able to take his best shot. Contrary to *Broadcasting*'s prediction, Democrat Bartley didn't favor an FCC inquiry into children's programming, but a new commissioner, Republican Thomas Houser, did. With Houser, Johnson, and H. Rex Lee, Burch had a one-vote majority to issue a notice of inquiry and proposed rulemaking "looking toward the elimination of sponsorship and commercial content in children's programming and the establishment of a weekly fourteen-hour quota."

Combining a notice of inquiry with a notice of rulemaking, an action suggested by Henry Geller, was unusual at that time. Under this procedure, a time-consuming step could be eliminated: an inquiry served only to establish that rules were needed and to suggest what they might be. The combined notice would allow the FCC to proceed "to take such action as the public interest may call for," the announcement made clear; such action might include "further notice of proposed rulemaking; a rule; a rule with a further notice of proposed rulemaking; a policy statement."

Because the Commission had never asked renewal applicants to provide information about past or proposed programs for children, little relevant information was available for the inquiry and rulemaking. The FCC said it "hopes and urges" that all TV networks and licensees would supply specific data on their children's programming: the identity of sponsors and host-salesmen, and the age group, if any, programs were aimed at. The FCC, noting the difficulty of defining "children's pro-grams," asked licensees to set forth the definition they used in the com-pilation of the data they submitted. The Commission then asked these five general questions: What types of now unavailable children's pro-grams should be presented? To what extent beyond holding their inter-est and attention does "children's programming" benefit children? What, generally speaking, is a definition of "children's programming"? What restrictions, short of prohibition on types of products or services, would be desirable for commercials? To what extent should any restric-tion on commercial messages in children's programs apply also to mes-sages adjacent to children's programs?

Commissioner Johnson, in a concurring statement, chided the ma-jority for not acting on ACT's original proposal; he called the inquiry "due processing them to death" and stated "we should at the very least be ready now to adopt specific proposals—those proposed by ACT or whatever our own ingenuity could devise—as a proposed rulemaking." Johnson quoted William F. Fore: "Saturday morning cartoons may not incite our nation's children to violence and rioting in the street, but they may put the best parts of their minds to sleep. Which is worse?" Johnson cited Joseph Seldin: "Manipulation of children's minds in the fields of religion or politics would touch off a parental storm of protest and a rash of Congressional investigations. But in the [pursuit] of com-merce children are fair game and legitimate prey." Johnson commended Burch for his leadership in attempting to get some action and said, "It is especially tragic and regrettable, therefore, that this commendable public leadership cannot see a flowering in something more substantial than this action."

Reaction to the Commission's further inquiry was predictable. Evelyn Sarson of ACT, who had hoped the Commission would propose specific rules, said, "We are disappointed but not defeated. We're glad that the FCC is still concerned with what television is providing for children, but we're disappointed that they feel they have to ask the kind of ques-tions they have." Sarson added, "We could give the Commission a sub-scription to *TV Guide*. At least half the questions they're asking are answered in it." Sarson referred the Commission to ACT's 87-page study, submitted May 4, 1970, and containing data supporting its position on children's programming.

ACT now had to try once more to drum up support from individual letter-writers around the country, for licensees—mobilized by the dan-ger of prospective rules—would be certain to comment in opposition. Moreover, ACT feared that the materials the Commission received wouldn't be truly representative because broadcasters were simply urged but not required to submit examples; stations that were doing very little, or perhaps nothing, might not respond.

To document their suspicions that only best-foot-forward material would be provided, ACT and three other media reform groups asked the FCC to require broadcasters to make available the following material: at least one film or videotape of all network programming and advertising aired in the composite week, film or tape of all children's product commercials approved by NAB's code standards during 1969 and 1970, and station program logs for the composite week. When the FCC pronounced their request "unduly burdensome" to broadcasters, ACT and its allies asked for just those films or tapes of children's programs and commercials carried by the three networks between 8:00 A.M. and 2:00 P.M. on the Saturday of the composite week. The Commission told ACT to submit this request directly to the networks and promised that the agency would "take whatever steps are required to secure additional information necessary to proper consideration" of the matters being examined.

ACT also requested 120 television stations to broadcast twice a week on separate days (during prime time) a 30-second message soliciting viewer letters to the FCC about "what you would like to see on TV for children; what you feel about commercials aimed to children." The ACT message was designed to inform the public of the Commission inquiry. Two Boston stations responded: one agreed to air a shorter version of the ACT statement; the other said the request had been referred to its Washington attorney. Throughout the crusade, ACT got little television coverage—for obvious reasons.

In April when the Commissioners appeared before the House subcommittees on appropriations and on communications, the chairman of the latter, the late Torbert Macdonald (D.–Mass.), referred to children's programming as "a terribly overlooked area," and expressed his hope that the FCC would consider "putting some specialists to work on this. I don't think a bureau within your commission would have to be all that big. I think just some specialists who have time to work on this, without being harried by all the other problems you have." Macdonald then mentioned ACT, a group of women "not from my district, but from Massachusetts who have been in touch with you very often." Burch responded that the questions raised by ACT "enter into a couple of terribly vital areas" but that the whole problem of children's programming "does involve the spectre of [Section 326 of the act] which is our censorship provision, and one that I am sensitive about." Macdonald replied that he thought it would be "a good area to get a test case on, and I think you would get a lot of help from Congress. Most Congressmen have young children or have had, and they are more aware of the problems than perhaps in other areas in communications."

During the spring of 1971, broadcasters continued to be pressured on children's programming. ACT designated May 1—two days before comments on its proposal were due at the FCC—as Turn Off TV Saturday (TOTS). The networks were concerned enough to order special Nielsen surveys to check the boycott's effectiveness in New York and Los Angeles—it was minimal. The decennial White House Conference on Children included a forum on media; the forum recommended that advertisers and networks be encouraged to introduce "meaningful innovations in the current TV advertising structure, including tests of clustering commercials," and to test elimination of all commercials in children's programming. The trade press was rumbling about the possible conclusions of the Surgeon General Study of Television and Violence, begun in 1969 at the urging of Senator Pastore and due for release in a matter of months.

Aside from the networks' constant concern about their image, they were acutely aware of the economic damage that banning commercials from kids' programs would cause. *Broadcasting* reported that children's programming provided networks some $75 million in revenues in 1970 —up from 68.9 million in 1969. The magazine listed the names and the 1970 network outlays of advertisers who would be forced to retrench: Kellogg, $8.9 million; Mattel toys, $7.8 million; General Mills, $7.1 million; General Foods, $6 million; Deluxe Topper, $4 million; Quaker Oats, $3.8 million; Miles Laboratories, $2.6 million; and Mars (candy) Inc., $2.3 million. The first three companies accounted for about one-quarter of children's program revenues; the rest, for another quarter. So the networks had other incentives, besides a deep and abiding morality and love of children, to do something to turn down the heat.

In May 1971, James Duffy, head of the ABC television network, told affiliates that ABC–TV would sponsor a June conference for networks and other broadcasters, sponsors, advertising agency executives, and programming experts to discuss ways to improve children's programming. He warned that the "clear and present danger" of government intervention could be read "in the light of the brush fires that are burning," and that the danger could be met only by facing the critical questions being asked:

> Have we, in our competitive zeal, been morally delinquent? Have we, in our predominant concern with adult programming, given short shrift to children's programming? Have we, in the face of mounting government and citizen-group criticism, undertaken a Band-aid application rather than the surgery that is called for in this area?

Duffy proposed abandoning regular ratings of Saturday-morning programs and substituting full-industry studies aimed at determining children's motivations and attitudes; Duffy argued that the substitution of psychological research for popularity ratings would redirect the emphasis in both selling and buying time from quantity to quality.

On June 23 and 24, 1971, ABC conducted the two-day conference. Although *Broadcasting* originally reported that probably one and perhaps both other networks would attend, neither CBS nor NBC sent representatives. However, more than 400 conferees were present. In his keynote speech, Duffy again suggested that Saturday morning ratings be dropped. Duffy also said, "I would hope that everything from government control to self-regulation standards and practices be ventured and voiced; that we meet the views and criticisms of everyone from the FCC to the burgeoning civic groups head-on and—whether violently agreeing with them or violently disagreeing with them—discuss them; that there is no issue we cannot at least try to come to grips with as a collective and responsible body." ACT President Evelyn Sarson told conferees that "the present situation is not healthy and I see very little change in children's programming in the new network schedules." She attacked stations for "carrying 16 minutes of commercials in Saturday-morning children's shows, while carrying only about half of that amount in adult shows"; and she criticized the practice of permitting program hosts to serve as product pitchmen.

Meanwhile, comments to the Commission's notice of rulemaking had been filed, and reply comments continued to come in. Significant among those suggesting that the Commission take action was the American Civil Liberties Union. ACLU noted its hesitancy to enter areas other than civil liberty issues and stressed that the Commission shouldn't violate broadcasters' First Amendment rights by getting into program or advertising content. However, said ACLU, the rights of children are at stake; to expand the diversity of material and to meet children's needs, the FCC should prohibit overcommercialization. In fact, ACLU claimed, the Commission had authority to require the stations' assessment of children's needs as an important part of community ascertainment and a commitment to localism.

As expected, broadcasters filed many comments with the FCC. NAB commented that "Parental emotion about their children must not be confused with actual facts about television's influence upon the young." NAB stressed the value of self-regulation through its code and noted that "significant improvements in programming and advertising content" have occurred at both network and local levels. CBS claimed that "commercial television has been made the whipping boy. It is berated for its success in producing entertaining programming for children and families, and it is ignored for its significant accomplishments in creating entertainment, informational, instructional, news, and other programming for children and families." CBS asserted that ACT and other organizations wanted commercial television to act as educator because of the "alleged failings of the multi-billion dollar educational system in the United States." NBC called the ACT proposals self-defeating; good programming couldn't be created without financing, and the Commission's aim should be to encourage broadcasters to invest in and to seek advertising support for quality programming. Metromedia, a large group owner, agreed that elimination of commercials would weaken its ability to present high-quality children's programs: eliminating commercials would cost Metromedia's four television stations a total of $3,809,624 annually. Broadcasters were hastening to counter ACT's proposals.

On the other hand, by July 12, 1971, roughly 80,000 letters in support of the ACT proposal had been sent to the Commission. Most of these letters were directed to the ACT proposal rather than to the detailed notice of inquiry that the Commission had issued. Because of the volume of letters, ACT recommended that the Commission assign "one or more" staff members "to make a systematic compilation and summary" of these documents. "We believe that the criteria and judgments which can be found in this material are of the highest importance because they come from disinterested public sources and reflect a mutual consensus which cuts across every significant economic, sectional, occupational and other division in American society."

After seeing the ACT request, Carol Oughton, confidential assistant to Commissioner Houser, called the Broadcast Bureau's Rules and Standards Division to learn how the letters were being processed. An official told her they were being stacked in large boxes for later filing in bound volumes. There was no timetable for examining the letters and no one on the staff was considering reading them: "What's the sense in reading them?" he asked. "They all say the same thing."

17

Self-regulation or the Heavy Hand of Government

17 While the letters continued to pour into the Commission, some broadcasters were making significant changes in their policies for children. Westinghouse Broadcasting Company announced the creation of a series of science-oriented programs designed for children between eight and 14; the programs would be run on all five of its stations and would be syndicated to other stations. Commercials during these programs would be limited to four two-minute breaks, only one of which would occur during the course of the program. Post–Newsweek announced its stations would increase their children's schedules to 14 hours per week—the amount proposed by ACT—through the addition of local programming. Each program would be labelled for a specific age group: preschool, grade school, or teenage—another ACT proposal; and commercials would be limited to clusters before and after each local program.

Such voluntary compliance with the spirit of the ACT petition was unusual. It was significant that neither Westinghouse nor Post–Newsweek was "in trouble" with the FCC and seeking some special advantage. The majority of station owners, however, persisted in considering the ACT recommendations as the opening wedge in splitting asunder the greatest free-enterprise communications system in the world.

In his second consecutive IRTS address on children's television in September 1971, Dean Burch planned to announce formation of the Broadcast Bureau's permanent children's unit, which Torbert Macdonald had urged. When Burch told the other commissioners of his plan several days before his speech, he encountered strong opposition; establishment of the unit was settled only after a vote: three commissioners voted against it, three others sided with Burch. One of those supporting the unit was Houser, who would be leaving the FCC in a month. He had been given what amounted to an interim appointment by President Nixon, who had named Illinois Congresswoman Charlotte Reid to succeed Houser. Reid was forbidden by law to join the Commission earlier because the Congress of which she was a member voted a pay raise to the FCC. When Congress adjourned in October, she was confirmed to the FCC.

Burch told the IRTS meeting in New York that the special children's unit would be staffed by Elizabeth Roberts, who had worked with the White House Conference on Children, and by Alan Pearce, who had just completed an Indiana University doctoral dissertation on the economics of network television. Burch stated: "I want to stress that this represents just the beginning of a standing commitment." He announced also that the FCC and FTC had initiated a formal liaison agreement to "devise an affirmative regulatory policy that will not undermine the commercial base of our broadcasting system, but will protect a uniquely impressionable audience." (In fact, nothing much ever came of this cooperative plan.)

Burch gave "a prognosis of cautious optimism" based on developments during the past year. Among "favorable indicators," Burch included each network's launching a new series with a significant number of better ideas in children's programming, a "deluge" of plans for better children's programming in the new season, and a new NAB toy advertising code with "teeth and all." He listed some negative factors, too: the networks' "caution" in scheduling some of the new programs for "only short seasons"; each network's insistence on slotting its hottest properties against the other networks' on Saturday morning while putting new programs in fringe times; and broadcasters' propensity to make weekday afternoons the "preserve of syndicated reruns, and whatever cartoons are left over from Saturday morning." Burch credited the improvements in children's programming to a changed climate of opinion: "Where children's television is concerned, the machinist's wife from Dayton—Mrs. Middle America in the flesh—has joined the ranks of the disaffected [who are] fed to the teeth with past performance and [are] not about to settle for mere cosmetics."

On the subject of commercialization, Burch was unequivocal. He felt there was "no room for debate" about the content of commercials aimed at children: "We must crack down hard on the hard-sell that shades off into downright deception and, if anything, err on the side of toughness." He suggested that the NAB code be tightened to limit the number of "commercial minutes" on Saturday morning. Such tightening "would earn you lots of Brownie points from grateful parents—and kids, too." As a Surgeon General's research team found, among sixth- and tenth-graders, 90 percent of kids were turned off by commercials generally—and more than half didn't believe what commercials said. Finally, Burch said, "The good ladies of ACT have gone to the core issue. They are asking, in effect, whether a commercially based broadcasting system is capable of serving up quality programming for an audience so sensitive and malleable as children. Or, by contrast, is there some sense in which 'commercialism' and good educational vibrations are fundamentally inconsistent?"

The FCC's permanent children's unit, whose formation Burch announced to the IRTS, began operations in October 1971. Its staff members found the work piled knee-high when they arrived: more than 100,000 persons had commented on the ACT proposal, and their comments filled 63 docket books. Although the children's unit was funded through the Broadcast Bureau, Burch situated Roberts and Pearce near Burch's office on the eighth floor where they could report directly to Burch and his aide, Charles Lichenstein. The chairman knew that bureau personnel were not enthusiastic about the unit's existence. Pearce was working on other problems involving broadcast economics, too.

The children's unit was soon increased by the appointment of Karen Hartenberger as assistant to Elizabeth Roberts. Mrs. Hartenberger, who was earning her doctorate in speech, was the wife of Werner Hartenberger, a lawyer who became Wiley's legal assistant when Wiley became a commissioner and who later became FCC general counsel. When Hartenberger first joined the Commission, she was convinced that a policy statement by the FCC would be the best way to dispose of the ACT petition; but her studies of former FCC proceedings eventually convinced her that rules, rather than a policy statement, would be needed because "a policy statement would just be put in someone's drawer and forgotten."

The Roberts-Hartenberger research revealed a definite correlation between outside pressure for change and broadcasters' upgrading of children's programming, an upgrading reflected in more live programs and less animation, and more instructional or educational programs instead of just entertainment. Roberts and Hartenberger, in a slide presentation to the commissioners, demonstrated what happened to children's fare during Newton Minow's crusade and following the complaints against violent programs after the assassinations of President Kennedy and Martin Luther King. The research clearly showed that when the pressure eased, the children's programs returned to their previous pattern.

The Surgeon General's January 1972 report on the effects of television violence would offer ammunition for both sides in the violence debate. The report would conclude, in general, that causal relationship had not been proved between TV programs that depict violence and aggressive behavior by the majority of children. The report would find that TV violence could trigger aggression in children who were predisposed to violence or were unstable. Surgeon General Jesse Steinfeld put forth his personal opinion, based on studies: potential danger of television's producing negative behavior patterns in children was sufficient to require some action.

In a September 1971 hearing before the Senate Communications Subcommittee, Burch said, "We are by no means just waiting around" for the Surgeon General's report. One of the first major efforts of the FCC's new children's programming unit would be to analyze and evaluate the Surgeon General's report and back-up research, and to advise the Commission "as to its possible future options." Burch added, "In our budget projections for the next several years, furthermore, we have penciled in under 'external contract research' a specific category for children's programming." Burch maintained that "it is not necessary that we have perfect knowledge about television's negative impacts before coming down hard on the side of the positive."

The contracts Burch had "penciled in" were never signed in ink. No contracts or research assignments on children's perception of TV were discussed in Commission meetings. Although members of Congress in various hearings queried commissioners about what they were doing in this area, no single member of Congress ever followed up on what had happened to Burch's plan.

By the end of 1971, a Commission memorandum from a lawyer in General Counsel Richard Wiley's office stated that the Commission had broad authority to act on matters of children's programming. Displeased with this conclusion, Broadcast Bureau officials did what they could to limit the memorandum's distribution. They worried that if the document were leaked, the commissioners would be increasingly pressured to take favorable action on the ACT petition.

In January 1972, the heat was on and the broadcasters knew it. They decided to act to stave off criticism. ABC–TV's James Duffy had announced in December that he would ask for an NAB code reduction in the number of commercial minutes permitted in weekend TV programs broadcast between 7:00 A.M. and 2:00 P.M.: from the current level of 16 minutes per hour to 11 minutes per hour. ABC would ask also that the code limit on program interruptions be reduced from four to two per half-hour, a proposal that was still less restrictive than the prime-time standards—9½ minutes of commercials per hour and no more than two interruptions per half-hour.

The NAB acted to change its code. Although the code board approved Duffy's suggested standards, to be effective January 1, 1973, almost a full year later, the board rejected a CBS proposal that commercial minutes per hour in *all* children's programs—not just weekend programs—be reduced from 16 minutes to 12. The NAB television board modified the code board's recommendations: nonprogram material on weekend mornings was limited to 12 minutes, rather than 11; and no time restriction was placed on other children's programming commercials. In or adjacent to children's shows, commercials by hosts or primary cartoon characters were forbidden. This prohibition had been strongly recommended at the FTC advertising hearings by Boston University's Dr. Earl Barcus, who cited the results of his ACT-financed study of *Romper Room:* the "teacher" spent a considerable amount of time selling commercial products. A third NAB code change halved the number of permitted commercial interruptions in children's programming during the specified Saturday and Sunday morning periods: no more than two interruptions within any 30-minute program, and no more than four within a 60-minute program. The NAB board instructed its TV code review board to study the CBS proposal to apply the restrictions to all children's programming seven days a week, and to phase in the reduction in nonprogram time in two stages.

The reaction of the three networks was quoted in *The New York Times* (January 22, 1972). ABC was "very pleased at the action of the Board." NBC said the proposal "to include all programs devoted to children on Saturday and Sunday mornings was advanced by us and we are pleased that it's been adopted." CBS believed that its proposal for restrictions throughout the week was better; but since it had been outvoted, "we will accommodate ourselves to the new ruling and hope that our position will be recognized at the June meeting." (It was not.)

An FCC study of the economics of children's programming, presented in July 1972 by economist Alan Pearce, examined the potential impact of ACT's proposal to eliminate commercials and the probable effect of the NAB's plan to reduce the number of commercials on such programs beginning in 1973. Although revenues from children's programs accounted for less than 5 percent of the networks' gross revenues—$75 million out of more than $1.7 billion in 1970—these programs did contribute a substantial share of the profits earned by CBS and ABC. CBS led the other networks in profits received from children's programming—$16.5 million on gross revenues of $33.5 million from weekend programming in 1970; ABC's 1970 weekend programming yielded $7 million on revenues of $19 million. Pearce estimated that a reduction in commercial minutes from 16 to 12 per hour would reduce CBS profit to $10 million, and ABC, to $3.5 million; and NBC "would barely break even." However, if networks increased the advertisers' rates, network profits would remain high. Pearce considered this development likely because a small number of advertisers would be competing for an increasingly small number of commercial minutes: "Most major advertisers will remain in children's television for the simple reason they have no other place to go where they can advertise as cheaply and as effectively." If advertising were banned altogether, as ACT had proposed, the networks would face "serious problems in recouping these losses," Pearce concluded. He saw little chance of alternative financing, such as foundation support or institutional advertising support.

Pearce attempted to avoid specific recommendations, but he did suggest that broadcasters should try "to convince advertisers to support age-specific programming so as to expose children to new ideas and to new experiences." Pearce also agreed with critics of existing practices that children's programming should be considered an aspect of public service:

> It should be said that it never has been contended that every segment of network programming should be profitable in and of itself: for example, many documentary programs lose money for the networks. Maybe some children's programming ought to be treated in this way. The networks have always been charged with the responsibility to present a diversified programming schedule, within the limitations of overall commercial viability. . . .

ACT was dissatisfied with Pearce's conclusions. Evelyn Sarson of ACT criticized his drawing them from "the framework of the status quo." What was needed, according to Sarson, was for the networks to "view children as something special, rather than just another consumer market." To refute the Pearce study, ACT used a grant to commission a study by William H. Melody, associate professor of communications economics at the University of Pennsylvania's Annenberg School. Melody struggled with Pearce's implication that if networks couldn't sell time on children's shows, the networks would simply drop the programs: "Whether external financing can be obtained for children's programming will remain a highly uncertain matter until it is attempted." Melody recommended that alternative financing be tried in phases. Broadcast stations would contribute their air time, either as a voluntary action or as an FCC public service requirement. Program decisions would be made by others than broadcasters. Melody certainly couldn't be accused of being bound by the structure of the status quo.

September 1972 brought the new network schedule of weekend children's programs. Many promised programs, which had occasioned Burch's "prognosis of cautious optimism," had been scratched before reaching the air. Other noncartoon programs with educational value had been truncated. In some cases, the network proposals for higher quality programs had been refused by a majority of the network affiliates in the belief that fewer children would watch these programs than would watch adventure cartoons. Ratings and studies seem to support this belief. A San Francisco survey, asked children to pick their favorite shows, and parents and teachers to list the best and worst programs for children. On the top of the kids' list were *Gilligan's Island, The Flintstones, I Dream of Jeannie, Speed Racer, Sabrina,* and *Three Stooges;* on the bottom were *Sesame Street, Mister Rogers' Neighborhood, Captain Kangaroo,* and *Romper Room.* Except for *Jeannie,* the children's favorites were on the bottom of the parents' list; the top choices of parents and teachers were last with the kids. (*Detroit Free Press,* September 3, 1972).

The Commission held public panel discussions on children's television on October 2, 3, and 4, 1972. Each panel was assigned a specified topic: content diversification treated animated vs. live programming, information vs. entertainment-only programming, and fictional vs. nonfictional presentations; age specificity covered current offerings and suggested changes; responsive scheduling questioned whether stations should be required to present a minimum number of hours and whether current offerings are adequate; children's television and advertising was divided into two sections, one on present commercial practices and one on alternative methods of financing and modifications; and self-regulation.

As expected, citizen groups maintained that children's programming was a disgrace while broadcasters defended current practices as what the audience wanted. One significant aspect of the discussion was an interim proposal by ACT's Evelyn Sarson: because eliminating commercials in children's programs might work extreme economic hardship on some small-market TV stations, Sarson proposed a "sliding scale" to differentiate between networks and major-market stations, which would give up commercials, and small stations, which would sell their own commercials.

The three-day panel discussion disappointed most of the commissioners and staff members. They agreed with *Broadcasting* (November 20, 1972) that the oral arguments in the public panel discussions had damaged the chances for FCC substantive action on children's programs. When some FCC observers criticized the panelists for failing to provide "scientific" backing for FCC action, when advertisers and broadcasters pointed to a lack of research demonstrating commercials' adverse effect on children, ACT's Peggy Charren responded: "There are millions of mothers out there who are not willing to wait for a lot of research. Generations of children are growing up. Research goes on for years."

Formal oral argument on the children's programming rulemaking took place in January 1973. When it was over, Burch told reporters that nothing "devastatingly new" had been presented by the 45 speakers, and described the inquiry as the "most open-ended" the FCC had undertaken while he was chairman. Admitting that he was uncertain what action the Commission might take or even when it might conclude the proceedings, he listed alternative actions: issuing a policy statement, changing the renewal forms, jawboning, or enforcing by raised eyebrow. He added, "I was disappointed that the networks didn't cover these hearings by decision-making personnel. It would have been an illuminating experience for people in the networks to learn what people think of their programming."

Shortly thereafter, the children's unit listed several options in an internal memorandum. The unit suggested the FCC might set rules for age-specific programming. Or the Commission could revive the idea of networks' rotating quality children's programs in certain time slots, provided the Justice Department did not block such an agreement on antitrust grounds. Networks might be allowed to feed affiliates children's programs in the prime-time access period otherwise barred to networks. Other issues raised included late-afternoon programming, reduction of commercials on children's programs, and product-promotion guidelines, such as forbidding hosts to sell products. The children's unit put forth four general "regulatory options": self-regulation, policy statement, ascertainment requirement, and "industry and public relations." The unit warned that "the weight of the evidence indicates that self-regulation is an ineffective means of regulation." The industry and public relations option would require each licensee to meet with an established body of community representatives "to evaluate children's programs and maintain a continuing dialogue to develop an understanding of children's needs and determine ways to meet those needs." When broadcast lobbyists learned from the trade press of the unit's suggestions, they descended on the FCC in force.

A special January 30, 1973, meeting of the Commission was held to discuss the children's unit memorandum and the Broadcast Bureau's preference for a policy statement, rather than rules. The bureau believed that the policy statement should express approval of certain practices, like age-specific programming, and should urge improvements, such as basing schedules on children's viewing patterns. The bureau strongly opposed requiring a particular type of program at a particular time. The bureau's internal memo said, "Inevitably, to call for educational/information programs will involve the Commission in making program content judgments on whether a particular program did or did not meet this test. The consequences would be disastrous." The bureau added, "Equally important, merely because a program met the test would not mean that the program in any way responded to the needs of children. . . . Simply call upon broadcasters to respond to the various needs of children, including educational/informational, leaving the means of implementation to them." Similarly, the bureau believed it was appropriate "to urge rather than mandate the phasing out of commercials to preschool children" if the Commission wished this practice discontinued. The bureau clearly favored general urging, suggesting, and reminding, rather than requiring.

Just after the FCC's special discussion of the children's unit's memorandum, the *Television/Radio Age* annual FCC issue (March 1973) led off with an article by Mal Oettinger that said, "Not in two FCC generations—some 14 years—have so many commissioners and staff members been so sympathetic to the problems of the regulated." The article predicted that the Commission would "probably issue some guidelines for children's programming, commending self-regulatory steps taken by the industry and assuring licensees that this area would be continually monitored." The article also noted a split among the commissioners on "how firm a stance to take" and suggested that the NAB's reduction of commercial time in children's programs and its edict against host-salesmen would persuade the FCC that the industry was righting any deficiencies. On the other hand, the article noted, "Some people at the Commission who favored the inquiry in the first place have said the situation is growing worse on many stations despite the industry code to the contrary." At about the same time, the viewer-oriented *TV Guide* titled its three-part series on the ACT petition "The Children's Crusade That Failed."

In a speech to the Broadcast Advertising Club, Commissioner Wiley, who became chairman a year later, said, "After all, children are not just little consumers. Accordingly, perhaps industry should reevaluate the kinds of products being advertised to children as well as the nature of the commercial messages they receive." On these grounds, he was endorsing important principles but on matters in the FTC's bailiwick, not his. If the industry doesn't act, Wiley warned, the government probably would, "with consequences which may be detrimental to our basic freedoms and to the fundamentals of our free-enterprise system."

The head of the Council on Children's Media and Merchandising, Robert Choate, who had previously concentrated on children's advertising issues before the FTC, asked the three television networks to devote "substantial amounts" of broadcast time to discussion of the quality and value of children's programming, with critics of television's performance and policies participating. He accused the networks of presenting only one side of the issue through the programming itself and promotion for those programs. Naturally enough, the networks weren't interested in providing Choate or his colleagues with a forum to stir up an issue that now appeared to be going the networks' way.

The NAB code review board in June 1973 did adopt a "statement of principles," specifying steps that broadcasters should take in producing and presenting commercials aimed at the young. Such reforms, if followed, would be unquestionably commendable steps, but they still fell short of what Choate and ACT had in mind.

Broadcasters and advertisers, like stock traders, are always looking for indicators of how the future is likely to go; and indicators abounded. In October 1973, Chairman Burch was still warning broadcasters that the FCC might be forced to curb advertising aimed at children; but rumor had it that Burch would be leaving the FCC, probably before the children's issue came to a vote. (The rumor was off on the timing but correct in the outcome.) At the same time, the FCC General Counsel John Pettit, who was being touted by *Broadcasting* as a future commissioner, was telling the Association of National Advertisers that broadcasters should not be apologetic about their Saturday morning children's fare: "Instead of suffering under the label of cartoon ghetto, why not refer to Saturday morning programming as 'the comic book of the airwaves'?"

ACT and its supporters were hoping the Commission would vote on its rulemaking petition before the FCC membership changed radically. In December 1973 the FCC mentioned children's programming in its order on prime-time access: during the half-hour that the stations, instead of the networks, would now be programming, licensees would be expected to provide "minority-affairs programs, children's programs, and programs directed to the needs and problems of the stations' community." *Broadcasting* (December 3) said, "There is talk at FCC that the movement to elevate children's television programming may have reached its high-water mark in the modification of the prime-time access rule voted last week."

That vote was one of the last in which Nicholas Johnson participated; the composition of the FCC was changing. When Johnson's term ran out in June 1973, Nixon had appointed James Quello to Johnson's seat; but Quello was tied up in confirmation hearings so Johnson stayed until late December. Burch said he intended to leave as soon as the Quello question was resolved; H. Rex Lee, who had earlier suffered a heart attack, announced his intention to resign. In March 1974 Burch left the

FCC to become a counsellor to President Nixon, and Richard Wiley was named chairman. It became apparent that the panel of commissioners taking the final vote would be different from the panel that first agreed to consider the question.

Who would handle the children's programming problems was uncertain after Elizabeth Roberts, head of the children's unit, left shortly before Burch. Her assistant, Karen Hartenberger, had already been reassigned to the Office of Plans and Policies. On Wiley's first day in office, at a hearing before the Senate Appropriations Committee, Chairman William Proxmire (D.–Wis.) asked Wiley the status of the FCC's children's unit. Wiley acknowledged that no one was specifically assigned to the unit, but "much of the staff work has been done in this area. What remains may be some judgmental factors that the Commission is going to have to face up to, and I think that will come in the near future." When Proxmire questioned whether the Commission had "any additional staff expert in the area of children's perspectives on broadcasting, so that you can judge unfair broadcast practice to children," Wiley responded that "the Commission is probably at this point not set up for deep psychological and sociological aspects of our work." Because the Commission relied on written comments in oral testimony that it received, the FCC had tried to develop the Office of Plans and Policy, "which would give us more of a research arm and would give us an opportunity to attract experts in some of these related and very important areas that you touch on." Later in Wiley's first week as chairman, congressmen concerned with violence in children's programming asked Wiley what experts the FCC had on its staff. He responded, "Again, the Commission is not made up of people who can judge the effects of violence on children. We do not have social scientists. We are an engineering, legal, and processing agency. I hope we can expand our scope so we can consider some of the sociological aspects of television."

Congress would raise this question in subsequent hearings. More than a year later, for example, in 1975, Torbert Macdonald offered the FCC funding for personnel to conduct research on children's TV. Chairman Wiley said he "would certainly have no objection" to the FCC commissioning outside research on children. A committee member, Timothy Wirth (D.–Colo.), responded: "When you say you have no objection that is an incredibly passive statement. This is something of extraordinary importance . . . and you should aggressively seek outside help." By the spring of 1977, only one person at the Commission had a primary responsibility for children's programming: Karen Hartenberger, who had left the FCC in August 1974, rejoined the staff as a member of the Plans and Policy Office in October 1975 after completing her doctoral dissertation. The head of the office, Dale Hatfield, told Cole in May 1977, "Most of the time she spends on children's programming is occupied in answering letters."

An abrupt change in public climate took place less than two weeks after Wiley assumed the helm of the FCC. A column by Jack Anderson was the catalyst. Its effect might be underestimated unless one savors its sensational style, so here it is, in full:

Buried FCC Study Blasts Broadcasts   *By Jack Anderson*

An explosive Federal Communications Commission study that would reform the inane world of children's television has been stuffed in a government safe. Meanwhile, the study's supporters on the commission have been replaced by bosom pals of big broadcasters.

The report demands an end to hard-sell ads to kids, cutbacks in witless cartoons and more decent children's shows scheduled at appropriate hours. Violators, no matter how powerful, would risk loss of their licenses.

Had the study been accepted by the FCC, it would have cost the broadcast industry tens of millions of dollars a year, compelling them to produce more programs for children and to slice their 32 commercials per hour to no more than 18—the generous allotment currently allowed to adult shows.

These and other dramatic changes were envisioned by former FCC Chairman Dean Burch. Outraged at what he had personally seen of children's programming, he set up a special children's Television Unit in September 1971.

At its head was tough-minded Dr. Elizabeth Roberts, an ex-coordinator of the White House Conference on Children and Youth. For months, the Roberts team studied children's TV.

Four months ago, she delivered the sizzling document to Burch, who forthwith locked it up in his office. Since then, Burch has moved to the White House, and his two staunchest allies in the matter, Commissioners Nick Johnson and Rex Lee, have left the FCC.

We have now obtained a bootleg copy of the suppressed document from under the nose of the new chairman, Richard Wiley. As general counsel and commissioner, Wiley, according to FCC sources, was kinder to network treasuries than to children's welfare. The report's recommendations, therefore, are now in jeopardy.

The 45-page document condemns the "noise, violence or frantic activity" that broadcasters use to keep children mesmerized before TV sets. Years ago, says the report, the networks aired imaginative, decent children's programs on weekdays. But now, cheap cartoons and other movies keep the broadcast coffers full while good shows have dwindled to extinction "with the notable exception of Captain Kangaroo."

The FCC study is even tougher on advertising. Children are "inundated with numerous commercial messages that may be misleading or false to the literal and immature mind of a child." The broadcasters "manipulate his needs" in a manner "destructive to the child's development . . ." the report charges.

"Common sense tells us that commercials presented to sell products to three-, four- and five-year-olds are improper under any civilized public-interest standard."

The Roberts report asks for an end to all advertising on shows for preschool children, saying it is "inherently deceptive." The study would also ban mention of advertised products by "hosts" on children's programs. Kids tend to build a "special relationship" with their hosts, some of whom seem intent on gulling them.

Finally, the study would cut back advertising on kid's show drastically, from the present 16 minutes per hour to a still-generous 9½ minutes, the present voluntary maximum for adult shows.

At the FCC, Chairman Wiley gave us a ringing declaration of independence from the past. He insisted that children's programming was "on the front burner" with him, and pointed out that he had been chairman with power to change things for only 10 days.

At the White House, a spokesman for Dean Burch said the ex-FCC chairman planned to keep an eye on progress. He insisted that there was no intentional stalling on the report, saying it took time to consolidate several studies on the subject.

Reprinted by permission of United Feature Syndicate.

The bulk of the Roberts report recommended rather mild changes. She called for rules that would make permanent what the NAB had already agreed to do voluntarily. The parts of her report that were quoted by Jack Anderson were the more radical recommendations, such as prohibiting commercials aimed at preschool children. She urged that commercials be restricted to 9½ minutes per hour all week instead of just on weekends. She was not proposing far-out solutions although she had certainly considered them, but she did not limit her recommendations to variations of self-regulation.

None of the "explosive" details in the Roberts report was unknown to members of Congress who had been following the FCC's deliberations on children's programming—and certainly no commissioner, however he or she stood on the issue, was unaware of Elizabeth Roberts's arguments. The trade press had discussed the significant portions of the report earlier. But when the issue was brought so forcefully to the public's attention, something had to be done about it publicly.

The network officials who had previously treated ACT officials with a condescending deference went on the attack. John Schneider, president of the CBS Broadcast Group, said, "We must recognize the enemy and they are the consumer groups who went to Washington and told the FCC that they must put an end to all advertising on children's programming. There is no way to negotiate with such a group." When ACT later quoted these remarks as evidence that self-regulation would not work so long as executives held this attitude, Schneider told Peggy Charren that he regretted making this public statement and asked her to stop quoting it.

The Anderson column appeared the morning the commissioners were to go before the Senate Communications Subcommittee for the annual oversight hearing. The senators demanded to see the "sizzling" Roberts report. Although Wiley showed some reluctance, Robert E. Lee, an old hand, suggested the commissioners would agree to hand the report over.

John Pastore, the Senate's force majeure in broadcasting, decided to advise the new FCC chairman on how to solve these thorny children's programming problems. Pastore said he recognized the constraints placed upon the Commission by the First Amendment and the Communications Act; "But on the other hand, it strikes me that from time to time you could sit down informally with the heads of these networks to review the whole matter as to their responsibility." Pastore said that when he himself had called three network presidents into his office, NBC President Julian Goodman remarked that he was unfamiliar with some of the programs being aired. Pastore quoted Goodman, who had a 12-year-old son, as saying, "I was amazed when I looked at our own children's program and then I did something about it." Pastore suggested that Goodman did something about it "because this committee called it to his attention. . . . I wonder if from time to time your Commission cannot sit down with these people and make them recognize they are participants, and they are citizens. Make them recognize what their obligations are. . . . Without twisting anyone's arm these people should be called from time to time to discuss their responsibility, and *if you do not want to do it, I will.*"

Wiley pointed out that in the two and one-half weeks he had been chairman, he had already met with the three networks' Washington vice presidents and also with their "code personnel."

In May 1974 Chairman Wiley expressed his support of reform in children's programming in a speech before the Atlanta branch of the Television Academy of Arts and Sciences. He noted that law and social policy made special provisions for the protection of children, and that the NAB code recognized a "special responsibility." He carried on the Burch tradition of jawboning and went further; Wiley noted that the weekend network schedule comprised 28 animated shows and only seven live shows; he questioned why children's weekends, their "prime time," should include more nonprogram material than adult's prime time included; and he warned that if the industry failed to take any action, the government would be forced to.

Wiley was shocked when Senator Marlow Cook (R.–Ky.), one of the communications subcommittee members who had been needling Wiley about release of the Roberts report, told a New York advertising agency symposium that Wiley's Atlanta speech was the kind of statement no government regulator should make. *Broadcasting,* which had generally supported Wiley, editorialized (June 3, 1974) that "not since Newton Minow ordered his vision of Eden to bloom in the vast wasteland has there been as overt a call for government control." And the Motion Picture Screen Cartoonists Local 839 called Wiley's speech "very irresponsible and ill-advised." Wiley had chosen to get out in front on the issue, and the flak was beginning to come in.

18
A Policy Emerges

18 In June 1974 Chairman Wiley, following the guidelines set forth by Senator Pastore, initiated a campaign to bring the children's programming issue to settlement. The industry would have to give. And although the NAB had agreed to go from 16 minutes to 12 minutes of nonprogram matter per hour on weekends, something additional would have to be ceded. Wiley proposed to NAB top officials that weekend commercial time be brought into line with prime time—a 9½-minute limit.

When Wiley went to work on a project, he displayed an industriousness and an intensity that may be unparalleled in FCC history. In this case he was dealing chiefly with two men: Grover Cobb, NAB senior executive vice president and a former broadcaster, and Vincent Wasilewski, NAB president. Consciously or not, Wiley employed the tactics of a Kojak. At the outset he made it plain that if the NAB code were amended to restrict commercials on children's programs to 9½ minutes per hour, and if the NAB would help him persuade *all* TV stations to adhere to these standards, the FCC would not—as long as he was chairman—pass rules that would cast these standards in concrete.

He met with Cobb one steamy June afternoon during the 1974 energy crisis, when the Government Services Administration, the official janitor of all agencies, had insisted that air conditioning be cut off in government buildings after 4:30 P.M. Because his own office was flooded with sunlight and unbearably hot, Wiley moved his meeting into another office, full of file cabinets and a duplicating machine, where he and Cobb, economist Alan Pearce, and Wiley's legal aide Lawrence Secrest sat on stools and filing cabinets to continue the discussion.

Wiley used the "good cop—bad cop" routine: he warned Cobb that if the industry stubbornly refused to regulate itself, key staff members like Pearce, who had developed figures proving the broadcasters could afford a cutback in commercials, and Secrest, who had cited the FCC's legal authority to set standards, would press for stronger measures than he, Wiley, would prefer. If the NAB went along with Wiley, the industry would be protected from binding regulation; if not, the views of the hotheads might prevail.

Wiley and his aides met frequently with the three networks' Washington vice presidents. Wiley recognized that network influence on the NAB in this matter was crucial. The network people knew him well enough to know that when he said he preferred self-regulation, he meant it; but they would understand his congressional mandate to turn up the heat. One network representative agreed to go along privately—but not in public pronouncements.

Wiley met also with the heads of INTV, an association of independent broadcasters, whose stations were not affiliated with networks. Since, unlike NAB code stations, most of them hadn't subscribed to cutting commercials on children's programs even to 12 minutes per hour, Wiley suggested they make reductions in stages. The eventual FCC policy statement would recognize differences between independent and network-affiliated stations.

When Cobb appeared before the NAB code review board on June 26, 1974, he set forth what he called "the political facts of life." Some members balked; but when the meeting was over, the NAB had agreed to cut commercials on weekend children's shows from 12 minutes per hour to 10 minutes effective December 31, 1974, and to 9½ minutes one year later; on weekday children's programs (mainly in the late afternoon), commercials would be cut from 16 minutes to 14 that year, and to 12 minutes a year later. The code board agreed also to prohibit commercials for vitamins or drugs during children's programs, to restrict selling by program hosts or heroes, to separate clearly program content from advertising messages, and to ensure that advertising products met generally accepted safety standards. By a close vote, the NAB television board approved of the code board's action although according to *Television Digest* (July 8), "There was open resentment to the role played by Wiley in forcing code action."

The independent stations agreed separately to follow the NAB's example and reduce nonprogram material in children's shows. Wiley was quoted in *Broadcasting* (July 29) as being "very pleased," and saying that the reductions were along the lines that he had proposed in Atlanta. "We're not looking for deeper cuts," he said.

And so it came to pass that in October 1974, the FCC labored and brought forth a children's programming policy statement. ACT would consider it a mouse, and broadcasters would consider it a camel's nose under the free enterprise tent.

When the Commission met to vote on the policy statement, the lineup was significantly different from the commissioners who voted on the original ACT petition for rulemaking in 1971. Only Robert E. Lee, who had voted against issuing the notice, was still on the Commission. The staff was different too. The children's unit members had departed. The policy statement was drafted by a task force headed by Lawrence Secrest and including members of the general counsel's office and the Broadcast Bureau. Secrest believed the FCC had authority to act firmly on the matter; the bureau had not changed its position since the recommendations of January 1973, but this position was not dominant in the drafted statement.

Even before the policy could be confirmed or announced, it leaked to the press. On October 7, 1974, the day before the commissioners were to discuss a draft of the policy statement, *Television Digest* printed pertinent parts of the staff draft with the news that "some commissioners are known to be opposed to strong program language, and will make effort to throw some of it out, tone down some." Broadcast lawyers, of course, understood the legal significance of the strong language and hastened to suggest how to tone it down. ACT had no comparable crack at urging retention of the stronger language. The leak to *Television*

the Roberts report, the Commission added no requirement beyond the generality that "we do believe that some effort should be made for both preschool and school-age children."

Leaving the content of children's advertising to the Federal Trade Commission, the FCC did caution licensees against "overcommercialization" on children's programs and specified that the NAB standard, as well as the 12 minutes per hour adopted by the less lucrative, independent stations, is "reasonable." "We recognize that there may be some independent VHF and UHF stations which cannot easily afford such a reduction in advertising; such stations should be prepared to make a substantial and well-documented showing of serious potential harm to support their advertising practices. However, we anticipate accepting very few other justifications for overcommercialization in programs designed for children." Specifying that broadcasters should separate program and commercial matter, the FCC described "host selling" as not in the public interest.

In conclusion, the FCC said, "We believe that in these areas every opportunity should be accorded to the broadcast industry to reform itself because self-regulation preserves flexibility and an opportunity for adjustment which is not possible with *per se* rules." The Commission left the proceeding open "in view of the fact that we plan to evaluate the improvements in children's programming and advertising which are now expected."

ACT was not pleased with the policy statement. Peggy Charren said:

By not making a rule at this time the FCC has said to the broadcaster, "You have gone far enough." No one who has followed the development of children's advertising as an issue of public importance expects the NAB to make further rules now that the FCC has indicated it will not act. . . . It would seem that all 100,000 letters the Commission received from the public, and all the comments from organizations concerned with children's health and development have been totally ignored by this policy statement. . . . It is not enough to rely on the sense of commitment of broadcasters. If it were, ACT would not have had to come into existence. (*Broadcasting*, October 28, 1974.)

Drawing a distinction between weekends and the rest of the week in determining commercal ceilings was, Charren said, "absurd."

ACT immediately appealed the FCC's action to the U.S. Court of Appeals in Washington, D.C. Charren told Cole that one reason ACT filed so quickly was fear that broadcasters might appeal the FCC statement for going too far and that an appeals court outside Washington would be given jurisdiction and would lack the D.C. circuit's familiarity with broadcasting issues.

In an editorial *Broadcasting* (November 4, 1974) said, "Now that the FCC has concluded its long inquiry into children's television with a policy statement instead of a rule, a good many broadcasters are privately celebrating. Perhaps they would be wiser to keep the champagne corked." The magazine characterized the FCC statement as an invitation to "pressure groups" to create regulatory standards through case-by-case attacks on licensees. Further, *Broadcasting* suggested that quality children's programming could be left to public television stations.

Henry Geller, former FCC general counsel who was working as a consultant to the RAND Corporation, and Karen Possner, his RAND colleague, asked the FCC to reconsider its policy statement because the "considerable vagueness" of its definition of goals would come back to haunt the Commission when citizen groups sought to measure licensee performance. Geller and Possner asked the FCC to "adopt more definitive guidelines; foster a cooperative effort by the networks (and stations) in the area of children's TV educational/informational programming, and find unlawful product commercials in programs designed specifically for preschool children (ages 2–5)."

In September 1975 the FCC rejected the Geller-Possner petition for reconsideration. Because the Commission was relying heavily on industry self-regulation, its statement "necessarily entails a greater degree of vagueness than would have been acceptable had we chosen to adopt formal rules.... [The] precise question of the relationship between those guidelines and license renewal standards was not addressed." As for banning advertising to preschool children, "it seems unrealistic on the one hand to expect licensees to improve significantly their program service to children and on the other hand, to withdraw a major source of funding for this task." The plea to encourage network cooperation was rejected on the rather quixotic grounds that "we do not believe *lessening* the competition in programming is the best way to encourage varied, imaginative children's programming." Commissioner Hooks dissented to the denial of reconsideration.

While the FCC had been deliberating about commercials on children's programs, broadcasters had been threatening that the losses of revenue would make such fare unprofitable and consequently would force cutbacks in the amount and quality of children's shows. Alan Pearce's economic study, cited by Hooks, estimated that networks could cut commercials back to 7½ minutes per hour on weekend *and* weekday children's shows and still show overall profit on this kind of programming. On weekends, Pearce suggested, the limit could be 6 minutes. Nonetheless, CBS's John Schneider testified before the House Communications Subcommittee in July 1975 that because of tightened commercial time restrictions and increasing production costs, "children's television has declined in recent years from a highly profitable area of activity at CBS to a marginal undertaking." When Chairman Torbert Macdonald challenged Schneider to produce revenue figures to document his complaint, the CBS executive declined to reveal profit information "for competitive reasons." Macdonald said later, "I do not approve of the tactics of some broadcasters who make economic arguments in public and then refuse to substantiate these arguments with facts and figures."

Pearce, working subsequently for the House subcommittee, reported in late 1976,

> The three networks combined have lost nothing in gross revenues by reducing the amount of advertising in children's programs. . . . gross advertising revenues for all three networks combined for both regularly scheduled and special children's programs reached an all-time high in 1975 ($90.8 million) . . . representing an overall increase of 16 percent over the previous year in spite of a reduction of from 12 to 17 percent in the amount of advertising allowed on children's programs.

In fact, he asserted, children's television continued to contribute proportionately higher percentages of profit than those of other portions of the networks' programming.

The policy statement contained some ringing declarations of what the FCC expected from broadcasters, but citizen groups like ACT wondered how the FCC expected to monitor licensees' performance and what mechanisms of enforcement the Commission had. In paragraph 43 of the policy statement, the FCC said, "To insure that the Commission will have adequate information on broadcasters' advertising practices in programs designed for children, we will, in a separate order, amend the renewal form to elicit more detailed information in this area." Licensees would be asked to indicate the number of commercial minutes per hour broadcast both on weekdays and weekends in programs designed for children. "The data provided by this question will serve, in part, as a basis for determining whether self-regulation can be effective." Because studies showed that $9\frac{1}{2}$ minutes on weekends and 12 minutes on weekdays were levels "economically feasible for most licensees to achieve over the next year and a half," after January 1, 1976, broadcasting more than the amount of advertising proposed by the NAB and INTV "may raise a question as to whether the licensee is subordinating the interests of the child audience to his own financial interests."

There was an irony in the Commission's reference to programs "designed for" children. During the drafting of the television renewal form adopted in 1973, ACT, its supporters, and some FCC staff personnel, including Cole, fought to include on the renewal application form meaningful data on children's programming policies. Staff members who believed such questions infringed on licensees' prerogatives campaigned successfully to word the question to allow licensees to list programs "directed to" children—which include habitually watched programs like reruns of *Gilligan's Island* or *I Love Lucy*—and avoid the embarrassment of admitting that very little programming was specifically "designed for" children.

When the FCC decided to add questions on commercials in children's programs, the industry was eager to have the affected category as narrow as possible. Broadcasters didn't want to explain why they had aired many commercials on programs that children just happened to watch. So the staff recommended that the question cover just those programs particularly designed for children. Since the wording was the same as that in the NAB code, there was no opposition.

Handling the question of commercials on children's programs in this way was inconsistent with the language in the general children's programming question that had been adopted in 1973. To resolve the inconsistency, the FCC adopted the narrower phrase "designed for children" in both cases. The FCC explanation for the change was this: "It has been our experience that some television licensees have responded to [the renewal form question] with information on programs which may be viewed by children, rather than programs designed particularly for them."

After issuing the children's programming policy statement, the FCC did revise the renewal form to query applicants on how many programs designed for children 12 years old and under contained commercials in excess of 12 minutes per hour and 6 minutes per half-hour on weekdays, or $9\frac{1}{2}$ minutes per hour and $4\frac{3}{4}$ minutes per half-hour on weekends. The form asks also about proposed commercial policies for programs designed for children 12 years old or under. Finally, the form asks the licensee to give a "brief description of programs, program segments or program series" designed for children 12 years old and under and broadcast during the past license period.

As with many other questions on the renewal form, the commissioners (as of June 1977) have shown no interest in learning what the answers are. Nor have the commissioners instructed the renewal staff as to what are acceptable levels of programming and commercials and what responses should trigger further scrutiny. As with other renewal problems, the staff doesn't want to stir up a hornet's nest on matters in which the commissioners have evinced no interest. If citizens file a petition to deny a station's license renewal on grounds that the licensee has violated the principles of the FCC's policy statement on children's programming for an entire license period, then there may be some commissioner response. Because the statement didn't become fully effective before 1976, no such petitions have been processed as yet. As they are filed in the future, the Commission will have a somewhat different cast from the one that approved the statement initially.

When Cole asked a renewal branch employee what the process is for monitoring compliance with children's standards, the employee said that as long as the licensee puts down some answer, the analysts of the form have been instructed to keep going—on to the next question.

"We've gotten some crazy answers as to what makes a kid's program, but we're not going to get into the problem of deciding what is and what isn't a children's program and how much is enough." As Henry Geller suggested, some future Commission may decide to take some action—and the 1974 policy statement is vague enough and broad enough to permit many alternatives of action.

*   *   *

"Sex 'n' violence" in children's programming is, of course, a separate issue—a favorite crusade of some members of Congress and the target of some citizen groups. This issue remains wide open, partly because Chairman Wiley attempted to duplicate almost step by step what he considered his success in the areas of commercials and children's fare. The saga of the "family viewing" hour could fill a book. This is what happened.

Barely two weeks before the FCC adopted the children's programming statement, Chairman Wiley made a speech to Illinois broadcasters urging the industry to do something voluntarily about violence in kids' shows. He was acutely aware that congressmen who'd been urging the FCC to do something about children's fare wouldn't be satisfied simply by the proposed statement on commercial policies. So he began a parallel course to jawbone the networks into a voluntary policy of preserving the earliest hour of prime-time network TV programs, when presumably young children would still be awake and viewing TV, as a "family viewing hour," when programming "inappropriate for viewing by a general family audience" would not be presented. As *Broadcasting* (October 21, 1974) noted with some prescience: "But Chairman Wiley lacks the leverage for dealing with his present problem that was available to him in connection with his determination to see ads on children's television cut back—the Commission's freedom to adopt rules to enforce a desired kind of conduct."

In fact, the family viewing circumstances differed from the children's program case in two other important respects: committees of both houses of Congress had given Wiley a December 31, 1974, deadline to report what he was doing about violent programs, and there had been no rulemaking announced nor comments solicited upon which Wiley could legally base action. Under these pressures, Wiley chose to follow the path of persuasion that had led to the children's policy statement.

Wiley met with officials from the networks, the NAB, and independent TV stations at different time. The networks agreed that 8:00 P.M.–9:00 P.M. would be reserved for family viewing; and despite protests from some NAB members, the trade organization revised its code.

However, the Writers Guild of America, West, whose membership scripts TV shows, sued the FCC in California for restricting freedom of expression and violating the Administrative Procedure Act. TV producer Norman Lear joined the suit and cited CBS for limiting the times when controversial fare such as he produced (*All in the Family, Maude, Mary Hartman*) could be shown. ACT and other groups, joining in the suit, charged that the FCC and broadcasters had made these changes without any public participation.

In November 1976, Judge Warren Ferguson of the U.S. District Court (Central District) of California (*Writers Guild of America* v. *FCC*) found against the FCC and for the plaintiffs, who "have evidenced a successful attempt by the FCC to pressure the networks and the NAB into adopting a programming policy they did not wish to adopt. The plaintiffs have proven that the FCC formulated and imposed new industry policy without giving the public its right to notice and its right to be heard." The judge made clear that he was not ruling on whether a family viewing hour was desirable or not; he decided simply that if government intervenes to control TV entertainment programming, "it shall do so not in closed-door negotiating sessions but in conformity with legislatively mandated administrative procedures."

Judge Ferguson emphasized that he wasn't denying the FCC's power to enforce protections for children, provided the agency established a public record; but the family viewing policy "is in large part a public relations gimmick" because it is confined to early evening viewing even though the FCC had stated that "children form a substantial segment of the audience on weekday afternoons and early evenings as well as on weekends." Conscious that the policy statement was being considered in another court, the judge said, "It may be that the rights of children to diversity of programming have been so severely ignored by broadcasters that affirmative requirements that broadcasters meet their needs in the times when children most frequently watch television could be constitutionally supported in a properly prepared administrative record."

The judge questioned not the accuracy of the FCC's gauging of public policy but the method the FCC employed in the family viewing matter. Judge Ferguson said:

> Here, ironically, the government and the networks, both acting as public trustees, negotiated public policy while refusing to comply with procedural safeguards designed to protect the public they serve. If this process is considered acceptable adminstrative procedure, the [Communications] Act's provisions will become meaningless. The government could sit down at a table with the regulated industry, negotiate policy, delegate to the industry the power to enforce the policy, mouth empty words of congratulation about self-regulation, issue cynical denials of government responsibility, and avoid the Act entirely. Such procedures would permit government and industry to seal out the public from the decisionmaking process and to frustrate judicial scrutiny.

The judge also pinpointed the reason the FCC was able to apply pressure on broadcasters: "The root of the power is the uncertainty of the relicensing process and the vagueness of the standards which govern it."

Judge Ferguson's decision was appealed by all losing parties. The NAB was particularly concerned because the judge threatened the future of the code when he stated,

> The NAB has no constitutional right to set up a network board to censor and regulate American television. . . . Even when station managers are willing to abdicate their responsibilities by delegating their programming authority in exchange for membership in the NAB (with the convenient advantages of access to lobbying and informational services together with whatever prestige attaches to membership), the First Amendment requirement of diversity in decision-making does not protect such tie-in arrangements.

Judge Ferguson was ruling in a case in which the FCC hadn't followed the procedures that require public comment, the rulemaking process where all interested parties may file, whether or not their arguments are heeded in the outcome. He ruled, among other things, that the public—the broadcast audience—hadn't sufficient opportunity to be heard by the FCC.

In the case of the ACT rulemaking and inquiry, circumstances were significantly different. ACT asked the Court of Appeals to rule that the FCC didn't go far enough in its policy statement. Earle K. Moore, who with Henry Geller and Ellen Shaw Agress represented ACT, acknowledged: "It's a tough procedure. It's like suing Congress for not passing a law. Our main argument is that the Commission did not take up ACT's primary point—the impact of advertising on program content."

On the day the court was to hear argument on ACT's appeal, Peggy Charren came to Washington. She conferred with various citizen groups and lawyers, and then went to the FCC building to get information on another matter. By chance, she ran into Chairman Wiley in the elevator.

"What brings you to town?" he asked pleasantly.

"Our case is being heard in the appeals court," she replied.

"Oh? Whom are you suing?"

"You."

"Oh yes," he recalled, "and who is on the panel [of three judges] hearing the case?"

When she named the panel, three judges considered the most conservative on broadcast matters, Wiley broke into a big smile and said, "Why, that's wonderful."

"You know, you're the first person I've spoken to all day who feels that way," Ms. Charren said.

The appeals court panel issued a ruling on July 1, 1977. Moore's forebodings and Wiley's optimism were justified: the FCC was affirmed. The court ruled, as it has in many cases in which the judges acknowledge the FCC's particular expertise, "The Commission did not act arbitrarily or otherwise abuse its broad discretion in declining to adopt ACT's proposed rules as its own, or, for that matter, in declining to adopt any rules whatsoever for the time being." The court said,

> It is true that self-regulation has not always worked out as desired, but this does not mean that self-regulation has never worked or that it cannot work in this case. Much, we suppose, depends on the degree to which such efforts are focused on specific problems and the extent to which the Commission and the public monitor the level of actual performance. We believe that the [FCC's policy statement] promises reasonable success from both standpoints.

Even while nodding to the FCC's role as "the expert agency entrusted by Congress with the administration and regulation of the crucial, dynamic, communications field," the court added a note that ought to cheer ACT. The judges said that while

> the Commission has chosen to accord licensees a substantial measure of their customary discretion in the areas of programming and advertising decisions . . . yet it has made it quite clear that general improvements must be forthcoming in the time devoted to advertisements, in separation of advertisements from program content, and in increased educational or informative programming.

While not referring to the family-viewing case opinion by Judge Ferguson, the court did discuss the extent of the public's and of the industry's participation in the ACT rulemaking.

> In holding that ACT's position was not prejudiced by the manner in which the Commission pursued the temporary resolution of these proceedings, we wish to emphasize that we are not insensitive to ACT's disenchantment with what it considered to be the agency's undue deference to the interest of those it was created to regulate. . . . Nevertheless, while it may have been impolitic for the Commission not to invite further comment on the NAB's proposals, especially in view of the fact that there was no necessity for deciding these difficult issues quickly, we still cannot say that the Commission abused its discretion in deciding not to . . . nor are we persuaded that ACT's interests in these proceedings were inadequately protected, much less subverted, by the Commission's action.

The court rejected the argument that the nature of the children's programming proceeding "made this rulemaking action susceptible to poisonous ex parte influence. Private groups were not competing for a specific valuable privilege. Furthermore, this case does not raise serious questions of fairness. Chairman Wiley met with representatives of NAB, as Chairman Burch had met with representatives of ACT, and there is no indication that he 'gave to any interested party advantages not shared by all.' "

The court decision came at a time when the authors thought they'd tied a ribbon around their particular box of FCC history. When asked for her reaction, Peggy Charren said ACT would ask the full nine-member court to reconsider the opinion. But she was encouraged by some of the language. "The judges said the FCC should give the industry some time to see if self-regulation works. Well, the FCC issued its statement in 1974, and things aren't much better today. So we're going to ask the Commission for new rules to enforce the standards." How goes the battle after all these years? "I'm optimistic," Peggy Charren replied, "I wouldn't be able to keep going in this business if I weren't."

APPENDIX A
FCC
Organizational
Chart

Federal Communications Commission
Organization Chart   May 1977

The Commissioners (47)*

RICHARD E. WILEY CHAIRMAN
ROBERT E. LEE   BENJAMIN L. HOOKS
JAMES H. QUELLO   ABBOTT M. WASHBURN
JOSEPH R. FOGARTY   MARGITA E. WHITE

Office of Administrative Law Judges (30)

Review Board (22)

Office of Opinions and Review (28)

Office of Plans and Policy (13)

Field Operations Bureau (494)

Enforcement Division
Engineering Division
Regional Services Division
Violations Division

Field Installations

Office of Executive Director (358)

Administrative Services Div.
Consumer Assistance Office
Data Automation Div.
Emergency Communications Div.
Financial Management Div.
Internal Review & Security Div.
Management Systems Div.
Personnel Div.
Procurement Div.
Public Information Officer
Records Management Div.
The Secretary

Office of Chief Engineer (144)

International &
Operations Division
Laboratory Division
Research &
Standards Division
Planning &
Coordination Staff
Spectrum Allocations Staff
Spectrum Management
Task Force

Office of General Counsel (60)

Administrative Rules &
Procedure Division
Legal Research &
Treaty Division
Legislation Division
Litigation & Enforcement
Division
Industry Equal Employment
Opportunity Unit

Safety and Special Radio Services Bureau (264)

Amateur & Citizens Division
Aviation & Marine Division
Industrial & Public Safety Facilities
Division
Industrial & Public Safety Rules
Division
Legal Advisory & Enforcement
Division

Regional Management Staff

Common Carrier Bureau (257)

Accounting & Audits Division
Economics Division
Facilities & Services Division
Hearing Division
Mobile Services Division
Policy & Rules Division
Tariff Division

International Programs Staff

Program Evaluation Staff

Field Offices

Cable Television Bureau (91)

Certificates of
Compliance Division
Policy Review
& Development Division
Research Division
Special Relief &
Microwave Division

Broadcast Bureau (343)

Broadcast Facilities Division
Complaints & Compliance Division
Hearing Division
License Division
Office of Network Study
Policy & Rules Division
Renewal & Transfer Division

FC COMMISSION USA FEDERAL COMMUNICATIONS (logo)

* Figures in parentheses are estimated employee totals at end of fiscal year 1977 (September 30, 1977).
Totals in offices of the commissioners include assistants and secretaries.

APPENDIX B
Forms
Relating to
License Renewal

FCC Form 303 A
September 1976

Form Approved
OMB No. 52- R0229

RETURN COPY WITH MAILING LABEL AND
ONE ADDITIONAL COPY TO THE FCC
RETAIN ONE COPY FOR YOUR FILES

FEDERAL COMMUNICATIONS COMMISSION
Washington, D. C. 20554
Reference 8630

1 9 7 6

ANNUAL PROGRAMMING REPORT

SEE INSTRUCTIONS ON REVERSE SIDE BEFORE COMPLETING THIS REPORT

RETURN TWO COPIES TO THE FCC; RETAIN ONE COPY FOR YOUR FILES

PLEASE TYPE OR PRINT

CALL SIGN	CHANNEL	LICENSEE'S NAME	COMMUNITY OF LICENSE	STATE
NETWORK AFFILIATION		LEAVE BLANK		

COMPOSITE WEEK DATA	FROM 6PM TO 11PM (5PM TO 10PM CENTRAL AND MOUNTAIN TIME)		FROM 6AM TO MIDNIGHT		FROM MIDNIGHT TO 6AM (SAME BROADCAST DAY)	
	Minutes of Operation (A)	% of Total Time (Line 1-Col.A) (B)	Minutes of Operation (C)	% of Total Time (Line 1-Col.C) (D)	Minutes of Operation (E)	% of Total Time (Line 1-Col. E) (F)
1. TOTAL TIME OPERATING (*Including commercial material*)	(Maximum 2100)	100.0	(Maximum 7560)	100.0	(Maximum 2520)	100.0
2. TOTAL NEWS (*Exclude commercial material*)		.		.		.
3. TOTAL PUBLIC AFFAIRS (*Exclude commercial material*)		.		.		.
4. TOTAL OTHER Non-entertainment/Non-sports (*Exclude commercial material*)		.		.		.
5. LOCAL NEWS (*Exclude commercial material*)		.		.		.
6. LOCAL PUBLIC AFFAIRS (*Exclude commercial material*)		.		.		.
7. LOCAL OTHER Non-entertainment/Non-sports (*Exclude commercial material*)		.		.		.
8. ALL LOCAL PROGRAMS — Include Entertainment & Sports (*Exclude commercial material*)[1]		.		.		.

LOCAL AND NON-LOCAL (rows 2–4)

LOCAL ONLY (rows 5–8)

[1] LINE 8 EQUALS THE TOTAL OF LINES 5, 6 AND 7 PLUS LOCALLY-PRODUCED ENTERTAINMENT AND SPORTS PROGRAMS

COMPLETE THE CERTIFICATE ON THE REVERSE SIDE AND ATTACH PROGRAM DESCRIPTIONS

INSTRUCTIONS FOR FCC FORM 303-A

Filing Requirements

All commercial television licensees/permittees must file this form annually before February 1. The data to be filed is to be taken from the programming for the composite week shown in the enclosed notice. Return two copies of the form (one with the mailing label) and two copies of the program descriptions to the FCC, Washington, D.C., 20554. A third copy of the form including program descriptions is to be placed in the licensee's public inspection file along with a copy of the program logs for the composite week in accordance with section 1.526(a) (8) of the Commission Rules.

For each program included in the categories of 'public affairs' and 'all others', the date and time of broadcast, duration, source (see definition 2 below) and a brief description should be submitted with this form. For each program in the category of 'news', the date and time of broadcast, duration, and source (see definition 2 below) should be submitted with this form. Write the station call sign on each page of these attachments.

Guidelines

1. Stations in the Central and Mountain Time zones are to use the time classification of 5-10 PM in place of 6-11 PM.

2. Report all time in minutes rounded to the nearest minute. Round all percentages to the nearest tenth of a percent.

3. Include commercial matter (see definition 1(e) below) in line 1, columns A, C and E. Exclude all commercial matter from all other program categories (lines 2, 3, 4, 5, 6, 7, and 8, all columns).

4. Satellite stations are to report as local programs only those programs that the satellite station originates itself. Definition 1 (d) below should be followed in determining what is considered local.

5. In reporting network affiliation, write ABC, CBS, or NBC if affiliated; write IND if not affiliated. If affiliated with more than one network during the composite week, write the primary affiliation first followed by the secondary affiliation(s).

Definitions

1. The following definitions are to be used in furnishing the information called for in the Annual Programming Report:

(a) News includes reports dealing with current local, national and international events, including weather and stock market reports; and commentary, analysis, or sports news when they are an integral part of a news program.

(b) Public Affairs Programs are programs dealing with local, state, regional, national or international issues or problems, including, but not limited to, talks, commentaries, discussions, speeches, editorials, political programs, documentaries, mini-documentaries, panels, roundtables and vignettes, and extended coverage (whether live or recorded) of public events or proceedings, such as local council meetings, congressional hearings and the like.

(c) All Other non-entertainment/non-sports includes all other programs which are not intended primarily as entertainment. (Entertainment includes music, drama, variety, comedy, quiz, etc.) Do not include play-by-play sports programs, pre- or post-game related activities and separate programs of sports instruction, news, or information (e.g. fishing opportunities, golfing instructions, etc.).

(d) A Local Program is any program originated or produced by the station, or for the production of which the station is substantially responsible, and which also employs live talent more than 50% of the time. Such a program, taped, recorded or filmed for later broadcast shall be classified as local. A local program fed to a network shall be classified by the originating station as local. All non-network and non-syndicated news programs may be classified as local. Programs primarily featuring syndicated or feature films, or other non-locally recorded programs shall not be classified as local, even though a station personality appears in connection with such material. However, identifiable units of such programs which are live and separately logged as such may be classified as local (e.g., if during the course of a feature film program a non-network 2 minute news report is given and logged as a news program, the report may be classified as local).

(e) Commercial Matter includes commercial continuity (network and non-network) and commercial announcements (network and non-network) as follows:

(1) Commercial Continuity is the advertising message of a program sponsor.

(2) A Commercial Announcement is any other advertising message for which a charge is made, or other consideration is received.

(a) Included are "bonus" spots, trade-out spots, and promotional announcements of a future program where consideration is received for such an announcement or where such announcement identifies the sponsors of the future program beyond mention of the sponsor's name as an integral part of the title of the program (e.g., where the agreement for the sale of time provides that the sponsor will receive promotional announcements, or when the promotional announcement contains a statement such as "TOMORROW SEE -- NAME OF PROGRAM -- BROUGHT TO YOU BY -- SPONSOR'S NAME --").

(b) Other announcements including but not limited to the following are not commercial announcements:

(1) Promotional announcements, except as defined above

(2) Station identification announcements for which no charge is made

(3) Mechanical reproduction announcements

(4) Public service announcements

(5) Announcements made pursuant to Section 73.654(d) of the Rules that materials or services have been furnished as an inducement to broadcast a political program involving the discussion of controversial public issues

(6) Announcements made pursuant to the local notice requirements of Sections 1.580 (pre-grant) and 1.594 (designation for hearing) of the Rules.

2. Sources of programs are defined as follows:

(a) A local program - See instruction 1 (d) above.

(b) A network program is any program furnished to the station by a network (national, regional or special). Delayed broadcasts of programs originated by networks are classified as network.

(c) A recorded program is any program not defined in (a) and (b) above, including without limitation, syndicated programs, taped or transcribed programs, and feature films.

CERTIFICATE

I certify that I am _____ of _____

Official title   (Exact legal name of licensee or permittee)

that all the statements made in this report and attached exhibits are considered material representations, and that all the exhibits are a material part hereof and are incorporated herein as if set out in full in the report; that the statements contained in this report are true, complete, and correct to the best of my knowledge and belief, and are made in good faith.

_____
(Signature)

Any person who willfully makes false statements on this report can be punished by fine or imprisonment. U.S. Code, Title 18, Section 1001.

_____ , 19 _____

Person to whom inquiries may be directed

(please type or print)

Name _____

Area Code _____ Phone _____

PROGRAMMING SECTION OF RENEWAL FORM
FOR COMMERCIAL TELEVISION LICENSEES

FCC Form 303	STATEMENT OF TV PROGRAM SERVICE	Section IV

NAME OF APPLICANT

CITY AND STATE WHICH STATION IS LICENSED TO SERVE	CALL SIGN

1. Has applicant placed in its public inspection file at the appropriate times the required documentation relating to its efforts to ascertain the community problems, needs and interests?

☐ YES ☐ NO ☐ DOES NOT APPLY

If NO, attach as Exhibit No.   a complete statement of explanation.

2. Attach as Exhibit No.   applicant's community leader check-list for the preceding license term.

☐ DOES NOT APPLY

3. Has the applicant placed in its public inspection file at the appropriate times its annual list of those problems, needs and interests which, in the applicant's judgment, warranted treatment by its station and typical and illustrative programming in response thereto?

☐ YES ☐ NO

If YES, attach those listings as Exhibit No.
If NO, attach as Exhibit No.   a complete statement of explanation.

4. Describe in Exhibit No.   the procedures applicant has or proposes to have for the consideration and disposition of complaints or suggestions from the public.

5. A. State for the most recent composite week (a) the total number of public service announcements broadcast and (b) the number of public service announcements broadcast between 8AM - 11PM.

(a)	(b)

B. Of the total number of public service announcements broadcast during the most recent composite week state (a) the number which in the licensee's judgment were primarily designed to promote programs, activities, or services of organizations or organizational units located in the service area, (b) the number which in the licensee's judgment were primarily designed to promote programs, activities or services of organizations or organizational units located outside the service area, and (c) the number which in the licensee's judgment do not readily fall into either category (a) or (b) and/or are a combination of both.

(a)	(b)	(c)

C. Attach as Exhibit No.   one exact copy of the program logs for the most recent composite week used as a basis for responding to Questions 5, 11, and 12 herein. Applicants utilizing automatic program logging devices must comply with the provisions of Section 73.670(f).

6. A. Was the applicant affiliated with one or more national television networks during the past license period?

☐ YES ☐ NO

If YES, give name(s) of network(s):

If the applicant had more than one such affiliation, which network was the principal source of network programs?

B. If a network affiliate, did the applicant regularly carry (i.e., carry more than 50% of the programs offered during the current license period) available network news and public affairs?

	YES	NO
(1) News	☐	☐
(2) Public Affairs	☐	☐

7. In Exhibit No.   give a brief description of programs, program segments or program series broadcast during the license period which were designed for children twelve years old and under. Indicate the source, time and day of broadcast, frequency of broadcast, and program type.

8. A. In the applicant's judgment, does the information supplied in the Annual Programming Reports (FCC Form 303-A) submitted during the current license period, the information supplied in the annual listings of typical and illustrative programs and program segments broadcast to help meet significant problems and needs of the service area for the current license period, and the information supplied in Questions 5, 6 and 7 above adequately reflect its programming during the current license period?

☐ YES ☐ NO

B. If the answer to A is NO, the applicant may attach as Exhibit No.   such additional information (including the listing of entertainment programs the applicant considers to be of special merit) as may be necessary to describe accurately and present fairly its program service.

C. If the applicant's programming reflected in the Annual Programming Reports submitted during the current license period varied substantially from the programming representations made in the last renewal application, the applicant may submit as Exhibit No.   a statement explaining the variations and reasons therefor.

9. Indicate the minimum amount of time the applicant proposes to devote normally each week to the categories below. Commercial time should be *excluded* in all computations except for the entries in columns 2, 6 and 10 of the total time operating line (line a).

| ANTICIPATED TYPICAL WEEK DATA | FROM 6AM TO MIDNIGHT | | | | FROM 6PM TO 11PM (5PM to 10PM CENTRAL AND MOUNTAIN TIME) | | | | FROM MIDNIGHT TO 6AM | | | |
| | ALL PROGRAMS | | LOCAL PROGRAMS ONLY | | ALL PROGRAMS | | LOCAL PROGRAMS ONLY | | ALL PROGRAMS | | LOCAL PROGRAMS ONLY | |
(1)	MINUTES OF OPERATION (2)	PERCENTAGE OF TOTAL TIME OPERATING (3) 2/	MINUTES OF OPERATION (4) 1/	PERCENTAGE OF TOTAL TIME OPERATING (5) 2/	MINUTES OF OPERATION (6)	PERCENTAGE OF TOTAL TIME OPERATING (7) 2/	MINUTES OF OPERATION (8) 1/	PERCENTAGE OF TOTAL TIME OPERATING (9) 3/	MINUTES OF OPERATION (10)	PERCENTAGE OF TOTAL TIME OPERATING (11) 4/	MINUTES OF OPERATION (12) 1/	PERCENTAGE OF TOTAL TIME OPERATING (13) 4/
a. TOTAL TIME OPERATING		100%				100%				100%		
b. NEWS 1/												
c. PUBLIC AFFAIRS 1/												
d. ALL OTHERS *(Exclusive of entertainment and sports)* 1/												

1/ Excluding Commercials
2/ Percentages are of the total minutes of operation reported at the top of column 2.
3/ Percentages are of the total minutes of operation reported at the top of column 6.
4/ Percentages are of the total minutes of operation reported at the top of column 10.

10. A. State (a) the minimum total number of public service announcements and (b) the minimum number of public service announcements between 8AM - 11PM the applicant proposes to broadcast during a typical week.

(a)	(b)

B. Of the total number of public service announcements the applicant proposes to broadcast during a typical week state (a) the number which it expects will be primarily designed to promote programs, activities or services of organizations or organizational units located in the service area, (b) the number which it expects will be primarily designed to promote programs, activities or services of organizations or organizational units located outside of the service area, and (c) the number which it expects will not fall readily into either category (a) or (b) and/or will be a combination of both.

(a)	(b)	(c)

PAST COMMERCIAL PRACTICES

11. State the number of 60-minute segments during the most recent composite week (beginning with the first full clock hour and ending with the last full clock hour of each broadcast day) containing the following amounts of commercial matter:

A. Up to and including 8 minutes	
B. Over 8 and up to and including 12 minutes	
C. Over 12 and up to and including 16 minutes	
D. Over 16 minutes	

List each segment in category D above, specifying the amount of commercial time in the segment, and the day and time of broadcast.

Segment	Amount of Commercial Time in Segment	Day and Time Broadcast

If more space is needed continue in Exhibit No.

12. State the number of 60-minute segments in the 6PM - 11PM (5PM - 10PM Central and Mountain Time) time period during the most recent composite week containing the following amounts of commercial matter:

A. Up to and including 8 minutes	
B. Over 8 and up to and including 12 minutes	
C. Over 12 and up to an including 16 minutes	
D. Over 16 minutes	

List each segment in category D above, specifying the amount of commercial time in the segment, and the day and time broadcast.

Segment	Amount of Commercial Time in Segment	Day and Time Broadcast

If more space is needed continue in Exhibit No.

13. **A.** In the applicant's judgment, does the information supplied in Questions 11 and 12 adequately reflect its commercial practices during the current license period?

  ☐ YES ☐ NO

 B. If NO, applicant may attach as Exhibit No.   such additional material as may be necessary to describe adequately and present fairly its commercial practices.

 C. If the applicant's commercial practices for the period covered by Questions 11 and 12 varied from the representations made in the applicant's last renewal application the applicant may explain in Exhibit No.   the variations and the reasons therefor.

14. Submit as Exhibit No.   each one hour or ½ hour segment of programming designed for children twelve years old and under broadcast during the license period which contained commercial matter in excess of:

  (a) 12 minutes per hour or 6 minutes per half-hour on weekdays (Monday through Friday), or
  (b) 9½ minutes per hour or 4 3/4 minutes per half-hour on weekends (Saturday and Sunday).

 For each programming segment so listed, indicate the length of the segment (i.e. one hour or ½ hour) and the amount of commercial matter contained therein.

PROPOSED COMMERCIAL PRACTICES

15. What is the maximum amount of commercial matter in any 60-minute segment which the applicant proposes normally to allow?

 If the applicant proposes to permit this amount to be exceeded at times, state in Exhibit No.   under what circumstances and how often this is expected to occur, and the limits that would then apply.

16. What is the maximum amount of commercial matter in any 60-minute segment between the hours of 6PM - 11PM (5PM - 10PM Central and Mountain Time) which the applicant proposes normally to allow?

 If the applicant proposes to permit this amount to be exceeded at times, state in Exhibit No.   under what circumstances and how often this is expected to occur, and the limits that would then apply.

17. **A.** What is the maximum amount of commercial matter per hour the applicant proposes to allow in programs broadcast on weekdays (Monday through Friday) which are designed for children twelve years old and under?

 If the applicant proposes to permit this amount to exceed 12 minutes, state in Exhibit No.   under what circumstances and how often this is expected to occur, and the limits that would then apply.

 B. What is the maximum amount of commercial matter per hour the applicant proposes to allow in programs broadcast on weekends (Saturday and Sunday) which are designed for children twelve years old and under?

 If the applicant proposes to permit this amount to exceed 9½ minutes, state in Exhibit No.   under what circumstances and how often this is expected to occur, and the limits that would then apply.

 NOTE: Unless otherwise indicated, it is assumed that proportional commercial time limits apply to ½ hour segments for the purpose of this question.

COMMUNITY LEADER ASCERTAINMENT CHECKLIST
(included in the renewal application of commercial radio and television licensees and noncommercial television licensees)

SAMPLE – COMMUNITY LEADER ANNUAL CHECKLIST

Institution/Element	Number	Not Applicable (Explain briefly)
1. Agriculture 2. Business 3. Charities 4. Civic, Neighborhood and Fraternal Organizations 5. Consumer Services 6. Culture 7. Education 8. Environment 9. Government (local, county, state & federal) 10. Labor 11. Military 12. Minority and ethnic groups 13. Organizations of and for the Elderly 14. Organizations of and for Women 15. Organizations of and for Youth (including children) and Students 16. Professions 17. Public Safety, Health and Welfare 18. Recreation 19. Religion 20. Other While the following are not regarded as separate community elements for purposes of this survey, indicate the number of leaders interviewed in all elements above who are: (a) Blacks (b) Hispanic, Spanish speaking or Spanish-surnamed Americans. (c) American Indians (d) Orientals (e) Women		

PROGRAMMING SECTION OF RENEWAL
FORM FOR COMMERCIAL RADIO LICENSEES

PART IV - PROGRAMMING

11. Has applicant placed in its public inspection file at the appropriate times the required documentation relating to its efforts to ascertain the community problems, needs, and interests?

  ☐ YES   ☐ NO   If NO, attach as EXHIBIT 11 a complete statement of explanation.

  ☐ DOES NOT APPLY.

12. Attach as EXHIBIT 12 applicant's community leader checklist for the preceding license term.

  ☐ DOES NOT APPLY.

13. Has the applicant placed in its public inspection file at the appropriate times its annual list of those problems, needs and interests which, in the applicant's judgment, warranted treatment by station and typical and illustrative programming in response thereto?

  ☐ YES   If YES, attach those listings as EXHIBIT 13.

  ☐ NO   If NO, attach as EXHIBIT 13 a complete statement of explanation.

14. (a) Attach as EXHIBIT 14 one exact copy of the program logs for the composite week used as a basis for responding to the questions herein. Applicants utilizing automatic program logging devices must comply with the provisions of Sections 73.112(f) and 73.282(f) of the Commission's rules.

(b) PROGRAM TYPES	Previously Proposed Minutes of Operation	% of Total Time	Composite Week Performance Minutes of Operation	% of Total Time	Minimum Proposed Minutes of Operation	% of Total Time
(1) News						
(2) Public Affairs						
(3) All other programs, exclusive of entertainment and sports						
TOTALS						
(4) Public Service Announcements	Number		Number		Number	

15. Attach as EXHIBIT 15 those programs in the composite week included in the public affairs and "all other" program categories (lines 2 and 3 of the above chart), indicating the title, source, type, brief description, time broadcast and duration of each program.

16. Did the amount of time applicant devoted to non-entertainment programming (lines 1, 2 and 3 of the above chart) during the composite week vary substantially from the representations made in applicant's last application?

  ☐ YES   ☐ NO   If YES, attach as EXHIBIT 16 a statement explaining the variations.

17. State the number of 60-minute segments in the composite week (beginning with the first full clock hour and ending with the last clock hour of each broadcast day) containing over 18 minutes of commercial matter;   segments. List in EXHIBIT 17 each segment and the day and time broadcast with headings of "Amount of Commercial Time in Segment" and "Day and Time Broadcast".

18. Do the applicant's commercial practices for the period covered by this application vary from the representations made in applicant's last application?

  ☐ YES   ☐ NO   If YES, explain in EXHIBIT 18 the variations and the reasons therefor.

19. State the maximum amount of commercial matter applicant proposes normally to allow in any 60-minute segment (Minutes   ). State the percentage of hourly segments per week this amount is expected to be exceeded (%   ), and the limits per hourly segment that would then apply under those circumstances to regular commercial (Minutes   ) and to political commercial matter (Minutes   ).

20. Describe briefly applicant's program format(s) during the past 12 months·

  Describe briefly applicant's proposed format

21. Does the applicant's station duplicate the programming of another radio station?

  ☐ YES   ☐ NO   If YES, state:

(a) the call letters of the duplicated station	
(b) the population of the community of license of the duplicated station	
(c) the population of the community of license of the station for which renewal is requested	
(d) the total number of broadcast hours in the composite week	
(e) the amount of programming duplicated during the composite week	%

22. Attach as EXHIBIT 22 any additional information which, in applicant's judgment, is necessary to adequately describe or to present fairly its services and operations in relation to the public interest.

PART V - EQUAL EMPLOYMENT OPPORTUNITY

23. Attach as Exhibit 23 a description of the program the applicant proposes to follow during the coming license term and, where applicable, the program implemented during the preceding license term to assure equal employment opportunity for minorities and women.

24. Attach as EXHIBIT 24 a brief description of any complaint which has been filed before any body having competent jurisdiction under federal, state, territorial or local law, alleging unlawful discrimination in the employment practices of the station, including the persons involved, the date of filing, the court or agency, the file number (if any), and the disposition or current status of the matter.

THE APPLICANT hereby waives any claim to the use of any particular frequency or of the ether as against the regulatory power of the United States, because of the previous use of the same, whether by license or otherwise, and requests an authorization in accordance with this application. (See Section 304 of the Communications Act.)

THE APPLICANT acknowledges that all the statements made in this application and attached exhibits are considered material representations and that all the exhibits are a material part hereof and are incorporated herein as set out in full in the application.

CERTIFICATION

I certify that the statements in this application are true, complete, and correct to the best of my knowledge and belief, and are made in good faith.

Signed and dated this _____ day of _____ 19 _____

NAME OF APPLICANT

BY SIGNATURE

TITLE

WILLFUL FALSE STATEMENTS MADE ON THIS FORM ARE PUNISHABLE BY FINE AND IMPRISONMENT. U.S. CODE. TITLE 18, SECTION 1001.

FCC NOTICE TO INDIVIDUALS

The solicitation of personal information requested in this application is authorized by the Communications Act of 1934, as amended. The principal purpose(s) for which the information will be used is to determine if the benefit requested is consistent with the public interest. The staff, consisting variously of attorneys, accountants, engineers, and application examiners, will use the information to determine whether the application should be granted, denied, dismissed, or designated for hearing. If all the information requested is not provided, the application may be returned without action having been taken upon it or its processing may be delayed while a request is made to provide the missing information. Accordingly, every effort should be made to provide all necessary information.

THE FOREGOING NOTICE IS REQUIRED BY THE PRIVACY ACT OF 1974, P.L. 93-579. DECEMBER 31, 1974, 5 U.S.C. 552 a (e) (3).

PROGRAMMING SECTION OF RENEWAL FORM
FOR NONCOMMERCIAL RADIO AND TELEVISION LICENSEES

FCC Form 342		Section IV

STATEMENT OF PROGRAM SERVICE OF BROADCAST APPLICANT	Name of applicant:	**FOR COMMISSION USE ONLY** File No.:

DEFINITIONS FOR PROGRAM DATA

1. Sources of programs are defined as follows:

   A local program (L) is any program originated or produced by the station, employing live talent more than 50% of the time, and using the studios or other facilities of the station. A local program recorded or filmed by the station for later broadcast shall be classified as local. A program produced by a station and fed to a network shall be classified by the originating station as local. Programs primarily featuring phonograph records, syndicated or feature films or taped or transcribed programs, shall not be classified as local even though a station personality appears incidentally to introduce such material.

   A record program (REC) (Radio only) is any program, not falling within the definition of "local" above, which utilizes phonograph records, electrical transcriptions or taped music, with or without commentary by a local announcer, or other station personnel.

   A network program (N) is any program furnished to the station by a network (national, regional or special) such as NET, NAEB Radio Tape Network, Eastern Educational Network, Educational Radio Network, etc.

   Other Programs (OTHER) are any programs not defined above, including, without limitation, syndicated film, taped or transcribed programs, and feature films.

2. Types of educational programs are defined as follows:

   Instructional (I) includes all programs designed to be utilized by any level of educational institution in the regular instructional program of the institution. In-school, in-service for teachers, and college credit courses are examples of instructional programs.

   General Educational (GEN) is an educational program for which no formal credit is given.

   Performing Arts (A) is a program, live or recorded, in which the performing aspect predominates such as drama or concert, opera or dance.

   Public Affairs (PA) includes talks, discussions, speeches, documentaries, editorials, forums, panels, round tables, and similar programs primarily concerning local, national, and international affairs or problems.

   Light Entertainment (LE) includes programs consisting of popular music or other light entertainment.

   Other (O) includes all programs not falling within the definitions of Instructional, General Education, Performing Arts, Public Affairs or Light Entertainment. Such programs as news or sports should be reported as "other."

PROGRAM DATA

1. (a) Attach as Exhibit No. _____ Program Logs for a full week of operation:

   (1) from the school term during which the application is filed, or

   (2) if such term began less than 90 days before the date of filing the application, from the school term immediately preceeding the school term during which the application is filed.

(b) State for the week submitted in 1(a) above the sign-on and sign-off time and total hours for weekdays, Saturday, and Sunday.

	Weekdays	Saturday	Sunday
Sign-on			
Sign-off			
Total hours on air			Total _____

(c) State for a full week submitted in 1(a) above the portion of the schedule obtained from the following sources (totals to equal 100%):

Source	Hours	Percentage
1. Local program		
2. Record program (Radio only)		
3. Network program		
4. Other		
Total		100%

(d) State for a full week submitted in 1(a) above the amount of time devoted to the following types of programs (totals to equal 100%):

Type of Program	Hours	Percentage
1. Instructional		
2. General Educational		
3. Performing Arts		
4. Public Affairs		
5. Light Entertainment		
6. Other		
Total		100%

2. Does applicant contemplate any material changes in future program service?   YES ☐ NO ☐

   If "Yes", submit as Exhibit No. _____ a statement indicating what they are.

3. Will the station be affiliated with any network?   YES ☐ NO ☐

   If "Yes", give the name of the network(s).

NOTE: The NET, NAEB Radio Tape Network, Educational Radio Network, and the Eastern Educational Network are examples of educational networks.

4. Is the station for which renewal is requested a Class D FM facility ("10-watt") as defined by Section 73.504 (b)(1) of the Commission's rules or is the programming of the station <u>wholly</u> "instructional" as that type of programming is defined above?

☐ YES   If Yes, omit questions 5 through 7.

☐ NO

5. Has the applicant placed in its public inspection file at the appropriate times the required documentation relating to its efforts to ascertain community problems, needs and interests?

☐ YES

☐ NO   If No, attach as Exhibit No.   a complete statement of explanation.

Radio applicants, attach as Exhibit No.   the narrative description of these efforts as required by Section 1.527 (b) of the Commission's rules.

Television applicants, attach as Exhibit No.   the narrative description of the public survey as required by Section 1.527 (c)(2)(ii) of the Commission's rules.

6. Television applicants, attach as Exhibit No.   your community leader checklist for the preceding license term.

7. Has the applicant placed in its public file at the appropriate times its annual list of those problems, needs and interests which, in the applicants judgment, warranted treatment by the station, and the typical and illustrative programming broadcast in response thereto?

☐ YES   If Yes, attach those listings as Exhibit No.

☐ NO   If No, attach as Exhibit No.   a complete statement of explanation.

APPENDIX C
The FCC
Children's
Policy Statement

FEDERAL COMMUNICATIONS COMMISSION

[Docket No. 19142; FCC 74–1174]

CHILDREN'S TELEVISION PROGRAMS

Report and Policy Statement

In the matter of petition of action for children's television (ACT) for rulemaking looking toward the elimination of sponsorship and commercial content in children's programming and the establishment of a weekly 14 hour quota of children's television programs, Docket No. 19142.

I. Introduction. 1. By notice issued January 26, 1971 (Docket 19142, 28 FCC 2d 368, 36 FR 14219) we instituted a wide-ranging inquiry into children's programming and advertising practices.

2. This inquiry was instituted at the request of Action for Children's Television (ACT) and our notice specifically called for comment on ACT's proposal that the Commission adopt certain guidelines for television programming for children. These guidelines are as follows:

(a) There shall be no sponsorship and no commercials on children's television.

(b) No performer shall be permitted to use or mention products, services or stores by brand names during children's programs, nor shall such names be included in any way during children's programs.

(c) Each station shall provide daily programming for children and in no case shall this be less than 14 hours a week, as part of its public service requirement. Provision shall be made for programming in each of the age groups specified below, and during the time periods specified: (i) Pre-school: Ages 2–5 7 a.m.–6 p.m. daily, 7 a.m.–6 p.m. weekends; (ii) Primary: Ages 6–9 4 p.m.–8 p.m. daily, 8 a.m.–8 p.m. weekends; (iii) Elementary: Ages 10–12 5 p.m.–9 p.m. daily, 9 a.m.–9 p.m. weekends.

3. In addition to comments on the specific ACT proposal, the Commission requested interested parties to submit their views on such issues as the proper definition of what constitutes "children's programming", the appropriate hours for broadcasting children's programs, the desirability of providing programs designed for different age groups, commercial time limitations, separation of advertising from programming content, and other areas of concern. The Commission also requested all television licensees and networks to submit detailed information on their current children's programming practices, including a classification of programs as being either entertainment or educational. We gave notice that this information might be used as a basis for formulating rules concerning programming and advertising in children's television.[1]

---

[1] The scope of the Commission's inquiry in this proceeding did not extend to the issues of violence and obscenity in television programming. The House and Senate Committees on Appropriations, however, have requested the Commission to submit a report by December 31, 1974, outlining the actions we plan to take in these areas. We will, therefore, address the problems of violence and obscenity at that time.

4. The response to our notice was overwhelming. More than 100,000 citizens expressed their opinions in writing and the accumulated filings fill 63 docket volumes. This material falls into three main categories: formal pleadings, programming data from stations and networks, and informal expressions of opinion (letters and cards).[2]

5. To apprise itself further of the various issues involved in children's television, the Commission conducted panel discussions focusing on specific areas of interest on October 2, 3, and 4 of 1972.[3] Forty-four individuals took part in these discussions, including representatives of citizens groups, broadcasters, advertisers and performers. These panel discussions were followed by oral argument which was presented before the Commission on January 8, 9, and 10 of 1973.[4] Forty-one persons participated in the oral argument, representing public interest groups, advertisers, educators, licensees, producers and performers.

6. The record in this proceeding includes 1252 pages of transcript in addition to further comments and the previously mentioned 63 docket volumes.

II. Children's Television Programming. 7. We believe that proposals for a set amount of programming for children of various age groups should appropriately be considered in terms of our statutory authority and against the background of the Commission's traditional approach to program regulation.

A. Scope of Commission authority concerning programming. 8. Section 303 of the Communications Act, 47 U.S.C. 303, confers upon the Commission broad authority to regulate broadcasting as the "public convenience, interest, or necessity" requires. On the basis of this standard, the Commission is empowered by section 303(b), 47 U.S.C. §303(b), to "[p]rescribe the nature of the service to be rendered by each class of licensed stations and each station within any class." (emphasis supplied.) The Commission is further authorized to: [c]lassify radio stations"; provide for experimental uses of frequencies, and generally encourage the larger and more effective use of radio in the public interest"; and "[m]ake such rules and regulations and prescribe such restrictions and conditions, not inconsistent with law, as may be necessary to carry out the provisions of this Act." 47 U.S.C. 303 (a), (g) and (r).

9. The Supreme Court has made it clear that these provisions do not limit the Commission to the role of a "traffic officer, policing the wave lengths to prevent stations from interfering with each other." "National Broadcasting Co. v. United States," 319 U.S. 190, 215 (1943). "[T]he Act," the Court held, "does not restrict the Commission merely to supervision of the traffic." Id. at 215–16. The Commission neither exceeds its powers under the Act nor transgresses the First

---

[2] A digest of comments appears in Appendix A.

[3] Participants in the panel discussions are listed in Appendix B.

[4] Oral argument participants are listed in Appendix C.

Amendment "in interesting itself in general program format and the kinds of programs broadcasts by licensees." "Red Lion Broadcasting Co. v. FCC," 395 U.S. 367, 390 (1969). But, while the Commission's statutory authority is indeed broad, it is certainly not unlimited. Broadcasting is plainly a medium which is entitled to First Amendment protection. "United States v. Paramount Pictures, Inc.", 334 U.S. 131, 166 (1948). Although the unique nature of the broadcasting medium may justify some differences in the First Amendment standard applied to it, it is clear that any regulation of programing must be reconciled with free speech considerations. In Section 326 of the Act, 47 U.S.C. 326, Congress has expressed its concern by expressly prohibiting "censorship" by the Commission. For these reasons, the Commission historically has exercised caution in approaching the regulation of programing:

[I]n applying the public interest standard to programing, the Commission walks a tightrope between saying too much and saying too little. In most cases it has resolved this dilemma by imposing only general affirmative duties—e.g., to strike a balance between various interests of the community, or to provide a reasonable amount of time for the presentation of programs devoted to the discussion of public issues. The licensee has broad discretion in giving specific content to these duties * * *. Given its long-established authority to consider program content, this approach probably minimizes the dangers of censorship or pervasive supervision. Banzhaf v. FCC, 405 F. 2d 1082, 1095 (D.C. Cir 1968), cert. denied "subnom. Tobacco Institute v. FCC," 396 U.S. 842 (1969).

We believe that this traditional approach is, in most cases, an appropriate response to our obligation to assure programing service in the public interest and, at the same time, avoid excessive governmental interference with specific program decisions.

B. History of general program categories. 10. In 1929, the Federal Radio Commission adopted the position that licensees were expected to provide a balanced program schedule designed to serve all substantial groups in their communities. "Great Lakes Broadcasting Co.", 3 F.R.C. Ann. Rep. 32, 34 (1929), rev'd on other grounds 37 F. 2d 993, cert. dismissed 281 U.S. 706 (1930). At this time, the Commissioner set forth a number of general programming categories which it believed should be included in the broadcast service of each station:

[T]he tastes, needs, and desires of all substantial groups among the listening public should be met, in some fair proportion, by a well-rounded program, in which entertainment, consisting of music of both classical and lighter grades, religion, education and instruction, important public events, discussions of public questions, weather, market reports, and news, and matters of interest to all members of the family find a place. Id.

In listing these programming categories, the Commission made it clear that it did not "propose to erect a rigid schedule specifying the hours or minutes that may be devoted to one kind of program or another." Id. Its purpose was only to emphasize the general character of programming to which licensees must conform in order to fulfill their public service responsibility. While the Commission's list did include "matters of interest to all members of the family", children's programs were not specifically recognized as a distinct category entitled to special consideration.

11. In 1946, the Federal Communications Commission reaffirmed the FRC's emphasis on a "well-balanced program structure", and noted that since at least 1928 license renewal applications had been required "to set forth the average amount of time, or percentage of time, devoted to entertainment programs, religious programs, educational programs, agricultural programs, fraternal programs, etc." FCC, "Report on Public Service Responsibility of Broadcast Licensees" 12–13 (1946) (hereinafter cited as The Blue Book). In line with the views of its predecessor, the FCC did not recognize programs for children as an independent category and no suggestion was made as the percentage of time that should be devoted to any category.

12. The Commission's first recognition of children's programs as a distinct category came in the 1960 statement of basic programming policy. "Report and Statement of Policy Re: Programming", 20 P&F R.R. 1901 (1960). In this report, "Programs for Children" was listed as one of fourteen "major elements usually necessary to meet the public interest, needs and desires of the community." Id. at 1913. The fourteen elements included such matters as educational programs, political broadcasts, public affairs programs, sports, entertainment and service to minority groups. No special emphasis was given to children's programming over and above these other categories, and again the Commission made it clear that its list was "neither all-embracing nor constant" and that it was not "intended as a rigid mold or fixed formula for station operation." Id. The ultimate decision as to the presentation of programs was left to the licensee, who was expected, however, to make a positive effort to provide a schedule designed to serve the varied needs and interests of the people in his community.

13. The Supreme Court, in its landmark decision in "Red Lion Broadcasting Co. v. FCC," 395 U.S. 367 (1969), gave considerable support to the principle that the FCC could properly interest itself in program categories. In this decision, the Court specifically affirmed the Commission's fairness doctrine and noted that the doctrine (in addition to requiring a balance of opposing views) obligates the broadcaster to devote a "reasonable percentage" of broadcast time to the discussion of controversial issues of public importance. The Court made it plain that the Commission is not powerless to insist that they give adequate . . . attention to public issues." Id. at 393.

14. While the holding of the Red Lion case was limited to the fairness doctrine, the Court's opinion has a significance which reaches far beyond the category of programming dealing with public issues. The Court resolved the First Amendment issue in broadcasting by stating that "[i]t is the right of the

viewers and listeners, not the right of the broadcasters, which is paramount." Id. at 390. It stated further, that "[i]t is the right of the public to receive suitable access to social, political, esthetic, moral, and other ideas and experiences which is crucial here. That right may not constitutionally be abridged either by the Congress or by the FCC." Id. This language, in our judgment, clearly points to a wide range of programming responsibilities on the part of the broadcaster.

C. *Programs designed for children*. 15. One of the questions to be decided here is whether broadcasters have a special obligation to serve children. We believe that they clearly do have such a responsibility.

16. As we have long recognized, broadcasters have a duty to serve all substantial and important groups in their communities, and children obviously represent such a group. Further, because of their immaturity and their special needs, children require programming designed specifically for them. Accordingly, we expect television broadcasters as trustees of a valuable public resource, to develop and present programs which will serve the unique needs of the child audience.

17. As noted above, the Federal Radio Commission and the Federal Communications Commission have consistently maintained the position that broadcasters have a responsibility to provide a wide range of different types of programs to serve their communities. Children, like adults, have a variety of different needs and interests. Most children, however, lack the experience and intellectual sophistication to enjoy or benefit from much of the non-entertainment material broadcast for the general public. We believe, therefore, that the broadcaster's public service obligation includes a responsibility to provide diversified programming designed to meet the varied needs and interests of the child audience.

18. In this regard, educational or informational programming for children is of particular importance. It seems to us that the use of television to further the educational and cultural development of America's children bears a direct relationship to the licensee's obligation under the Communications Act to operate in the "public interest." Once these children reach the age of eighteen years they are expected to participate fully in the nation's democratic process, and, as one commentator has stated:

Education, in all its phases, is the attempt to so inform and cultivate the mind and will of a citizen that he shall have the wisdom, the independence, and, therefore, the dignity of a governing citizen. Freedom of education is, thus, as we all recognize, a basic postulate in the planning of a free society. A. Meiklejohn, The First Amendment is an Absolute, in 1961 Supreme Court Review 245, 257 (Kurland ed.); see generally Brennan, The Supreme Court and the Meiklejohn Interpretation of the First Amendment, 79 Harv. L. Rev. 1 (1965).[5]

[5] In the words of the Supreme Court, "[a] democratic society rests, for its continuance, upon the healthy, well-rounded growth of young people into full maturity as citizens, with all that implies." Prince v. Massachusetts, 321 U.S. 158, 168 (1943).

We believe that the medium of television can do much to contribute to this educational effort.

Amount of programming for children. 19. While we are convinced that television must provide programs for children, and that a reasonable part of this programming should be educational in nature, we do not believe that it is necessary for the Commission to prescribe by rule the number of hours per week to be carried in each category. As noted above, we are involved in a sensitive First Amendment area, and we feel that it is wise to avoid detailed governmental supervision of programming whenever possible. Furthermore, while the amount of time devoted to a certain category of program service is an important indicator, we believe that this question can be handled appropriately on an ad hoc basis.[6] Rules would, in all probability, have been necessary had we decided to adopt ACT's proposal to ban advertising from children's programs. As explained below, however, we have not adopted that proposal and it may be expected that the commercial marketplace will continue to provide an incentive to carry these programs.

20. Even though we are not adopting rules specifying a set number of hours to be presented, we wish to emphasize that we do expect stations to make a meaningful effort in this area. During the course of this inquiry, we have found that a few stations present no programs at all for children. We trust that this Report will make it clear that such performance will not be acceptable for commercial television stations which are expected to provide diversified program service to their communities.

Educational and informational programming for children. 21. Our studies have indicated that, over the years, there have been considerable fluctuations in amount of educational and informational programming carried by broadcasters—and that the level has sometimes been so low as to demonstrate a lack of serious commitment to the responsibilities which stations have in this area.[7] Even today, many stations are doing less than they should.

22. We believe that, in the future, stations' license renewal applications should reflect a reasonable amount of programming which is designed to educate and inform—and not simply to entertain. This does not mean that stations must run hours of dull "classroom" instruction. There are many imaginative and

[6] We are just beginning to receive complete information on the children's programming performance of stations through question 6 in section 4-B of the new renewal form. FCC Form 303. It may be that the question of rules will be revisited as we gain experience under the new form. The Commission's Notice of Inquiry requested licensees to provide it with complete information on their program service to children on a voluntary basis; unfortunately, too few responded to provide a valid sample.

[7] In 1968 and 1969, for example, none of the networks carried a single informational program in its Saturday morning line-up of children's shows, and only one network presented an educational program during the week.

exciting ways in which the medium can be used to further a child's understanding of a wide range of areas: History, science, literature, the environment, drama, music, fine arts, human relations, other cultures and languages, and basic skills such as reading and mathematics which are crucial to a child's development. Although children's entertainment programs may have some educational value (in a very broad sense of the term), we expect to see a reasonable amount of programming which is particularly designed with an educational goal in mind.[8]

23. We would like to make it clear, however, that we do not necessarily expect the broadcaster to have programs designed to cover every subject or field of interest. We simply expect the licensee to select the particular areas where he believes that he can make the best contribution to the educational and cultural development of the children in his community—and then to present programming designed to serve these needs. The Commission will, of course. defer to the reasonable, good faith judgments which licensees make in this area.[9]

Age-specific programming. 24. In its original petition, ACT requested the Commission to require broadcasters to present programming designed to meet the needs of three specific age groups: (1) Pre-school children, (2) primary school aged children, and (3) elementary school aged children. During the panel discussions before the Commission, however, ACT and several of the other parties agreed that the presentation of programming designed to meet the needs of just two groups, pre-school and school aged children, would be sufficient to meet the broadcaster's responsibilities to the child audience.

25. While we agree that a detailed breakdown of programming into three

[8] As a general matter. programs of this type are logged as "Instructional" in accord with the provisions of Section 73.670 of the Commission's rules. The rule defines instructional programming so as to include "programs * * * involving the discussion of, or primarily designed to further an appreciation or understanding of, literature, music, fine arts, history, geography, and the natural and social sciences * * *" 47 CFR 73.760, Note 1(f). Typically, such programs as Captain Kangaroo, Multiplication Rock, and Wild Kingdom are logged as instructional.

[9] Another area of concern to many of the critics of children's programming in this proceeding was the emphasis on fantasy in the animated cartoons and in other "fanciful" programs which dominate the children's schedule. Such programming, it is argued, does not offer children the diversified view of the world of which television is capable. While the Commission recognizes that cartoons can do much to provide wholesome entertainment for young children, we note that the networks have broadened their schedules for this Fall to include more live-action shows and more representations of "real" people interacting with their families and the world around them. We commend the networks for being responsive to these concerns and for having made an effort to provide programming which meets the varied needs and interests of the child audience.

or more specific age groups is unnecessary, we do believe that some effort should be made for both pre-school and school aged children. Age-specificity is particularly important in the area of informational programming because pre-school children generally cannot read and otherwise differ markedly from older children in their level of intellectual development.[10] A recent schedule indicated that, although one network presented a commendable five hours a week for the pre-school audience, the others did not appear to present any programs for these younger children. In the future, however, we will expect all licensees to make a meaningful effort in this area.

Scheduling. 26. Evidence presented in this inquiry indicates that there is tendency on the part of many stations to confine all or most of their children's programming to Saturday and Sunday mornings. We recognize the fact that these are appropriate time periods for such shows, but are nevertheless concerned with the relative absence of children's programming on weekdays. It appears that this lack of weekday children's programs is a fairly recent development. In the early 1950's, the three networks broadcast twenty to thirty hours of children's programming during the week. During the late fifties and early sixties many popular shows such as "Howdy Doody", "Mickey Mouse Club" and "Kukla, Fran and Ollie" disappeared, and by the late sixties, "Captain Kangaroo" was the only weekday children's show regularly presented by a network. While some stations, particularly those not affiliated with networks, do provide weekday programming for children, there is nevertheless a great overall imbalance in scheduling.

27. It is clear that children do not limit their viewing in this manner. They form a substantial segment of the audience on weekday afternoons and early evenings as well as on weekends. In fact, the hours spent watching television on Saturday and Sunday constitute, on an average, only 10 percent of their total viewing time. (A.C. Nielsen Company, February, 1973). Accordingly, we do not believe that it is a reasonable scheduling practice to relegate all of the programming for this important audience to one or two days. Although we are not prepared to adopt a specific scheduling rule, we do expect to see considerable improvement in scheduling practices in the future.

III. *Advertising practices—A. Background.* 28. The second major area of concern in this inquiry has to do with advertising practices in programs designed for children. In its original peti-

[10] With regard to entertainment programming, there is considerable evidence that pre-school children, unlike older children, cannot distinguish fantasy from reality. It does not follow, however, that because a program is not age-specific, it cannot provide wholesome entertainment for all ages. Therefore, while there may be some value in age-specific entertainment programming, we cannot say that this is necessary in every case.

tion, ACT requested that the Commission eliminate all commercials on programs designed for children and prohibit any other use or mention of any product by brand name. During the course of the proceeding various parties criticized the amount of commercial matter now directed toward children, the frequency of program interruptions and a variety of other specific advertising practices: these included the use of program talent to deliver commercials ("host selling") or comment on them ("lead-ins and/or outs"); the prominent display of brand name products on a show's set ("tie-ins"); the presentation of an unrealistic picture of the product being promoted; and the advertising generally of products which some parties consider harmful to children (e.g., snack foods, vitamins and drugs).

29. The Commission's statutory responsibilities include an obligation to insure that broadcasters do not engage in excessive or abusive advertising practices. The Federal Radio Commission warned in 1928 that "advertising must not be of a nature such as to destroy or harm the benefit to which the public is entitled from the proper use of broadcasting." 2 F.R.C. Ann. Rep. 20 (1928). In 1929 the FRC again considered the advertising problem in the context of the licensee's responsibility to broadcast in the public interest. Great Lakes Broadcasting Co., 3 F.R.C. Ann. Rep. 32 (1929). The Commission noted that broadcasters are licensed to serve the public and not the private or selfish interests of individuals or groups. It then stated that "[t]he only exception that can be made to this rule has to do with advertising; the exception, however, is only apparent because advertising furnishes the economic support for the service and thus makes it possible." *Id.* The FRC recognized "that, without advertising, broadcasting would not exist, and [that it] must confine itself to limiting this advertising in amount and in character so as to preserve the largest possible amount of service for the public." *Id.* at 35. The FCC, over the years, has maintained a similar position. See "The Blue Book," supra, 40–41; "Report and Statement of Policy Re: Programming," supra, at 1913.

30. Traditionally, however, the Commission has not attempted to exercise direct supervision over all types of advertising abuses. Since the Federal Trade Commission has far greater expertise in, and resources for, the regulation of false or deceptive advertising practices, the FCC has largely confined its role in this area to notifying stations that the broadcast of material found to be false or deceptive by the FTC will raise questions as to whether the station is operating in the public interest. See Public Notice entitled "Licensee Responsibility with Respect to the Broadcast of False, Misleading, and Deceptive Advertising, FCC 61–1316 (1961); "Consumers Association of District of Columbia," 32 FCC 2d 400 (1971). We do not believe that it would be appropriate to change this policy at the present time. The Federal Trade Commission is currently conducting inquiries into ad-

vertising practics on children's programs (F.T.C. File No. 7375150) and food advertising (F.T.C. File No. 7323054) which cover many of the advertising practices objected to by the parties before the Commission. In light of the actions of the FTC, we have chosen not to address some of these specific promotional practices. On the basis of this proceeding, however, we are persuaded that an examination of the broadcaster's responsibility to children is warranted in the areas of the overall level of commercialization and the need for maintaining a clear separation between programming and advertising.

B. *Overcommercialization*. 31. While it is recognized that advertising is the sole economic foundation of the American commercial broadcasting system and that continued service to the public depends on broadcasters' ability to maintain adequate revenues with which to finance programming, the Commission has a responsibility to insure that the "public interest" does not become subordinate to financial and commercial interests. Although this proceeding marks the first instance in which the level of advertising on programs designed for children has been singled out as possibly abusive, the Federal Government has been concerned about the problem of overcommercialization in general since the beginning of broadcast regulation. In 1929, the Federal Radio Commission took the position that the "amount and character of advertising must be rigidly confined within the limits consistent with the public service expected of the station." "Great Lakes Broadcasting Co.," 3 F.R.C. Ann. Rep. at 35 (1929). The Federal Communications Commission has continued this policy. In 1946, for example, the Commission noted that, "[a]s the broadcasting system itself has insisted, the public interest clearly requires that the amount of time devoted to advertising shall bear a reasonable relation to the amount of time devoted to programs." "The Blue Book, supra." 56. In the definitive 1960 policy statement, licensees were admonished to "avoid abuses with respect to the total amount of time devoted to advertising continuity as well as the frequency with which regular programs are interrupted for advertising messages." "Report and Statement of Policy Re: Programming, supra," at 1912-1913.

32. Although some of the parties to this proceeding questioned the Commission's authority to limit the level of commercialization on children's programs, the Commission believes that it has ample authority to act in this area. This issue was raised in conjunction with the Commission's general inquiry into overcommercialization in 1963-1964, when the Commission concluded that it could adopt rules prescribing the maximum amount of time a licensee may devote to advertising:

Numerous sections of the act refer to the public interest, one element of which clearly is the appropriate division as between program material and advertising • • •. We conceive that our authority to deal with overcommercialization, by whatever reasonable and appropriate means is well established. Amendment of Part 3 of the Commission's Rules and Regulations with Respect to Advertising on Standard, FM, and Television Broadcast Stations, 36 FCC 45, 46 (1964).

If a licensee devoted an excessive amount of his broadcast time to advertising, the Commission could certainly consider that factor in deciding whether a renewal of the license would serve the "public interest". See WMOZ, 36 FCC 201 (1964); Gordon County Broadcasting Co., 24 P&F R.R. 315 (1962); Mississippi Arkansas Broadcasting Co., 22 P&F R.R. 305 (1961). If a given policy is an appropriate consideration in individual cases, then, as the Supreme Court has suggested, "there is no reason why [the policy] may not be stated in advance by the Commission in interpretative regulations defining the prohibited conduct with greater clarity." "Federal Communications Commission v. American Broadcasting Company," 347 U.S. 284, 289-290, note 7 (1954).

33. A restriction on the amount of time a broadcaster may devote to advertising does not constitute censorship or an abridgment of freedom of speech. The courts have traditionally held that commercial speech has little First Amendment protection. "Valentine v. Christensen," 316 U.S. 52 (1942); "Breard v. City of Alexandria," 341 U.S. 622 (1951). A Congressional ban on cigarette advertising on television was held not to violate the First Amendment, in part, because broadcasters "[had] lost no right to speak—they [had] only lost an ability to collect revenue from others for broadcasting their commercial messages." "Capital Broadcasting Co. v. Mitchell," 333 F. Supp. 582, 584 (1971); aff'd 405 U.S. 1000 (1972).

34. If our policy against overcommercialization is an important one, and we believe that it is, it is particularly important in programs designed for children. Broadcasters have a special responsibility to children. Many of the parties testified, and we agree, that particular care should be taken to insure that they are not exposed to an excessive amount of advertising. It is a matter of common understanding that, because of their youth and inexperience, children are far more trusting of and vulnerable to commercial "pitches" than adults. There is, in addition, evidence that very young children cannot distinguish conceptually between programming and advertising; they do not understand that the purpose of a commercial is to sell a product. See Report to the Surgeon General, "Television and Growing Up: The Impact of Televised Violence," Vol. IV at 469, 474 (1970). Since children watch television long before they can read, television provides advertisers access to a younger and more impressionable age group than can be reached through any other medium. See "Capital Broadcasting Co., supra," at 585-6. For these reasons, special safeguards may be required to insure that the advertising privilege is not abused. As the Supreme Court

stated, "[i]t is the interest of youth itself, and of the whole community that children be . . . safeguarded from abuses." "Prince v. Massachusetts," 321, U.S. 158, 165 (1943).

35. Despite these concerns, we have chosen not to adopt ACT's proposal to eliminate all sponsorship on programs designed for children. The Commission believes that the question of abolishing advertising must be resolved by balancing the competing interests in light of the public interest.[33] Banning the sponsorship of programs designed for children could have a very damaging effect on the amount and quality of such programming. Advertising is the basis for the commercial broadcasting system, and revenues from the sale of commercial time provide the financing for program production. Eliminating the economic base and incentive for children's programs would inevitably result in some curtailment of broadcasters' efforts in this area. Moreover, it seems unrealistic, on the one hand, to expect licensees to improve significantly their program service to children and, on the other hand, to withdraw a major source of funding for this task.

36. Some suggestions were made during the proceeding that institutional advertising or underwriting would replace product advertising if the latter were prohibited. Although we would encourage broadcasters to explore alternative methods of financing, at this time there is little evidence that the millions of dollars necessary to produce children's programs would, in fact, be forthcoming from these sources. Since eliminating product · advertising could have a serious impact on program service to children, we do not believe that the public interest would be served by adopting ACT's proposal.

37. The present proceeding has indicated, however, that there is a serious basis for concern about overcommercialization on programs designed for children. Since children are less able to understand and withstand advertising appeals than adults, broadcasters should take the special characteristics of the child audience into consideration when determining the appropriate level of advertising in programs designed for them. Many broadcasters substantially exceed the level of advertising that represents the best standard followed generally in the industry. The Television Code of the National Association of Broadcasters, for

---

[33] At one time the Commission maintained the position that "sustaining" programming (which was not commercially sponsored) played an important role in broadcasting. The Commission's 1949 policy statement placed considerable emphasis on sustaining programs to assure balanced programming and to serve minority tastes and interests. The Blue Book, supra, 12. In 1960, however, the Commission reversed its position on the grounds that "under modern conditions sponsorship fosters rather than diminishes the availability of important public affairs and 'cultural' broadcast programming." Report and Statement of Policy Re: Programming, supra, at 1914.

example, permits only nine minutes and thirty seconds of non-program material (including commercials) in "prime-time" programming (i.e., 7:00–11:00). In contrast, many stations specify as much as sixteen minutes of commercial matter an hour for those time periods in which most children's programs are broadcast.

38. Although advertising should be adequate to insure that the station will have sufficient revenues with which to produce programming which will serve the children of its community meaningfully, the public interest does not protect advertising which is substantially in excess of that amount. These revenues, moreover, need not be derived solely from programs designed for children.

39. On the basis of this proceeding, the Commission believes that in many cases the current levels of advertising in programs designed for children are in excess of what is necessary for the industry to provide programming which serves the public interest. Recently, following extensive discussions with the Commission's Chairman, the National Association of Broadcasters agreed to amend its code to limit non-program material on children's programs to nine minutes and thirty seconds per hour on weekends by 1976; the Association of Independent Television Stations (INTV) has agreed to reduce advertising voluntarily to the same level. By these actions the industry has indicated that these are advertising levels which can be maintained while continuing to improve service to children.

40. The Commission's own economic studies support this assumption. The economic data indicates that there is an "inelasticity of demand" for advertising on children's programs. It appears, therefore, that the level of advertising on children's program can be reduced substantially without significantly affecting revenues because the price for the remaining time tends to increase. In 1972, for example, the NAB reduced the permissible amount of non-program material on weekend children's programs from 16 to 12 minutes per hour; although the amount of network advertising was cut by 22 percent, the networks' gross revenues for children's programs fell by only 3 percent. The Commission anticipates similar results if advertising were further limited to nine minutes per hour: There should be minimal financial hardship on networks and affiliates, although the problem could be somewhat more significant for independent stations. Most independent stations, however, have already agreed to make reductions, and the fact that 12 minutes per hour will still be permitted on weekdays (when most of these stations program for children) should soften any adverse economic effect.

41. The issue remains, however, whether the Commission should adopt per se rules limiting the amount of advertising on programs designed for children or await the results of the industry's attempt to regulate itself. The decisions of the NAB and the INTV to restrict advertising voluntarily are recent developments which occurred during the course of this inquiry and after consultation with the Commission's Chairman and staff. The Commission commends the industry for showing a willingness to regulate itself. Broadcasting which serves the public interest results from actions such as these which reflect a responsive and responsible attitude on the part of broadcasters toward their public service obligations.

42. In light of these actions, the Commission has chosen not to adopt per se rules limiting commercial matter on programs designed for children at this time. The standards adopted by the two associations are comparable to the standards which we would have considered adopting by rule in the absence of industry reform.[13] We are willing to postpone direct Commission action, therefore, until we have an opportunity to assess the effectiveness of these self-regulatory measures. The Commission will expect all licensees, however, to review their commercial practices in programs designed for children in light of the policies outlined by the Commission and the standards now agreed upon by substantial segments of the industry, and to limit advertising to children to the lowest level consistent with their programming responsibilities. If it should appear that self-regulation is not effec-

[13] The actual proposals of the two industry groups are as follows: (1) Beginning in January, 1975, the NAB Code will permit broadcasters 10 minutes of non-program material per hour on Saturday and Sunday children's programs and 14 minutes during the week; beginning in January, 1976, these levels will be further restricted to 9 minutes and thirty seconds on weekends and 12 minutes during the week; (2) beginning in January, 1975, the Association of Independent Television Stations will reduce its advertising to 12 minutes per hour on Saturday and Sunday and 14 minutes during the week; beginning in January, 1976, advertising will be limited to 9 minutes and thirty seconds on the weekend and 12 during the week.

The Commission is willing to accept the phased-in reduction proposed by the industry. Although the Commission's economic studies indicate that affiliates probably would not suffer significant economic hardship from an immediate reduction, non-affiliated broadcasters could be affected. The Commission's own economic analysis suggested a gradual implementation of the proposed reduction. Since the NAB members include non-affiliated stations, we believe that both the NAB and INTV proposals are reasonable.

The Commission, in addition, finds the proposed differentials between weekend and weekday programming to be acceptable. Unlike Saturday and Sunday morning when there is no significant audience other than children, weekday mornings and afternoons are attractive periods to program for adults. The more substantial the differential between the permissible level of advertising on children's and adult programs during the week, the greater is the disincentive to program for children on weekdays. Since we are already concerned about the concentration of children's programming on the weekend, we are willing to accept the balance which the industry has struck on this issue.

tive in reducing the level of advertising, then per se rules may be required.

43. To insure that the Commission will have adequate information on broadcasters' advertising practices in programs designed for children, we will, in a separate order, amend the renewal form to elicit more detailed information in this area. All licensees will be asked to indicate how many minutes of commercial matter they broadcast within an hour in programs designed for children both on weekends and during the week. The data provided by this question will serve, in part, as a basis for determining whether self-regulation can be effective. In addition, since the Commission's own economic studies and the actions of the industry indicate that nine minutes and thirty seconds on weekend children's programs and twelve minutes during the week are levels which are economically feasible for most licensees to achieve over the next year and a half, the broadcast of more than the amount of advertising proposed by the NAB and the INTV after January 1, 1976,[13] may raise a question as to whether the licensee is subordinating the interests of the child audience to his own financial interests.

44. For the present, compliance with the advertising restrictions adopted by the industry and endorsed by the Commission will be sufficient to resolve in favor of the station any questions as to whether its commercial practices serve the public interest. Licensees who exceed these levels, however, should be prepared to justify their advertising policy. We recognize that there may be some independent VHF and UHF stations which cannot easily afford such a reduction in advertising; such stations should be prepared to make a substantial and well-documented showing of serious potential harm to support their advertising practices. However, we anticipate accepting very few other justifications for over-commercialization in programs designed for children.

45. We emphasize that we will closely examine commercial activities in programs designed for children on a case-by-case basis. Overcommercialization by licensees in programs designed for young children will raise a question as to the adequacy of a broadcaster's overall performance. The Commission will, in addition, continually review broadcasters' performance on an industry-wide basis.[14]

[13] Broadcasters who are not members of either the NAB or the INTV are, of course, not bound by their proposed phased-in reductions. As noted in the conclusion to this Report, however, the Commission expects all licensees to make a good faith effort to bring their advertising practices into conformance with the policies established herein over the period preceding January 1, 1976.

[14] We wish to stress that self-regulation can only be acceptable in this area if it is effective generally throughout the industry. As the Chairman has stated: "it is important that certain standards apply industry wide and not solely to those broadcasters who voluntarily live up to the highest principles of public service responsibility." Address before the National Academy of Television Arts and Sciences, Atlanta Chapter, Atlanta, Georgia, May 23, 1974.

If self-regulation does not prove to be a successful device for regulating the industry as a whole, then further action may be required of the Commission to insure that licensees operate in a manner consistent with their public service obligations.

C. *Separation of program matter and commercial matter.* 46. The Commission is concerned, in addition, that many broadcasters do not presently maintain an adequate separation between programming and advertising on programs designed for children. The Commission has ample authority under the Communications Act to require broadcasters to maintain such a separation. Any practice which is unfair or deceptive when directed to children would clearly be inconsistent with a broadcaster's duty to operate in the "public interest" and may be prohibited by the Commission. Section 317 of the Communications Act, in addition, specifically requires that all advertisements indicate clearly that they are paid for and by whom. 47 U.S.C. 317. The rationale behind this provision is, in part, that an advertiser would have an unfair advantage over listeners if they could not differentiate between the program and the commercial message and were, therefore, unable to take its paid status into consideration in assessing the message. Hearings on H.R. 5589 before the "House Committee on the Merchant Marine and Fisheries," 69th Cong., 1st Sess., at p. 83 (1926). If inadequate separation contributes to an inability to differentiate programming from advertising, then Commission action designed to maintain a clear separation would further the policies of section 317.

47. On the basis of the information gathered in the course of the Commission's inquiry, it has become apparent that children, especially young children, have considerable difficulty distinguishing commercial matter from program matter. Many of the participants knowledgeable in the areas of child development and child psychology maintained that young children lack the necessary sophistication to appreciate the nature and purpose of advertising. Also, a study sponsored by the government concluded that children did not begin to understand that commercials were designed to sell products until starting grade school. Report to the Surgeon General, "Television and Growing Up: The Impact of Televised Violence," Vol: IV at 469 (1970). Kindergartners, for example, did not understand the purpose of commercials; the only way they could distinguish programs from commercials was on the basis that commercials were shorter than programs. Id. at 469, 474. The Commission recognizes that, as many broadcasters noted, these findings are not conclusive; psychological and behavioral questions can seldom be resolved to the point of mathematical certainty. The evidence confirms, however, what our accumulated knowledge, experience and common sense tell us: That many children do not have the sophistication or experience needed to understand that advertising is not just another form of informational programming.

48. The Commission believes, therefore, that licensees, when assessing the adequacy of their commercial policies, must consider the fact that children—especially young children—have greater difficulty distinguishing programming from advertising than adults.[15] If advertisements are to be directed to children, then basic fairness requires that at least a clear separation be maintained between the program content and the commercial message so as to aid the child in developing an ability to distinguish between the two.

49. Special measures should, therefore, be taken by licensees to insure that an adequate separation is maintained on programs designed for children. One technique would be to broadcast an announcement to clarify when the program is being interrupted for commercial messages and when the program is resuming after the commercial "break."[16] Another would be to broadcast some form of visual segment before and after each commercial interruption which would contrast sufficiently with both the programming and advertising segments of the program so as to aid the young child in understanding that the commercials are different from the program. In this context, again following discussions with the Commission's Chairman and staff, the NAB Code Authority has recently amended its advertising rules to require a comparable separation device. We applaud this action by the industry to improve advertising practices directed to children.[17]

50. We recognize that this may be an incomplete solution to the problem. Indeed, in view of the lack of sophistication of the child audience, no complete solution may be possible. The broadcast of an announcement and/or a visual device can only aid children in identifying commercials. The Commission believes, however, that the licensee who directs advertising to children has a responsibility to take action to insure that it is presented n as fair a manner as possible.[18]

51. The Commission is also concerned that some broadcasters are now engaging in a commercial practice which takes unfair advantage of the difficulty children have distinguishing advertising from programming: the use of program characters to promote products ("host-selling"). In some programs designed for children, the program host actually delivers the commercial in his character role on the program set. In others, although the host does not actually deliver the commercial, he may comment on the advertisement in such a manner as to appear to endorse the product ("lead-in/lead-out").

52. The Commission does not believe that the use of a program host, or other program personality, to promote products in the program in which he appears is a practice which is consistent with licensees' obligation to operate in the public interest. One effect of "host-selling" is to interweave the program and the commercial, exacerbating the difficulty children have distinguishing between the two. In addition, the practice allows advertisers to take unfair advantage of the trust which children place in program characters. Even performers themselves recognize that, since a special relationship tends to develop between hosts and young children in the audience, commercial messages are likely to be viewed as advice from a friend.[19] The Commission believes that, in these situations, programming is being used to serve the financial interests of the station and the advertiser in a manner inconsistent with its primary function as a service to children. In this regard, it should be noted that many stations, in particular NAB Code member stations, have already eliminated host selling.[20]

[15] Although the evidence indicates that this problem is most acute among pre-school children, they can be expected to make up a substantial portion of the audience of virtually all children's programming.

[16] The Commission notes in this context that similar practices are found in adult programs. Moderators on talk shows and announcers on sports programs often finish a program segment by announcing that the program will resume after the commercial break; sections of entertainment programs are sometimes entitled "Part I," "Part II," and so forth.

[17] The Commission notes in this context that while INTV does not have a code, it has established a committee to consider adopting general standards and guidelines on commercial practices in children's programs in addition to time limitations.

[18] In this connection, broadcasters may wish to consider a suggestion made by several of the parties that limiting the number

of program interruptions by grouping commercials can contribute to maintaining a clear separation between programming and advertising. We do not believe that it is necessary at this time for the Commission to require "clustering" of commercials, although further consideration of this matter may be appropriate in the future. But, as we noted in the 1960 Programming Report, licensees should "avoid abuses with respect to . . . the frequency with which regular programs are interrupted for advertising messages." Report and Statement of Policy Re: Programming, supra, at 1912–1913. In this regard, particular care should be taken to avoid such abuses in programs designed for the pre-school audience.

[19] As a children's show hostess testified before the Commission: "I watched [a program host] sell Wonder bread for years. I bought Schwinn bicycles because I felt that they were a good thing and because I trusted him. The same thing applies to me in my neighborhood, in my town. I want the children to trust me. I want them to know that when I say something is good, to believe in me, the same way as if I suggested that they attend their school carnival or don't step off the curb when the bus is coming." Lorraine F. Lee-Benner, Transcript of the Panel Discussion, Vol. II, p. 339 (1972).

[20] Public interest questions may also be raised when program personalities or characters deliver commercial messages on programs other than the ones on which they appear. Although this practice would not have the effect of blurring the distinction between programming and advertising, some

53. Finally, the Commission wishes to caution licensees against engaging in practices in the body of the program itself which promote products in such a way that they may constitute advertising." The inquiry revealed that some broadcasters weave the prominent display of the brand names of products into the program sets and activities. One program's set, for example, featured a large billboard announcing the "[Brand Name] Candy Corner" under which children were regularly given samples of the brand name candy as prizes. The hostess on another program, before serving a snack to the children on the show, concluded a prayer with the words, "Now you may have your [Brand Name] orange juice from the [XYZ] Dairy." The analysis of the same program showed, in addition, that the children had been given "[the title of the show]" brand toys with which to play; these were carefully displayed to the viewing audience and children were encouraged to purchase these toys so that they could play along at home. One of the clearest examples of incorporating promotional matter into a program was a cartoon series entitled "Hot Wheels" which was the trade name of a toy manufacturer's miniature racing cars; the manufacturer developed an additional line of cars modeled after those featured in the cartoon series. The Commission found that the program itself promoted the use of the product and required the licensee to log more of the program as commercial matter. See Topper Corporation, 21 FCC 2d 148 (1969); American Broadcasting Companies, 23 FCC 2d 132 (1970).

54. Licensees should exercise care to insure that such practices are in compliance with the sponsorship identification requirements of section 317 of the Communications Act and the Commission's rules on logging commercial matter. Not every mention of a brand name or prominent display thereof necessarily constitutes advertising. All such mate-

rial, however, should be strictly scrutinized by the broadcaster to determine whether or not it should be treated as commercial matter. See 47 U.S.C. 317(a); FCC Public Notice 63-409, entitled "Applicability of Sponsorship Identification Rules" (1963); 47 CFR 73. 670(a)(2), Note 3.

55. Licensees who engage in program practices which involve the mention or prominent display of brand names in children's programs, moreover, should reexamine such programming in light of their public service responsibilities to children. We believe that most young children do not understand that there is a "commercial" incentive for the use of these products and that it is, in fact, a form of merchandising. Any material which constitutes advertising should be confined to identifiable commercial segments which are set off in some clear manner from the entertainment portion of the program. When providing programming designed for children, the conscientious broadcaster should hold himself to the highest standard of responsible practices.

56. The Commission, thus, wishes to stress that this policy statement does not cover every potential abuse in current advertising practices directed to children. Licensees will be expected to reduce the current level of commercialization on programs designed for children, maintain an appropriate separation between programming and advertising, and eliminate practices which take advantage of the immaturity of children. The failure by the Commission to comment on any particular practice, however, does not constitute an endorsement of that practice. Many of these matters are currently under investigation at the Federal Trade Commission. Licensees are again reminded that the broadcast of any material or the use of any practice found to be false or misleading by the Federal Trade Commission will raise serious questions as to whether the station is operating in the public interest. Broadcasters have, in addition, an independent obligation to take all reasonable measures to eliminate false or misleading material. See Public Notice entitled "License Responsibility with Respect to the Broadcast of False, Misleading and Deceptive Advertising," supra. We will expect licensees to exercise great care in evaluating advertising in programs designed for children and refrain from broadcasting any matter which, when directed to children, would be inconsistent with their public service responsibilities.

IV. *Conclusion.* 57 It is believed that this Report will help to clarify the responsibilities of broadcasters with respect to programming and advertising designed for the child audience. We believe that in these areas every opportunity should be accorded to the broadcast industry to reform itself because self-regulation preserves flexibility and an opportunity for adjustment which is not possible with per se rules. In this respect, we recognize that many broadcasters may not currently be in compliance with the policies herein announced. Since this

Report constitutes the first detailed examination of broadcasters' responsibilities to children, we do not wish to penalize the media for past practices. The purpose of this Report is to set out what will be expected from stations in the future.

58. We also realize that it will necessarily take some period of time for broadcasters, program producers, advertisers and the networks to make the anticipated changes." Stations, therefore, will not be expected to come into full compliance with our policies in the areas of either advertising or programming until January 1, 1976. In the interim period, however, broadcasters should take immediate action in the direction of bringing their advertising and programming practices into conformance with their public service responsibilities as outlined in this Report.

59. In the final analysis, the medium of television cannot live up to its potential in serving America's children unless individual broadcasters are genuinely committed to that task, and are willing—to a considerable extent—to put profit in second place and the children in first. While Government reports and regulations can correct some of the more apparent abuses, they cannot create a sense of commitment to children where it does not already exist.

60. In view of the fact that we plan to evaluate the improvements in children's programming and advertising which are now expected, the proceedings in Docket No. 19142 will not be terminated at this time.

Adopted: October 24, 1974.

Released: October 31, 1974.

FEDERAL COMMUNICATIONS COMMISSION,"

[SEAL] VINCENT J. MULLINS,
Secretary.

---

advantage may be taken of the trust relationship which has been developed between the child and the performer. We recognize, however, that it may not be feasible, as a practical matter, for small stations with limited staffs to avoid using children's show personnel in commercial messages on other programs. While we are not prohibiting the use of selling by personalities on other programs, broadcasters should be cognizant of the special trust that a child may have for the performer and should exercise caution in the use of such selling techniques. This may be particularly important where the personality appears in a distinctive character costume or other efforts are made to emphasize his program role.

** ACT originally requested that we ban any mention of products by brand name during the body of a children's program. We are concerned, however, that such a ban would go so far as to prohibit even the critical mention of products and other comment for which no consideration is received. Such a rule would, we believe constitute a form of illegal censorship of programming. Cf., Capital Broadcasting Co. v. Michell, supra. Indeed, it would have a chilling effect on any effort to provide consumer education information for children.

** The Commission anticipates that the networks will take the lead in producing varied programming for children. The networks are responsible for the bulk of the programs now being broadcast: they provide most of the children's shows carried by network-owned or affiliated stations and originally produced most of the syndicated material presented by independent stations. Changes in network programming will, therefore, have both an immediat and a long-range impact as programs gradually become available on a syndicated basis. It is also clear that the networks have the financial resources to make a significant effort in this area. The Commission's economic studies indicate that network children's programming has been consistently profitable for many years.

** Commissioners Lee and Reid concurring in the result; Commissioner Hooks concurring and issuing a statement; Commissioner Washburn issuing additional views; Commissioner Robinson issuing a separate statement. Separate statements of Commissioners Hooks, Washburn and Robinson filed as part of the original document.